ANNALS OF COMMUNISM

Each volume in the series Annals of Communism will publish selected and previously inaccessible documents from former Soviet state and party archives in a narrative that develops a particular topic in the history of Soviet and international communism. Separate English and Russian editions will be prepared. Russian and Western scholars work together to prepare the documents for each volume. Documents are chosen not for their support of any single interpretation but for their particular historical importance or their general value in deepening understanding and facilitating discussion. The volumes are designed to be useful to students, scholars, and interested general readers.

The Road to Terror

*Stalin and the Self-Destruction
of the Bolsheviks, 1932–1939
Updated and Abridged Edition*

J. Arch Getty
and
Oleg V. Naumov

*Archival Research Team
N. V. Muraveva, E. P. Karavaeva, and E. E. Kirillova*

Translations by Benjamin Sher

Yale University Press

New Haven and London

Documents that are held by the Russian State Archive of Social and Political History (RGASPI), the Russian State Archive of Contemporary History (RGANI), and the State Archive of the Russian Federation (GARF) are used with the permission of these archives.

Set in Sabon type by The Composing Room of Michigan, Inc., Grand Rapids, Michigan.
Printed in the United States of America by Sheridan Books.

Library of Congress Cataloging-in-Publication Data

Getty, J. Arch (John Arch), 1950–
    The road to terror : Stalin and the self-destruction of the Bolsheviks, 1932–1939 / J. Arch Getty and Oleg V. Naumov; translations by Benjamin Sher. — Updated and abridged ed.
        p.   cm. — (Annals of communism)
    "Archival research team: N. V. Muraveva, E. P. Karavaeva, and E. E. Kirillova."
    Includes bibliographical references and index.
    ISBN 978-0-300-10407-3 (pbk. : alk. paper)   1. Political purges—Soviet Union—History—Sources.   2. Soviet Union—Politics and government—1917–1936—Sources.   3. Soviet Union—Politics and government—1936–1953—Sources.   4. Kommunisticheskaia partiia Sovetskogo Soiuza—Purges—Sources.   5. Terrorism—Soviet Union—Sources.   6. Stalin, Joseph, 1879–1953—Sources.   I. Naumov, Oleg V.   II. Sher, Benjamin.   III. Title.
    DK267.G45 2010
    947.084′2—dc22

                                                                    2009020426

A catalogue record for this book is available from the British Library.

10 9 8 7 6 5 4 3 2 1

Yale University Press gratefully acknowledges the financial support given for this publication by the National Endowment for the Humanities and Open Society Fund (New York).

This volume has been prepared with the cooperation of the Russian State Archive of Social and Political History (RGASPI) in the framework of an agreement concluded between RGASPI and Yale University Press.

Contents

Preface   ix
Acknowledgments   xi
Notes on Transliteration and Terminology   xiii
A Note on Sources and Citations   xv

Introduction   1

PART I. The Fork in the Road

1. The New Situation, 1930–32   21
2. Party Discipline in 1932   45
3. Repression and Legality   55
4. Growing Tension in 1935   71
5. The Fork in the Road   95

PART II. The Terror

6. The Face of the Enemy, 1936   109
7. The Sky Darkens   143
8. The Storm of 1937: The Party Commits Suicide   165
9. Ending the Terror, 1938   196
10. Two Bolsheviks   217

Conclusion: Quicksand Politics   231

Appendixes
1. Numbers of Victims of the Terror   241
2. Biographical Notes   246

Notes   253
Index   279

Illustrations follow page 106

Preface

This volume is an updated and abridged version of our documentary monograph *The Road to Terror: Stalin and the Self-Destruction of the Bolsheviks, 1932–1939* (New Haven, 1999). The lengthy archival documents in the first edition have been removed or dramatically shortened, and the text has been rewritten both to stand alone as an interpretation and to reflect new sources and studies that have appeared since the first edition.

In the ten years since the first edition of *Road to Terror* appeared, a substantial amount of new archival documentation has become available, through either published works or the ongoing process of archival declassification in Russia. Despite the weariness of the Russian public with gruesome revelations from the Stalin period, some important monographs have also appeared there. Wherever relevant, the new documentation and the recent scholarly studies have been incorporated into this edition.

The archival declassification process in Russia has unfortunately slowed in recent years, which makes historians even more grateful for some remarkable documentary publication projects organized by prominent scholars in Russia. The late Alexander Yakovlev's *Rossiia XX Vek* series, published by his Mezhdunarodnyi Fond "Demokratiia," has produced more than fifty substantial volumes of documents on all periods of Soviet history. The volumes of Viktor P. Danilov's *Tragediia sovetskoi derevni* have provided voluminous and detailed documentation on collectivization and agriculture in general.

In fact, in the past decade the bright lights in Russian publishing on the Stalin period have been documentary collections. Unfortunately, with very few exceptions, scholarly studies have been tendentious and of uneven quality. Given that Stalin so dominated twentieth-century Russia, we should probably not be surprised that he also dominates today's historical writing. Russian scholars are almost completely focused on the person of Stalin and sensational revelations. Most of the serious historical works that have been published in the past ten years have been either narrowly focused pro- or anti-Stalin polemics, or sensational works on spies and the secret workings of police agencies. With some important exceptions, these works contain little if any documentation, few if any footnotes. Social history, political economy, or historical treatments of the Soviet period as something other than the manifestation of Stalin's personality or dictatorship are hard to find.

Historians are always pleased when the appearance of new source material supports rather than contradicts the conclusions they had previously reached. We can confidently report that although a few details have changed or become clearer, the conclusions we had reached ten years ago remain substantially unchanged.

Acknowledgments

This research was supported in part by a grant from the International Research and Exchanges Board, with funds provided by the U.S. Department of State (Title VIII program) and the National Endowment for the Humanities. I received additional support from the National Endowment for the Humanities and from the University of California's Academic Senate.

People who have influenced this work either personally or through their scholarship are too numerous to mention but would include Ken Bailes, Bill Chase, Sheila Fitzpatrick, James Harris, Hiroaki Kuromiya, Roberta Manning, Robert McNeal, Alec Nove, Lewis Siegelbaum, Peter Solomon, Jr., Ronald Suny, and Lynne Viola. I have benefited greatly from conversations with O. V. Khlevniuk, V. A. Kozlov, V. P. Naumov, A. P. Nenarokov, and A. K. Sokolov (and the *rebyata* in his laboratory). I received indescribable additional help from Nancy Getty, T. V. Goriacheva, N. V. Muraveva, L. V. Poliakov, Mary Rakow, Irina Renfro, and N. P. Yakovlev. Alice, Earl, and Floyd know who they are and what they did. I owe a unique debt to my friend Gábor T. Rittersporn, who aided me in all the above categories. I always feel fortunate to benefit from the deep knowledge of the 1930s which he so generously shares.

None of the organizations or people mentioned above are responsible for the views expressed in this book. They deserve due credit for anything good in what follows; I alone am to blame for any errors. Finally, I could not have completed this work without the warm and tolerant support of my family. Nancy, Amanda, Jessica, and John tolerated Moscow, my absences when I was there without them, and my occasional mental absences when I was at home.

Arch Getty
Santa Monica, California, 2009

Notes on Transliteration
and Terminology

In rendering Russian to English we use a modified version of the standard Library of Congress system in the text and documents.

In final position:
ii = y (Trotsky, not Trotskii)
iia = ia (Izvestia, not Izvestiia)
nyi = ny (Nagorny, not Nagornyi)
In initial position:
E = Ye (Yezhov, not Ezhov)
Ia = Ya (Yaroslavsky, not Iaroslavsky)
Iu = Yu (Yudin, not Iudin)

In citations and translator's notes, we follow the Library of Congress system.

In the 1930s the Communist Party was known as the All-Union Communist Party (Bolsheviks), Vsesoiuznaia Kommunisticheskaia Partiia (bol'shevikov) or VKP(b) in its Russian acronym. In practice, its highest policy-making body was the Politburo, which in the 1930s consisted of roughly ten full (voting) members and five candidate (nonvoting) members. In the beginning of the period covered by this study, the Politburo met about once per week; by the end of the period it was meeting about once a month. Each meeting technically had dozens or even hundreds of items on the agenda, but increasingly these were decided without formal meetings, by polling the members. Other top party committees included the Secretariat and the Orgburo, both of which were largely concerned with personnel assignments.

The Central Committee of the VKP(b) (of which the Politburo, Orgburo, and Secretariat were formally subcommittees) consisted of about seventy full voting members and about seventy candidate members in the 1930s. A meeting of the Central Committee (hereafter CC) took place from two to four times a year and was known as a plenum. Minutes (stenograms) were taken at CC plenums, and many of them are available in Russian archives.

Below the level of the CC, the party was divided into a hierarchy of regional party committees based on republics, provinces, territories, districts, and places of work. These bodies also conducted plenums, but the real work was usually done in an inner executive committee known as a buro. Parallel with this hierarchy, and subordinated to the Central Committee, was another structure of party committees known as the Party Control Commission (KPK). The KPK was charged with various kinds of inspection and discipline in the party apparatus. Its mission was to investigate and punish cases of ideological deviance, corruption, and violation of party rules.

A parallel state apparatus was formally separate from the party but in reality subordinated to it. Topped by a Congress of Soviets with hundreds of delegates, formal state power resided in a Central Executive Committee (TsIK) of Soviets, consisting of several dozen members. Day-to-day administration and confirmation of legislation at this level was conducted by the Presidium of the Central Executive Committee, whose chair served as nominal president of the USSR. Below the Central Executive Committee and formally subordinated to it was the government cabinet, known in this period as the Council of People's Commissars (Sovnarkom), which consisted of ministers (commissars) representing various branches of the economy and state administration. Finally, below this central state structure was a hierarchy of elected national republic, provincial, city, and district soviets that might be thought of as organs of local administration.

The USSR was a union of republics, with each republic being the political organization of a nationality. The Russian Republic (RSFSR) and the Ukrainian Republic (USFSR) were the largest of a series of "states" that included Belorussians, Georgians, Armenians, Uzbeks, and the other constituent peoples of the USSR. The RSFSR was clearly the most powerful, and its administration overlapped in general with that of the USSR.

A Note on Sources and Citations

Most of the documents on which this book is based are from the Russian State Archive of Social and Political History (Rossiiskii gosudarstvennyi arkhiv sotsial'no-politicheskoi istorii, hereafter RGASPI), the former Central Party Archive of the Institute of Marxism-Leninism of the Central Committee of the Communist Party (TsPA IML pri TsK KPSS). For an outline of the history and holdings of the archive, see J. Arch Getty, "Researcher's Introduction to RTsKhIDNI," in *Rossiiskii Tsentr Khraneniia i Izucheniia Dokumentov Noveishei Istorii: Kratkii Putevoditel'*, ed. J. Arch Getty and V. P. Kozlov, Moscow, 1993, v–xix. Some documents were from the Russian State Archive of Contemporary History (Rossiiskii gosudarstvennyi arkhiv noveishei istorii, hereafter RGANI), the former archive of the General Department of the Central Committee, and from the State Archive of the Russian Federation (Gosudarstvennyi arkhiv Rossiskoi Federatsii, hereafter GARF), the main archive of central state institutions. A few documents are from the Central Archive of the Federal Security Service of the Russian Federation (Tsentral'nyi arkhiv Federal'noi sluzhby bezopasnosti Rossiiskoi Federatsii, hereafter TsA FSB).

Russian archival documents are cited and numbered by collection (fond or f.), inventory (opis' or op.), file (delo or d.), and page (list or l., or in plural, ll.): thus, for example, RGASPI, f. 17, op. 165, d. 47, l. 3 means RGASPI archive fond number 17, inventory number 165, file number 47, page 3.

The Road to Terror

Introduction

BY 1936 ALEXANDER YULEVICH TIVEL was enjoying a successful career as a journalist and editor. He was born just before the turn of the century in Baku, not far from where a young Stalin was pursuing his career as an underground revolutionary. Despite his parents' status as white-collar employees of a joint-stock company, Alexander's life possibilities had seemed limited by his birth in 1899 into a Jewish family in the provinces. But he was a clever boy who at an early age had somehow managed to learn a passable amount of English, German, and French.

He was also political. At age sixteen he had joined a Zionist student organization in Baku. With two strikes against him (the Imperial system had little use for politically active Jews from non-Russian provinces of the empire), he finished high school at age eighteen and wondered what he would do with his life. As it turned out, the determining factor was his graduation year of 1917, the year of the Russian Revolution.

We do not know what role he played in the dramatic events of that year, but in 1918 he was working first in the military office of the Piatigorsk Soviet, then in Moscow in the propaganda department of the new Bolshevik government. By the end of the year he had joined the editorial staff of the Soviet government's press agency, ROSTA. During the Russian Civil War (1918–21), he served as a correspondent for ROSTA and for several Soviet newspapers in Moscow, the Volga region, and Tashkent. His editing

1

and language skills stood him in good stead with a new regime desperate for such talents.

After the Civil War, Alexander Tivel worked as a editor and writer in Moscow for the Communist International (Comintern), where he met and married Eva Lipman. In 1925 he moved to Leningrad to work in the foreign news department of *Leningradskaia pravda,* but in 1926 it was back to Moscow for editorial work in the Secretariat of the Central Committee of the Communist Party and in the CC's department of Culture and Propaganda. Despite his previous jobs working for the Communist press, he had never joined the party. But his new job in the apparatus of the party's Central Committee required him to be a member. His editorial experience and knowledge of languages made him a valued worker; by special order of the CC Secretariat, he was admitted directly to the party in December 1926 without the required period of candidate membership. During the next ten years, Tivel continued to work in Moscow party headquarters, eventually rising to the position of assistant chief of the International Information Bureau of the Central Committee of the Communist Party.

On the surface, his record seemed exemplary. True, between 1930 and 1936 Tivel had received three party reprimands for such minor infractions as misplacing a telegram or losing his party card, but it was not unusual for party members to have several such small technical blots on their records. Behind the scenes, however, there was a growing fear in the top party leadership that was leading to heightened scrutiny of one's past. Normal work relationships with political dissidents or with losers in political intrigues were increasingly examined and given sinister interpretations. Alexander had two such suspicious associations. During his year in Leningrad back in 1925, he had worked with followers of the leftist oppositionist Grigory Zinoviev and for a time had been Zinoviev's secretary. Tivel had been in the wrong place at the wrong time: since Zinoviev was party boss of Leningrad at the time, his supporters had naturally controlled the newspaper where Tivel worked. And by 1936, Tivel's immediate supervisor in the Information Bureau was the ex-Trotskyist Karl Radek, a well-known and bitingly sarcastic critic of Stalin in the 1920s.

Such suspicions reached new heights in the aftermath of the August 1936 show trial of Zinoviev and other former leftists. The trial had sentenced these dissidents to death, and in its wake those who, like Radek, had sided with the leftists came under intense scrutiny. At the end of August, Radek was arrested and Tivel was taken by the secret police (NKVD) at the same time. His wife and young son never saw him again.

Tivel spent the next six months in prison under interrogation. We do not know whether he was physically tortured by his interrogators, but there is ample evidence that countless others were. Even high-ranking officials under arrest were beaten or, as Molotov would put it, "worked over."[1] Ten years later, a high-ranking police official wrote to Stalin describing interrogation procedures. First, prisoners were to be offered better conditions—better food, mail, and so on—in return for a confession. If that failed, appeals to the prisoner's conscience and concern for his family followed. The next step was a solitary confinement cell without exercise, a bed, tobacco, or sleep for up to twenty days. Food was limited to three hundred grams of bread per day, with one hot meal every third day. If all this failed, the use of "physical pressure" was authorized in accordance with a Central Committee decree of 10 January 1939.[2] These procedures refer to a later, less terrible period, but the routine was hardly lighter in the 1930s when Tivel was in custody.

In 1936 the Stalinist leadership's paranoia reached new heights. A wave of arrests engulfed former party dissidents of both the left and the right. Prominent Bolsheviks with oppositional pasts, including diplomat Grigory Sokolnikov, Deputy Commissar of Heavy Industry Georgy Piatakov, and many others, found themselves in prison. All were accused of the most fantastic crimes: sabotage, espionage, and a variety of other treasonable actions. The Bolshevik elite was consuming itself.

Even within the precincts of the Central Committee where Tivel had worked, the wave of suspicion reached ludicrous proportions. In one of the paranoid waves, someone remembered that two young women party workers in the central apparatus, Toropova and Lukinskaya, had been seen with Tivel at a social event. M. F. Shkiriatov, the high-ranking chairman of the Party Control Commission, dashed off a memo to the NKVD requesting that Tivel be asked about the women, frustrated that "we cannot verify everybody with whom Tivel had danced."

On 7 March 1937, the NKVD replied that there was nothing incriminating from Alexander Tivel against the women. But on the same day, the Military Collegium of the Supreme Court convicted Tivel not only of knowing about terrorists' intentions to assassinate Bolshevik leaders but of directly "preparing to commit a terrorist act against [NKVD chief]

Yezhov." Tivel was shot, probably on the same day. Unlike many others who were badgered and tortured by the NKVD, he had not confessed.

But the Tivel story does not end here; the terror that swallowed him also destroyed the families of those "repressed." Immediately after Tivel's arrest, his wife Eva had been fired from her job "for political motives" and now found it impossible to find any work with this notation on her record. Shortly thereafter, she was evicted from her Moscow apartment and, facing destitution on the streets, she and her sickly young son moved into her mother's crowded flat. But in May of 1937 she and her son were banished from Moscow altogether and exiled to the far-off Omsk province in Siberia. Her mother lost her apartment and was exiled along with her daughter and grandson, apparently for sheltering them.

In October 1937 Eva Tivel was herself arrested in Omsk. After eight months in the Tobol'sk jail, she was sentenced by the NKVD's Special Board (which had the right to sentence people even if they had committed no crime) to eight years in a labor camp for being a "member of the family of a traitor to the Motherland." The savage human destruction of the terror did not stop even there. Shortly after Eva's arrest, the NKVD arrived at her mother's apartment and took the Tivels' nine-year-old son to an orphanage. He would not see his mother for nearly two decades.

After completing her eight-year sentence in the camps, Eva, like so many others, received an additional term: eight more years in Siberian exile. She was freed only in 1953, the year of Stalin's death, when she returned to Moscow. She soon began a campaign to have her husband's name cleared. Even though Tivel had been dead for sixteen years and Eva was now free, their twenty-five-year-old son still carried a stigma as a "child of an enemy of the people," which limited his work and educational possibilities. From the beginning of 1955 Eva began to write letters to party authorities seeking posthumous rehabilitation of Alexander Tivel "in order to remove this false conviction from the father of my son." Her first letter was in January 1955; another followed in March.

Such letters from relatives and survivors were numerous in 1955, and would eventually lead to Nikita Khrushchev's de-Stalinization campaign, with its mass rehabilitations. But the process began slowly. Eva received no answer until January 1956, when Major Tishchenko, a case worker in the Military Procuracy, informed her that her appeal had not been acted upon. She then demanded an appointment with the procuracy but was told there that "the question of rehabilitating Tivel cannot now be decided because he had been accused in connection with a group of people [evidently Radek] convicted at an open trial in 1937." Eva now joined the legion of widows, relatives, and former convicts who trudged from office to office in search of justice.

Khrushchev's anti-Stalin "Secret Speech" of February 1956 stimulated the reconsideration of old cases, but even then the pace was slow. Shortly after Khrushchev's speech, Eva wrote once again to the Military Procuracy asking for Tivel's case to be reopened. This time, Major Tishchenko actually took up the matter and began an investigation of Tivel's conviction. But again there was no movement. In September 1956 Eva had another appointment at the procuracy and received another infuriating bureaucratic answer: "Because A. Y. Tivel was accused in connection with a group of people whose cases are now being reexamined, the question of his rehabilitation cannot be decided until the reexamination of those cases is completed." In December of 1956 Eva wrote another letter, this time to the Party Control Commission.

Finally, on 23 May 1957, more than twenty years after Tivel's execution, the Military Collegium of the USSR Supreme Court reversed his 1937 conviction, which, in the court's words, "had been based on contradictory and dubious materials of the preliminary investigation, which the court [in 1937] did not verify." A month later, on 18 June, Tivel's August 1936 expulsion from the party was reversed and his party standing posthumously restored.[3]

Questions and Culprits

Alexander Tivel was not a high party leader. He was a minor figure whose records in no way stand out in the archives, and we will not meet him in the corridors of power. Despite his obscurity, his fate illustrates many of the elements of the terror process; personal and work connections became crimes that spurred insane and paranoid investigations. The physical pain and deep suffering of the Alexander Tivels and their families have been well documented in a huge corpus of powerful memoir literature, including Eugenia Ginzburg's *Into the Whirlwind,* Anna Larina's *This I Cannot Forget,* and Alexander Solzhenitsyn's *The Gulag Archipelago,* to name only a few.

What led the Soviet Communist Party elite to destroy its own? Why were valuable but politically harmless people like Alexander and Eva

Tivel destroyed in what might otherwise have been a historically common internecine fight among the elite? Why did it take so long, even after Stalin's death, to begin to reverse the miscarriages of justice? What was the mindset of the Stalinist and post-Stalinist party elite?

Although we have had memories and powerful portrayals of the process from its victims, until the recent opening of some of the political archives of the former Soviet Union we have been forced to guess about the process at the other end, from the top. We have not been able to write the history of the origins of the terror from the standpoint of those who administered it. The laconic official documents at our disposal until recently have been tips of Soviet historical icebergs. In the past two decades, a tremendous quantity of heretofore secret documentation from the Soviet period has been declassified and made available to us. We now have the texts and words of those in power; we can hear and study their language.

Historians have often posed the question "How did one man—Stalin—manage to inflict such wholesale terror on an experienced political elite?" The historical literature refers to Stalin's careful plans, cunning, deception, threats, and blackmail.[4] In some views, Stalin simply decided to kill a lot of people and then tricked or intimidated large numbers of otherwise intelligent people into helping him do it. Society plays no role in these explanations, and there is no real politics at work here. The only factors worth mentioning are the plans of the ruler; everyone else was a passive recipient. Many basic accounts of the terror operate at this interpretive level: once one decides who is guilty, there are no more questions to ask, and research becomes the further enumeration of foul deeds by the evil prince.[5] The road to terror seems straight, direct, and brightly lit.

The figure of Iosif Vissarionovich Stalin does indeed hover like a specter over these events. As the most powerful political leader of the state and the center of a growing semireligious cult, he is personally responsible for much of the bloodshed. His motives and plans and the exact sequence of his actions are still not completely clear, but we do have sufficient evidence of his enormous guilt. Although we do not have a diary or journal, a clear list of his orders and commands, or even many documents with his signature, we have enough to posit for him a vicious and cold participation in the killing. His fingerprints are all over the archives.

We shall see in the course of this study how Stalin's power grew so dramatically throughout the 1930s that by the end of the decade he was a virtual autocrat. Although Russia had always been a country ruled by men rather than laws, more and more in the 1930s people would refer to Stalin or other leaders to guide their behavior and solve their problems. We shall also see, however, that this process was uneven and characterized by zigs and zags. Sometimes Stalin was a referee or makeweight, balancing various interests and groups against one another. He made and changed alliances with different groups at different times either by explicit pronouncements or by implicitly allowing them to use his name and authority. At other times, he directly asserted his personal authority. Although by the end of the decade he was unquestionably the supreme leader, he was never omnipotent and always functioned within a matrix of other groups and interests.

In the witch hunts of the seventeenth century, to which the Stalinist terror bears many similarities, a small number of authoritative persons identified the victims and organized their execution. Behind and around them, though, were other groups and constituencies that abetted the proceedings, acquiesced in the process, or simply looked on, believing that all of this was necessary, reasonable, or at least acceptable. These included members of religious and political hierarchies, policemen of various kinds, and ordinary citizen-members of "the crowd." As Hugh Trevor-Roper wrote, "[No] ruler has ever carried out a policy of wholesale expulsion or destruction without the cooperation of society. . . . Great massacres may be commanded by tyrants, but they are imposed by peoples. . . . Afterwards, when the mood has changed, or when the social pressure, thanks to the blood-letting, no longer exists, the anonymous people slinks away, leaving public responsibility to the preachers, the theorists, and the rulers who demanded, justified, and ordered the act."[6] Our curiosity and attention are drawn to those who helped, approved, or simply accepted the necessity of fatal purges of perceived enemies. Both in colonial America and in Stalinist Russia, there were bureaucratic constituencies and popular masses who went along with the bloodletting and who thought it was right and even proper.

It is, after all, possible to analyze and even on some level to understand a homicidal maniac or a serial murderer. Such phenomena are unfortunately common events in today's newspapers, and the tools of modern psychoanalysis give us quite a few clues to the motivations of such criminals. In the case of Stalin, a good bit has been written on his presumed personality.[7] Yet to understand how a generalized terror erupted in the USSR in the 1930s we must look further afield. Why were his orders carried out?

Why was there fertile soil for terror to grow? Even if we decide that Stalin was always the main actor, unless we study the party and the political system, the scale and spread of the terror would remain incomprehensible.

The Bolshevik (or Communist) Party was the administrative tool for Stalin's policies, the forum for conflicting and feuding bureaucracies, and the only politically articulate stratum of a politically fractured society. It was the priesthood, the military commander, the chief of police, and the sole landowner. This elite represented and was representative of society, including as it did workers, peasants, foremen, collective farm chairmen, local political bosses, economic administrators, and others in a wide array of social and political roles. The party was the state. It had a monopoly on political organization and control of the press, courts, army, and police. It established and defended the only permissible ideology; it suppressed and controlled traditional religion and promulgated its own system of beliefs in the Communist millennium, complete with saints and demons.

Yet the party, which could have stopped the terror, actively cooperated in its own destruction. It embarked on a series of policies that disorganized its regime, fractured society, and destroyed itself. This bears explaining.

The Bolshevik Party was descended from idealistic, egalitarian, and socially progressive strands in the Russian intelligentsia and working class. By the 1930s much of the original idealism had been lost or transformed as Bolshevik revolutionaries became state officials. But even the remaining idealists—and there were many—supported and followed policies that facilitated terror, not only against traditional "enemies" but against themselves. This too requires an explanation.

By dealing with such questions, we hope to give some insight into the most difficult question of the terror: how was it all possible?

We shall see that the terror was facilitated by certain interests that wanted to increase or decrease repression, by traditional Bolshevik Party unity that mutated into a fanatical party discipline, by customary and ritual practices, and by the transformation of political sins into judicial crimes.

One key to these processes is the position and corporate self-interest of the party elite. Since the early 1920s, full-time professional party leaders had become the administrators of the country. They became accustomed to giving commands, enjoying privileges, and living well. The process of the formation of an official social stratum had begun. This had been the gist of Lev Trotsky's critique of the Stalin regime and one of the reasons the ruling elite had been so fierce in its destruction of Trotsky's group. This ruling segment of the party, its elite, became more and more conscious of itself as a group separate from the party rank and file and from the population in general. Self-selected and replenished by a system of hierarchical personnel appointment, the party elite, or *nomenklatura,* enjoyed increasing power, prestige, and privilege as time went on.[8]

It was an elite that included members and staffs of the Politburo and Central Committee, first secretaries of provincial party committees, and full-time paid officials and organizers at many levels down to urban and rural districts. But although these various subgroups had differing parochial interests that sometimes conflicted with those of other nomenklatura groups, they shared a group identity as "insiders." They were the ones with power, great or small, whose membership in the ruling caste distinguished them from the multitudinous "outsiders."

If the regime fell, their various privileges and immunities would disappear. The more exclusive and authoritative they could be, the more secure were their personal fortunes. On another level, though, there is no reason to believe that they were not also true believers in communism. In fact, there was little contradiction between the two. In the worldview they had constructed, the future of humanity depended on socialism. Socialism depended on the survival of the Soviet revolutionary experiment, which in turn depended on keeping the Bolshevik regime united, tightly disciplined, and in control of a society that frequently exhibited hostility to that regime. The long-standing Bolshevik self-image as "midwives of the revolution" was alive and well through the 1930s. Even without crass self-interest as a conscious motive, this Bolshevik tradition made it easy to equate nomenklatura power with the good of the country.

Stalin was simultaneously creator, product, and symbol of the nomenklatura. As chief of Central Committee personnel, he controlled the most important appointments. But he was also a product and representative of the new official stratum; they supported him as much as he supported them. As several scholars have noted, Stalin had "won over a majority cohort of high- and middle-ranking party leaders" rather than creating that cohort.[9] Trotsky agreed, and indeed maintained that Stalin was simply the representative of the new official stratum.

Schisms in the party, which were neither about ideology nor limited to the articulate political stratum, constitute an important key to this story.

Fault lines ran not so much between "right" and "left," as they had in the 1920s, but between and among strata. The party was by no means a united organization, and there are several ways to disaggregate it into its component groups. Various players jockeyed with one another in a system bound by rules they did not always control.

Even Stalin's room for maneuver was limited. Stalin and his Politburo together made a collective player in the matrix, with their own interests. Frequently, as we will show, they sided with the centralization-minded elements of the elite nomenklatura when their mutual interests coincided. At other times, they united with the regional chiefs. But again, along with the central and regional elites, Stalin and the Politburo made up part of the broader governing stratum that more often than not closed ranks against the party rank and file. He needed these elites to maintain power and run the country. His dilemma, therefore, was how to rein in other players' powers without advertising elite discord to the spectators outside the arena of politics. Although groups within the elite feuded with one another and combined and recombined in various coalitions, their fears of splitting the party or "going public" to reveal internal divisions to the outside world provided strong incentive to keep their squabbles hidden.[10]

Stalinist Mentalities and Language

Much of this delicate and covert maneuvering was accomplished (and hidden) with language. In the past two decades, a tremendous quantity of previously secret documentation from the Soviet period has been declassified and made available to us. We now have the texts and words of those in power; we can hear and study their language.

In fact, language plays a major role in this book, as it did in the unfolding of the terror. The regime's official language was as much a tool of rule as police, ideology, education, and propaganda. It was deployed by those on high, but was also modified by those who received it. Common folk learned the official language in order to speak properly and get what they wanted. Officials at all levels used official texts in ways that suited them. Language was used and abused, prescribed and proscribed, detailed and twisted in the service of the Stalinist regime and its component constituencies. This book is also about how language created and determined people and events, as much as vice versa.

The Bolsheviks were active creators and deployers of words. Lenin had spent much of his life producing and debating political programs. For the Bolsheviks before the revolution (and especially for the intellectual leaders in emigration), hairsplitting over precise points of revolutionary ideology was much of their political life. To a significant extent, Bolshevik politics had always been inextricably bound with creating and sharpening texts. Leninists and then Stalinists were professional wordsmiths as well as professional revolutionaries; their very founding events—including the 1903 break with their Menshevik Russian Social Democratic rivals—were about how to word a resolution.

Their close attention to language continued once they were in power. Statements emanating from the top Stalinist leadership were produced and written with great care and were meant to provide rules and parameters for political and social behavior according to the needs of those creating them. Phrasing was exact, reflecting prescribed linguistic formulations and agreed-upon slogans and phrases. Thus the Central Committee announced the official slogans of the season, which were then republished for study across the country.[11] Typically, *Pravda* issued a list of numbered official slogans for the new year on January 1, and even high officials were taken to task for using incorrect or unapproved formulations. As we shall see, variant texts of the same document were deliberately produced for different audiences in an attempt to shape precisely the behavior of those audiences by providing targeted narratives, which were mandatory for use by various groups. In turn, texts from on high were studied and combed by those below for explicit rules and implicit codes and clues to guide political life. The relationship among written laws and regulations, transcripts of authoritative political meetings, and oral speech often held the key to proper behavior, and the successful politician was the one who best understood the relative powers of various texts.

Much of our story involves Stalinist attempts to create an interpretive template, a collective representation of reality that made sense of a society in crisis, and a corresponding rationale for a dominant hegemony to control that society. As many social theorists have shown, elites attempt to control societies by creating and promulgating an ideology: a "master discourse" or "master narrative" for society to follow. Whether we call it a ruling myth, a transcript, or a hegemonic ideology, elites everywhere support a basic system of beliefs, assumptions, and tenets.[12] Whether they are about democracy, socialism, fascism, patriarchy, or religion, they provide an organizing thought pattern and validation of the existing order (even if that order be revolutionary). They seek to legitimize the existing class and status order: "This is the way things are, and this is the way things should be." They also provide a "self-portrait of dominant elites as they would have themselves seen."[13] They facilitate a unified elite self-representation, cohesion, and integration and offer a means of social control by insisting that citizens adhere to the belief system; they thereby provide a definition of heresy in the form of nonadherence.

Every regime creates and uses symbols, which are often crafted with language. Stalinist rhetoric was attributive, rather than strictly definitional, in its categories, symbols, and images. Labels (really symbolic codes) like *kulak* or *Trotskyist,* along with many types we shall encounter, like the "politically careless" official, the "heartless bureaucrat," the "provocateur," and the "little person," represented not so much categories as tropes, or metaphors, meant to carry symbolic content that changed over time. Rebels are labeled as "bandits"; reluctant peasants become "kulaks"; dissenters become "Trotskyists." Any unauthorized political organization becomes ipso facto a "counterrevolutionary organization." Such official high-level use of symbols was a convenient tool of rule. But it was also unpredictable in its effects because the same flexibility to define each symbol enjoyed by the Politburo was employed at every step down the chain of command. As we shall see, regional and local party leaders could fill and refill these tropes with meaning in order to deflect the fire from their friends and focus it on their opponents.

Official texts and transcripts tolerated no competing discourses, branding them as "anti-Soviet agitation" or "enemy propaganda," and finally making them equivalent to treasonous acts. Competing ideologies and texts, whether oral or written, were not considered simply to be heretical or slanderous but were rather equivalent to overt political rebellion. Hostile language and hostile actions were seen as the same thing. The regime had mechanisms to enforce adherence to the dominant line, including the party and the secret police. Deviation from the line was even a specific state crime: "anti-Soviet agitation."

Use of approved language ("speaking Bolshevik") was an obligatory part of functioning in Stalinist society.[14] Using the official mode of speech was a way to survive and maneuver within the Stalinist system and was practiced by everyone from the poorest peasant to the most senior official. It was a way in which individuals reacted to and made their way within the prescribed parameters of the system. Whether they were producing official documents, writing letters, or speaking at party meetings, many members of the Stalinist elite consciously "spoke Stalinist" as a matter of group conformity and even individual survival. Even more pragmatically, it was important for the top leaders to use the official language because they were producing texts for use by others at lower positions in the party hierarchy and in society. If they expected everyone to use the *lingua stalina,* they had to use it themselves.

But language was not only a vehicle to cloak politics, promote self-interest, or maintain social control. Language did work: it had the power to make politics as well as express politics. And it could make people as well as portray them. Their language created them as much as vice versa.

The ways Stalinists used official language, metaphors, and symbols were not necessarily cynical or false. One of the big surprises in party documents is that the Stalinists said the same things to one another behind closed doors that they said to the public: in this regard their "hidden transcripts" differed little from their public ones. The Stalinists were themselves products of the symbolic construction—the ideology—that they created. They were ultimately no more capable of escaping it than is the priest of any religion. "The 'great' are those who can least afford to take liberties with the official norms. . . . The price to be paid for their outstanding value is outstanding conformity to the values of the group, the source of all symbolic value."[15]

It may be useful to think of another possible effect of language: its impact on the self-understanding and consciousness of those using it.[16] Educational systems stressing recitation and religious practices of liturgical repetition have long been based on the simple notion that if one repeats something often enough in a particular form, one will come to believe it. Employing language in this way, therefore, is more than using it as a personal tool. It involves complex processes of identity-shaping and formation and the creation of personal subjective meaning through use of language. Belief, therefore, can be understood as a dynamic and evolving process as much as an a priori motivation. As the Stalinists used language instrumentally and obligatorily, they were also being shaped by that language. Their political identities were a product of the texts they created just as much as that language was a tool for individual advancement.

But the question of belief was and is a complicated one, connected to collective representations common both to the elite and the general population and to language. Some have pointed out that language can be "con-

stative" or "performative." Constative speech makes descriptive statements that state facts or characterize reality. Performative speech, on the
other hand, changes or creates reality in some way. Constative speech can
be true or false; performative utterances do work and are neither true nor
false. They do their work not because of the intention of the speaker but
because of the accepted conventions and circumstances surrounding its
utterance. It is therefore not the intention of the speaker that characterizes
speech or makes it successful or not; it is the extent to which it follows prescribed codes in certain venues and contexts.

For others, the speaker does not necessarily determine meaning in advance, only to perform a discourse later on. Instead, she or he is "enabled"
(but not completely determined) by the performative speech itself. Through
the repetition of ritualized events and speech, persons are themselves
transformed or produced. It is not, therefore, the case that a "real," finalized person "precedes" his ritualized speech, and then either lies (wears a
mask) or "reveals truth," depending on what she or he believes. This view
has important implications for our Stalinists and their beliefs. Speakers
were "ritualized agents," partially produced in the very process of speech
performance in ritual settings. Therefore we must allow for the possibility
that things—and persons—are in fact *created* by speech in ritualized contexts: political truth, the meaning of symbols and political words, the
"meaning" and role of persons themselves, and what in fact they believe,
all as a result of their performative speech.[17]

Therefore it follows that any speech act can break with convention in
unforeseen ways and come to mean things that were not intended in advance. As with the previously discussed politician-creates-language mode,
the language-defines-politics phenomenon could unfold in unpredictable
ways. If, for example, performative speech in a certain ritual setting did
not precisely follow the norms, it could create unforeseen and inconvenient meanings: comrades could be redefined as enemies, enemies as
friends, regardless of the presumed intentions of the speaker or the plans
of those managing the event.

We can see a strange confluence of Stalinist and postmodern under-
standings of speech as politics and politics as speech. For both, to a considerable extent it was speech and action that defined and created the subject, not vice versa. In critical theory, it is the ritualized performance that
helps create and shape the subject, as much as or even regardless of his
previous subjective intent. For Stalinists it was the political "objective

consequences" of one's speech, not one's subjective intent, that defined and governed one's "political physiognomy." As we shall see, in ritualized party meetings one's adherence to proper performative speech created meaning, both for those present and for others who would receive the performed text, and to a considerable extent made politics and defined the speaker himself.

Fear

Finally, we must introduce another element that strongly affected politics in the 1930s: fear inside the elite. The Stalinists never felt that they really controlled the country. Transportation and communication were poor, and the regime's representatives were few in number, especially outside the cities. There was not even a telephone line to the Soviet Far East until the 1930s. In the relatively developed European part of Russia, most communications with party committees were by telegraph or letters delivered by couriers on motorcycles. Mud and snow isolated numerous villages from any contact with the regime for months out of the year. Local party officials frequently interpreted and misinterpreted Moscow's directives in ways that suited their local purposes. The Central Committee complained constantly throughout the decade about the lack of "fulfillment of decisions" and spent a great deal of time creating mechanisms to check up on miscreant and disobedient local leaders.[18]

Established regimes that rest on a base of general popular acceptance and consensual order do not need to resort to terror; they can rely on consensus (and/or hegemony in a Gramscian sense) to ensure stability and compliance. As Pierre Bourdieu noted, "Once a system of mechanisms has been constituted capable of objectively ensuring the reproduction of the existing order by its own motion, the dominant class have only to *let the system they dominate take its own course* in order to exercise their domination; but until such a system exists, they have to work directly, daily, personally, to produce and reproduce conditions of domination which are even then never entirely trustworthy." The Bolsheviks, even into the 1930s, never enjoyed this level of acceptance and constantly feared for the safety of their regime. They could not simply "let the system they dominate take its own course" and felt that they had to work at it. They thought they had "to work directly, daily, personally, to produce and reproduce conditions of domination which are even then never entirely trustworthy."[19]

The regime's monopoly on force, the sheer scale of the terror, and the apparent grim, mechanical efficiency of the secret police have produced a literature dominated by images of an unstoppable, monstrous, and omnipotent "terror machine." Indeed, from the vantage point of the victim, or that of observers who associate themselves with the victim, the objective reality seems clear. To civilians killed by an artillery barrage, the force seems huge and powerful. Yet to those firing the shots, the nature of the persons targeted might seem quite different; they are perceived as invisible, evil, monstrous, and threatening. To these shooters, the weapons of the state might seem dubious or even weak. Ultimately, of course, there is no difference: people are killed by a terrible mechanical process. But for an understanding of the event as phenomenon, the subjective perceptions of those administering terror are important. To date, studies of the terror, when they have dealt with the motives of those carrying out terror, have treated them simply as evil men who killed a lot of people. But the perpetrators were also, collectively, frightened of their surroundings. And they were as afraid of political and social groups below them as of authorities on high.[20]

This was a political system in which even Politburo members in the 1930s carried revolvers. Recalling in the 1930s their formative experiences in the Civil War, the Stalinists always felt figuratively surrounded, constantly at war with powerful and conniving opponents. Twenty years after the event they reflexively fell back on Civil War metaphors and branded all categories of enemies as "white guards."

Of course, should one discover that the Bolshevik recourse to terror involved regime anxiety, the awful results of that terror remain unchanged. There is no insanity defense or excuse for the Stalinists; given the scale of the suffering they caused, there can be none. But if we are interested in the "why" surrounding the terror (or that part of it sponsored from above) it is relevant to inquire into the leaders' construction of reality and their place in it.

More than a few caveats are in order. First, our study does not touch on all questions relating to the terror. Because our sources are predominantly internal political records of the upper Communist Party, we are unfortunately not able to deal comprehensively with foreign policy, agricultural or industrial affairs, or cultural matters. We rather focus on party policy as it relates to internal repression of perceived and identified "enemies," and hope that this exercise may shed some light on other areas. Our concentration on high politics in this collection does not imply that other factors were unimportant or even less important. Local conflicts between leaders and led, social and status conflicts on the shop floor or the kolkhoz, populist resentment from below, even popular culture played active roles that have been documented in other studies. But because of the categories of documents we present, these important elements cannot receive a great deal of attention here except as the objects of central concerns and policies. This is a bias of the source base, not necessarily a reflection of historical reality.

Second, even within a subject focus, all scholars are necessarily selective in their use of sources. Because our subject is the Communist Party, much of our source base is from the former Central Party Archive of the Soviet Communist Party, which is technically responsible for party documents for the period to 1953. Accordingly, we have not made extensive use of the collections in the various state, economic, and cultural archives.

Similarly, for a variety of reasons, we have not used much of the large corpus of memoir literature. This reflects no claim that Stalinist archival documents are inherently trustworthy or that they are inherently superior to literary accounts in general. Because of the special relation of Stalinist discourse to the truth (or more accurately because the Stalinists were "creating truth" through their documents), archival documents must be handled with utmost critical care.[21] With that in mind, it is important also to observe that they were produced by the people in power. On the other hand, the vast majority of existing memoir accounts were not written by persons in a position to report accurately the maneuvers of high politics we are studying. Much of the information they provide is in the form of second- or thirdhand gossip and hearsay. Even secret police memoirs were written decades later by agents stationed outside the USSR during the 1930s. Such memoirs are suspect not only because of their distance from the events they discuss; they also contain major mistakes and errors of fact. For example, concerning only some key events of the terror discussed in this volume, the two most important police memoirs misdate (sometimes by years) the Riutin opposition, the purge of 1933, the implication of Marshal Tukhachevsky, the arrest of Piatakov, and the execution of the army generals in 1937.[22]

Memoirs of victims who were not part of the elite or who were far removed from the seat of power, although they contain poignant and revealing material, cannot be taken as sources for central decision making even when they provide tantalizing rumors repeated in the labor camps. By contrast, Molotov's and Kaganovich's memoirs, although they were written decades after the events they recount, are more important sources because of the key positions their authors held in the 1930s. Nevertheless, they deserve the most strict critical treatment because of their ideological and self-serving nature.

The Great Terror of the 1930s in the Soviet Union was one of the most horrible cases of political violence in modern history. Millions of people were detained, arrested, or sent to prison or camps. In 1937 and 1938 alone, three-quarters of a million supposed "enemies of the people" were shot, many without any trial or other legal proceedings. Countless lives, careers, and families were permanently shattered. Honest, loyal people were destroyed. Relatives were persecuted and descendants lived with stigma and tragedy for decades. Beyond this, the experience left a national trauma, a legacy of fear that lingered for generations. When confronted with undeniable and unimaginable evil, our natural impulse is to condemn and to denounce. Although these are righteous and appropriate responses, they should not substitute for our duty as scholars and social scientists to explain phenomena, both positive and negative. Cancer researchers are no doubt repelled by the ravages of the disease they study, but they do not write of their repulsion in their scholarly works or allow it to replace or obviate their need to analyze and explain dispassionately. Their question, like ours, is "how was this all possible?"

I
The Fork in the Road

CHAPTER ONE

The New Situation, 1930–32

I believe that the implementation of a plan of such exceptional difficulty as that
which confronts us in 1931 demands solid unity between the top echelons of
the Soviet and Party leadership. Not the slightest cleft should be permitted.
—V. V. Kuibyshev, 1930

THESE WERE TERRIBLE YEARS in the Soviet Union. It was the fif-
teenth year of the Revolution, and the country faced the paradox of rapid
industrial expansion combined with the starvation of millions of people.
How had things come to such a pass?

In 1917 the Bolsheviks had come to power in a relatively backward
country suffering through a wartime crisis. As Marxists, they believed that
socialism was the inevitable future for mankind but that it depended on
the existence of an advanced economy. As Leninists, they were convinced
that this future could be brought about through a highly disciplined party
of professional revolutionaries acting as "midwives of history" to guide
the masses toward their future. These beliefs associated with the Leninist
version of Marxism were understood differently by various groups within
the Bolshevik Party, but by and large they were fundamentals of Bolshevism and crucial factors in the futures of both the party and the country.

Almost immediately, the new regime was plunged into the three-year
Civil War that pitted the Reds (Bolsheviks and their allies) against the
Whites (politically almost everyone else). The Civil War saw not only mil-
itary intervention by more than a dozen capitalist states against the Bol-
sheviks, but also almost unimaginable violence and cruelty on both sides.
Torture and massacres of prisoners were common, epidemic and famine

racked the country, and the economic base of the country was severely damaged.

The Civil War was an important formative experience for the Bolsheviks. To stay in power—to save the Revolution—they had launched a Red Terror and organized a secret police (CHEKA) with unlimited powers to arrest, try, and execute. The war had forced on the Bolsheviks a kind of military discipline that valued obedience, strict party unity, and a combative mentality. Words like *implacable* and *pitiless* came into the Bolshevik vocabulary as positive attributes for party members. Moreover, the life-and-death struggle against domestic and foreign enemies of the Revolution had nurtured in their minds a kind of siege mentality that saw enemies and conspiracies everywhere and allowed little in the way of compromise or toleration. Concerns for legality and civil rights were seen as "rotten liberalism" that was dangerous to the Revolution, and it was in this period that the Bolsheviks banned other parties and took monopolistic control of the press. Even after 1921, when the Civil War was won, these wartime measures were extended indefinitely. The regime never felt confident about its hold on power; domestic and foreign enemies were still out there, and to weaken the state seemed an unnecessary risk. Intolerance, quick recourse to violence and terror, and generalized fear and insecurity were the main legacies of the Civil War. The ends justified the means, and it was the Civil War that turned revolutionaries into dictators.[1]

Indeed, so concerned were they with maintaining iron discipline in their own ranks that at the very moment of victory they passed a resolution banning the formation of factions within their own party. Lenin's ideas of party organization, known as "democratic centralism," held that party policies should be adopted democratically, but once a decision was taken it was the duty of all party members publicly to defend and support those policies whether or not they personally agreed with them. Rather loosely observed in the party before and during 1917, these norms received strong reinforcement in the desperate emergency of the Civil War, and party leaders of all kinds had little trouble institutionalizing them as a "ban on factions" at the Tenth Party Congress in early 1921.

Economically, the Bolsheviks faced a bleak outlook at the end of the Civil War. During that struggle, their policies had been a patchwork of nationalizations, labor mobilizations, food requisitions, and state-sponsored barter known as War Communism. The Russian peasants, a large majority of the population, had in their own spontaneous revolution seized and redistributed the land during 1917. They tolerated Bolshevik forced grain requisitions during the war only because the alternative was a restoration of the Old Regime with its landlords. But with the passing of the wartime emergency the peasants were unwilling to sacrifice their harvests for the Bolshevik state, and a series of revolts convinced Lenin of the need to placate peasant farmers to save the regime.[2]

The result was the New Economic Policy (NEP), adopted in 1921. Free markets were allowed in agriculture and in small and medium industry (the Bolsheviks retained nationalized heavy industry in their own hands). Lenin saw this concession to capitalism as a necessary measure to appease the peasants and to allow market forces to help rebuild the shattered economy. NEP always enjoyed mixed popularity among the Bolsheviks, depending on their political views.[3]

For some "moderate" or "rightist" Bolsheviks, NEP was a strategic "retreat" that implied a fairly long road to the eventual socialist goal. Traversing that long evolutionary path would require patient socialist indoctrination of the population, education, and above all maintaining the goodwill of the peasant majority as it "grew into" socialism. For "leftist" Bolsheviks, NEP was more of a tactical "breathing spell," a temporary rest period before restarting the socialist offensive. For these leftists, NEP was always a dangerous concession to capitalism, and they believed that reaching socialism was a revolutionary process that would inevitably involve a "class struggle" with "capitalist elements" among the peasantry.

Regardless of their political disposition toward the mixed economy of NEP, virtually all Bolsheviks agreed that the basic problem was an economic one. If Russia was to reach socialism, it would have to undergo a dramatic industrial expansion. Marx had taught that socialism followed developed capitalism and was based on a modern technological and industrial base. Nobody in the party believed that Russia was anywhere near that stage, so the question was how (and how fast) to industrialize.

Rightist Bolsheviks, who clustered around the economic theoretician and *Pravda* editor Nikolai Bukharin (and eventually around the trade union leader Mikhail Tomsky and Premier Aleksei Rykov), saw NEP as a long-term strategy in which the party should maintain its alliance (*smychka*) with an increasingly prosperous peasantry. Funds for industrialization would be generated by rational taxation and the general growth of the economy. Leftist Bolsheviks, on the other hand, favored "squeezing" resources from the peasantry at a faster rate. Led by the Communist International chief and Leningrad party boss Grigory Zinoviev, Moscow party chief Lev Kamenev, and the brilliant Lev Trotsky, the leftists, impatient with what they considered coddling of the peasantry, pressed for a more militant and aggressive industrial policy. Rightists accused them of court-ing disaster by provoking the peasantry. Leftists retorted by arguing that the rightist version of NEP was a sellout to capitalist elements that were holding the Bolsheviks hostage and delaying industrialization.

Overlaying and sharpening these disagreements was a classic struggle for succession that followed Lenin's death in 1924. Responding to per-sonal loyalties, patron-client networks, and sometimes policy platforms, Bolshevik leaders began to gravitate to various high personalities of the party who contended for Lenin's mantle. Bukharin spoke for the pro-NEP rightist Bolsheviks. Zinoviev became the leading spokesman for the more aggressive economic leftists. Trotsky, always an iconoclast, took varying—although generally leftist—positions on economic questions but was best known as an advocate of antibureaucratism and increased party democracy.

Iosif Stalin, as general secretary of the party, had influence among the growing apparat, or full-time corps of professional party secretaries and administrators. The party had grown tremendously from its relatively humble size in early 1917. As it became larger and more complex and took on the tasks of government rather than those of insurrection, Lenin and other leaders saw the need to regularize the party's structure. Toward the end of the Civil War the party's governing body, the Central Committee (CC), formed three subcommittees to carry out the party's work between sittings of the full body. The Political Bureau (Politburo) was to decide the grand strategic questions of policy. An Organizational Bureau (Orgburo) was to organize implementation of these decisions by assigning cadres to the necessary tasks. Finally, a Secretariat was charged with the day-to-day mundane matters of handling correspondence and communication, mov-ing paperwork through the party bureaucracy, and preparing agendas for the other bodies. Stalin, pushed forward by Lenin as a good organizer, sat on all three subcommittees.[4]

Most party leaders believed that the Politburo would be the locus of real political power, and to a great extent it was. But as the struggle for per-sonal power heated up in the 1920s, real power—as is always the case in a large organization—was as much a question of patronage as of theory, and from his vantage in the Orgburo and Secretariat, Stalin was able to influence personnel appointments throughout the party. While the other leaders stood on economic policy platforms and theoretical formulations, Stalin's power was that of the machine boss. Throughout the country, territorially based party committees were led by a network of party secretaries who, in theory, carried out the Politburo's policy in the provinces. More and more in the 1920s, this full-time party secretarial apparatus looked to Stalin as its leader.[5]

And he was an attractive leader for many reasons. Unlike the other top leaders, Stalin was not an intellectual or theoretician. He spoke a simple and unpretentious language not unattractive to a party increasingly made up of workers and peasants. His style contrasted sharply with that of his Politburo comrades, whose complicated theories and pretentious demeanor won them few friends among the plebeian rank and file. He also had an uncanny way of projecting what appeared to be moderate solutions to complicated problems. Unlike his colleagues, who seemed shrill in their warnings of fatal crises, Stalin frequently put himself forward as the calm man of the golden mean with moderate, compromise solutions.

The personal struggle for power among the Olympian Bolshevik leaders was complicated but can be summarized quickly. Beginning in 1923 Trotsky launched a trenchant criticism of Stalin's "regime of professional secretaries," claiming that they had become ossified bureaucrats cut off from their proletarian followers. Trotsky also argued that the survival of the Bolshevik regime depended on receiving support from successful workers' revolutions in Europe, and he accused Stalin and other leaders of losing interest in spreading the revolution. To the other Politburo leaders, Trotsky seemed the most powerful and the most dangerous. By common recognition he was, after Lenin, the most brilliant theoretician in the party. More important, he was the leader of the victorious Red Army and regarded as personally ambitious, a potential Napoleon of the Russian Revolution.

Bukharin, Zinoviev, Kamenev, and Stalin closed ranks to isolate Trotsky, accusing him of trying to split the party because of his personal ambition to lead it. They argued that Trotsky was only using "party democracy" as a phony political issue: during the Civil War he had never been for anything less than iron discipline. Now, they charged, his criticism weakened party unity. Stalin in particular played a nationalist card by noting that the world revolution was not coming about as soon as they had thought, and in any case "we" Bolsheviks and "we" Soviet people do not need the help of foreigners to build socialism. "Socialism in One Country" was a real possibility, he argued, and Trotsky's insistence on proletarian revolutions abroad betrayed a lack of faith in the party's and country's possibilities. Faced with the unity of the other Politburo members, the party's near-religious devotion to party unity and discipline, and Stalin's influence among the party apparatus, Trotsky could not win. He was stripped of his military post in 1924 and gradually marginalized in the top leadership.[6]

The following year, in 1925, Zinoviev and Kamenev split off from the "party majority" by launching a critique of NEP from the leftist point of view. They said that the NEP policy of conceding constantly increasing grain prices to the peasantry was depriving the state of capital for industrialization, bankrupting industry, confronting the proletariat with high bread prices, and indefinitely postponing the march to socialism. In 1926 Trotsky joined Zinoviev and Kamenev in the "New" or "United Opposition." To the Leningrad and Moscow machine votes controlled by Zinoviev and Kamenev, Trotsky brought the remnants of his supporters.

Stalin and Bukharin denounced this United Opposition as another attempt to split the party by challenging the existing policy and violating the centralism part of democratic centralism. Moreover, they defended NEP as the only viable and safe policy. Their arguments seemed far less incendiary than those of the left. Bukharin's impressive pragmatic and theoretical defense of "Lenin's" NEP, combined with Stalin's low-key pragmatic approach, made a formidable combination. The votes from the party secretarial apparatus, loyal to Stalin and not eager to provoke a dangerous turn in party policy, won the day, and the United Opposition went down to defeat in 1927.[7]

In a final bid for power, followers of Trotsky organized a street demonstration on the anniversary of the October Revolution in 1927 to protest the Central Committee majority and defend the leftists. Stalin and Bukharin used the police to break up this demonstration, characterizing it as an illegal and disloyal blow against the party. It was one thing to disagree with the leadership by voting against it in conferences and congresses, but quite another to take to the streets. Such a move horrified the party majority because it threatened to take the inner-party struggle into the public eye, where real ("White," "counterrevolutionary") enemies, disgruntled workers, and discontented "elements" of all kinds could take advantage of the friction in the party to threaten the regime as a whole. Trotsky seemed to be putting his own interests above those of the Bolshevik government, thereby endangering the entire Revolution. As we shall see, any attempt to carry politics outside the confines of the party was the one unpardonable sin. Zinoviev and Kamenev were stripped of their most powerful positions. Trotsky was expelled from the party and exiled to Central Asia. Two years later, in 1929, he was deported from the country.

Bukharin and Stalin were in charge. Bukharin handled theoretical matters and the powerful party press. His associates Tomsky and Rykov ran the trade unions and the government ministries. Stalin, for his part, led the growing party apparatus, aided by a corps of Old Bolshevik lieutenants that included Viacheslav Molotov, Lazar Kaganovich, Kliment Voroshilov, and Sergo Ordzhonikidze. By all accounts, Stalin and Bukharin became close friends in this period. They called each other by familiar nicknames neither of them had used for Trotsky, Zinoviev, or Kamenev, and their arduous but successful struggle against the left certainly was a source of personal bonding. Their families saw each other socially, and Bukharin was a frequent guest in Stalin's home, sometimes spending entire summer months at Stalin's country house.[8]

But their political victory did not mean that the economy of NEP was working satisfactorily. Paying high prices for the peasants' grain drained the treasury and was not increasing the market for industrial goods by raising peasant buying power. After the industrial base was repaired and returned to the level of 1914, industrial growth was stagnating. Workers faced high food prices and intensification of labor discipline from various "labor rationalizations" designed to increase efficiency. By the late 1920s unemployment had reared its head, threatening the Bolsheviks' social base of support among the working class. The real and immediate threat, however, and the factor that would change everything, came from agriculture.

Despite what the Bolsheviks considered to be favorable prices, the Russian peasantry was not marketing an adequate quantity of grain to satisfy urban and military needs. The reasons for this were complicated and included poor agricultural technology, bad harvests, and market manipulation by peasants who held back grain to force higher prices. To Stalin in particular, all this smelled of peasant sabotage, and, while never admitting it outright, he doubtless began to wonder whether perhaps the leftists had not been right about the impossibility of allying with the peasants forever.

Beginning in 1927 Stalin sponsored a series of forced grain requisitions across the country. Squads of Bolshevik loyalists fanned out across the countryside, and local party officials were mobilized to force peasants to market their grain reserves at fixed prices. Bukharin was horrified. He was not a blind partisan of the market and had been in favor of a controlled squeezing of the well-to-do peasant (*kulak*). But Stalin's "extraordinary measures" went too far, striking at the "middle peasant" as well; such radical and voluntarist campaigns threatened to alienate the peasantry as a whole and destroy the market foundations of NEP. Bukharin, Rykov, and Tomsky protested in the Politburo.[9]

Tempers flared, positions hardened, and the gulf between Stalin and Bukharin widened quickly. Neither side would compromise and a break became inevitable. The Stalin faction accused Bukharin and his comrades of forming a pro-peasant "Right Opposition" against the "majority policy" of the Central Committee. In a series of Politburo and Central Committee meetings in 1928 and 1929, Stalin was able to mobilize enough votes to defeat the rightists by portraying the situation as a potentially fatal crisis for the regime. By 1930 Bukharin, Rykov, and Tomsky were stripped of their key positions. But unlike the leftists, the Right Opposition went quietly. They did not take the struggle outside the party corridors and never attempted to mobilize support "outside" in society. Rykov later said that the rightists had been afraid of provoking a civil war.[10] Accordingly, their treatment in defeat was much milder. They recanted their "mistakes" in party forums and with good party discipline affirmed their support for Stalin's line. Although they were removed from the Politburo, they remained on the Central Committee and were not expelled from the party. Those of their followers who refused to recant were expelled, and a few of most recalcitrant were arrested.

Their power now unchallenged, the Stalinists plunged ahead with a truly radical "Second Revolution," sometimes called the Stalin Revolution. In agriculture, the "extraordinary measures" of 1927–28 became a violent campaign of "dekulakization," in which hundreds of thousands of peasant families were deprived of their farms and deported to distant regions. By 1930 dekulakization had become the "full collectivization" of agriculture. Private farming and private property were ended, and agricultural production was organized into state-controlled collective farms. The public goal was to end capitalism and bring about the long-awaited socialism. The private goal was to end the economic power of the peasantry and establish control over food production.[11]

At the same time, the Stalinists abolished capitalism in industry and trade. All production was nationalized, and growth was to be planned without market mechanisms according to "Five-Year Plans" of the national economy. Based on the notions that socialism could be built immediately and that national defense required quick growth, industrialization was to be carried out at a breakneck pace. Production targets were set extremely high, and the country was mobilized for the campaign of development. A new "Soviet technical intelligentsia" was to be created to staff industry. Professional engineers trained under the old regime but still working in industry ("bourgeois specialists") were pushed aside, removed, and arrested in large numbers to make way for a new generation of rapidly trained and politically loyal Red Engineers. Factory workers were taken from production and sent to school in large numbers to staff this new cadre in a kind of massive affirmative action program for the proletariat.[12]

The Stalin Revolution was an enthusiastic campaign, not a policy. Scientific industrial "norms" and rational calculations of agricultural potential were cast aside in favor of enthusiastic mobilization. "Bolsheviks can storm any fortresses" became a watchword of the new revolution; speed and quantity rather than accuracy and quality became the criteria for success. Cautious warnings were denounced as sabotage or "capitalist wrecking," and careful analysis was suspect. No one could stand aside in the great push for modernization and socialism. And few did. The period of the first Five Year Plan (1928–32) was one of exuberance and excitement. Millions of workers went to school and moved into management. Millions of young peasants escaped the villages and flocked to new lives in construction. Young people volunteered in large numbers to work for the common effort, to help with collectivization, and to improve their work qualifications. For the young Nikita Khrushchevs and Leonid Brezhnevs, this was the best of times. It was the period of optimism and dynamism and the era that launched their careers. The enthusiastic upward mobility for plebeians looked very much like the fruition of the Revolution: the workers were taking power and building socialism!

The Bolsheviks believed that they were involved in a life-or-death "class war" against the remaining "capitalist elements" in society. They issued slogans about class warfare and constantly stressed the need to win a quick victory, not only for the sake of socialism but to prevent an expected foreign intervention by capitalist states eager to protect their kulak and capitalist class allies. Party discipline took on an even more military character than before; party "mobilizations" on this or that "front" were always in the air. Even the military tunic of Civil War days came back into fashion for party leaders and militants.

The first Five Year Plan was a resounding success. Production indexes in mining, steel, and chemicals increased severalfold in four years. Factories and mines sprang up everywhere, and the country was proud of the new giant dams, plants, and railroads whose construction contrasted so sharply with the industrial doldrums of the Great Depression in the West. Unemployment disappeared, and although real wages actually fell (another casualty of capital accumulation), education, opportunity, and mobility were available to everyone willing to work. In the lives of the rapidly increasing urban masses, on the factory wall charts of production, and in the rapidly growing network of educational institutions, everything was onward and upward.

But taken on the basis of its effect on the lives of the peasantry, the agricultural part of the Stalin Revolution was an unqualified disaster, provoking one of the greatest human tragedies of modern times. Wild radical collectivizers descended on the villages, closing churches and attacking priests and other traditional village leaders. Grain was seized without any regard for peasants' need for food and seed. Any resistance was attributed to "kulak sabotage" and was punished with deportation to Siberia, arrest, or execution. Many peasants were unable to plant because the seed had been taken; others, in protest, refused to plant. Rather than give up their animals to the new collective farms, peasants slaughtered horses, cows, pigs, and sheep in huge numbers. When the meat was gone, the peasants starved. Soviet meat production would not recover for decades. The loss of animal traction power and the regime's inability to provide tractors in adequate numbers paralyzed agriculture. The regime's inability or unwillingness to calculate rational targets for planting and harvesting combined with chaos in the countryside and bad weather to produce mass starvation. Millions died from hunger, disease, or the terrible conditions of remote exile.

By and large, party militants had responded loyally to the Stalinist "socialist offensive" of 1929–34. Believing that they were fighting the final battle for the communist millennium, masses of party members responded enthusiastically to the leadership's calls for rapid collectivization and escalating industrial production targets. In some cases, local militants' zeal outstripped the plans of the center, and Moscow often had to rein in excessive "dekulakizations," forcible collectivization, and ultraleftist zeal in persecuting religion. At other times, local party officials and activists balked at the grain requisitions and more extreme forms of dekulakization and collectivization. Most of the time, though, the hard-line activities of party collectivizers on the ground were a reflection of the extreme policies of the Stalin leadership. The result was a disastrous famine and social violence and persecution on an unimaginable scale.

As we have noted, the Right Opposition of N. I. Bukharin, M. P. Tomsky, and A. I. Rykov had bucked the leftist course of collectivization back in 1928. But it had been defeated by 1929, and its leaders had recanted their mistakes in order to remain in the party. These mandatory recantations were designed not only to show a united face to the world but also to "disarm" the lower-level followers of the leading oppositionists. Former dissident leaders were required to show their agreement with the Stalinist party line in order to demonstrate to their former adherents that resistance was wrong. One scholar has aptly described such public apologies as a ritual payment of "symbolic taxes" or "symbolic capital": public display of acceptance of error in order to reaffirm the status quo.[13]

The former dissidents were further expected to work loyally and diligently to fulfill that line and to combat the party's enemies. This was the essence of party discipline, as the Bolsheviks understood it. The following document is one of N. I. Bukharin's recantations. In 1930, however, such rituals did not have the solemnity that they would take on later. Oppositionists could still recant in a virtual colloquy with the Stalinist audience; Bukharin's text contained puns, and his reference to executing dissidents drew laughter.

BUKHARIN: The Party leadership had to crush [*razgromit'*] the most dangerous rightist deviation within our Party.

VOROSHILOV: And those infected with it.

BUKHARIN: If you are talking about their physical destruction [*razgrom*], I leave it to those comrades who are, to one degree or another, given to bloodthirstiness. (Laughter) . . . I feel compelled to show my wit by recalling a certain ditty [*chastushka*], which was published in its time in the now defunct *Russian Gazette* [*Russkie Vedomosti*]: "They may beat me, they may beat me senseless, they may beat me to a pulp, but nobody is gonna kill this kid, not with a stick, a bat or a stone." (Laughter breaks out throughout the room). I cannot say, however, that "nobody is gonna kill me."

KAGANOVICH: Who, may I ask, is the kid here and who the person wielding a stone?

> BUKHARIN: Oh, how witty you are! Obviously, it was I who was struck and beaten with a stone. And now not a single member of the Plenum—I dare say—thinks that I am concealing some sort of a "stone" of resentment, not even the stone-faced Kamenev.[14]

In his speech, Bukharin, addressing the ruling Stalinist group, observed that "all power and authority are in your hands." Shkiriatov and Molotov chided him for this breach of party etiquette: Bukharin's remark contradicted the party unity he was preaching and suggested a hierarchy within the nomenklatura leadership, the very situation his recantation and profession of support was supposed to end, or at least hide. Even though such passages were not released publicly, it was necessary for the elite to maintain a unified rhetorical affirmation of power and solidarity to and for themselves. As James Scott has noted, such apologetic transcripts and rituals were meant not only for subordinates. They served to affirm unanimity within and for the elite itself, because "the audience for such displays is not only subordinates; elites are also consumers of their own performance."[15]

Despite the generally light tone of Bukharin's confession, Kaganovich had pointedly interrupted him with the demand that the oppositionists must not only recognize their mistakes but must sincerely convince others among their former followers. This was the real purpose of recantation. V. V. Kuibyshev, speaking for the Stalinist majority, laid down this law in no uncertain terms in a December 1930 speech: "It is absolutely clear that at such a time it should be demanded of a leader of the Party or Soviet state, first and foremost, that he lead the battle for the general line, that he take his place in the front ranks of this campaign. It is not enough that he should say that he 'is doing the best he can.'"[16]

Kuibyshev's terms were tough. Indeed, there is reason to believe that Stalin's lieutenants took a more aggressive stance toward the opposition than he did. One month before Bukharin and Kuibyshev spoke, a Politburo meeting had considered punishments for two high-ranking Central Committee members (Syrtsov and Lominadze) who had taken a "right-opportunist" line against the excesses of collectivization. In the Politburo, Stalin proposed demoting them to the status of candidate members of the Central Committee. The majority, however, "strongly" disagreed and voted to expel them from the CC.[17]

By 1932 there was no formal organized opposition faction in the party's highest leadership. The vast majority of the leading leftist and rightist oppositionists had recanted. Although it seems that the majority of the party, both in the leadership and the rank and file, dutifully implemented the Stalin Revolution, the chaos of 1932 produced doubts, grumbling, and eventually outright opposition among some veteran Old Bolsheviks. And below the very top level, among the second- and third-rank oppositionists, resistance to Stalin's policies was still strong; in 1932 it began to coalesce. We can document three such groups: the Riutin group, a reactivated Trotskyist organization, and the Eismont-Tolmachev-Smirnov group.

M. N. Riutin had been a district party secretary in the Moscow party organization in the 1920s and had supported Bukharin's challenge to Stalin's policy of collectivization. But unlike Bukharin and the other senior rightist leaders, he had refused to recant and to formally support Stalin's course. As a result, he had been stripped of his party offices and expelled from the party in 1930 "for propagandizing right-opportunist views."[18] Riutin remained in contact with fellow opponents inside the party, and in March of 1932 a secret meeting of his group produced two documents. One of these was a seven-page typewritten appeal "To All Members of the VKP(b)," which gave an abbreviated critique of Stalin and his policies and called on all party members to oppose them in any ways they could.[19] At the bottom of the appeal from the "All Union Conference 'Union of Marxist-Leninists'" was the request to read the document, copy it, and pass it along to others.

By far the most important document drafted at the March 1932 meeting was the so-called Riutin Platform, formally entitled "Stalin and the Crisis of the Proletarian Dictatorship." This manifesto of the Union of Marxist-Leninists was a multifaceted, direct, and trenchant critique of virtually all of Stalin's policies, his methods of rule, and his personality. The Riutin Platform, drafted in March, was discussed and rewritten over the next few months. At an underground meeting of Riutin's group in a village in the Moscow suburbs on 21 August 1932, the document was finalized by an editorial committee of the Union. (Riutin, at his own request, was not formally a member of the committee because at that time he was not a party member.)[20] At a subsequent meeting, the leaders decided to circulate the platform secretly from hand to hand and by mail. Numerous copies were made and circulated in Moscow, Kharkov, and other cities.

It is not clear how widely the Riutin Platform was spread, nor do we know how many party members actually read it or even heard of it. The evidence we do have, however, suggests that the Stalin regime reacted to it in fear and panic. The document's call to "destroy Stalin's dictatorship" was taken as a call for armed revolt.

One of the contacts receiving the platform turned it over to the secret police. Arrests of Union members began as early as September 1932. The entire editorial board, plus Riutin, was arrested in the fall of 1932; all were expelled from the party and sentenced to prison for membership in a "counterrevolutionary organization." Riutin himself was sentenced to ten years in prison. There is a persistent myth that Stalin unsuccessfully demanded the death penalty for those connected with the Riutin Platform but was blocked by a majority of the Politburo.[21] At any rate, by early 1937 all the central figures in the Riutin opposition group had been shot for treason.

At the end of 1932 many of the former leaders of opposition movements, including G. E. Zinoviev, L. B. Kamenev, Karl Radek, and others, were summoned to party disciplinary bodies and interrogated about their possible connection to the group; some were expelled anew from the party simply for knowing of the existence of the Riutin Platform, whether they had read it or not. Indeed, in coming years having read the platform, or even knowing about it and not reporting that knowledge to the party, would be considered a crime. In virtually all inquisitions of former oppositionists from 1934 to 1939, this "terrorist document" would be used as evidence connecting Stalin's opponents to various treasonable conspiracies. By providing a cohesive alternative discourse around which rank-and-file party members might unite against the elite, the platform threatened nomenklatura control:

> To place the name of Stalin alongside the names of Marx, Engels and Lenin means to mock at Marx, Engels and Lenin. It means to mock at the proletariat. It means to lose all shame, to overstep all bounds of baseness. To place the name of Lenin alongside the name of Stalin is like placing Mt. Elbrus alongside a heap of dung. To place the works of Marx, Engels and Lenin alongside the "works" of Stalin is like placing the music of such great composers as Beethoven, Mozart, Wagner and others alongside the music of a street organ-grinder. . . .
>
> Lenin was a leader [vozhd'] but not a dictator. Stalin, on the contrary, is a dictator but not a leader. . . .
>
> The entire top leadership of the Party leadership, beginning with Stalin and ending with the secretaries of the provincial committees are, on the whole, fully aware that they are breaking with Leninism, that they are perpetrating vi-

olence against both the Party and non-Party masses, that they are killing the cause of socialism. However, they have become so tangled up, have brought about such a situation, have reached such a dead-end, such a vicious circle, that they themselves are incapable of breaking out of it.

The mistakes of Stalin and his clique have turned into crimes. . . .

In the struggle to destroy Stalin's dictatorship, we must in the main rely not on the old leaders but on new forces. These forces exist, these forces will quickly grow. New leaders will inevitably arise, new organizers of the masses, new authorities.

A struggle gives birth to leaders and heroes.

We must begin to take action.[22]

To those who defended the monopoly version of political reality, this text inspired fear and anger. It is not an exaggeration to say that the Riutin Platform began the process that would lead to terror, precisely by terrifying the ruling nomenklatura. Why did this document provoke such fury in the highest levels of the party leadership? First of all, it was a text, and to those who took such pains to produce political documents, the appearance of an actual alternative written text carried special significance. So anxious was the regime to bury the Riutin Platform that it has proved impossible to find an original copy in any Russian archive. (The surviving text is taken from a typescript copy made by the secret police in 1932.) Indeed, it seems that the words themselves were considered dangerous. Reaction to them recalls Foucault's description of the speech of a "medieval madman" whose utterances were beyond the limits of accepted speech but at the same time had a power, a prescience, and a kind of magic revealing a hidden and dangerous truth.[23] Similarly, Trotsky's writings in exile were sharply proscribed but were carefully read by Stalinist leaders in the 1930s.[24] To the Stalinists, the words of Riutin and Trotsky seem to have had a special kind of threatening quality, and the reaction of the elite to them seems to reflect a fear of the language itself.

Second, the Riutin Platform subjected the Stalin leadership to a sustained and withering criticism for its agricultural, industrial, and inner-party policies that remained the most damning indictment of Stalinism from inside the Soviet Union until the Gorbachev period. Even Nikita Khrushchev's 1956 "Secret Speech" was neither as comprehensive nor as negative in its assessment of Stalin. The language was bitter, combative, and insulting to anyone in the party leadership.

Third, the Riutin Platform could not have come at a more dangerous time for the party leadership. The industrialization drive of the first Five Year Plan had not brought economic stability, and although growth was impressive, so were the chaos and upheaval caused by mass urbanization, clogged transport, and falling real wages. The situation in the countryside was even more threatening. Collectivization and peasant resistance to it had led to the famine of 1932; eventually millions of "unnatural deaths" from starvation and repression would be recorded. Faced with this disaster, the Stalinist leadership held its cruel course and refused to abandon its forced collectivization of agriculture. On lower levels of the party, however, many in the field charged with implementation began to waver. Reluctant to consign local populations to mass death, many local party officials refused to push relentlessly forward and actually argued with the center about the high grain collection targets. The country and its ruling apparatus were falling apart. In such conditions, any dissident group emerging from within the besieged party was bound to provoke fear, panic, and anger from a leadership that worshiped party unity and discipline.

Finally, and politically most important, the platform threatened to carry the party leadership struggle outside the bounds of the ruling elite, the nomenklatura. The leftist opposition of the mid-1920s had attempted to do this as well by organizing public demonstrations and by agitating the rank and file of the party. The response of the leadership at that time— which included not only the Stalinists but also the moderate Bukharinists and indeed the vast majority of the party elite—had been swift and severe: expulsion from the party and even arrest. Although leaders might fight among themselves behind closed doors, any attempt to carry the struggle to the party rank and file or to the public could not be tolerated. Such a struggle not only would open the door to a split in the party between left and right but would raise the possibility of an even more dangerous rift between top and bottom within the party. Such a danger was particularly acute in 1932, with the reluctance of some local party members to press collectivization as hard as Moscow demanded. Such a split would almost certainly destroy the Leninist generation, which saw itself as the bearers of communist ideology and as the vanguard of the less politically conscious working class and the mass of untutored new party members inducted since the Civil War. But the idea of Leninism was not the only thing at stake. Isolated as they were in the midst of a sullen peasant majority—relatively few communists in a sea of peasants who wanted nothing more than private property—the Bolsheviks realized that only military discipline and party unity could keep them in power, especially during a crisis in which their survival was threatened. The nomenklatura was therefore personally threatened by opposition movements that sought to set the rank and file against the leadership. Back in the 1920s the Trotskyist opposition had taken the argument outside the party leadership and literally to the streets; Trotskyists had organized a public demonstration against the party leadership. After this dangerous experience, the elite at all levels understood the dangers posed by a politicization of the masses on terms other than those prescribed by the elite.

It was this understanding of group solidarity that had prevented the rightist (Bukharinist) opposition from lobbying outside the ruling stratum. The risks were too high, especially in an unstable social and political situation where the party did not command the loyalty of a majority of the country's population. Accordingly, the sanctions taken against the defeated rightists were much lighter than those earlier inflicted on the Trotskyists. Although some of the rightists were expelled from the party, and its leaders lost their highest positions, Bukharin and his fellow leaders remained members of the Central Committee. They had, after all, played according to the terms of the unwritten gentleman's agreement not to carry the struggle outside the nomenklatura.

Although the Riutin Platform is notable for its assault on Stalin personally, it was also attacking the ruling group in the party and the stratified nomenklatura establishment that had taken shape since the 1920s. That elite regarded the platform as a call for revolution from within the party. After the Riutin incident, the ruling stratum reacted more and more sharply to any criticism of Stalin, not because they feared him—although events would show that they should have—but because they needed him to stay in power. In this sense, Stalin's interests and those of the nomenklatura coincided.

Although the Riutin Platform originated in the right wing of the Bolshevik party, its specific criticisms of the Stalinist regime were in the early 1930s shared by the more leftist Lev Trotsky, who also had sought to organize political opposition "from below." Trotsky had been expelled from the Bolshevik Party in 1927 and exiled from the Soviet Union in 1929. Since that time, he had lived in several exile locations, writing prolifically for his *Bulletin of the Opposition*. Like the Riutin group, Trotsky believed that the Soviet Union in 1932 was in a period of extreme crisis provoked by Stalin's policies. Like them, he believed that the rapid pace of forced collectivization was a disaster and that the hurried and voluntarist nature of industrial policy made rational planning impossible, resulting in a disastrous series of economic "imbalances." Along with the Riutinists, Trotsky called for a drastic change in economic course and democratization of the dictatorial regime within a party that suppressed all dissent. According to Trotsky, Stalin had brought the country to ruin.[25]

At the same time the Riutin group was forging its programmatic documents, Trotsky was attempting to activate his followers in the Soviet Union. Most of the leaders of the Trotskyist opposition had capitulated to Stalin in 1929–31, as Stalin's sharp leftist change of course seemed to them consistent with the main elements of the Trotsky critique in the 1920s. Trotsky himself, however, along with a small group of "irreconcilables," had refused to accept Stalin's leftist change of course and remained in opposition.

Sometime in 1932 Trotsky sent a series of secret personal letters to his former followers Karl Radek, G. I. Sokolnikov, and E. Preobrazhensky and others in the Soviet Union.[26] And at about the same time, he sent a letter to his oppositionist colleagues in the Soviet Union by way of an English traveler: "I am not sure that you know my handwriting. If not, you will probably find someone else who does. . . . The comrades who sympathize with the Left Opposition are *obliged* to come out of their passive state at this time, maintaining, of course, all *precautions*. . . . I am certain that the menacing situation in which the Party finds itself will force all the comrades devoted to the revolution to gather actively about the Left Opposition."[27]

More concretely, in late 1932 Trotsky was actively trying to forge a new opposition coalition in which former oppositionists from both left and right would participate. From Berlin, Trotsky's son Lev Sedov maintained contact with the veteran Trotskyist I. N. Smirnov in the Soviet Union. In 1932 Trotsky accepted Smirnov's proposal of a united oppositional bloc that would include both leftist and rightist groups in the USSR. Trotsky favored an active group: "One struggles against repression by anonymity and conspiracy, not by silence."[28] Shortly thereafter, Smirnov relayed word to Sedov that the bloc had been organized; Sedov wrote to his father, "It embraces the Zinovievists, the Sten-Lominadze group, and the Trotskyists (old '_____')."[29] Trotsky promptly announced in his newspaper that the first steps had been taken toward formation of an illegal organization of "Bolshevik-Leninists."[30]

Back in the Soviet Union, the authorities smashed Trotsky's bloc before it got off the ground. In connection with their roundup of suspected participants in the Riutin group, nearly all the leaders of the new bloc were pulled in for questioning. Many of them were expelled from the party and sentenced to prison or exile. Sedov wrote to his father that although "the arrest of the 'ancients' is a great blow, the lower workers are safe."[31]

As with the Riutin episode, it was these "lower workers" that troubled the leadership the most, and Trotsky no doubt knew this. A few months later Trotsky wrote a letter to the Politburo. Trotsky pointed out that he had tried to make the Stalinist leadership see the error of its ways and invite him back into the fold. This having failed, he offered Stalin one last chance to make peace and to integrate the Trotskyists back into the ruling elite. Speaking as one nomenklatura member to another, he issued the ultimate threat: if the Stalinists refused to deal with him, he would feel free to agitate for his views among rank-and-file party members.[32] As with the Riutinists, Trotsky's new initiatives promised to take the political struggle outside the elite and thereby strike at the heart of the nomenklatura.

The Stalinist leadership was well informed about the dissident and "conspiratorial" activities of the Riutin and Trotsky groups. It was in possession of the Riutin Platform weeks after it was written and managed to neutralize the group in short order. We also know that senior leaders in Moscow read Trotsky's *Biulleten' oppozitsii* and were aware of I. N. Smirnov's secret communications with Trotsky. Two years later, when N. I. Yezhov had become head of the NKVD, he disclosed that the secret police had been aware at the time of Smirnov's 1932 connections with Trotsky through Sedov.[33] But what about the "lower workers," as Sedov had called them? As the preceding documents show, both Riutin and Trotsky had practically given up on the well-known leaders of the oppositions of the 1920s and had pinned their hopes on rank-and-file members to carry the banner against Stalin.

From the point of view of the elite, the climate "out there" gave little cause for optimism. Secret police reports on the mood of the population in the larger cities showed that many common folk thought of themselves as "us" and the regime as "them."[34] Popular poems, songs, and ditties (*chastushki*) expressed hostility to the regime:

Stalin stands on a coffin
Gnawing meat from a cat's bones.
Well, Soviet cows
Are such disgusting creatures.
How the collective farm village
Has become prosperous.
There used to be 33 farmsteads
And now there are five.
We fulfilled the Five Year Plan
And are eating well.
We ate all the horses
And are now chasing the dogs.
Ukraine!
Breadbasket!
She sold bread to the Germans
And is now herself hungry.
O commune, O commune,
You commune of Satan.
You seized everything
All in the Soviet cause.[35]

We know very little about actual lower-level dissidence. The archives contain only sporadic evidence of such activity. We know, for example, that underground Trotskyists in the Bauman district of Moscow (the "Moscow Group of Bolshevik-Leninists") published a newsletter called "Against the Current" in 1931.[36] We also have ambiguous evidence of the existence of other underground groups.[37]

It is possible that the organizations in question were simply inventions of zealous police investigators who rounded up some marginal people and beat false confessions out of them. As an institution, the secret police had a vested interest in periodically producing "conspiracies" to justify their position and funding. Similarly, hard-liners within the party at various levels, anxious to show the need for repression, also had an interest in magnifying the importance of such "organizations," which could be portrayed as a real threat to the nomenklatura elite. Nevertheless, given the chaos and hardship that Stalin's policies provoked in the country at the time, it would be surprising if such groups were a complete figment of the police imagination.

It is clear that the Stalin regime was not very popular among certain segments of the political public, and it knew it.[38] Among "Old Bolsheviks" of both left and right, rank-and-file party members, and students there was anti-Stalin grumbling. And outside the politically articulate strata, the regime was still waging virtual civil war with the majority of the peasantry. There can be no doubt that the regime was worried about the discontent and the implications for its continued rule. The very fact that the highest leadership would solicit and circulate reports on clumsy groups of students (whose "platform" could not even be produced and whose criticisms had already been voiced and acknowledged semipublicly) is in itself symptomatic of the nomenklatura's malaise.

Still, from the point of view of internal party self-representation, it was possible for Stalinist Bolsheviks to rationalize this opposition and reconcile it with their Leninist self-image. Thus the Trotskyist and rightist oppositions had long been categorized not as deviant tendencies within Bolshevism but as representatives of hostile class and political forces, usually the kulaks or White Guards. Their proposals to remove Stalin and change the party leadership could thus be branded as un-Leninist and outside the pale of the Lenin-Stalin orthodoxy that was the ideological pillar of the regime.

It was more difficult to rationalize the massive discontent, resistance, and famine among the peasantry in terms of orthodoxy and regime legitimacy. Of course, the enemy class attribute was always available: acts of resistance were attributed to kulaks—"bourgeois" peasant ringleaders—or to their "influence," just as "Trotskyist" would become an attributive category later for any form of political deviation. Despite massive evidence to the contrary, the regime maintained (and perhaps even believed) that the middle and poorer peasants were on their side. This public position allowed the Bolsheviks to claim that a majority of the country was behind them. Even within the party's secret counsels, their "hidden transcript" was the same as their public one. Mechanisms and explanations were found to rationalize peasant resistance and even a widespread famine that the Bolsheviks were anxious to hide and to deny even to themselves. The mental gymnastics of rationalization—not only in public propaganda but also in the top secret documents of the regime—made it possible to avoid questioning the basic policy both out loud and even to oneself. All the problems were the result of conspiracies or incompetent local officials. Even hunger was a kulak conspiracy.[39]

A regime that feels it necessary to arrest groups of marginal students in small towns or that panics about a dissident program that was narrowly circulated and never published is not a confident one. This government and its leaders were afraid of their own shadows and of anything that might challenge their political monopoly and privilege. As former revolutionaries who had used propaganda to come to power, they feared the printed word. The attentive efforts and technical workings of Bolshevik censors to control the production of texts have been well documented.[40] What has been perhaps less well known is the extent to which the top leadership was preoccupied with such questions. Typewritten pamphlets by student groups attracted the attention of the Politburo and found their way into its files.[41] The Politburo reviewed individual books and decided on their removal from libraries. Lists of such books were prepared as official orders of the Politburo.[42]

At the same time, though, leaders' fear was not accompanied by self-doubt about policies or means. What alternatives did the Bolsheviks have for interpreting and understanding the situation in the country? One way—perhaps the most rational way—to grasp the situation would have been in terms of mistaken policies. It is obvious to us today that collectivization and breakneck industrialization were ill advised and reckless. Of course, this interpretation of events was not available to the general population or even to most layers of the party-state administration; articulation of this view brought instant repression. But in a different way it was also impossible for leading Bolsheviks within the Stalinist faction to accept that their policies were wrong. Everything in their background and intellectual baggage told them that there was a "correct" solution to every situation and that they had in Stalin's General Line found the correct solution to Russia's backwardness, to class oppression, and to the problems of capitalism. Their nineteenth-century rationalist faith in scientific solutions to human problems, combined with their facile understanding of Marx's stages of historical development, told them that they were on the right track. Their victory in 1917 and dramatic rise to power seemed to validate them and their place as midwives of history. Aside from the desire to protect their privileged position, they really believed in socialism and their own key importance in realizing it. It was genuinely impossible to imagine that their policies were wrong. Nevertheless, their conviction was no doubt strengthened consciously or subconsciously by the recognition that their personal positions and collective fortunes were tied to those policies.

So when things went wrong, when disasters occurred, it was necessary for them to find answers and solutions that avoided self-questioning. The most available explanation for problems, and one with resonance in Russian culture, was that conspiratorial "dark forces" were at work to sabotage the effort. If the policies were correct and if they were being implemented by the right people, there could be no other explanation. Schooled in the brutal Civil War of 1918–21, when there were real conspiracies, Stalinist leaders and followers found it easy to believe that enemies of various kinds were responsible for every problem. Of course, for the top leaders, there was a convenient element of scapegoating in blaming everything on "alien enemy forces." At the same time, reading the transcripts of closed party meetings, Central Committee sessions, and even personal letters among the senior leaders gives the strong impression that it was more than scapegoating. To a significant extent, even Politburo members seemed to have genuinely believed in the existence of myriad conspiracies and considered them real threats to the regime.

The regime's fear of everything from elite platforms to gossiping students was conditioned by a silent recognition that its control was in fact weakly based in the country. The leaders' recourse to spasmodic mass violence in place of ordered administration would be another proof of weakness disguised by brute force. This fragility was combined with a fanatical lack of self-doubt, a belief in conspiracies, a traditional Russian intolerance of opposition, and a conditioned recourse to violence to produce the Stalinist mentality.

The Stalinist leadership in the coming years would refer repeatedly to the "new situation" that began in 1932. In the repression of 1936–39, many party leaders would be accused of involvement in the "Riutin affair." This was a key accusation against Bukharin in 1937, and even his last letter to Stalin from prison dealt with the charge. Yezhov, the head of the secret police, would frequently refer to the Riutin Platform and the Trotskyists' 1932 activities as evidence of a massive plot against the government. The fear that such "plots" could set the party membership and the population against the regime would haunt the nomenklatura for years after the plots themselves had been smashed.

To insure themselves against the perceived threat of party splits based on either ideology or status conflict, the party's leading stratum began in 1932 a series of measures to protect their monopoly on power. These measures included stiffening party discipline in the nomenklatura itself, screening the party's membership for "dubious elements" of all kinds, strengthening the repressive apparatus (both police and party organizations), reforming the judiciary in various ways, tightening ideological and cultural conformity, redefining the "enemy" in broader and broader ways, and eventually blind, mass terror. These are the subjects of the chapters that follow.

These measures often evolved in a series of contradictory oscillations, moves and countermoves, rather than in a straight-line trend toward a particular goal. At the same time, however, the twisting road to terror was paved by an amazing group consensus within the nomenklatura, bordering on paranoia, about the need to tighten controls and generally to "circle the wagons" against a variety of real and imagined threats from the peasantry, the former opposition, rank-and-file members, and even their own ranks.

CHAPTER TWO

Party Discipline in 1932

One must not discuss anything behind the Party's back. In view of our present situation, this is a political act, and a political act behind the Party's back is manifestly an anti-Party action, which could only be committed by people who have lost all connection with the Party.—A. P. Smirnov, 1932

Both our internal and external situation is such that this iron discipline must not under any circumstances be relaxed. . . . That is why such factions must be hacked off without the slightest mercy, without being in the slightest troubled by any sentimental considerations concerning the past, concerning personal friendships, relationships, concerning respect for a person as such and so forth. We are currently at war and we must exercise the strictest discipline.
—N. I. Bukharin, 1932

THE CENTRAL COMMITTEE plenum of January 1933 took place in a crisis atmosphere. Famine was still widespread. Because of the hunger and the rapid industrialization, population movements took on a titanic scale as millions of peasants moved about seeking food and employment. As a result of mass recruitment drives in 1929–32, the party's membership had swelled from 1.5 to 3.5 million.[1] Many of these were raw, "untested" recruits about whom the party leadership knew little. As we have seen, significant numbers of lower-level cadres had balked at the stern measures of collectivization, and the Riutin and Trotsky episodes had threatened to mobilize these lower cadres against the nomenklatura leadership. From the point of view of that senior leadership, things had slipped out of control in a threatening way.

Desperate to establish control, the senior party leadership took several measures. After having encouraged peasant migration to labor-short industrial areas in 1931, the Bolsheviks were faced with a loss of control of population movement as masses of peasants streamed into the cities. As a response to the famine, the regime established an internal passport system at the end of 1932 to stabilize residency.[2] To defuse the threat from its local cadres, the Central Committee in January 1933 established political departments in the rural Machine Tractor Stations in order to purge recalcitrant local party officials. At the same time, a purge of these local cadres was under way, and the January 1933 plenum ordered a general purge of the swollen party ranks.[3]

Given its loss of control over the country and the various threats it faced, the nomenklatura could not afford any splintering of its own ranks. The members of the Riutin and Trotskyist groups in the fall of 1932 were, from the point of view of party position, marginal figures, and it is difficult to imagine that they constituted a real threat to the regime. They had been deprived of their party posts years before, and their leaders (Riutin and Trotsky) had been expelled from the party. But at precisely this moment, in November 1932, another dissident group was "unmasked" by the police. This time its members were high-ranking members of the current party leadership.

In 1932 N. B. Eismont was People's Commissar for Supply of the RSFSR government. His apartment was the scene of a series of gatherings of friends and comrades who were critical of the Stalin line on collectivization and industrialization. Among these were V. N. Tolmachev (a department head in one of the transport sections of the RSFSR) and E. P. Ashukina (chief of the Personnel Planning Department of the USSR Commissariat of Agriculture), but the most influential member of the circle was A. P. Smirnov, an Old Bolshevik party member since 1898 and chairman of the Public Housing Commission of the Central Executive Committee. Smirnov had been a member of the party Central Committee since 1912 (the year Stalin became a member) and in 1932 sat on its powerful Orgburo.

At one of these gatherings on 7 November 1932 (ironically, the anniversary of the 1917 Bolshevik revolution) Eismont had a conversation with one I. V. Nikolsky, an old friend recently arrived from work in the Caucasus. It is not clear exactly what Eismont said to Nikolsky, but it seems that there was considerable drinking and talk about removing or replacing Stalin as party leader. In any case, to Nikolsky the conversation had an "antiparty character," and he reported Eismont's statement to his friend M. Savelev, who in turn wrote a letter to Stalin about it.[4] The police quickly rounded up Eismont and his circle, all of whom were quickly interrogated. A. P. Smirnov was not present at Eismont's gathering, but was on close working and personal terms with many of those present. Although he was not arrested, he was summoned to the Politburo for an "explanation" and face-to-face confrontation with Eismont.[5]

The participants in this affair were of sufficient rank and stature that their "case" was the subject of a debate at the next plenum of the Central Committee in January 1933. M. F. Shkiriatov and Ya. Rudzutak were the main accusers from the party's disciplinary body, the Central Control Commission. Smirnov spoke in his own defense: "First of all, I would like to resolutely and categorically disavow the vile, counter-revolutionary words concerning Comrade Stalin ascribed to me. . . . One must not discuss anything behind the Party's back. In view of our present situation, this is a political act, and a political act behind the Party's back is manifestly an anti-Party action . . . It's absolutely clear."[6]

The attack on Smirnov at the meeting illustrates a number of aspects of the party leadership's attitude toward oppositionists in the 1930s, including guilt by association or by subjective attitude even in the absence of a specific act or violation. They also show the stricter demands that the Stalinist leadership made of former oppositionists. It was no longer enough for repentant oppositionists repeatedly to admit their mistakes, condemn their former positions, and take responsibility for the continued offenses of their former partisans. Such a position was considered too passive—"standing to one side" in the "active struggle with anti-party elements [and] for the general line of the party." For the Stalinists, it was now necessary for the former dissidents actively to attack their followers, to inform on those still in opposition, and to work visibly to affirm the Stalinist version of reality.

As a member of the party leadership, Smirnov was obliged to oppose and to report any nefarious activities or speech to disciplinary authorities. Smirnov's "confession" was only partial. Because he wasn't present at the ill-fated drinking party, he did not think that he was personally guilty, or at least as guilty as the others. Moreover, he expressed reservations by not denying his crimes, "if there are any." His speech was constative, about true and false charges. Subsequent remarks made it clear that this was not enough. The party leadership wanted performative speech. It expected Smirnov and the others to carry out a full apology ritual: to admit their guilt, to outline the dangerous consequences of their previous actions, and thereby to affirm the truth of the charges and the right of the leadership to make them. Smirnov had not played that role completely, and his critics were quick to renew their attack.

Stalinist political practice involved considerable symbolism and ritual, and it is well known that all revolutionary regimes try to establish legitimacy and consolidate support with rituals and cults.[7] In the Soviet period, the officially sponsored cults of Lenin, Stalin, and the Great Patriotic War are famous.[8] Until the recent release of internal documentation, however, we have not been able to analyze elite ritual practice. Elites "justify their existence and order their actions in terms of a collection of stories, ceremonies, insignia, formalities, and appurtenances. . . . It is these—crowns and coronations, limousines and conferences—that mark the center as center and give what goes on there its aura of being not merely important but in some odd fashion connected with the way the world is built."[9]

The inseparable connection between politics and ritual can be seen in the Stalinist "apology ritual" used to censure an important official. The official, who was either removed or merely censured, played his part by recognizing that Moscow's position was "completely correct," reiterating Moscow's critique in the context of "self-criticism." These apologetic rituals were designed to affirm unanimity and were "a show of discursive affirmation from below" to demonstrate that the dissident "publicly accepts . . . the judgment of his superior that this is an offense and reaffirms the rule in question."[10]

Such rituals had public versions that were performed before the population. The most obvious examples are the show trials of the 1930s, which were crude morality plays involving apologies, confessions, and obvious scapegoating. Yet these rituals were also acted out by, and it seems for, the elite itself in private venues. In Central Committee plenums and other secret texts which never saw public light of day, we see these ritual performances being carried out in the secret confines of the elite as a kind of "fellowship of discourse" within a closed community.[11] The affirmation and validation provided by such practices seem to have been no less important for the elite than for the population it ruled.

Several of Smirnov's critics, including Control Commission members Shkiriatov and Rudzutak, practically equated Smirnov's behavior with treason. The unfelicitous type of performative speech he had uttered had in fact defined him as an opponent of the party, regardless of his intentions.

Stalin's cult of personality had already grown to such proportions that discussions of removing him from his post were regarded as calls for a "counterrevolutionary" coup. Several speakers referred to Stalin repeatedly as the *vozhd'*, a word that carries connotations of "chief" above and beyond a simple "leader." Since replacement of Stalin by routine electoral procedures was considered inconceivable, to remove him by other means implied illegal or treasonous acts. And, the logic went, such a removal could be successful only if it were violent.

Indeed, Yan Rudzutak maintained that even talk of reelecting the general secretary was a betrayal of the party. According to the new discourse —Party = Central Committee = Stalin—criticism of one was betrayal of all. As A. I. Akulov put it in his speech to the January 1933 meeting, "Stalin's policy is our policy, the policy of our entire Party. It is the policy of the proletarian revolution, it is the policy not only of the proletarian revolution in our country but of the proletarian revolution in the world. That's what Stalin's policy is all about. And these gentlemen will never succeed in separating us from our leader [vozhd']."[12]

As M. F. Shkiriatov put it,

> Regarding the leader of our Party, Comrade Stalin—what means did they employ in their struggle against Comrade Stalin? . . . They said that they were prepared to remove Comrade Stalin, whereas, in their testimony, Eismont and others tried to replace one [particular] word with another: they had spoken not of "removing" [*ubrat'*] but of "dismissing" [*sniat'*] him. . . . We, on the other hand, consider that all of these words—"change" [*smenit'*], "dismiss," "remove"—are one and the same thing, that there is no difference whatsoever between them. In our opinion it all amounts to violent dismissal. . . . Now Comrade Smirnov declares that he loves Stalin. But love has nothing to do with it. . . . The matter has nothing to do with love. Love consists of carrying out the line pursued by the Party headed by Comrade Stalin.[13]

Shkiriatov's was an extreme statement of an extremist position. Even though Smirnov had never been a member of an opposition group, Shkiriatov had shifted the burden of proof to Smirnov and demanded that he prove the history of his struggle against the opposition, that he prove that he had *not* been an adherent.

For Shkiriatov, even jokes and stories carried a dangerous counterrevolutionary character and could have no place in the prescribed loyal narrative. During NEP in the 1920s, jokes and ditties had not been sources for official obsession. In the 1930s, however, the onset of collectivization, its height, the period following Kirov's assassination, and the terrible year 1937 each brought dramatic increases in persecution for "anti-Soviet agitation." Jokes, songs, poems, and even conversations that in any other political system would have been ignored as innocent were now seen as dangerous crimes. Shkiriatov called them "sharp weapons" against the party. The regime's agents carefully recorded jokes, poems, and the like, and these were matters for attention and concern by the country's highest political circles.[14] Osip Mandelstam was arrested for a poem. Because he was a prominent writer, his writings could in fact be seen as a propagandistic "weapon" against the party. But it is harder to classify as dangerously political the hundreds of thousands of utterances by ordinary citizens. Nevertheless, the regime was deeply concerned.

Yan Rudzutak, another Control Commission official, spoke for much of the elite nomenklatura, which believed that Stalin was their symbol and partner. To remove him was to remove them. As Rudzutak put it,

> These, the finest people of the Party, did not fear many years in prison and in exile, and now these revolutionaries, who devote themselves to the victory of the Revolution, these old revolutionary warriors, according to Smirnov, are afraid to vote against Comrade Stalin? Can it be that they vote for Stalin from a fear for authority while, behind his back, they prepare—if anything comes up—to change [meniat'] the leadership? You are slandering the members of the Party, you are slandering the members of the CC, and you are also slandering Comrade Stalin. We, as members of the CC, vote for Stalin because he is ours (applause). EXCLAMATIONS. Right! (applause).[15]

These apology rituals had several aspects. Pragmatically, from the point of view of the elite as a whole, when the accused played his role properly, the scene provided a scapegoat who could be used as a negative example to those below and a symbol or signpost for a change in policy. Secondly, these scenes allowed Stalin to mobilize the united (and nearly always unanimous) support of the Central Committee behind him in his moves to isolate and discredit his opponents.

The unitary rituals had other effects as well. Speaker after speaker rose to join the unanimous criticism of the accused. The collective denunciations and pronouncements worked: they served to affirm and validate the organized collective (the Central Committee in this case) as an authoritative body. Although Stalin and his circle certainly chose the accused in this case, the collective elite were being asked to validate not only his choice but their right to pass judgment on such matters. As any ritual does, these Central Committee meetings allowed the participants to make a group affirmation of their organization as a "society" or even a political subculture in the system.

Finally, like all rituals, these meetings contributed to the construction of self-identity and self-representation of the participants as individuals. By being present as a member, by participating in what might appear to be meaningless repetitive speech, the participants implicitly made statements about who they were individually. Self-identity is, of course, a function of many complex variables, including class, kin, nationality, gender, personal experience, and others. Among these components are political status and place in the social hierarchy. Participation in apology and other rituals was to say "This is who I am: I am a revolutionary and a member of the party elite. I along with my comrades are part of the governing team of Stalinists. I insist on party discipline and stand against those who break it. In that position, I am making a contribution toward party unity and therefore toward moving the country historically toward socialism."

The former rightist oppositionists N. I. Bukharin, A. I. Rykov, and M. P. Tomsky were also called upon to speak and make their position clear in relation to the Smirnov group. Rykov, in his speech, repeated the ritual self-criticism demanded of former oppositionists and tried to demonstrate his lack of any connection with the group. Tomsky took a more contrary stand. Although he also criticized his former oppositionist positions, he pointed out that the party should not make too much of careless and drunken conversations at evening parties. Bukharin's speech was much more repentant and his position was judged more acceptable; those of Rykov and Tomsky were not and they were roundly denounced in the discussion.

Bukharin accepted the premise that the new situation and new threats demanded strong discipline and unconditional unity. He understood the need for a unifying, affirming text that would make clear his continued membership in the elite. In distinction to other speakers, though, Bukharin did not invoke Stalin's name as vozhd', nor did he explicitly equate Stalin with the Central Committee: "Comrades, with regard to Aleksandr Petrovich Smirnov's group, it seems to me that no Party member can be of two minds about it: if it is necessary for us, on the whole, to indignantly re-

pudiate a group of this sort, then it should especially—twice and thrice—
be repudiated *now*, and severe punishment should be meted out."[16]

It may be instructive to compare these tougher demands with the relatively civil treatment of oppositionists back in 1930. As we have seen,
Bukharin in his 1930 speech made several witty comments that were received with friendly laughter by his audience. His colloquies with Kaganovich and Molotov were like gentlemanly debates aimed at seeking compromise, and his critics behaved in a polite and civilized manner.

But in 1933 the mood was quite different; it had become tense and anxious. While Bukharin could joke about opposition in 1930, Shkiriatov in
1933 asserted that "jokes against the party are agitation against the
party." The texts of Smirnov's critics were laced with nostalgic references
to party discipline in Lenin's time, but in 1932 they were demanding much
more: "iron discipline" required Central Committee members to become
informers on each other. Bukharin's jest in 1930 about "physically destroying" members of the opposition elicited laughter from the Central
Committee. One wonders whether it would have done so in 1932.

For their parts, several of the opposition leaders accepted the logic of
the new situation. Bukharin's speech emphasized the main point: "If it is
necessary for us, on the whole, to indignantly repudiate a group of this
sort, then it should especially—twice and thrice—be repudiated *now*, and
severe punishment should be meted out." Smirnov himself recognized the
dangers inherent in the new situation and accepted the notion that discussing Stalin's removal was "a political act, and a political act behind the
Party's back is manifestly an anti-Party action." Smirnov found no fault
with the logic of the accusation in principle; he simply denied that he had
done it.

But Smirnov, Tomsky, and Rykov did not fully accept that formal guilt
or innocence was not the question. For the Stalinists, on the other hand,
the party made the truth. After all, it had been Trotsky who had said that
one cannot be right against the party. As a party member and member of
the Central Committee, Smirnov was a soldier. His duty, if so ordered, was
to confess, to report on others, and to proclaim his "crimes" in order to
help the party in its struggle. To disagree, or even to defend oneself against
an accusation, was tantamount to insubordination, to "taking up arms
against the party" in wartime, to counterrevolution. Bukharin, on the
other hand, understood. Another former oppositionist, Karl Radek, also
grasped the new requirements and quickly did his duty:

Dear Comrade Rudzutak—After reading Comrade A. P. Smirnov's statement, in which he rejects with great indignation the very possibility of being held in suspicion in Right-wing factional work, I am hereby informing you of the following:

In 1927, sometime during the summer, G. A. Zinoviev notified those who were then the leaders of the Trotskyist opposition of a proposal made to him, i.e. to Zinoviev, by A. P. Smirnov, for the formation of a block against Comrade Stalin. As related by Zinoviev, Smirnov complained about the regime that was numbing the Party, [that] the Party had no clear policy concerning the peasantry, at times making concessions to the peasants, at times revoking them. . . .

The fact that A. P. Smirnov has denied this factional past of his in general sheds light on his statements regarding the charges brought against him today of working for the opposition.

With a Communist salute,

K. Radek.[17]

Another important element of the nomenklatura's treatment of the opposition was the distinction between personal and political factors. Bolsheviks had always separated their political and personal lives; the bitter political disputes between Lenin and Zinoviev over the question of seizing power in 1917 did not prevent them from maintaining cordial personal relations. But by 1932 the stakes were considered so high that fond personal relations and one's "good will" were specifically sacrificed to political needs. Consider the following 1933 remarks from Commissar of Defense Voroshilov:

Comrade Tomsky, one more piece of advice, as a friend,—after all, you and I were once close friends: please do not think that you are so clever (laughter). You spoke before us here, and I was ashamed for your sake. You were once an intelligent person, but owing to the fact that you slept through the past four years, you poured out such rubbish here that I was simply ashamed for your sake. Even a Marxist circle of the lowest rank would be ashamed to read this. It's all elementary. All those peas pushed here and there by the nose—all of this is nothing but utter rubbish. We expected a different kind of speech from you, different words.[18]

In the end, A. P. Smirnov was expelled from the Central Committee and the Orgburo but was allowed to remain in the party with the warning that his continued membership depended on his future behavior. Those party members present at the ill-fated soiree were expelled from the party. Eismont and several others were sentenced to three years in labor camps. Technically, discussing the removal of Stalin was not a crime covered by the criminal code, but the Special Conference (*Osoboe Soveshchanie*) of the secret police (*Obedinennoe gosudarstvennoe politicheskoe upravlenie*, OGPU), had the right to sentence people to camps for such things as "anti-Soviet agitation" or being a "socially dangerous element."

All of the participants still living in 1937 would be arrested and shot for "counterrevolutionary activities"; thus the punishments meted out in 1933, especially to Smirnov, seem relatively light and show that despite the fiery rhetoric of some Stalinists, there was still some indecision about how hard to push the dissidents. Repression of real or imagined opposition groups in this period was becoming more common. But the sources we have from the 1932–34 period paint a rather ambiguous picture of the direction of party policy. Sampling the archives from this period, we shall find a mixture of hard- and soft-line policies on matters relating to political dictatorship and dissidence.

Some have argued that Stalin and his closest associates may already have been preparing for a major purge and attempting to set in place a series of decisions, personnel, and practices designed to facilitate a subsequent unleashing of terror. According to this explanation, the countervailing soft-line measures were the result of a liberal (or at least antiterror) faction within the leadership that tried to block Stalin's plans. Said to consist of S. M. Kirov, V. V. Kuibyshev, Sergo Ordzhonikidze, and others, this group would have favored a general relaxation of the dictatorship; now that capitalism and the hostile class forces had been defeated, there was no reason to maintain a high level of repression.[19]

But the documents now available make this view untenable. There is little evidence for such a plan on Stalin's part or of the existence of a liberal faction within the Politburo. Above and beyond routine squabbles over "turf" or the technicalities of implementation, neither the public statements nor the documentary record shows any serious political disagreement within the Stalin group at this time. Rather, the simultaneous pursuit of both soft- and hard-line policies was the result of indecision within an anxious leadership that reacted on an ad hoc basis to events rather than proceeding according to grand plans.[20]

CHAPTER THREE

Repression and Legality

Anyone who feels like arresting does so. It is no wonder, therefore, that with such an orgy of arrests, the organs having the right to make arrests, including the organs of the OGPU, and, especially, of the police, have lost all sense of proportion.—Central Committee Circular, 1933

At this congress, however, there is nothing to prove and, it seems, no one to fight. Everyone sees that the line of the Party has triumphed.—Stalin, 1934

LITERARY CENSORSHIP in this period provides an example both of ambiguous policies and of direct attempts to construct the regime's dominant rhetoric and narrative. Since 1917 the Bolsheviks had suppressed publication of books and newspapers from their political opponents. But during the 1920s the Stalinist leadership had often permitted the publication of statements and articles from various oppositionists within the party, at least until the moment of their defeat and expulsion. Trotsky's works were published until the mid-1920s, and Bukharin continued to publish, albeit within controlled parameters, until his arrest in 1937; he was in fact editor of the government newspaper *Izvestia* until that time.[1]

Writing and Rewriting History

The content of historical works had always played a role in Bolshevik politics. Part of the public dispute between the Stalinists and the Trotskyists in the early 1920s had revolved around Trotsky's historical evaluation of the role of leading Bolsheviks in his *Lessons of October*. And in 1929 a letter to the editor of a historical journal on an apparently obscure point of party history touched off a political purge in the historical profession and a general hardening of the line on what was acceptable and what was not.[2]

By the early 1930s the Stalinists were generally more intolerant of publications from ex-oppositionists, whose writings were scrutinized more carefully. At the end of 1930 Bukharin could still publish statements about his position on various matters, but their content was checked word for word by the Politburo before approval. In one such case, a Politburo directive of October 1930 noted that "Comrade Bukharin's statement is deemed unsatisfactory. . . . In view of the fact that the editors of *Pravda*—were Comrade Bukharin to insist on the publication of his statement in the form in which it was sent by him to the CC—would be forced to criticize it, which would be undesirable, Comrade Kaganovich is entrusted with talking to Comrade Bukharin in order to coordinate the definitive wording of the text of his statement."[3] Bukharin's statement was eventually published, but only after considerable haggling over its content.

By 1932, however, things had become harder even for veteran party litterateurs. A. S. Shliapnikov, a prominent Old Bolshevik and one of the leaders of the defeated Workers' Opposition in the early 1920s, was taken to task for some of his writings on the 1917 Revolution. In this case, though, it was not a matter of prior censorship of historical works; Shliapnikov's *1917* and *On the Eve of 1917* had already been published.[4] This time, the new situation required a formal recognition of "mistakes" and a published retraction from the author; otherwise he would be expelled from the party. In the "new situation," the worried nomenklatura was taking command of history itself by reshaping historical texts that had already been promulgated. In the Stalinist system, public disquisitions—which were necessarily political—could be "repaired" and history itself could be changed along with them. Chaotic times make ideology and ideological control important in order to "render otherwise incomprehensible social situations meaningful."[5]

Despite the general tightening of literary "discipline," the policy of censorship in the 1932–34 period was uneven. In June 1933 a circular letter from the Central Committee formally prescribed policies for "purging of libraries." Back in 1930, during the ultraleft upsurge of the "cultural revolution," the party had insisted on removing literary and historical works by "bourgeois" and oppositionist authors from all libraries. The June 1933 circular, while approving the removal of "counterrevolutionary and religious literature," along with the works of Trotsky and Zinoviev, took a relatively moderate line on library holdings in general. Works representing "historical interest" were to remain in the libraries of the larger towns, and closed or "special" collections were forbidden, as were mass purges of libraries.[6]

Even here, the Politburo had difficulty taking control of the situation. The June 13 order was ignored by hotheaded local activists who continued to strip the libraries of books they considered counterrevolutionary. Yemelian Yaroslavsky and other party leaders complained about this to the Politburo, prompting Molotov and Stalin to issue stronger strictures that characterized the purging of the libraries as "anti-Soviet" and again ordered it stopped.[7]

Later, beginning in 1935, the policy would harden again as Stalin assumed supervision of the Culture and Propaganda department of the Central Committee from Andrei Zhdanov.[8] Large numbers of books would be removed from circulation and Stalinist censorship would emerge in its full form. But in the 1930–34 period, policy was still in flux.

Judiciary and Police

Similar ambiguity characterized judicial policy in this period.[9] At the beginning of the 1930s an ultraleftist version of "socialist legality" had prevailed. A class-based justice differentiated "class-alien" defendants from the "bourgeoisie," and those from the working class or peasantry, with the former receiving much sterner treatment at the bar. Legal protections were minimal, with the secret police (OGPU until 1934) having the right to arrest, convict, and execute with only the most cursory (or no) judicial proceedings. Indeed, the Collegium of the OGPU had the right to pass death sentences entirely in secret and "without the participation of the accused."

During the period of "dekulakization" and collectivization, such legality as existed was completely thrown aside. Lawlessness was the rule as squads of party officials, police, village authorities, and even volunteers arrested, exiled, and even executed recalcitrant peasants without any pretense of legality.[10] As early as March 2, 1930, even Stalin recoiled from the chaos and wrote his famous "Dizziness with Success" article, in which he called for a halt to forced collectivization and ordered a reduction in the use of violence against peasants.[11] Although the article did result in a general decline in mass terror against peasants, it did not curb the powers of the police (and others) to make arrests as they chose.

Indeed, in the 1932–34 period, the regime sent mixed signals on the general question of judicial repression. Consider the policy toward technical specialists from the old regime. In June 1931 Stalin's "New Conditions—New Tasks" speech seemed to call a halt to the radical, class-based persecution of members of the old intelligentsia and said that the party's policy should be "enlisting them and taking care of them." "It would be stupid and unwise to regard practically every expert and engineer of the old school as an undetected criminal and wrecker."[12] The following month, the Politburo forbade arrests of specialists without high-level permission.[13] In the subsequent period, the Politburo intervened on several occasions to protect persecuted members of the intelligentsia and to rein in the activities of secret police officials persecuting them.

An apparently contradictory "hard" signal came a few months later, when a new decree (said to have been drafted by Stalin personally) prescribed the death penalty (or long imprisonment with confiscation of one's property) for even petty thefts from collective farms. Such harsh measures testify to the climate of paranoia in the top leadership in this period. They also bespeak panic and an inability to control the countryside through any means but repression.

Despite the draconian nature of this law, its application was uneven and confused. The following month, September 1932, the Politburo ordered death sentences prescribed by the law to be carried out immediately.[14] Nevertheless, of those convicted under the law by end of 1933, only 4 percent received death sentences, and about one thousand persons had actually been executed.[15] In Siberia, property was confiscated from only 5 percent of those convicted under the law. Although the law seemed aimed at collective farm members, commentators argued that class bias should be applied and that workers and peasants should be shown leniency.[16] In 1933 the drive was reoriented away from simple peasants and against major offenders; at that time, 50 percent of all verdicts passed under the law had been reduced. By mid-1934 most sentences for theft did not carry prison or camp time.[17] It is interesting to note that the Commissariat of Justice was unwilling or unable to report to higher authorities exactly how many people were convicted under its provisions, giving figures ranging from 100,000 to 180,000 as late as the spring of 1936. Despite Stalin's strictures in the original decree against leniency, by August 1936 a secret decree had ordered the review of all sentences under the "Law of August 7, 1932." Four-fifths of those convicted had their sentences reduced and more than 40,000 of them were freed at that time.[18]

In April 1933 a show trial of engineers was held in Moscow in which technicians "of the old school" were accused of espionage and sabotage on behalf of Great Britain.[19] The "Metro-Vickers" trial was the latest in a series of such open proceedings against engineers and technicians of the old regime that included the Shakhty trial of 1928 and the trial of the Industrial Party in 1930. The symbolism conveyed in these proceedings, which seemed to reinforce repressive trends, was that older technical specialists from the old regime were not to be trusted and that party members and Soviet citizens must be increasingly vigilant against enemies. Even here, though, there was ambiguity. Several of the defendants were released on bail before the trial. No death sentences were handed out, and two of the defendants received no punishment at all. According to the most recent study of the trial, the proceedings seemed to indicate indecision within the Soviet government, perhaps reflected in the court's hedging statement that it "was guided by the fact that the criminal wrecking activities of the aforesaid convicted persons bore a local character and did not cause serious harm to the industrial power of the USSR."[20] Nevertheless, a political trial is a political trial, and the Metro-Vickers prosecutions sent a hard signal.

Almost immediately, the regime did another volte-face back in the direction of sharply relaxing repression. During the Civil War and again during collectivization, the secret police had operated tribunals for the purposes of handing down drumhead sentences of death or hard labor for political enemies. The vast majority of those executed during the storm of dekulakization and collectivization were victims of three-person police "troikas." On 7 May 1933 the Politburo ordered the troikas to stop pronouncing death sentences.[21]

The next day, a document carrying the signatures of Stalin for the Central Committee and V. M. Molotov for the government ordered a drastic curtailment of arrests and a sharp reduction in the prison population. Half of all prisoners in jails (not, in should be noted, in camps or in exile) were to be released. The power to arrest was sharply restricted to police organs, and all arrests had to be sanctioned by the appropriate judicial procurator. The "Instruction to All Party-Soviet Workers, and All Organizations of the OGPU, Courts, and Procuracy" ordered an end to "mass repression" of the peasantry:

The Central Committee and the Council of People's Commissars, (SNK) [the government] are of the opinion that, as a result of our successes in the countryside, the moment has come when we are no longer in need of mass repression, which affects, as is well known, not only the kulaks but also independent peasants [*yedinolichniki*] and some kolkhoz members as well. . . . Information has been received by the Central Committee and the Council of People's Commissars that makes it evident that disorderly arrests on a massive scale are still being carried out by our officials in the countryside. . . .

It is no wonder, therefore, that with such an orgy of arrests, the organs [of state] having the right to make arrests, including the organs of the OGPU, and, especially, of the police [*militsia*], have lost all sense of proportion. More often than not, they will arrest people for no reason at all, acting in accordance with the principle: "Arrest first; ask questions later!" . . .

It would be wrong to assume that the new situation and the necessary transition to new methods of operation signify the elimination or even the relaxation of the class struggle in the countryside. On the contrary, the class struggle in the countryside will inevitably become more acute. It will become more acute because the class enemy sees that the kolkhozy have triumphed, that the days of his existence are numbered, and he cannot but grasp—out of sheer desperation—at the harshest forms of struggle against Soviet power. . . .

Therefore, we are talking here about intensifying our struggle against the class enemy. The point, however, is that in the present situation it is impossible to intensify the struggle against the class enemy and to liquidate him with the aid of old methods of operation because these methods have outlived their usefulness. The point, therefore, is to improve the old methods of struggle, to streamline them, to make each of our blows more organized and better targeted, to politically prepare each blow in advance, to reinforce each blow with the actions of the broad masses of the peasantry.[22]

The language was ambiguous: although the former sharply repressive policy had been correct and successful, it must end. Although the level of "class struggle" with enemy elements in the countryside would "inevitably sharpen" and the party's struggle with the class enemy "must be strengthened," it was nevertheless time for a relaxation in arrest and penal policy.

On the face of it, such language represents the usual and cynical attempt to initiate a new policy by praising the discarded one and blaming local implementers who had "distorted" it. After all, the center had encouraged much of the violence it now condemned in what appears to be a break with previous policy. But in another sense, the document was consonant

with others of the period that sought to concentrate more and more authority in Moscow's hands. In addition to admitting that blind mass repression was inefficient, the leadership wanted to get control of the situation by putting repression into the hands of Moscow officials rather than
those of local organs: blows against the enemy would thus be "more organized" and "better targeted." In this sense, the document did not in
itself necessarily imply less violence but rather violence more tightly directed from the center. In any case, there is evidence that this decree had
concrete results. In July 1933 Stalin received a report that in the two
months since 8 May 1933 the population of prisons had indeed been reduced to a figure below four hundred thousand.[23]

In the following two months, the Politburo decided to make two administrative changes that also seemed to point in the direction of enhanc-
ing legality: the creation of Office of Procurator of the USSR (roughly,
attorney general) and of an all-Union Commissariat of Internal Affairs
(NKVD). Up to this time, each constituent republic of the USSR had its
own procurator, who had limited powers to supervise or interfere in the
activities of central administrative, judicial, and punitive organs (including the secret police). In principle, the new procurator of the USSR was to
have jurisdiction over all courts, secret and regular police, and other
procurators in the entire Soviet Union. Legally speaking, an all-Union
"civilian" judicial official thus received supervisory powers over the secret
police. As with procurators, each republic had previously had its own
Commissariat of Internal Affairs, with supervisory responsibilities over
republican soviets, regular police, fire departments, and the like.

The position of procurator is an element of continental and Russian
law. Unlike Anglo-Saxon "prosecutors," a procurator is not only the representative of the people in an adversary proceeding against defense counsel. Indeed, the principal function of Russian procurators from the time of
Peter the Great was administrative as much as judicial; it was to exercise
supervision (variously *nadzor* or *nabliudenie*) over state bodies and over
their proper and legal implementation of state measures.[24]

A February 1934 decree announced the formation of the NKVD USSR,
abolished the OGPU and incorporated its police functions into the new
organization.[25] Moreover, according to the new regulations, the NKVD
did not have the power to pass death sentences (as had the OGPU and its
predecessors the GPU and CHEKA) or to inflict extralegal "administrative" punishments of more than five years' exile. Treason cases, formerly

under the purview of the secret police, were, along with other criminal matters, referred to the regular courts or to the Supreme Court. Similarly, at this time the secret police lost the power to impose death penalties on inmates of their own camps. Special territorial courts under the control of the Commissariat of Justice, rather than of the police, were established in the regions of the camps, and cases of crimes (like murder) committed in the camps were now heard by those judicial bodies.[26]

Combined with the decrees on the USSR Procuracy, the formation of the NKVD seemed to herald a new era of legality, and contemporary observers were favorably impressed with what appeared to be moves in the direction of reduced repression.[27] Other decisions support the impression of a relaxation in 1933–34. As we shall see, though, in 1937 and 1938 legal protections would become dead letters, as the unfettered sweeps of the police netted huge numbers of innocent victims who were jailed, exiled, or shot without procuratorial sanction or legal proceedings or protection of any kind. But this was 1934, and a number of key events between then and 1937 would dramatically change and harden the political landscape; these included the assassination of Politburo member S. M. Kirov at the end of 1934.

In June 1934 a Politburo resolution quashing the sentence received by one Seliavkin strongly censured the OGPU for "serious shortcomings in the conduct of investigations."[28] In September a memo from Stalin proposed the formation of a Politburo commission (chaired by V. V. Kuibyshev and consisting of Kaganovich and State Procurator Akulov; A. A. Zhdanov was later added) to look into OGPU abuses. Stalin called the matter "serious, in my opinion" and ordered the commission to "free the innocent" and "purge the OGPU of practitioners [nositely] of specific 'investigative tricks' and punish them regardless of their rank."

Thus, in response to Stalin's recommendation, the Kuibyshev Commission prepared a draft resolution censuring the police for "illegal methods of investigation" and recommending punishment of several secret police officials. Before the resolution could be implemented, however, Kirov was assassinated. The mood of Stalin and the Politburo changed dramatically, and the recommendations of the Kuibyshev Commission were shelved in a period characterized by personnel changes in the police, scapegoating of a poor harvest and industrial failures in 1936, the rise of German fascism, and the resurgence of spy mania in 1937.[29]

Another 1934 decree complicates the picture even further. Simultane- ously with the decision to create the NKVD, the Politburo—at future NKVD chief Genrikh Yagoda's request—created a Special Board of the NKVD (*Osoboe Soveshchanie*) to handle specific cases. Yagoda and other police officials had worried about losing all judicial-punitive functions and had lobbied to retain some of them. Officials of justice and procuracy agencies pressed to concentrate all punitive functions in judiciary bodies. Stalin refereed the dispute, siding with the legal officials but giving the new NKVD the Special Board.[30] According to the new scheme, all crimes chargeable under the criminal code were to be referred to and decided by one of the various courts in a judicial proceeding. But the Special Board had the right to exile "socially dangerous" persons for up to five years to camps, abroad, or simply away from the larger cities.[31]

Certainly, compared to the former powers of the OGPU, the general trend of 1934 represented a sharp restriction on the independent punitive power of the police. On the other hand, several aspects of the Special Board ran quite contrary to legality. First, the Special Board consisted only of secret police officials. Aside from the "participation" ex officio of the USSR procurator, no judicial officials, judges, or attorneys were involved. Second, the "infractions" coming under the purview of the Special Board were not criminal offenses as defined in the criminal code; formally it was not a crime to be a "socially dangerous" person, but under these provi- sions it was punishable by the police in a nonjudicial proceeding. It was therefore up to the police to decide what was "socially dangerous" and who could be punished under that category. Third, the Special Board passed its sentences without the participation or even presence of the ac- cused or his or her attorney, and no appeals were envisioned. Because of the ability to punish persons who had committed no definable crime (an "advantage" later touted by Yezhov), the activities come under the head- ing of administrative, extrajudicial punishments, a category hardly consis- tent with formal legality.

These contradictory judicial texts lend themselves to several possible interpretations: conflicting hard and soft factions, a terrorist Stalin try- ing to cover his purposes with "liberal" maneuvers, or a genuine moder- ate trend that was later derailed. But all of them point toward regular- ization and centralization of police powers in the hands of fewer and fewer people.

Screening the Party Membership

Leadership attitudes toward party composition provide our final example of ambiguous elite policies in the 1932–34 period. In early 1933 the party leadership decided to conduct a membership screening, or purge [*chistka*, meaning a sweeping or cleaning], of the party's membership. Purges had been traditional events in the party's history since 1918 and had been aimed at a wide variety of targets. Most often, the categories of people specified for purging were not explicitly related to political oppositional or dissidence but included targets like careerists, bureaucrats, and crooks of various kinds.[32] Members of oppositionist groups were not mentioned in the instructions. Still, the inclusion of categories like "double-dealers," "underminers," and those who refused to "struggle against the kulak," in a purge announced at the same plenum that attacked A. P. Smirnov, clearly invited the expulsion of ideological opponents.[33]

It would be a mistake to regard the 1933 chistka as having been directed solely against members of the opposition. The largest single group expelled were "passive" party members: those carried on the rolls but not participating in party work. Next came violators of party discipline, bureaucrats, corrupt officials, and those who had hidden past crimes from the party. Members of dissident groups did not even figure in the final tallies.[34] Stalin himself characterized the purge as a measure against bureaucratism, red tape, degenerates, and careerists, "to raise the level of organizational leadership."[35] The vast majority of those expelled were fresh recruits who had entered the party since 1929, rather than Old Bolshevik oppositionists. Nevertheless, the 1933 purge expelled about 18 percent of the party's members and must be seen as a hard-line policy or signal from Moscow.

Moreover, such purges potentially affected not only ideological groups but also various strata within the party. Traditionally, purges could strike at the heart of local political machines insofar as Moscow demanded strict verification of officials. On the other hand, the sword could strike the other way. Because they were usually carried out by local party leaders or their clients, party purges could be used by them to rid the party of rank-and-file critics or people the local party "family" considered troublemakers.

The chistka can be seen in another light not directly connected with real or imagined political dissidents or possible plans for terror. If, as we have argued, the dangerous "new situation" of 1932 threatened the regime's control (that is, the nomenklatura's position), it would make sense for the elite to close ranks, prune the party, and thereby restrict the size of the politically active strata of society. The chistka served these interests by "regulating its composition" and closing off access to it by "crisis" or "unstable" elements in a time of troubles. Thus the chistka may have been seen by the leadership not as a prelude to anything but rather as a survival mechanism for the nomenklatura.

At the beginning of 1934 Stalin spoke to the 17th Party Congress (dubbed the Congress of Victors by the party leadership). On the one hand, he noted that the oppositionist groups had been utterly defeated, and their leaders forced to recant their errors. Indeed, former oppositionists Bukharin, Rykov, Tomsky, and others were allowed to speak to the congress in order to demonstrate a new party unity that Stalin proclaimed. On the other hand, however, he noted that "unhealthy moods" could still penetrate the party from outside: "the capitalist encirclement still exists, which endeavors to revive and sustain the survival of capitalism in the economic life and in the minds of the people of the USSR, and against which we Bolsheviks must always keep our powder dry." Stalin's ambiguous (or perhaps dialectical) text thus combined the policies of stabilized legality with continued vigilance.

He criticized those who favored a weakening of state power and controls, arguing that even though the party was victorious and the class enemies were smashed, the state could not yet "wither away." Rightists and moderates had suggested that the victory of the party's General Line in industry and agriculture meant that the state could relax its control and reduce the power of its repressive mechanisms. In this connection, Stalin repeated his theoretical formula that as the Soviet Union moved toward victorious socialism, its internal enemies would become more desperate, provoking a "sharper" struggle that precluded "disarming" the state. Thus, while proclaiming victory and implying the end of mass repression, Stalin left the theoretical door open for the continued use of repression on a more selective basis. (He had previously ordered an end to mass repression in the countryside while simultaneously arguing that the struggle with enemies was becoming "sharper.") Nevertheless, the specific remedies he proposed for the remaining "problems" were in the benign areas of party education and propaganda rather than repression.

Stalin's nomenklatura listeners, beset by crises on all sides, certainly were glad to squelch any talk of "disarming." On the other hand, they must have been less pleased by the second part of his remarks, "Questions of Organizational Leadership." Here, he complained about high-ranking "bureaucrats" who rested on their laurels and were lax about "fulfillment of decisions." The "incorrigible bureaucrats" he chastised were members of the nomenklatura. Rudzutak had spoken for this elite the year before when he said of Stalin, "he is ours." Now, however, Stalin sounded a more sour note when he implied that the nomenklatura officials must themselves obey their own party line—and that of the leader of the party. This was the beginning of diverging interests between Stalin and the elite that backed him, and although their alliance would continue, signs of a rift were already present in early 1934.[36]

The year 1934 evokes positive memories in the Soviet Union. It began with famine and violent class war in the countryside, but also saw a series of reforms in the direction of a kind of legality, or, to use Gramsci's terms, hegemony rather than domination. Memoirs recall 1934 as a "good" year when the mass repression of the previous period had ended, and it seemed that official statements and new judicial arrangements heralded a period of relative stability and relaxation. Arrests by the secret police fell by more than half (and political convictions by more than two-thirds) from the previous year, reaching their lowest level since the storm of collectivization in 1930 (see table 1 and the appendix). The regime had made peace with the old intelligentsia and seemed to be replacing repression with political education as its main political tool. After the tumult of collectivization and hunger, the economy was improving, and the year ended with the abolition of bread rationing throughout the country.

Given the eruption of terror just a few years later, we now know that the stability of 1934 was temporary. In fact, as we have seen, moderation and softening of the regime alternated and indeed coexisted with the diametrically opposed policy of repression. On the questions of treatment of dissidents, literature, and judicial policy, we have seen that moderate and hardline policies were jumbled together in a contradictory way that suggested a series of vacillations more than any coherent pattern.

In one view, these oscillations represented a kind of jockeying for position between hard and soft factions in the top leadership. The question, of course, is what was Stalin's position? Because he was a crafty politician always careful not to reveal too much, it is exceedingly difficult to divine his thoughts and plans. Some observers saw the political situation of 1932–34

Table 1

Secret Police (GPU, OGPU, NKVD) Arrests and Sentences, 1921–39

	Arrests		Of "counterrevolutionary crimes," those for "anti-Soviet agitation"	For other crimes	Total convicted	Sentences			
Year	Total	For "counterrevolutionary" crimes				Shot	To camps and prison	Exiled	Other
1921	200,271	76,820		123,451	35,829	9,701	21,724	1,817	2,587
1922	119,329	45,405	0	73,924	6,003	1,962	2,656	166	1,219
1923	104,520	57,289	5,322	47,231	4,794	414	2,336	2,044	0
1924	92,849	74,055	0	18,794	12,425	2,550	4,151	5,724	0
1925	72,658	52,033	0	20,625	15,995	2,433	6,851	6,274	437
1926	62,817	30,676	0	32,141	17,804	990	7,547	8,571	696
1927	76,983	48,883	0	28,100	26,436	2,363	12,267	11,235	171
1928	112,803	72,186	0	40,617	33,757	869	16,211	15,640	1,037
1929	162,726	132,799	51,396	29,927	56,220	2,109	25,853	24,517	3,741
1930	331,544	266,679	0	64,865	208,069	20,201	114,443	58,816	14,609
1931	479,065	343,734	100,963	135,331	180,696	10,651	105,683	63,269	1,093
1932	410,433	195,540	23,484	214,893	141,919	2,728	73,946	36,017	29,228
1933	505,256	283,029	32,370	222,227	239,664	2,154	138,903	54,262	44,345
1934	205,173	90,417	16,788	114,756	78,999	2,056	59,451	5,994	11,498
1935	193,083	108,935	43,686	84,148	267,076	1,229	185,846	33,601	46,400
1936	131,168	91,127	32,110	40,041	274,670	1,118	219,418	23,719	30,415
1937	936,750	779,056	234,301	157,694	790,665	353,074	429,311	1,366	6,914
1938	638,509	593,326	57,366	45,183	554,258	328,618	205,509	16,842	3,289
1939					63,889	2,552	54,666	3,783	2,888

Source: GARF, f. 9401, op. 1, d. 4157, ll. 201–5.

as one in which different groups contended for Stalin's favor.[37] According to this line of reasoning, Stalin allowed his subordinates to contend with one another, with the result being the alternation of initiatives and emphases. Indecision therefore made 1934 a kind of crossroads at which several alternative paths—including a continuation of moderation—were open and terror was neither planned nor inevitable but rather a function of contingent factors that arose later.

From another view these waverings of 1932–34 constituted a prelude to terror. Indeed, many scholars believe that even then Stalin was predisposed toward repression and mass violence. According to this view, the hard-line policies of the period can be associated with a Stalin who promoted repressive policies in order to lay a groundwork for terror but was blocked by a moderate faction that favored relaxation and was often able to implement softer policies or at least force Stalin to back down temporarily. Opposition to Stalin, therefore, created a situation in which it would be necessary for him to neutralize the moderates in order to continue and indeed expand his repressive plans. In this view 1934 was merely an illusion, a hiatus in which there was little potential for any outcome other than terror.[38]

On this point it may be worthwhile to reflect briefly on what the 1932–34 period shows us about repression and Bolshevik mentality. Looking at the repressive or hard-line strand of policies, it is easy to have the impression of a fierce regime exercising strong totalitarian control. Without a doubt, the regime was capable of launching bloody and violent repression, as the collectivization of agriculture had shown.

But such repressive policies may well betray another side of the regime and its self-image. Regimes, even those with transformational goals, do not need to resort to terror if they have a firm basis of social support. They do not need messy, inefficient, out-of-control campaign-style politics, including mass campaigns of terror, if they have reliable and efficient administrations that govern with any degree of popular consensus. If governments are sound and firmly based, they do not need continued repression to survive and to carry out their goals. The Stalinist regime clearly did need such repression, or at least thought it did.

Given what must appear to us to be a paranoid and pathological institutional mentality and history of political violence, it is all the more remarkable that moderate and legalist policies periodically surfaced among the Stalinists. How can we explain the other, more moderate strand in Bolshevik policies in this period? Although such initiatives, sometimes bordering on constitutionalism and legalism, lost ground to the repressive alternative after 1935, they did not die out completely; they appeared even at the height of the terror and after.[39]

The answer is that in addition to being ideological fanatics willing to use any means, including violent "revolutionary expediency," the Stalinists were also state builders attracted to "socialist legal consciousness." USSR Procurator Andrei Vyshinsky saw no contradiction between these two goals, noting that they were compatible parts of the party's policy of "revolutionary legality."[40] Bolsheviks—including Stalin at various times —recognized that modern economies required modern states, efficient bureaucracies, predictable administration, and some measure of security for the political elite. The tension between voluntarist campaigns and arbitrary repression on the one hand and state building and orderly administration on the other marked the entire Stalin period; these two sets of policies alternated and overlapped with each other. As one scholar has noted, the Stalinist system was "two models in one," and tension between the two ran throughout the Stalin and post-Stalin periods.[41] We shall see this dynamic at work in the next period, when a political assassination raised the political temperature but provoked familiar contradictory responses.

In the summer of 1934 Politburo members advocated releasing several political figures convicted of anti-Soviet crimes. In one such case, Commissar of Defense Voroshilov noted that this was possible because "the situation now has sharply changed, and I think one could free him without particular risk."[42] There was the feeling at the top that the social struggle was calming down and that the previous policy of class struggle and maximum repression was being replaced by one in which the regime could feel strong enough to grant a certain measure of democracy without fear of being overthrown. L. M. Kaganovich wrote that the reform of the secret police "means that, as we are in more normal times, we can punish through the courts and not resort to extrajudicial repression as we have until now."[43]

Of course, no one in the Politburo was advocating abandoning the party-state dictatorship. As Stalin had said at the 17th Party Congress, "We cannot say that the fight is ended and that there is no longer any need for the policy of the socialist offensive." On the other hand, Stalin explicitly joined other Politburo members in proposing some kind of relaxation of that dictatorship, at least experimentally. The increased repression in later years "should not cast doubt on the intentions of Stalin and his colleagues in 1934."[44] At the beginning of 1935 he proposed a new electoral system with universal suffrage and secret-ballot elections. Confident that the regime was more and more secure and that sharp repression could be tempered with legality, Stalin wrote in a note in the Politburo's special folders, "We can and should proceed with this matter to the end, without any half-measures. The situation and correlation of forces in our country at the present moment is such that we can only win politically from this."[45] Even as late as 1937, when many of these "reforms" had been abandoned, there seems to have been some kind of attempt to democratize the electoral process and to "trust" the population to support the Bolsheviks.[46]

Thus one need not necessarily find the apparently hard and soft policies of 1932–34 to be mutually exclusive or sharply contradictory. Each was a means to an end: taking and maintaining control over the country in order to further the revolutionary program. Peasant revolt and starvation, conspiracies and platforms of former party leaders, dissident youth groups, and even a lack of iron discipline among serving Central Committee members had combined to frighten the nomenklatura elite and threaten its hold on power. In response, leaders sought to increase party discipline, strengthen judicial and police controls, and regulate the composition of their party. In these areas, both hard and soft policies had one common aspect: they sought to increase power exercised by the Moscow center. Even the legalist policies reviewed above, including reducing the number of arrests and insisting on judicial procedures, had the effect of tightening Moscow's control over these activities. By regulating arrest procedures, even in the direction of legality and procuratorial control, the Stalinists were asserting their right to control the entire judicial sphere. In this light, both hard and soft initiatives were parts of a drive (a defensive drive, in the nomenklatura's view) to centralize many spheres in a climate that was improving but still perceived to be dangerous.

CHAPTER FOUR

Growing Tension in 1935

To execute 60 people for one Kirov means that Soviet power is showing weakness by relying on terror to put down the growing discontent.—Komsomol member Ryabova, 1935

The main reason given for the commutation of sentence from death by shooting to ten years' imprisonment was the argument that this case did not involve a fully constituted counterrevolutionary group. . . . Do these people really need the fact of a perpetrated crime in order to convict such an obvious terrorist?! —M. F. Shkiriatov, 1935

NINETEEN THIRTY-FIVE BEGAN IN 1934. On 1 December 1934, the Politburo member, Leningrad party secretary, and Stalin intimate Sergei Kirov was shot in the corridor outside his office in the Smolny building. Over the next four years, the Stalinist leadership used the assassination as evidence of a widespread conspiracy against the Soviet state and its leaders and as a pretext for the Great Terror of the 1930s. Because millions of people were arrested, imprisoned, or shot in the aftermath of the assassination, and because it provided a key justification for Stalinist terror, the crime has rightly been called "the key moment which determined the development of the Soviet system."[1]

The assassin, one Leonid Nikolaev, was apprehended at the scene and along with several others was executed in short order. Three days after the killing, the Politburo approved an emergency decree whereby persons accused of "terrorism" could be convicted in an abbreviated procedure, denied the right of appeal, and summarily shot. This decree became the "legal" basis for thousands of summary executions over the next four years.

Moreover, complicity in organizing the Kirov murder was attached to al-most every high-level accusation made against Old Bolsheviks in the three famous Moscow show trials and many other proceedings.

Constructing the Kirov Assassination

Stalin used the Kirov assassination as a justification for persecution of his enemies. In fact, most historians believe that he organized the assassina-tion for this very purpose. The question is of more than antiquarian inter-est for two reasons. First, if Stalin was involved, it would be possible to ar-gue convincingly that he had a long-range plan to launch a terror of the elite and, indeed, of the entire Soviet Union. If, on the other hand, the as-sassination was not his work, the subsequent terror might appear to be less planned, and explanations of it would have to be sought outside the framework of a grand plan. Debates about Stalin's possible involvement in procuring the Kirov murder have been fierce but inconclusive because of the lack of official documentation.

In the 1930s various writers cast doubt on the official Stalinist story of an assassin working at the behest of an anti-Soviet criminal conspiracy. Leon Trotsky ("The Kirov Assassination," 1935) theorized that the killing may have been the accidental result of an operation by the secret police to stage an attempted assassination. Boris Nicolaevsky (*The Letter of an Old Bolshevik,* 1936) wrote that Kirov's killing was related to power struggles within the Politburo, with hard-liners standing to gain from the removal of Kirov's "liberal" influence with Stalin.

Beginning in the 1950s memoirs from some Soviet defectors began to suggest that Stalin may have arranged the crime in order to provide a jus-tification for terror or to eliminate Kirov as a rival. Then, in his speeches to party congresses in 1956 and 1961, Nikita Khrushchev hinted that in-deed "much remained to be explained" about the assassination (although he stopped short of actually accusing Stalin).

Working from the memoir literature, Western historians began to piece together the known events surrounding the assassination and its after-math, and elaborated a compelling case for Stalin's involvement. In addi-tion to creating a pretext for terror, Stalin's motives are said to include re-moving a popular rival and neutralizing a liberal, conciliatory voice on the Politburo that had opposed the Stalinists' hard-line policies. Kirov was said to be the choice of a secret group of high party officials who, in 1934, cast about for a possible replacement for Stalin. It is believed that this group encouraged a large number of delegates to the 17th Party Congress in 1934 either to abstain or to vote against Stalin's candidacy to the Central Committee. It is said that Kaganovich personally destroyed anti-Stalin ballots. In this view, Stalin knew about the attempt and decided to remove the alternative candidate and, eventually, all the officials behind the plan.

The strange incompetence of the Leningrad police in failing to prevent the assassination, coupled with possible connections between them and the assassin—it seems that they had previously detained him for questioning—suggested complicity of security officers in the murder. The fact that they received light punishments after the killing also pointed to Stalin's complicity, and their subsequent executions (along with almost everyone connected to Kirov or to the investigation of his murder) suggested a strategy of removing all witnesses. It seemed possible that Stalin, working through secret police channels, had procured the assassination of Kirov.[2]

In the 1980s the Politburo launched a new official investigation into the assassination. Assembling an interagency team from the Communist Party, KGB, and other bodies, this committee reexamined the evidence. But as with all previous investigations, the commission failed to produce a report. Their efforts dissolved into mutual recriminations among the members that leaked into the press, as some pressed for a conclusion implicating Stalin while other members argued that the evidence pointed the other way.[3] Proceeding from the mainstream Western theories, historians associated with the official rehabilitation effort supported the idea that Stalin was involved. The official party journal in the Gorbachev years promised its readers a full historical account but never produced one. Instead, its coverage of other cases in the Stalin period obliquely suggested Stalin's involvement in the killing.[4]

As early as 1973 some historians raised doubts about the prevailing view and made the first sustained Western case against Stalin's involvement.[5] Beginning in the 1980s other Western and Soviet historians also questioned the theory of Stalin's complicity, the origins of the story, and Stalin's motive and opportunity, as well as the circumstances surrounding the event. They noted that the sources for the theory derived originally from memoirists whose information was second- and thirdhand and who were in all cases far removed from the event. During the Cold War, a flood of Soviet defectors had generated a huge and sensational literature that largely repeated and echoed itself while providing few verifiable facts, and that sometimes seemed primarily designed to enhance the status and importance of the author. These historians also noted that despite at least two official Soviet investigations and the high-level political advantages of accusing Stalin in the Khrushchev years, none of the investigations by even the most anti-Stalin Soviet administrations had accused Stalin of the crime, even though he was directly accused of murdering many equally famous politicians.[6]

Historians also raised questions about Kirov's supposed liberalism and resistance to Stalin.[7] The evidence for an anti-Stalin group in the leadership that backed Kirov seems quite weak and based on hearsay that was often contradicted by other firsthand accounts.[8] In this view, the evidence seems to suggest that Kirov was nothing if not a staunch Stalinist who did his share of persecuting Stalin's enemies. Similarly, the most recent (Gorbachev-era) official investigation into the supposed anti-Stalin votes at the 17th Party Congress cast doubt on this story, finding that many witnesses reported the matter differently and that it was not possible to verify the story on the basis of personal testimonies or archival evidence.[9]

The question of Leningrad police complicity also seems murky. Recent evidence discounts the alleged connections between police and the assassin. The NKVD official who supposedly directed the assassin was not even in the city during the months he was supposed to have groomed the killer.[10] While it is true that most Leningrad police officials and party leaders were executed in the terror subsequent to the assassination, so were hundreds of thousands of others, and there is no compelling reason to believe that they were killed "to cover the tracks" of the Kirov assassination, as Khrushchev put it. Moreover, they were left alive (and in some cases at liberty) and free to talk for three years following the crime. It has seemed to some unlikely that Stalin would have taken such a chance for so long with pawns used to arrange the killing.

Shortly after the assassination, N. I. Yezhov (representing the party) and Ya. Agranov (representing the NKVD) took charge of the investigation in Leningrad. Yezhov's archive shows that they pressed assassin Nikolaev hard on any possible connections he may have had with the NKVD and turned up nothing. More than two thousand NKVD workers in Leningrad were interrogated or investigated by Yezhov's team; three hundred were fired or transferred to other work for negligence. Yezhov reported to Stalin that the men of the Leningrad NKVD were incompetent, careless, and incapable of operating intelligence networks that could have prevented the assassination.[11]

The head of the secret police in 1934, Genrikh Yagoda (through whom Stalin is said to have worked to kill Kirov), was produced in open court and in front of the world press before his execution in 1938. Knowing that he was to be shot in any event, he could have brought Stalin's entire house of cards down with a single remark about the Kirov killing. Again, giving a coconspirator this opportunity would appear to have been an unacceptable risk for a complicit Stalin.

Finally, in analyzing the regime's reaction immediately after the crime, it has seemed to some historians that the events surrounding the crime suggest more surprise than premeditated planning. The Stalinists seemed unprepared for the assassination and panicked by it. Indeed, it took them more than eighteen months to frame their supposed targets—members of the anti-Stalin Old Bolshevik opposition—for the killing.[12] Everyone agrees that Stalin made tremendous use of the assassination for his own purposes; it eventually enabled him to make cases against his political enemies, to settle old scores, and to launch a generalized purge. But although there is consensus on his actions *after* the assassination, there remains great disagreement about his involvement in arranging the crime itself.

Today many Russian scholars are less sure than they once were about Stalin's involvement. The leading scholars on opposition to Stalin in the 1930s now make no judgment on the matter, and the memoirs of V. M. Molotov (perhaps unsurprisingly) observe that Kirov was never a challenger to Stalin's position.[13] The most recent scholarly work on the Kirov assassination from a Russian scholar, based on Leningrad party and police archives, concludes that Stalin had nothing to do with the killing.[14] Similarly, a recent comprehensive study by an American scholar concludes that Stalin was not involved in the assassination.[15]

Although the instigation of the murder is still unclear, the aftermath and results are not. Stalin used the killing for political purposes. After some initial confusion, the regime blamed the assassination (albeit indirectly) on the former oppositionists of Leningrad led by G. E. Zinoviev.[16] Deputy commissar of the secret police Agranov was brought in to supervise a special investigation of the crime to be aimed at Zinoviev and his associate Lev Kamenev.[17] The assassin and several former associates of Zinoviev were quickly tried and shot, and in mid-December Zinoviev and Kamenev were arrested. But after one month of questioning, Agranov reported that he was not able to prove that they had been directly involved in the assassination.[18] So in the middle of January 1935 they were tried and convicted only for "moral complicity" in the crime. That is, their opposition had created a climate in which others were incited to violence. Zinoviev was sentenced to ten years in prison, Kamenev to five.

Repression also intensified beyond the circle of party members and oppositionists. In the immediate aftermath of the killing, the regime's reaction was locally savage but spasmodic and unfocused. As they had done in the Civil War, the police immediately executed groups of innocent "hostages" with no connection to the crime. Several dozen opponents, labeled as "whites" and already languishing in prison, were summarily executed in cities around the Soviet Union.[19] By February 1935 Yezhov wrote to Stalin that he had rounded up about one thousand former Leningrad oppositionists. Three hundred of these had been arrested, while the remainder were exiled from the city. Yezhov's archive shows that in this period he put together elaborate card files on the Leningrad oppositionists and kept them under surveillance in their exile locations. More than eleven thousand persons in Leningrad, described as "former people" (nobles, pre-Revolutionary industrialists, and others) were evicted from the city and forced to move elsewhere.[20] Characteristically, though, this action provoked disagreement in high places, with Stalin once again acting as referee. Yagoda had protested the exiles, arguing that they would generate bad publicity abroad; Stalin, at Yezhov's recommendation, approved them. A few months later, however, Procurator Vyshinsky protested against the wholesale, careless, and procedurally illegal nature of the deportations, and Stalin sided with him in reopening many of the cases and allowing the deportees to retain many of their electoral and labor rights.[21]

In his postmortem investigation of the Kirov killing, Yezhov cast doubt on NKVD chief Yagoda's competence. Although Yezhov turned up no incriminating evidence against the Leningrad NKVD, he made a strong case for incompetence bordering on the criminal: officers had "put aside their weapons and fallen asleep."[22] Yezhov wrote a detailed report to Stalin on 23 January 1935, ostensibly about his overall impressions of the work of the Leningrad police. But he transformed the report (which he reworked through several drafts) into an indictment of the NKVD in general.[23] This letter is a crucial landmark in Yezhov's career because it represents his first open salvo in his campaign against NKVD chief Yagoda, a campaign that he would prosecute relentlessly for the next eighteen months until Stalin gave him Yagoda's job: "I decided to write this memo in the hope that it might be useful to you in correcting the work of the ChK [secret police] generally. . . . Deficiencies evidently exist not only in Leningrad but in other places and in particular in the central apparatus of the NKVD. . . . Judging from what I saw in Leningrad, I must say that these people do not know how to conduct an investigation."[24] According to Bolshevik discursive and social conventions, this was a bold personal attack on Yagoda. It did not take a genius to see that Yezhov's implication was that Yagoda's performance had created a situation in which the regime, and the lives of Stalin and other Politburo members, were in danger. In terms of implications and possible consequences, therefore, the matter was serious; Yezhov was throwing down the gauntlet to Yagoda.[25] For the time being, however, Stalin kept the balance. He encouraged Yezhov's inquiries but continued to defend and retain Yagoda.

Unfortunately, documents from the former party archive shed no direct light on high-level involvement in the Kirov assassination. They do, however, clearly support known trends in arrest statistics: the Stalin leadership chose to politicize the crime and to interpret it as a political conspiracy. Shortly after the trial, the Politburo drafted a circular letter to all party organizations about the "lessons" to be drawn from the Kirov assassination. It sought to educate party members about the danger posed by "two-faced" oppositionists who claim to support the party but work against it:

> Now that the nest of villainy—the Zinoviev anti-Soviet group—has been completely destroyed and the culprits of this villainy have received their just punishment—the CC believes that the time has come to sum up the events connected with the murder of Comrade KIROV, to assess their political significance and to draw the lessons that issue from an analysis of these events.
>
> The villainous murder was committed by the Leningrad group of Zinoviev followers calling themselves the "Leningrad Center" under the leadership of the "Moscow Center" of Zinoviev followers, which, apparently, did not know of the preparations for the murder of Comrade KIROV but which surely knew of the terroristic sentiments of the "Leningrad Center" and stirred up these sentiments.[26]

Prescribed Transcripts

Although the January 1935 letter turned up the heat on current and former dissidents, it was not a call for terror. The first sentence of the letter claimed that "the nest of villainy—the Zinoviev anti-Soviet group—has been completely destroyed." By implication, in the view of the letter's authors, there were no further nests of villains. A party purge did not follow the letter for nearly five months, and then the screening instructions did not mention the Kirov killing. Zinoviev and Kamenev would not be charged with direct organization of the Kirov killing for more than a year and a half, and then on the basis of "new materials" unearthed in 1936. The January 1935 letter identified the "followers of Zinoviev" (but not Zinoviev himself) and other former oppositionists as counterrevolutionary enemies. This political transcript was read out at all party organization and cell meetings. Party leaders at all levels were ordered to conduct "discussions" of the letter to promulgate its conclusions. These discussions also served a ritual purpose. When they went as planned, they were to be forums for rank-and-file party members and citizens to repeat and affirm the proffered political narrative.

The letter invited local party organizations to identify present and former dissidents. The local discussions suggest, though, that there was a shortage of real Zinovievists remaining in party organizations. Accordingly, various marginal and unpopular characters were identified as oppositionists and punished. Sometimes the discussions of the Kirov assassination and the January 1935 letter tended to be routine and ritualistic, reflecting apathy and "weak participation" in the prescribed discourse. Frequently the meetings "unmasked" some unfortunates as "enemies," but such targets tended to be defenseless marginal types. On other occasions the meetings seem to have been more emotional, either encouraging further investigations or unearthing "anti-Soviet moods."[27]

Statistics on overall repression in the months following the Kirov assassination reveal some curious trends. In terms of police arrests, overall repression did not increase in 1935. The number of NKVD arrests in 1935 was lower than it had been even in the previous, calm year of 1934 (see table 1). The secret police made fewer arrests in 1935, in fact, than in any year since 1929. NKVD arrests had been declining steadily every year since 1931, and they would fall even lower in 1936.

But the character of those arrests was changing. Inside the lower aggregate arrest totals, arrests for political reasons were increasing: compared with 1934, there were 10 percent more arrests for "counterrevolutionary" crimes and two and a half times as many arrests for "anti-Soviet agitation" in 1935.[28] The proportion of NKVD arrests for nonpolitical offenses fell correspondingly. In other words, while total arrests were down, those arrests that did take place in the wake of the Kirov assassination were increasingly defined as "political."

In 1935 the NKVD arrested about 193,000 persons on all charges. In previous years, various proportions of those arrested were ultimately convicted, but in 1935 convictions *exceeded* arrests by more than 74,000 persons. In the months following the Kirov killing, thousands of people already under arrest before the assassination were reconvicted under more political charges. Unfortunately, we have no information on their new sentences, but the statistics we do have do not suggest that their new politicized sentences were necessarily more harsh. In 1935, although the total number of convictions was three times higher than in 1934, the proportion of sentences to prison or labor camp fell from 75 percent to 70 percent; executions as a proportion of all sentences fell from 2.6 percent to 0.4 percent. Less severe types of sentences increased: exile (either to a specific place or as denial of right to live in major cities) from 7.5 percent to 12.5 percent and other (mostly noncustodial) sentences from 14.5 percent to 17.3 percent.

Police repression of the former opposition intensified in the wake of the Kirov assassination. Aside from the January 1935 trial of Zinoviev and Kamenev, there were several less publicized judicial proceedings against former oppositionists in Leningrad, Moscow, and other cities. The trial of the "Leningrad Counterrevolutionary Zinovievist Group of Safarov, Zalutsky, and others" sentenced 77 defendants to camp and exile terms of four to five years.[29] Altogether in the two and one half months following the assassination, 843 former Zinovievists were arrested in Leningrad; most were exiled to remote regions and not sentenced to camps.[30] As one investigator told a detainee, formal guilt or innocence was not the point: "The proletariat demands the exile of everyone directly or indirectly connected with the opposition."[31]

The Nomenklatura and the Face of the Enemy

N. I. Yezhov had been a Petrograd worker who joined the Bolsheviks in the summer of 1917. Active as a political organizer and commissar during the Civil War, he worked in several provincial party committees in the 1920s and had a reputation as a solid party worker.[32] Perhaps spotted by L. M. Kaganovich, who ran the Organizational-Assignment Department of the Central Committee in the 1920s, Yezhov was brought to Moscow to work in the central party apparatus and by 1930, at Kaganovich's suggestion, was attending Politburo meetings.[33]

In the early 1930s he worked in the Central Committee's Industrial and Cadres (personnel) departments. By 1933 he had become a kind of personnel "checker." By January of that year he was heading the Central Committee's personnel assignment department. He played a leading administrative role in the 1933 party screening (*chistka*) and in a number of other bureaucratic verification operations.[34] From early 1934 his rise was meteoric. At the 17th Party Congress in early 1934 he headed the Mandate (credentials) Commission of the Congress and was elected a full member of the Central Committee (skipping over candidate member status altogether), a member of the Orgburo, and Deputy Chairman of the Party Control Commission (KPK).[35]

By 1934 Yezhov ranked high enough to earn the privilege of traveling abroad for rest cures, funded by hard currency from party coffers. It was common for high-ranking party leaders to go abroad for rest and relaxation in health spas. In 1934 Yezhov went abroad to a spa with a disbursement of twelve hundred rubles in foreign currency. He was apparently so dedicated to his work that the Politburo had to forbid him to return until the end of his rest, forwarding him an additional one thousand gold rubles to complete his rest vacation.[36]

In early 1935, as part of a series of security checks following the Kirov assassination, the NKVD began investigating the staff of the Kremlin. Arrests began in February, and by early summer 110 employees of the Kremlin service administration (including some of Kamenev's relatives) were accused in the "Kremlin Affair" of organizing a group to commit "terrorist acts" against the government. Ultimately, two were sentenced to death; the remainder received prison or camp terms of five to ten years.[37]

A. S. Yenukidze, as secretary of the Central Executive Committee of Soviets, was responsible for administration of and security in the Kremlin. The Kremlin Affair, in which dozens of Kremlin employees were arrested for conspiracy, cast suspicion on Yenukidze's supervision. The suspicion was compounded by Yenukidze's softhearted tendency to aid old revolutionaries who had run afoul of Soviet justice. Yezhov made his debut as a visible player in the Central Committee at the June 1935 plenum of the Central Committee, where he delivered the official accusation against Yenukidze.[38]

The Kremlin Affair of 1935 provided the basis for a further sharpening of the political atmosphere in mid-1935 by casting doubt for the first time on high-ranking party officials who had always sided with Stalin. The scene for this escalation was the June 1935 plenum of the Central Committee, where Yenukidze was accused of aiding and abetting the "terrorists." Yezhov was the agent for this heightening of tension and made his national political debut at the June plenum as Yenukidze's accuser and bearer of the latest narrative from on high.

It was a curious text. He began not by criticizing Yenukidze, but rather with a lengthy digression on the crimes of Zinoviev and Kamenev. To this point, they had been accused of only "moral complicity" in the death of Kirov. Now, however, Yezhov for the first time accused them of direct organization of the assassination and introduced the idea that Trotsky was also involved from his base in exile. Despite Yezhov's claim to the contrary, this was a radical new theory and one that could give no comfort to political dissidents.[39]

Yezhov's speech had treated the Yenukidze affair almost as a sidelight, and it is tempting to see the Yenukidze accusation as a pretext for introducing a new prescribed version of the transgressions of Zinoviev, Kamenev, and Trotsky. If this is true, and Yezhov's speech was a kind of trial balloon (either Yezhov's or Stalin's), it was a strange and unsuccessful attempt to recast the prevailing political line on the opposition.

First of all, Stalin did not speak in support of Yezhov's theory. This in itself was not strange; Stalin often used his henchmen to make his points while remaining silent. But this time, the usual chorus (Kaganovich, Rudzutak, Shkiriatov, and others) did not strongly back Yezhov. Second, despite Yezhov having posited "direct participation by Kamenev and Zinoviev in the organizing of terroristic groups" and having said that "the murder of Comrade Kirov was organized by Zinoviev and Kamenev," no new charges were brought against them, and it would be more than a year after Yezhov's speech that these two were brought to trial for the crime. During that period, their names almost never appeared in the press or in party speeches, even though a high-ranking party official had accused them of organizing the assassination of a Politburo member. Finally, Yezhov's failed new narrative was never published.

Why the strange delay in following up on Yezhov's thesis? No one spoke in defense of Zinoviev and Kamenev and no one suggested moderation or delay at the plenum, at any subsequent plenum, or in any documents at our disposal. Indeed, it is hard to imagine that the nomenklatura would want to defend them. After all, by identifying these has-beens as the enemy, the new theory suggested that any and all problems could be blamed on their treason, rather than on "bureaucrats" who did not "fulfill decisions."

There would appear to be two possible explanations for the failure of Yezhov's initiative against Zinoviev and Kamenev in June 1935. On the one hand, there could have been quiet opposition in the Central Committee that forced Stalin to stay his hand. Or it may well have been Stalin himself who was unsure about what to do with Zinoviev and Kamenev. He might have allowed Yezhov to float his trial balloon, then left him dangling by telling him that it was possible to follow up only if Yezhov could prove the charges. It would take Yezhov a year to get the "proof" by forcing Zinoviev and Kamenev to confess.

Although Yezhov's wild denunciation of former oppositionists was met with inaction, the members of the Central Committee did discuss the Yenukidze accusation, and the discussion shows the "lessons" party members were to draw. As always, the target of an accusation was expected to perform an apology ritual. Yenukidze, however, refused to play his part:

> YENUKIDZE: No one was hired for work in the Kremlin without their security clearance. This applies to all officials without exception.
>
> YAGODA: That's not true.
>
> YENUKIDZE: Yes, it is.
>
> YAGODA: We gave our security report, but you insisted on hiring. We said not to hire, and you went ahead and hired.
>
> YENUKIDZE: Comrade Yagoda, how can you say that?[40]

Yenukidze did not fully grasp what was required of him. Like his CC comrades, he recognized the propriety and gravity of the accusation, but he claimed that he was not guilty of anything. He refused to take his medicine and carry out the apology ritual. In his speech he had claimed that his organization was no better or worse than others and had blamed the NKVD and Control Commission officials for vetting the personnel who had been accused. Politically, he was still reading from a different page. His speech was constative, about true and false assertions, when what was required was performative speech that would do work. That work involved becoming a ritualized agent, transforming himself through language in a particular ritual setting into a serviceable "other," a "lesson" that the Central Committee could use politically.

Genrikh Yagoda, head of the NKVD, had to say something. According to formality and logic, his organization should have discovered the crime and reported on it. Instead, Yezhov, from the party secretariat, had uncovered and reported the "treason," a fact that already cast doubt on Yagoda's competence.[41] Yenukidze had blamed the NKVD in his remarks. The NKVD was explicitly and implicitly under fire. Yagoda had to speak, and in his own defense had to be tough and uncompromising. He had to be more Catholic than the pope: "I think that by his speech Yenukidze has already placed himself outside the bounds of our Party.

"What he said here, what he brought here to the Plenum of the Central Committee, is the pile of rubbish of a philistine. Everything that Yenukidze has said here is nothing but unadulterated lies."[42]

Yagoda proposed the expulsion of Yenukidze from the party, going beyond Yezhov's recommendation only to remove him from the Central Committee. In his remarks Yagoda had made an interesting point about Yenukidze's "parallel 'GPU'" and revealed that as late as 1935, high-ranking members of the nomenklatura had been able to thwart the secret police. In Yagoda's words, whenever Yenukidze "recognized one of our agents, he immediately banished him."

It fell to L. M. Kaganovich, as a real insider, to make the main point, to provide the main "lesson" of the Yenukidze affair. Recalling one of the themes of Stalin's speech to the 17th Party Congress, Kaganovich insisted that everyone—no matter how exalted his rank—must adhere to the master narrative and to the rituals of party discipline: "Our Party is strong by virtue of the fact that it metes out its punishment equally to all members of the Party, both in the upper and lower echelons. . . . This matter, of course, is important not only as it pertains to Yenukidze but also because we undoubtedly have in our Party people who believe that we can now 'take it more easily': In view of our great victory, in view of the fact that our country is moving forward, they can now afford to rest, to take a nap."[43]

So for Kaganovich the point was not whether or not the NKVD had missed the boat (although that lesson was lost on no one). The crux of the matter was not even whether or not Yenukidze was formally guilty or not. The point was that no one, not even those who had always been senior Stalinists, was above party discipline. Not even highly placed members of the nomenklatura who ruled their fiefs with an iron hand were immune to control or to the demands of the party. Yenukidze's duty as a Bolshevik was to discuss how enemies had stolen their way into the apparat, how he had protected dubious people. The party had demanded that Yenukidze help it teach a lesson, and Yenukidze had failed to play his role.

For years, the nomenklatura had demanded that lower-ranking party functionaries play the roles assigned to them: to help provide negative examples and changes in policy by making formal apologies and posing as scapegoats. Members of opposition groups who found themselves on the losing side had been expected to do the same to win readmission to the nomenklatura. What was new in the 1930s was the expectation that the highest-ranking members of the Stalin coalition do the same when duty called. As Kaganovich had said, "Our Party is strong by virtue of the fact that it metes out its punishment equally to all members of the Party, both in the upper and lower echelons." A. P. Smirnov in 1933 and now Yenukidze in 1935 had failed to understand that.

Kaganovich's discussion of the decision-making process shows that the inner leadership, including Stalin himself, had difficulty deciding what to do with Yenukidze. Various punishments had been discussed. Yezhov's personal papers contain three draft decrees on Yenukidze prepared before the meeting. The first proposed only removing him from his Central Executive Committee (TsIK) position and appointing him TsIK secretary in Transcaucasia. By the third draft, because of "new facts coming to light," the punishment had been escalated to "discussing Yenukidze's Central Committee membership." This was the proposal that Yezhov brought to the meeting.

Speaker after speaker denounced Yenukidze's sins in a ritual display of nomenklatura unity and anger. By joining to isolate Yenukidze, the members of the Central Committee were not only supporting Stalin's charges (but not, as we shall see, Yezhov's) but implicitly affirming their individual status as well as their collective right to decide punishment. CC apology rites had a transactional component; the final sanction depended on how well the subject had played his part. In this case, Yenukidze's declining the prescribed rite infuriated the group. The increasingly angry nature of the discussion at the plenum led to a second motion to expel him from the party altogether. At the end of the plenum, both proposals were put to the vote. Yezhov's motion to expel him from the CC passed unanimously; another proposal to expel him from the party passed by a simple majority.[44]

The split vote (itself an extreme rarity in the Central Committee) on the disposition of Yenukidze's fate was not something the top party leadership wanted to broadcast to the party rank and file. In the version of the plenum minutes printed for distribution in the party, the event was portrayed differently. History was rewritten to make it seem that there had been only one proposal and that the ultimate decision—to expel him from the party—was based on an original Yezhov motion, which he never made. The image of a united leadership had to be maintained with a single text.[45]

It is of course possible that the second, harsher proposal—to expel Yenukidze from the party—came from Stalin through his representatives. In this case, the strategy would have been to have Yezhov put forward a suggestion for moderate punishment of a key nomenklatura member in order not to alarm the elite, to gauge the reaction, and then to see what developed.

It is more likely, however, that the ad hoc harsher punishment came from the nomenklatura itself in the course of the plenum. In such a case, the nomenklatura was more radical in its punishment than Stalin himself. It could well be that Yenukidze's refusal to carry out the apology that elite discipline required infuriated the elite in the Central Committee. It may well have been that the elite went into the plenum with a quid pro quo in mind: in return for his formal apology, Yenukidze would be spared a full scapegoating and could remain in the party. His refusal or failure to comply thus led to the harsher punishment.

There is some reason to suspect that in the end Yenukidze was punished rather more harshly than Stalin had originally intended. At the first plausible opportunity, two plenums later in June 1936, Stalin personally proposed that Yenukidze be permitted to rejoin the party. At that time, Stalin explained that this was the earliest moment Yenukidze's readmission could take place: "Otherwise, it would be like expelling him at one plenum and readmitting him at the next." Readmitting Yenukidze then was a curious irony. For it was at that plenum that the Politburo announced the upcoming capital trial of Zinoviev and Kamenev for the assassination of Kirov, the theory Yezhov had put forward at the plenum that expelled Yenukidze.

Central Committee members must have taken several lessons from the June 1935 plenum. First, they were introduced to the idea that Zinoviev's and Kamenev's guilt might be greater than previously thought. Second, Yezhov was now a visibly important player before the Central Committee: he had brought down the secretary of the Central Executive Committee and stepped forward as the herald of a modified (albeit temporarily un successful) narrative. Third, Yagoda and the NKVD had been discredited. Fourth, and most uncomfortable for them, one of the highest-ranking members of the nomenklatura (and a personal friend of Stalin's) had violated discipline. For some members of the elite, this action must have been personally disquieting: if Yenukidze could fall, no one was safe. For others, however, the lesson was that the dangers and threats of the new situation had infected even the inner circle of the nomenklatura.

As was so often the case, Stalin remained in the shadows of the plenum. What did he think? What did he want? What, if any, were his plans? The events of the Yenukidze plenum are consistent with a plan to escalate repression and prepare the way for terror. Incriminating Zinoviev and Kamenev (along with Trotsky) in capital crimes clearly raised the stakes in defining enemies and punishments. Similarly, casting a shadow on a serving member of the upper nomenklatura—some speakers like the hysterical Yagoda had practically equated Yenukidze's guilt with Zinoviev's—could open the door to persecution of the elite itself in an unfolding terror.

On the other hand, Stalin's failure to take a position could reflect his own indecision about launching generalized repression. He personally softened many of the sentences that Yagoda proposed for those convicted in the Kremlin case, including commuting some death sentences and ordering the release of several defendants. When in May 1935 Yagoda jumped on Yezhov's bandwagon against the opposition by arguing that Kamenev was "organizer of an attempt on the life of Comrade Stalin," Stalin rejected the accusation and reduced Yagoda's proposed death sentence for Kamenev to ten years in jail.[46]

Moreover, if these June 1935 events were part of a scheme to move against major oppositionists, it remained stillborn for so long a time that their purported lessons were lost or devalued. Yezhov's accusations against Zinoviev and Kamenev were not followed up for a year; this was hardly striking while the iron was hot. To insiders skilled at reading the tea leaves of Central Committee plenums, the unitary lesson that Yenukidze's fall apparently provided was muted by Kaganovich's admission that the Politburo had had trouble deciding what to do, and was erased by Yenukidze's clean bill of health at Stalin's hands in June 1936. No ranking nomenklatura members would be arrested until the end of 1936, more than a year and a half after the Yenukidze plenum.

Finally, Yezhov's debut in the role of hatchetman against "enemies" was not an unqualified success. Not only was his main "thesis" ignored, but the proposal he put forward on Yenukidze was overruled. Given that everyone must have known that his recommendation on Yenukidze must have been approved by Stalin and the Politburo beforehand, the impression created was that the radical Yezhov had been taken down a peg at the moment of his triumph. No one except the master balancer—Stalin— could have permitted that.

Other documents from June and July 1935 nevertheless suggest a more "vigilant" and repressive atmosphere on the local level. For example, in the Azov–Black Sea Territory, there was a new crackdown against rural opponents. New loyalty checks were to screen officials for dubious pasts, and for good measure, fifteen hundred "kulaks and counterrevolutionaries" were to be deported from the province.[47]

Intensified Ideological Controls

New central decrees also sought to tighten controls over subversive book collections in libraries (perhaps in light of reports that the Kremlin Affair conspiracy had been centered in the Kremlin Library). A June 1935 decree ordered a list of "Trotskyist-Zinoviev" books to be removed from libraries but warned against "an uncontrolled and ungovernable 'purge' of libraries . . . and damaging of library resources."[48]

Increasing ideological and literary controls also extended to the members of the nomenklatura itself. Stalin, having emphasized "political education" and ideology since 1934 (see his speech to the 17th Party Congress) had personally taken control of the Culture and Propaganda Department of the Central Committee in April 1935. His personal interest and control over ideology is reflected in a document in which a ranking member of the nomenklatura was brought up short. No one was to be allowed to alter the public rhetoric about the supreme leader, even in the direction of glorification, without permission.[49]

Legal and Police Policy: Moderation vs. Legal Nihilism

Typically, however, even as things swung in the direction of harder and harder policies, there continued to be countervailing texts that suggested softer, legal tactics. Some documents reflect a liberalization of the policy enforced on exiled "enemies." Such granting of "privileges" was uncharacteristic of either the preceding period or the subsequent terror and represents a kind of isolated text in an otherwise darkening picture. The new rules permitted condemned "enemies" to work in their specialties; all memoir accounts agree that such a possibility was important to detainees. These new regulations also removed the legal stigma from children of the regime's victims. The central leadership had not yet decided on the completely brutal and severe treatment of its victims that would follow in 1937.[50]

In mid-June the Central Committee produced a regulation on procedures for conducting arrests. As with all such documents, it sent mixed signals. On the one hand, it seemed to tighten up the requirements for arrest by insisting that all arrests without exception had to be approved by the relevant procurator. On the other hand, though, in spelling out the approvals necessary for detaining persons in various positions, it foresaw the possibility—which could not have been lost on Stalinist officials—that high-ranking persons might in the future be arrested.[51]

It is also likely that this and similar decrees had another purpose: restriction of the powers of regional party leaders to conduct their own arrests in the provinces without judicial supervision. In Belorussia, for example, party provincial secretaries had sought to control railroad personnel through mass arrests. One Control Commission representative said that "tens, hundreds were arrested by anybody and they sit in jail." In the Briansk Railroad Line, 75 percent of administrative-technical personnel had been sentenced to some kind of "corrective labor." In Sverdlovsk and Saratov, Control Commission inspectors sent from Moscow reported that locals had "completely baselessly arrested and convicted people and undertaken mass repressions for minor problems, sometimes for ineffective leadership and in the majority of cases, arrested and convicted workers who merely needed educational work."[52] By insisting on the procurator's permission in order for an arrest to be made, the Central Committee was taking unlimited arrest powers out of the hands of regional party leaders.

On the other hand, the fall of 1935 also brought a political hardening and a kind of legal nihilism inconsistent with many of 1934's initiatives that had seemed to augur an era of legality and rule of law. In September 1935 Yezhov gave a secret speech to a closed meeting of party personnel officials from the provinces. Contradicting written party and state texts, he advised party officials sharply to restrict the rights of expelled members to appeal, and not to be restrained by procurators' insistence on procedural legality. "What guarantee do we have that a crook may not somewhere succeed in slipping through? Besides, for all we know, a certain liberalism may have been shown in respect of individual Party members. . . . Here our Procuracy has, to some extent, made a mess of things." He also encouraged his audience to make use of extralegal bodies to convict "dangerous elements" not guilty of a specific chargeable offense. Finally, he chided party organizations and the NKVD for stepping on each other's toes, referring to "certain officials who have gotten the NKVD involved where it is not needed, who have dumped work on the NKVD that they should have done themselves and who, on the other hand, do not permit the NKVD to concern itself with that which the NKVD should concern itself with."[53]

A few weeks later, M. F. Shkiriatov, a hard-line Party Control Commission functionary, wrote to Stalin about the case of one V. A. Gagarina, a "counterrevolutionary" who had been freed upon appeal by the Supreme Court. His description of the case also shows the tendency to override legal procedures, and is a classic statement of Bolshevik voluntarism and expediency at the expense of legality. It also indicates, however, that some judicial officials were willing to follow the letter of the law rather than the Shkiriatov version of political expediency. Such documents show that the "moderate" legalistic documents upholding procuratorial sanction and process, while more and more observed in the breach, did sometimes have an effect.[54]

Screening Cadres, 1935

Another party membership screening operation, or purge, came in the middle of 1935: the verification (*proverka*) of party documents. Planned even before the Kirov assassination, this purge was in the tradition of party screenings since 1921 and was designed to rid the party of "ballast": corrupt bureaucrats, those who had hidden their social origins or political pasts, those with false membership documents.[55] The order for the operation ("On Disorders in the Registration, Distribution, and Safekeeping of Party Cards and on Measures for Regulating This Affair") had characterized the verification as a housekeeping operation to bring some order to the clerical registration of party membership documents. Although the proverka did not specifically call for the expulsion of former oppositionists, it was inevitable that many of them would be targeted in this background check.[56]

According to a report by Yezhov, who was in charge of the screenings, as of December 1935, 9.1 percent of the party's members had been expelled in the proverka, and 8.7 percent of those expelled had been arrested; he gave a corresponding figure of 15,218 arrests out of 177,000 expulsions, or a little less than 1 percent of those passing through the verification.[57] The level of arrests varied considerably from province to province, and there is strong evidence that relations between party and police were not always smooth. The NKVD generated documents attesting to their close cooperation with party committees.[58]

Such reports were meant to show unanimity to the middle party leaders. But the hidden transcript was different. In a September 1935 meeting, Yezhov noted that cooperation between party and police organizations was not good. Party organizations had been reluctant to concede a political monitoring role to the NKVD, preferring instead the former system in which the NKVD investigated state crimes not involving members of the party and left political offenses to the party organs.[59] The information in table 2 shows, in fact, that party and police organizations worked badly together and frequently disagreed on who was "the enemy." Yezhov gave the 1935 operation a combative stamp by calling for verifiers in the party organizations to concentrate on expelling ideological enemies of all kinds. "One thing is clear beyond dispute: It seems to me that Trotskyists undoubtedly have a center somewhere in the USSR." His remarks emphasized the hunt for enemies.

Despite Yezhov's concentration on Trotskyists and other enemies, the results of the verification, like previous party screenings, struck hardest at

Table 2

Party Expulsions and Police Arrests, 1935

Party organization	Files sent by NKVD (A) to party	Number and %age of (A) expelled by party organizations (B)	Number and %age of (B) arrested by NKVD	%age of (A) ultimately arrested
Ukraine	17,368	6,675 (38%)	2,095 (31%)	12%
Ivanovo	3,580	1,184 (33%)	261 (22%)	7%
Western	3,233	1,337 (41%)	312 (23%)	10%

Sources: RGASPI, f. 17, op. 120, d. 184, ll. 63–66; f. 17, op. 120, d. 183, ll. 60–65, 92.

Table 3
Reasons for Expulsion, 1935–36 (%ages of all expelled)

	Yezhov 1935 report	*Malenkov 1937 memo[a]*
Spies	1.0	0.9
Trotskyists/Zinovievists	2.9	5.5
"Swindlers"	7.9	8.0
Former Whites, kulaks, etc.	19.1	27.5
Moral corruption		20.6
Incorrect documents		15.6
"Other"		17.7
Unexplained	69.1	4.2

Sources: RTsKhIDNI f. 17, op. 20, d. 177, ll. 20–22; f. 17, op. 120, d. 278, l. 2.
[a]Includes persons expelled in 1936 after the completion of the *chistki*.

rank-and-file party members with irregularities in their documents, many
of whom were charged with generally nonideological offenses having to
do with malfeasance or "alien" class background. Two reports, one from
Yezhov's 1935 report and another from an internal Central Committee
memo written by G. M. Malenkov, are summarized in table 3 and show
the categories expelled.

Local Cadres and Family Circles

The conduct of the proverka shows some interesting aspects of the relationship between central and provincial party organizations. Since the late
1920s provincial party leaders had become powerful political actors on a
par with feudal barons. They controlled the police, courts, trade unions,
agriculture, and industry in their territories. Responsible to Moscow for
fulfillment of plans, they ran hierarchical organizations based on patronage and personal power. Stalin had referred to them in 1934 as "feudal
princes," who pigeonholed Moscow's orders rather than fulfilling them,
did their best to conceal the real situation from Moscow, and "thought
[Moscow's] decisions were written for fools, and not for them."[60] Formally, they represented central authority in the provinces, but in reality
they ran powerful political machines that dominated economic, political,
and social life in their territories.

The instructions locals received had been vague. On the one hand, the document instigating the verification made it out to be a clerical rectification of party files and membership cards, fully consistent with a mass screening of the rank and file (those most likely to have defective or dubious cards). On the other, Yezhov had characterized it as an operation to uncover oppositionist elements, including Trotskyists and Zinovievists.

Because membership in the Trotskyist or Zinovievist organizations implied party membership dating back into the 1920s, "genuine" ex-oppositionists were likely to have worked their way up from the rank and file into leadership positions in local political machines. Yezhov's call, therefore, was implicitly a demand for local members of the nomenklatura to purge their own "families," doubtless an unpopular idea. The tendency of local elites to deflect the purge downward to the rank and file was almost certainly a response to the need to find enemies somewhere without risking the loss of experienced members of their own machines, even if they had dubious backgrounds. Purge discourse was flexible.

The Central Committee was not satisfied with this result. The frequent interventions from Moscow to stop and restart local verifications, along with subsequent criticism of local administrations, provide evidence of Moscow's displeasure. Documents also show that central party officials gathered information on how many members of local political machines had been identified and expelled.[61] In response, local machines tried to show that they had screened their own people. Here we see further evidence of a rift inside the nomenklatura elite, in this case between Moscow-based party leaders and regional party officials. From Yezhov's point of view, by entrusting the purge to party organizations themselves (rather than to control commissions or special purge committees, as had previously been the practice), he was giving them the chance to put their own houses in order.[62] Instead, they had protected their own and displayed their "vigilance" by expelling large numbers of helpless party members outside the local nomenklaturas.

Regional party committees had begun the proverka in May 1935. The following month, however, many of them were brought up short by the Central Committee, which criticized them for paying only cursory attention to the process and for hastily expelling large numbers of ordinary rank-and-file members (and few leading comrades) from their own machines.[63] Following accepted party ritual, the local and provincial committees quickly admitted that the Central Committee was right, confessed their mistakes, and tried to demonstrate their vigilance even against a few members of their own machines. Nevertheless, the overwhelming majority of those expelled remained rank-and-file members with suspicious biographies ("white guards and kulaks").

Moscow party leaders were concerned that the mass expulsions could create embittered enemies among ex-party members.[64] By the end of 1935 Moscow was investigating the numbers of expelled and finding that some party organizations had as many former members as current ones.[65] Moscow party officials not only kept an eye on those expelled, they checked into their moods.[66] Sometimes these ex-members were characterized as "enemies." A report from the Azov–Black Sea NKVD had it that "the available facts concerning the attitudes and conduct of persons expelled from the VKP(b), in connection with the verification of Party documents, indicate that a significant number of persons expelled is beginning to manifest counter-revolutionary activity, committing counter-revolutionary attacks against leading Party officials and threatening revenge for being unmasked and expelled from the Party."[67] On other occasions, though, Yezhov and others explicitly noted that the behavior of most ex-members was benign.

1935: The Personal Element

The membership screenings not only embittered those expelled. For some committed Communists, the loss of party membership meant not only a loss of privilege and elite status but a crushing psychological blow from which they could not recover. On many fronts at the end of 1935, the number of personal tragedies was increasing. Suicides and suicide notes attracted the attention of the party leadership.[68]

For the Stalinists in the 1930s, almost everything carried a threatening political content. Even suicide, which might be seen to represent to the Stalinists a welcome self-destruction of opponents, was seen as a dangerous political "blow against the party" by a dishonest person. As Stalin mused in 1936, "A person arrives at suicide because he is afraid that everything will be revealed and he does not want to witness his own public disgrace. . . . There you have one of the last sharp and easiest means that, before death, leaving this world, one can for the last time spit on the party, betray the party."[69]

Indeed, the most "famous" suicide of the 1930s, that of Sergo Ordzhonikidze, posed special problems for the regime. Ordzhonikidze had always been a staunch Stalinist; yet in February 1937 he killed himself. Unlike others, his suicide was never characterized as political betrayal. Rather, the embarrassing political fact of his suicide was hidden by the regime. His death was publicly announced as heart failure, and Nikita Khrushchev, a member of the Politburo, did not learn the truth about Ordzhonikidze's death for many years.

It was not only suicides of prominent politicians that worried them; the Stalinists feared even the suicides of their opponents. During the 1930s suicides of rank-and-file party members and even ordinary citizens attracted the attention of the top leadership. Even if they involved the most minor party members, such events were routinely investigated by the Special Political Department of the NKVD and found their way into Central Committee files.[70]

The Kirov assassination had come as a shock to the political life of the Soviet Union from top to bottom. Everyone, from Stalin to the lowest party secretary, had to reorient himself and figure out how to use the new political texts and situations. There was no authoritative decision on the extent of the oppositionists' guilt or, indeed, on who was an oppositionist or who needed to be expelled from the party. Hard and soft policies continued to coexist, and nobody knew exactly where Stalin stood.

CHAPTER FIVE

The Fork in the Road

Comrades, a significant number of the expellees is made up of people whom we cannot include in the category of our enemies. . . . You realize that such an incorrect attitude to the expellees is dictated not by reasons of vigilance but by a striving by certain Party officials to protect themselves against any eventuality.
—N. I. Yezhov, 1936

DOCUMENTS FROM ROUGHLY the first half of 1936 indicate a continuing desire by the top party leadership to ease up on uncontrolled repression. Each year from 1933 to 1936 the number of both political and nonpolitical arrests declined. In this period there was a two-thirds decrease in arrests for "political," counterrevolutionary crimes (Article 58 of the criminal code), from 283,029 in 1933 to 91,127 in 1936. Arrests for nonpolitical offenses fell by more than 80 percent in the same period, from 222,227 in 1933 to 40,041 in 1936.[1] Numerous texts relate to judicial policy and pertain to nonparty urban and rural victims of previous waves of repression in 1933–35. Several of these are connected to Andrei Vyshinsky, procurator general of the USSR, who has sometimes been seen as an advocate of procedural legalism (if not legality) and even as an opponent of indiscriminate terror (if not terror itself).[2] For example,

> Residence in localities in the USSR subject to special measures is to be permitted to dependents of persons removed from these localities: to dependents, whose family is engaged in socially useful work or to students, that is, to those people who are in no way personally to blame for anything.[3]

> It is proposed to the Central Executive Committee of the USSR and the All-Union Central Council of Trade Unions that persons deported from Leningrad

in 1935 who had not been found guilty of any specific crimes, not be deprived of their voting and pension rights during their period of exile.[4]

Local Cadres and Family Circles: Rift in the Nomenklatura

Local party secretaries had expelled large numbers of party members in the verifications and exchanges of party documents in 1935. Everyone could find political advantage in these screenings. For the nomenklatura as a whole, they made party membership more exclusive and thus restricted membership in the elite strata of political participation. By weeding out nonparticipant and inactive members who simply used party membership for their own interests, the purges would supposedly make the party a more efficient machine.

The purges also had particular advantages for particular groups and strata, and these advantages illustrate conflicting interests within the nomenklatura elite. For Stalin and the upper circle, purges could be used to discipline local leaders by pruning their patronage machines, or "family circles," and also offered the possibility of catching a few political dissidents and conspirators in the process. For the regional and local party secretaries who actually carried out the operations on the ground, the purges provided an opportunity to rid themselves of bothersome critics and individuals with political aspirations who did not belong to the local machine. Local leaders could also demonstrate their "vigilance" by expelling rather large numbers to run up the total for Moscow.

Even though we saw in the last chapter that Moscow sought to control, focus, and rein in the indiscriminate local expulsions, the screening operations remained in the hands of local leaders, who naturally used them to their own advantage. The archives for early 1936 are filled with long lists of persons whose expulsion was routinely confirmed at the provincial level in early 1936. Typically, they took the following form, with dozens on each page and without any personal details or individual circumstance:

> From the protocol of the meeting of the Buro of the _____ Provincial Committee of the VKP(b) on [date]:
>
> [Name of expelled], party card no. _____.
>
> The decision of the [district] District Committee of the Party no. _____ of [date] on the expulsion from the ranks of the party of _____—is confirmed.[5]

Sometimes, though, the expulsions threatened well-connected members of local political machines. This often happened at local purge meetings when rank-and-file party members made accusations against their superiors. Such criticism from below had to be blunted and reversed by the local elite in order to protect "their people." Local machines closed ranks to protect their own from popular criticism, using the power that regional and local party leaders had over administration of justice, and expulsions of protected persons were often reversed by their protectors as being "inexpedient." Convenience for the party family circle outweighed any consideration of formal justice, and the possible guilt or innocence of the factory director had no bearing on the political decision of his case.

Friction between rank-and-file party members and their local leaders was often more serious, and lower-level victims of party expulsions were able to use status differences and conflicts within the nomenklatura to fight back. Complaints and appeals from expelled members, accompanied by denunciations of the officials who had expelled them, reached the highest echelons of the party. There, in some cases, Moscow-based senior party leaders took up the cause of the "little person," as appellants were often called. Such intervention might happen when the accused official had highly placed enemies eager to embarrass him, when the Politburo wanted to strike some balance or inflict some blow against the middle level, or when Stalin decided to make a propaganda point by publicly posturing as a defender of "little people."

The Nomenklatura Against Itself in Early 1936: Who Is to Blame?

The June 1936 plenum of the Central Committee took up these questions of expulsions from the party and appeals from those expelled. The minutes of this meeting illustrate important points about variant texts, multiple narratives, levels of information, and how they were used in party leadership struggles.

Minutes of the discussions of Central Committee plenums exist in the archive in several versions. The raw minutes were taken down by stenographers, typed up into an "uncorrected stenogram," and distributed to the speakers, who had the right to edit and correct their remarks to produce a second textual version, the "corrected stenogram." The top party leadership (Stalin and his staff in the Secretariat) then prepared and printed a "stenographic report"—a third version—for formal distribution to members of the Central Committee and other important party officials charged with implementing and interpreting the decisions of the meeting. Finally, at the fourth level, abridged and sanitized versions of some of the resolutions and speeches were presented to the general public in *Pravda,* as printed speeches, summary editorials, or didactic articles.

For this reason, it is instructive to think of Central Committee plenums as ritualized performances intended to produce authoritative and useful texts for particular audiences. Such variant texts fulfilled a function that one scholar has called "concealment" within the master transcript. "By controlling the public stage, the dominant can create an appearance that approximates what, ideally, they would want subordinates to see."[6] Moreover, one's role in the production and distribution of texts was a sign of power. Access to information—and, just as important, access to knowledge about what was missing from or added to the less complete transcripts below one's position—was an important part of the stratification of power. Knowledge of the different transcripts *was* power.

The following texts illustrate these points. They are part of Yezhov's report to the June 1936 plenum of the Central Committee, combined with what may have been a short speech by Stalin. The subject was the appeal and readmission process for those expelled in the party membership screenings of 1935–36. This was a sensitive and extremely important personal issue for the rank-and-file members who had been expelled: would it be possible to reenter the party? For the nomenklatura, assessing blame for the "mistakes" was a political issue.

Although the lowest-level, public transcript revealed very little about the plenum, it was not completely devoid of information. A short notice in *Pravda* announced that a plenum of the Central Committee had taken place during 1–4 June 1936. According to the laconic announcement, attendees had discussed adoption of a new constitution, questions of rural economy, and procedures for considering appeals from those expelled in the just concluded verification and exchange of party documents. In connection with this last issue, *Pravda* noted that Yezhov had given a report and that decisions were reached on the basis of his report as well as on "words from Comrade Stalin."[7] No corresponding Central Committee resolution was published, but a subsequent series of press articles reported that lower-level party officials had taken a "heartless attitude" toward party members, had expelled many of them for simple nonparticipation in party life, and had been slow to consider appeals and readmissions of those wrongly expelled.[8]

Careful readers of even this minimal public text could discern the outlines of something a bit broader. First, the press formulation "on the basis of Comrade Yezhov's report and words from Comrade Stalin" was unusual. It suggested that somehow Yezhov's speech was not sufficient or completely authoritative: additional "words" from Stalin had been required. What were these "words"? A speech? An order? Second, by blaming low-level party officials for "mistakes," the Central Committee's formulation suggested a rift within the nomenklatura elite about who was to blame for the repression of innocent rank-and-file members. Those with access to more authoritative transcripts knew more. There were important and revealing differences among the various accounts and texts.

We move now to private and public versions of the transcript: the printed text prepared for distribution to party insiders versus the original transcription. Yezhov's speech and Stalin's remarks are the keys here.

In the original version of Yezhov's speech, transcribed at the time, he said:

> Yezhov: Comrades, as a result of the verification of Party documents, we have expelled over 200 thousand Party members.
> Stalin: That's quite a lot.
> Yezhov: Yes, quite a lot. I'll talk about it. . . .
> Stalin: If we expel 30,000—(inaudible), and if we also expel 600 former Trotskyists and Zinovievists, then we would gain even more from that.
> Yezhov: We have expelled over 200 thousand Party members. Some of the expellees, Comrades, have been arrested.[9]

But in the final version from the printed Stenographic Report prepared for broad party leadership distribution, the text became:

> Yezhov: You know, Comrades, that during the verification of Party documents we have expelled over 200 thousand Communists.
> Stalin: That's quite a lot.
> Yezhov: Yes, that is quite a lot. And this obligates all Party organizations all the more so to be extremely attentive to members who have been expelled and who are now appealing.[10]

Stalin's interjection, recorded only in the most private transcript, that it would have been better to expel six hundred "real" enemies than thousands of rank-and-file members suggests dissatisfaction with the results of the membership screenings that Yezhov had administered. But it also raised dangerous questions about the basic relationship between leaders and led in the party. This incendiary remark could be interpreted to mean that those who carried out the verification and exchange of party documents (including Yezhov and the network of regional secretaries) had missed the boat, failing to get the real targets of the operation and expelling inno- cent people. Were the "enemies" expelled not "real enemies"? Although Yezhov and other leaders were at pains to repeat that the expulsions had been more or less necessary, Stalin's remark could suggest the opposite to rank-and-file victims of the screenings: loyal and innocent party members like they (who even Yezhov had admitted were not enemies) had their lives ruined because of nomenklatura "mistakes." Suggesting as it did ques- tions of basic justice, hierarchy, and the legitimacy of the party leadership, the nomenklatura did not want such sentiments aired. That part of the text therefore had to be kept secret and was reserved for the private elite version of reality.

Accordingly, Stalin's original remark was excised even from the printed stenographic report of the plenum, which contained a more benign ver- sion designed to indicate Stalin's fatherly concern, while shielding the rep- utation of the party elite.[11] According to the archives, it is not clear that he made a speech to the plenum at all. There is no original transcript of any speech from him. Nevertheless, in the final created text, we find remarks from him:

> I would like to say a few things concerning certain points which in my opinion are especially important if we are to put the affairs of the Party in good order and direct the regulating of Party membership properly.
>
>   First of all, let me say something concerning the matter of appeals. Natu- rally, appeals must be handled in timely fashion, without dragging them out. They must not be put on the shelf. This goes without saying. But let me raise a question: Is it not possible for us to reinstate some or many of the appellants as candidate members?[12]

The sanitized version also allowed Yezhov to associate himself with Stalin's populist concern, even though he never actually said, "And this obligates all Party organizations all the more so to be extremely attentive to members who have been expelled and who are now appealing."

In the final version of the plenum transcript, the upper nomenklatura was not particularly eager to reveal that the criticism of regional party secretaries was more severe, and that one of them, the powerful first secretary in Kiev Pavel Postyshev, had been a specific target, even a scapegoat, for the excessive expulsions. The following passage, from Yezhov's original speech, was cut from the disseminated version:

YEZHOV: In the small district organizations it is the Secretary of the District Committee who directly handles the exchange of documents. He is under obligation to talk to the Party member whose card he is replacing.

POSTYSHEV: What do you mean "talk to"?

YEZHOV: You see, Pavel Petrovich, what I mean by "talking," there are cases in your organization, in Kiev, for instance.

POSTYSHEV: In what district?

YEZHOV: I'll tell you in a minute . . . petty questions of the following sort: "What is the law of diminishing fertility? What is money?" etc.

POSTYSHEV: Such a discussion is important.

YEZHOV: That discussions take place is important. . . . [But] we are against [this kind of] discussion. The CC did not have such discussions in mind when it said that a Party member must be summoned.[13]

If this section were not excised, the text would have sent the message that some powerful party secretaries were being harshly attacked, and this could undermine obedience up and down the party chain of command.

Even in the absence of useful performative speech, a final textual reality had to be produced for an expanded audience of party officials below Central Committee rank whose job it was to explain the plenum to the rank-and-file members. The intended message of this "semiprivate" (party) transcript was carefully crafted: (a) there had been some incorrect expulsions from the party, but they were a minority, (b) most of those expelled were not dangerous enemies, (c) too many "passive" members had been expelled, (d) "certain Party officials" had been careless about all this and were to blame, and (e) Stalin had taken a personal interest in these questions, adopting the position that many of those expelled—perhaps more than Yezhov had envisioned—could be readmitted to the party.[14] Thus Yezhov's "final" text included liberal sentiments he was not known for:

YEZHOV: We cannot, however, place the great mass of the expellees in the category of our enemies. . . . A part of them shall be reinstated after their appeals have been reviewed or they may be allowed to return to the ranks of our Party after amending their conduct. Meanwhile, Party organizations deal indiscriminately, mechanically, with all of the expellees from this category without looking into the reasons why they were expelled from the VKP(b). . . .

Out of the total number of Communists who had participated in the exchange of Party documents, approximately 3.5% were not issued their Party cards, and the question of their expulsion from the Party has been raised. From these 3.5%, about a half fall into the category of so-called passive membership or, as they are called in many places, "ballast."

STALIN: What percent?

YEZHOV: 3.5% have not been issued Party cards,—out of this group half fall into the passive category. Not an insignificant percent, as you can see. Such a percentage of Party members and candidate members belonging to the passive category is too high.[15]

The differences between the printed stenographic report and the public press version reveal that the Politburo's condemnation of party secretaries for excessive expulsions of the rank and file was harsher and more far-reaching than it wished to advertise. The public version, in contrast to the one for the middle level of the Party, vaguely suggested that some regional secretaries were to blame for unjust repression of the party rank and file. The secret uncorrected stenogram was even harsher, castigating party secretaries with the pejorative *chinovnik* (a tsarist-era arbitrary bureaucrat), "worse than our enemies," and directly accusing them of a perversion of vigilance by inflicting punishment on party members to "insure themselves" against being considered soft. The stenogram also specifically attacked a very high ranking official for such arbitrary punishment of innocent party members, an event missing from versions aimed at broader audiences.

Stalin interrupted Yezhov twice (on the question of total numbers expelled and on the percentage of "passives" expelled), indicating both his disapproval of the extreme way Yezhov had conducted the screenings and a desire to pose as the righter of wrongs against "little people." Only his sanitized interjections "How many?" and "What percent?" were printed in the stenographic report. This, along with the public transcript associating "words of Comrade Stalin" with the liberalized attitude toward appeals, communicated the symbol of Stalin as defender of the little person. Yet his actual interruption of Yezhov's speech at the point when the numbers of expulsions was discussed suggests more than just posturing or tactics.

After the June plenum, substantial numbers of expelled rank-and-file members were readmitted on appeal. But most were not. Even if Stalin had decided that the mass screenings had not hit the right targets, it was politically impossible to admit it or openly to correct the "mistake" on a large scale. To do so would have cast doubt not only on his own leadership but on the legitimacy and prerogatives of the nomenklatura itself, which had carried out the operation against those beneath it. Those capriciously expelled therefore paid the price to save the nomenklatura's face.

Stalin's interjections and his concluding remarks implied a generous approach to rank-and-file members. According to the original uncorrected stenogram, his remarks to the June 1936 plenum speech had not been foreseen in the preplenum agenda, a document traditionally planned by the Politburo and distributed in advance to Central Committee members. His words, if they were in fact uttered, were "not stenogramed." This notation and a blank page appear in the original plenum version in the archives.[16] What, then, were the origins of the remarks that appeared in the printed stenographic report? It is entirely possible that Stalin never said these words at the plenum but prepared them later for inclusion in the stenogram text.

His concluding remarks are also relevant to another puzzle of the June 1936 plenum. The most important item on the plenum's agenda was never mentioned in any of the accounts of the meeting, and discussion of it was not recorded in any of the stenograms or reports. This ultrasecret transcript concerned the upcoming show trial of Zinoviev and Kamenev for treason.[17] We suspect from subsequent accounts that Stalin spoke on this matter, possibly delivering a Politburo report on the question. He probably announced the upcoming trial and gave an overview of the charges against the accused, based on evidence that Yezhov had been gathering since the beginning of 1936. Moreover, the original version of the minutes notes that the plenum heard a "Communication" [soobshchenie] from NKVD chief Yagoda. Subsequent minutes from the February–March 1937 plenum refer to this Yagoda "report" to the June plenum and make it clear that he spoke about the upcoming show trial of Zinoviev and Kamenev.[18]

The June 1936 plenum presents us with a series of contrasts and apparent contradictions. The leadership denounced careless mass expulsions from the party and encouraged speedy appeals and readmissions. But it also announced the beginning of organized terror against former members of the opposition. Stalin implicitly criticized Yezhov for excessive expulsions but promoted him to head the terror less than three months later.

There was no real contradiction between Stalin's condemnation of the party membership purges and his launching of terror against Old Bolsheviks. The former had been carried out by members of the nomenklatura, while the latter would be directed against it, even enlisting the support of the rank-and-file victims of the screenings. No one at the time thought that the recently completed screenings had anything to do with the purge trials.

Stalin once again revealed himself to be a master of compromise, balance, and political maneuver inside and outside the nomenklatura. No one knew exactly where he stood, and no one (including, perhaps, Stalin himself) knew exactly where events were leading. Regional officials were criticized strongly, but the affair was hidden from the party masses and no one from that group was punished: Postyshev was raked over the coals but retained his position and rank. The regional secretaries' sins were deliberately hidden from rank-and-file anger, but enough was leaked to suggest to party members that all might not be quite right with their immediate superiors.

Despite the severe attacks on regional party leaders, when all was said and done, Stalin, Molotov, Postyshev, and the network of regional secretaries were all members of the same club, the nomenklatura. While they might thrash each other in the private confines of the Central Committee, such intragroup conflicts had to be muted or hidden from the public. Serious discord must be hidden so as not to disturb "the smooth surface of euphemized power."[19] Thus the public transcript only vaguely hinted that unnamed, low-level party functionaries had made "mistakes." Nevertheless, Stalin could, in the interests of party unity before the public, simply have kept the entire episode out of the public view. By even hinting in the public press that there was a shadow of some kind over the regional secretaries, Stalin and his circle were able to hold a kind of sword over these officials: they were not entirely immune from censure and disclosure of their sins.

These textual variations show more than mere censorship of secret party meetings. They illustrate alternative political transcripts, constructed realities, that presented different versions of politics to different audiences. The public received a hazy general picture that nevertheless communicated something significant: some unnamed individual party secretaries had made mistakes, but the senior leadership was united, Stalin and Yezhov were attending to the problems. To insiders, the problem of wrongful expulsions was portrayed as being more serious. Stalin had personally intervened (textually if not orally) and had been more critical of the party secretaries and, implicitly, of Yezhov. To those in the senior nomenklatura and the Central Committee, Stalin had been sharply critical of the entire screening process, suggesting that the process had targeted the wrong people. A senior nomenklaturchik, Postyshev, had been directly attacked.

Finally, it is interesting that Stalin chose to reveal anything of the conflicts outside the top leadership. Attentive readers of even the laconic public versions must have noted something in the way of disharmony. Why, for example, was Stalin's intervention necessary at all? Similarly, party members also received clues about possible discord in the top ranks. It may well be that Stalin decided to leak these tidbits as a way of chastising the nomenklatura by suggesting to its members that in the future, the solid facade of elite unity was not necessarily obligatory, and their public image would depend on their conduct.

G. M. Malenkov

Top left: From left, L. M. Kaganovich, I. V. Stalin, V. M. Molotov, 1920s
Bottom left: G. K. Ordzhonikidze, left, and N. I. Yezhov
Above: L. P. Beria

P. P. Postyshev

M. N. Riutin

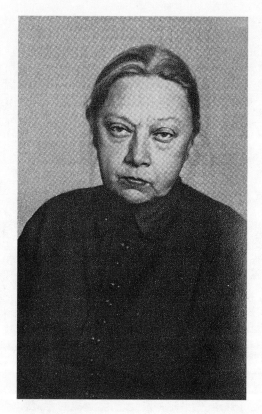

N. K. Krupskaia

II
The Terror

CHAPTER SIX

The Face of the Enemy, 1936

> The interests of the Revolution demand that we put an immediate end to the activities of this gang of rabid murderers, agents of fascism. —Azov–Black Sea Party committee resolution, 1936

> Surely, things will go smoothly with Yezhov at the helm.—L. M. Kaganovich to G. K. Ordzhonikidze, 1936

IN THE FIRST DAYS of 1936 one Valentin Olberg, a former associate of Trotsky, was arrested by the NKVD in the city of Gorky, apparently in connection with his suspicious history of foreign travel.[1] Under interrogation, he admitted to being Trotsky's "emissary" who had carried news to the exiled leader and "instructions" from him back into the USSR. This "information," along with reports from NKVD informers about other couriers, was passed to Stalin in the Central Committee. Stalin decided to reopen the Kirov investigation. According to Yezhov's later account, "Stalin, correctly sensing in all this something not quite right, gave instructions to continue [the investigation] and, in particular, to send me from the Central Committee to oversee the investigation."[2]

The Face of the Enemy

Extracting confessions, no doubt under pressure, from successive interrogations, NKVD investigators working for Yagoda but under Yezhov's supervision expanded the circle of the "conspiracy," and by spring they had arrested several important former Trotskyists. Yezhov, eager to make a case and a name for himself, used his mandate from Stalin to expand the

109

circle of arrests. By late spring he had elaborated a conspiracy theory in which Zinoviev and Kamenev, acting under instructions from Trotsky in exile, had directly and personally plotted the assassination of Kirov, Stalin, and other members of the Politburo. Effectively, then, Stalin had reopened the investigation into the Kirov assassination more than a year after it had been pronounced closed and several months after Yezhov's failed attempt to reopen it in June 1935. Zinoviev and Kamenev, who had been in prison since early 1935, were reinterrogated.

Yagoda had been under a cloud since early 1935. After all, the "negligence" of his NKVD had permitted Kirov's assassin to get close enough to fire the shot. We have also seen that the Kremlin Affair of mid-1935 was pointedly "uncovered" by Yezhov and party organs, rather than by the NKVD, whose job it should have been. Now, in the first half of 1936, Yagoda was being undermined by Yezhov again. Subsequent accusations in 1937 suggested that during Yezhov's 1936 "supervision" of the investigation, Yagoda and his deputy Molchanov had downplayed the importance of the Trotsky-Zinoviev connection and had tried to deflect or limit Yezhov's efforts. At one point, Yagoda had called the evidence that Trotsky was ordering terrorism in the USSR "trifles" and "nonsense" (chepukha, erunda). At another point, Stalin telephoned Yagoda and threatened to "punch him in the nose" if he continued to drag his feet.[3]

No doubt in response to this pressure, Yagoda now proposed drastic measures against Trotskyists—even those already in prison—in a 25 March 1936 memorandum to Stalin. As means of "liquidating the Trotskyist underground," Yagoda proposed summary death sentences for any Trotskyists suspected of "terrorist activity." Stalin referred Yagoda's memo to Vyshinsky for a legal opinion; the procurator replied, "From my point of view, there is no objection to transferring the cases of Trotskyists whose guilt in terrorist activities had been established, that is, of preparing terrorist acts, to the Military Collegium of the Supreme Court with application of the law of 1 December 1934 and the highest means of punishment—shooting."[4]

After this, the roundup and persecution intensified. Five hundred eight Trotskyists were under arrest by April 1936. In May the Politburo ordered all Trotskyists in exile and those formerly expelled from the party for "enemy activity" to be sent to remote camps for three to five years. Those convicted of participation in "terror" were to be retried and executed.[5] By July, Yezhov had secured confessions from a number of former Trotskyist leaders, as well as from Zinoviev and Kamenev. There are persistent rumors that Zinoviev and Kamenev agreed to confess to the scenario in return for promises that their lives would be spared, but no documentary evidence or firsthand testimony has been found to support this story.[6] Others argue that they may have confessed out of loyalty to the party, which needed their confessions as negative examples.[7] This explanation of the confessions of Old Bolsheviks in the show trials of the 1930s is supported by Bukharin's last letter to Stalin from prison. And, as Zinoviev wrote in prison in a manuscript called "Deserved Sentence," "Whoever plays with the idea of 'opposition' to the socialist state plays with the idea of counterrevolutionary terror. . . . Be born again as a Bolshevik! Finish your human days conscious of your guilt before the Party! Do everything in order to erase this guilt."[8]

The stage was now set for the first in a series of public treason trials of former oppositionists, announced to Central Committee members at the June 1936 plenum. Now it was time to inform a broader party audience, and in July 1936 the Central Committee sent an explanatory letter to party organizations. Written by Yezhov and edited by Stalin, the letter had to answer several questions that were bound to arise in connection with this announcement: Why did it take so long to discover the conspiracy, especially when the NKVD had closed the case in 1935? How could these Old Bolsheviks, who fought in the Revolution and Civil War, have conspired with evil forces to cede part of the country?[9] Given the 1936 pendulum swing toward strong persecution of the opposition, it was necessary to amend the existing master narrative on the opposition leaders and to change the content of the Trotskyist trope. Recently discovered "new materials" were the explanation:

> On the basis of new materials gathered by the NKVD in 1936, it can be considered an established fact that Zinoviev and Kamenev were not only the fomenters of terroristic activity against the leaders of our Party and government but also the authors of direct instructions regarding both the murder of S. M. Kirov as well as preparations for attempts on the lives of other leaders of our Party and, first and foremost, on the life of Comrade Stalin.[10]

The subsequent political trial could not have come as much of a surprise in the top party leadership. The supervision of the investigation from the beginning of the year by Yezhov, who had tried to make the case against Zinoviev and Kamenev at the June 1935 CC plenum, was widely known in the upper leadership. Stalin had discussed the upcoming repression with the Central Committee in June 1936, and the July letter was read out to all party organizations.[11] The amended narrative could not have given NKVD chief Yagoda much comfort; his NKVD had uncovered the "new materials" only under Yezhov's imposed and unwanted supervision.

Like other public accusations and show trials of this period, the 1936 trial scenario was based on a kernel of truth that had been embellished and exaggerated. We know that in the fall of 1932 a single bloc of opposition-ists uniting Trotskyists and Zinovievists had in fact been formed at Trot-sky's initiative.[12] But there is no evidence that this bloc was oriented toward organizing "terrorist acts" or anything other than political con-spiracy. In the hands of the Stalinists, though, this event was magnified into a terrorist conspiracy aimed at killing the Soviet leaders.

From 19 to 24 August 1936, Zinoviev, Kamenev, I. N. Smirnov, and thirteen other former oppositionists were tried in Moscow for treason. With the exception of Smirnov, who retracted his confession, all of the accused admitted to having organized a "terrorist center" at Trotsky's in-structions and to have planned the assassinations of Kirov, Stalin, Kaga-novich, and other members of the Politburo. As with all the major show trials, Yagoda, Yezhov, and Vyshinsky assembled the scenario, but Stalin played an active role in rewording the indictment, selecting the final slate of defendants, and prescribing the sentences.[13] The death sentences meted out to the defendants (as with all death sentences in political cases for years before) were decided beforehand by the Politburo.[14] Altogether throughout 1936, 160 persons were arrested and shot in connection with "terrorist conspiracies" related to this trial.[15]

The first show trial of the opposition sent a strong signal through the ranks of the nomenklatura and the party in general: former leftist opposi-tionists could no longer be automatically trusted to work loyally, even if they had recanted their views. Leaders of party organizations understood the signal and the required ritual. In line with directives from Moscow to mobilize support for the trial, they organized meetings of party members and ordinary citizens to produce supporting resolutions and letters. Such collective resolutions ostensibly came from below, but because of their so-licitation and formulaic nature should be considered elements of central, public rhetoric designed to affirm the desired unanimity. As the loyal Bol-sheviks of Makhachkala telegraphed to Stalin,

THE PARTY AKTIV OF MAKHACHKALA, HAVING DISCUSSED THE PROGRESS OF THE
TRIAL OF THE TROTSKYIST-ZINOVIEVIST GANG, DEMANDS THAT THE SUPREME
COURT EXECUTE THE THREE-TIME CONTEMPTIBLE DEGENERATES, WHO HAVE
SLID INTO THE MIRE OF FASCISM AND AIMED THEIR GUNS AT THE HEART OF
OUR PARTY, THE GREAT STALIN. . . . LONG LIVE THE GREAT LEADER OF ALL THE
OPPRESSED AND ENSLAVED OF THE WORLD, OUR DEAR AND BELOVED STALIN!
DEATH TO THE MURDERERS, TO THE TERRORISTS, TO THE VILE TRAITORS OF THE
SOCIALIST MOTHERLAND![16]

Thus the language surrounding the Zinoviev-Kamenev trial consisted
of several parts. The CC's July letter elaborated the discursive line; the prescribed letters and telegrams provided symbolic affirmation from below;
the trial itself provided the ritual performance of the new line. This was a
classic example of the mechanism for changing Stalinist policies; tropes
were filled with new content. However, the fact that actors at the various
levels played their roles does not mean that they did so insincerely or that
they did not believe the new line. Obviously, the new transcript could not
have been successful had it not filled particular needs or found resonance
at various levels. It could not create reality from scratch; it could only
adapt and redirect it.

The official face of the enemy was reconstructed in the summer of 1936:
he was a former leftist oppositionist who had taken the path of terror. He
was an agent of Trotsky, a spy, an assassin. This version had advantages
for several segments of the party. For Stalin and his circle, it provided a rationale for finally destroying personal and political enemies whose opposition went back more than a decade, and it created a climate in which
future opposition to him obviously carried life-and-death risks. For the
nomenklatura at all levels, it justified the obliteration of and final victory
over a possible alternative leadership whose leaders had argued for years
that the Stalinist team should be removed. This definition—or attribution—of the enemy also benefited the ruling elite as a whole insofar as it
presented a clearly defined evil and opposite "other": the groups behind
Zinoviev, Kamenev, and Trotsky. They had for years stood for an alternative team to lead the country. If they won, however unlikely that might
seem, the current team would be replaced in quick order. Although there
seemed little chance that Zinoviev or Trotsky would return to power in
the mid-1930s, the possibility always existed. Nomenklatura members'
memories told them that stranger things had happened. Lenin's ascension

to power in 1917 must have seemed at least as far-fetched in 1915. This evil force could be conveniently blamed for a variety of sins of the moment, including industrial failure, agricultural shortfalls, and other policy shortcomings more properly attributable to the nomenklatura itself.[17] The leftist opposition made perfect scapegoats.

But they were scapegoats of a particularly believable kind, given the prevailing mentalities of the time. The 1917 revolutions, the Civil War, and party struggles of the 1920s had created a kind of conspiracy mentality among the Bolsheviks. The vicious and violent civil war, which was rich with real conspiracies and constant, nagging insecurity, was the formative experience for this generation of nomenklatura and party member. In their view of reality, politics was inconceivable without conspiracy, and it was not hard for them to believe that professional revolutionaries and skilled conspirators like Zinoviev and Trotsky probably *had* been up to no good on some level. Similarly, for the Russian populace, with its cultural legacies of good versus evil, belief in the machinations of dark forces of all kinds, and a traditional suspicion of educated intellectuals, it was not difficult to accept the notion that Jewish Bolshevik intellectuals probably were involved in some sort of dark business.

There seem to have been no protests or questions raised in party leadership circles about executing these former oppositionists. Part of the reason was fear; knowing that police investigations were continuing, who would question Stalin's leadership on such a serious matter and risk being regarded as defenders of enemies? Another part of the answer was party discipline. In the crisis atmosphere of the times, which was perceived as a continuation of the "new situation" following the Riutin affair, there was strong incentive in the party to close ranks against the perceived threat.

The Zinoviev and Trotsky oppositions had broken the rules of the nomenklatura. In the 1920s (and as recently as the Riutin Platform) they had threatened to organize politically outside the party elite. Their strategy had been to agitate among the party's rank and file to gain support for their platforms against the ruling group. This was the unpardonable sin. By threatening to split the party (a split that, since the Civil War, was the Bolsheviks' worst nightmare), this strategy threatened the survival of the regime and thus of the Revolution.

At bottom, the strategy threatened to turn the membership against the ruling stratum. This could not be tolerated. The opposition therefore represented a continuing danger to the corporate interests of the Stalinist nomenklatura that outweighed any nostalgia leaders may have felt for their former Old Bolshevik oppositionist comrades-in-arms. The party elite did not regard the annihilation of Zinoviev and Kamenev as threatening to itself. It was not hard, then, for the current serving party leadership to support the final decimation of the leftist opposition. Once again, Stalin and the nomenklatura had common interests.

Cadre Issues in the Party

However useful it may have seemed to scapegoat the opposition and to identify officially approved enemies for public consumption, the tactic carried risks for the party elite. It was convenient for regional party secretaries to use a fluid definition of Trotskyism to marginalize, expel, and even arrest professional dissidents in their localities. On the other hand, an increasingly plastic definition of enemies and "Trotskyists" could be a loose cannon for the nomenklatura itself. The new rhetoric opened dangerous doors.

It was not only the serving members of the nomenklatura who could use the new accusatory narrative against its opponents. Ideological fanatics, careerists, opportunists, and ordinary party members with grudges to settle adopted the new line for their own purposes. In the aftermath of the July closed letter and the first trial, denunciations had increased at all levels.

Denunciations posed a new question: aside from marginalized has-beens like Zinoviev, were "Trotskyists" at work among serving officials in the state and party apparatus? The testimony of the Zinoviev trial had given a signal. Almost as an aside, some of the defendants had suggested conspiratorial links with long-recanted, apparently loyal ex-Trotskyists who were currently serving in the state apparatus. G. Piatakov, deputy commissar of Heavy Industry, and the prominent journalist Karl Radek had sided with the Trotskyist opposition in the 1920s. Although they had forsworn Trotskyism early in the 1930s, they were implicated in the trial testimony, as were rightist leaders Bukharin, Rykov, and Tomsky. Could it be that even high-ranking captains of industry with ancient Trotskyist connections were guilty of treason? Evidently, Stalin had authorized Yezhov to root out all former active Trotskyists and Zinovievists; to follow the trail of their personal connections wherever it led. And since such people with politically compromised pasts were working in the apparatus, the path of investigations began to wind itself into the bureaucracy. Regional leaders of the nomenklatura picked up on the increasingly ambiguous definition of the enemy's face.

What had seemed a useful definition of the enemy was mutating in dangerous ways. If captains of industry with compromising pasts were at risk, what about their own subordinates with or without similarly blemished political records? Although the regional secretaries were obliged to promulgate the new ideological transcript, it could have given them no pleasure to incorporate into their resolutions the notion that their own machines needed to be "checked and re-checked."

This checking and rechecking would by early 1937 result in the removal and sometimes arrest of a number of lower-level party officials in the provinces. By that time, according to data provided by chief of the Central Committee's party registration sector, G. M. Malenkov, some thirty-five hundred party members across the USSR had been removed from office as "enemies," representing about 3.5 percent of all those checked.[18]

Beginning in the fall of 1936, criticism of these officials escalated as the hunt for Trotskyists expanded. But in late 1936 through the first half of 1937, no regional party secretary was accused of disloyalty or association with "enemy conspiracies." In the fall of 1936 the only implication was that some had been lax in keeping their own political houses in order, and as late as the February–March 1937 plenum of the Central Committee, Stalin would go out of his way to publicly absolve them, arguing that they were by no means "bad" in this regard.[19]

On the other hand, it is possible to see in these moves the first step in a devious Stalin plan to destroy the provincial party leaders and apparatus. Several months later, in the second half of 1937, he would do just that. One could thus explain the new political line of late 1936 as the first tactical step in weakening the regional leaders preparatory to finishing them off later. The apparent restraint by Stalin at this point may have been part of a cat-and-mouse game. Or it may have been a means of threatening the regional leaders while at the same time giving them a clean bill of political health in order to secure their support in the upcoming move to destroy Bukharin, the military, or others.

But Stalin could simply arrest and remove regional leaders individually or en masse at any time, and it is hard to see what he would have gained by playing cat-and-mouse with them. Stalin did not need to entice or encourage the regional secretaries to support a move against Bukharin. Experi-

ence had shown that they were perfectly willing to take the lead in con-
demning former oppositionists without much encouragement. In other
words, if at this time he planned to destroy them, he had nothing to gain
by waiting, a tactic that would also carry a certain risk.

A possible plan to destroy the regional nomenklatura is not necessary to
explain Stalin's criticism and political text about political carelessness in
the party apparatus. In its own right, such criticism was a useful tool that
Stalin could use to control and discipline regional leaders. Party secretaries, as we have seen, were powerful satraps in their territories, domi-
nating the legal, police, cultural, ideological, and everyday lives of the
population. Many of them were petty tyrants, operating their own regional and local personality cults.

In Azerbaijan, progress in the oil industry was attributed to the wise
guidance of the party first secretary in Baku. Stalin had observed that in
the Caucasus there was not one real party committee but rather rule based
on the will of individual party chieftains (he used the Cossack term *ata-
man*). In Ukraine an authoritative text on literature noted that the development of Ukrainian and Russian literature was in considerable measure
due to the opinions of the party secretary in Kiev. One issue of a local
newspaper mentioned the first secretary's name sixty times. (The fact that
the secretary's wife ran the ideological institute no doubt helped.) The first
secretary of the Western Region, whose photograph frequently adorned
the regional newspaper, was "the best Bolshevik in the region." In Ka-
zakhstan the republican party politburo even tried to rename the highest
peak in the Tien Shan mountain range after the first secretary.[20]

From Moscow's point of view, this situation was profoundly troubling
and required considerable subtlety. On the one hand, Stalin needed these
satraps to carry out Moscow's policies in the far-flung regions of the country. It had been necessary to vest them with tremendous authority to implement collectivization and industrialization. They were Moscow's only
presence in the countryside and thus indispensable to the party. On the
other hand, their near-absolute powers had permitted them to use patronage to create their own political machines: miniature nomenklaturas under their personal control, complete with regional personality cults.

Often, as Yezhov admitted in 1935, Moscow did not even know the
identities of many local party leaders who staffed the regional machines.[21]
Appointment of district party secretaries had been subject to Central Committee confirmation only since early 1935. Even by early 1937 the list of

party officials subject to Central Committee confirmation (the list known as the Central Committee nomenklatura) included only 5,860 officials of a the national stratum of party secretaries and officials numbering well over 100,000.[22] In the mid-thirties, squabbles between regional leaders and the Central Committee secretariat about the appointment of this or that person were common and involved continuous negotiation. Generally, though, the regional party secretaries could prevail, if they pushed the point hard enough, and were thus able to staff their machines with "their people" more often than not.

How, then, could Moscow control the activities of the provincial governors? Stalin created various parallel hierarchies and channels of information (the NKVD and Party Control Commission were examples), but experience showed that even these nominally independent institutions sooner or later came under local machine control.[23]

Another tactic which Stalin frequently used was "control from below," a policy that he would discuss at some length at the upcoming February–March plenum of the Central Committee.[24] The often arbitrary rule of regional leaders created resentment from below, and it was possible for Stalin to encourage criticism of the party apparatus from those quarters. Of course, it was in the interests of neither Stalin nor the nomenklatura to permit a full and open discussion of the problem of government, so this discourse had to be kept within strict limits. The real reasons for local misconduct, dysfunctional administration, and corresponding popular resentment could not be discussed; things could not be named by their names. A genuine analysis of administrative problems would include discussion of the dictatorship itself and would threaten the governing myths of the regime. Such a discussion would touch on the lack of national consensus on Bolshevik dictatorship, the undemocratic selection of leaders at all levels, the constant recourse to terror as a substitute for consensual government, and the shifting voluntarist policy mistakes that characterized Bolshevik rule.[25]

The trick, then, for Stalin, and the essence of "control from below" was to encourage rank-and-file criticism of the middle-level leaders on particular issues of nonfulfillment or negligence. In this way, Stalin could receive specific information from the grass roots that bypassed the nomenklatura's normal information filters. He could solicit grassroots information and input about official misconduct, suspicious characters in high positions, and the nonfulfillment of decisions. Moreover, he could play the role of the good tsar, posing as a caring and attentive friend of the little guy against the highhanded actions of the "feudal princes," as he had called the regional secretaries at the 1934 party congress. It was desirable to use the rank and file as a stick over the heads of the midlevel apparatus without inciting riot from below. Because of the power of the local party leaders, such criticism could not happen without high-level license and approval.

The new public rhetoric about nomenklatura "political laxity" provided a vehicle for underlings to criticize the regional party elite around the country. As such, it emphasized the long-standing tension between leaders and led. This policy walked a fine line; it was desirable to blame (and thereby control) the middle party apparatus for the sins of the regime without destroying them completely. Stalin wanted to hold the regional secretaries' feet to the fire without setting the whole house ablaze. In his speech to the February–March plenum, he pointed out that although the regional party officials were not themselves bad, the rank-and-file members often knew better than they who was suspicious and who was not.[26]

As the continuing hunt for Trotskyists spread into the level of serving officials, it disturbed the leaders of the party apparatus. They gave up some of their valued assistants with dubious pasts when they had to, but they also used their power to try to limit the application of the "Trotskyist" label and to protect their own. Courts and procurators controlled by the local party machines frequently adopted a narrow definition of Trotskyism (and the criminality associated with it).

Central organs often complained about the practice. The easiest thing to do to deflect the heat was to expel large numbers of rank-and-file party members for suspicious pasts, speech, or connections. But Moscow was wise to this and had outlawed the practice. The next-most-expendable group comprised economic and technical specialists who worked for Moscow-based ministries rather than for the local party machine. At the beginning of 1937, however, the CC noted that several regional party secretaries,

> wishing to avoid reprimand, were very freely giving permission to the NKVD to arrest directors, technical directors, engineers, technicians and construction specialists in industry, transport and other economic branches. The CC reminds you that provincial party secretaries, much less local party officials, do not have the right to give permission for such arrests. The CC obliges you to follow the rules, obligatory for both party and NKVD, according to which ar-

rests of [such specialists] can be carried out only with the agreement of the relevant ministry.[27]

There were several competing definitions of Trotskyism. Traditionally,
Trotskyists were those who had formally or openly participated in the leftist opposition (from 1923 as Trotskyists or from 1926 as "United Oppositionists," together with the Zinoviev group). By the early 1930s the definition was expanded to include those who might at some time have voted
for a Trotskyist platform at a party meeting or defended a known Trotskyist from party punishment. Such actions were considered "incompatible with party membership" and had resulted in expulsion from the party.
Trotskyism, although a party crime, was not a punishable offense under
the state's criminal code. It was therefore necessary to use extralegal bodies like the NKVD's Special Conference to punish oppositionists, often by
exile. In the course of 1936, however, both the definition of Trotskyism
and the prescribed sanctions against it became much more severe. Already
in the summer of 1936, Trotskyists suspected of "terrorism" were being
executed. The Zinoviev trial made this new line public: some oppositionists were said to have crossed the line from political dissidence to treasonable criminal activity. But not all elements in the party-state hierarchy
were eager to apply the new standard.

On 29 September 1936 the Politburo made a firm statement on the matter. Trotskyists were no longer to be considered to be polemical opponents
on the left; now, as a category, they were defined as fascist spies and saboteurs. This document provides an excellent example not only of attributive definition of enemies, but also of explicit and self-conscious narrative
construction through a prescriptive text. The political-linguistic process
of attribution was quite open: a "directive" defined "our stance" on certain groups who "must now therefore be considered" in a different way.
The form of the enemy was now filled with new content.

a) Until very recently, the CC of the VKP(b) considered the Trotskyist-Zinovievist scoundrels as the leading political and organizational detachment of
the international bourgeoisie. The latest facts tell us that these gentlemen have
slid even deeper [into the mire]. They must therefore now be considered as
foreign agents, spies, subversives and wreckers representing the fascist bourgeoisie of Europe.

b) In connection with this, it is necessary for us to make short shrift of these
Trotskyist-Zinovievist scoundrels. This is to include not only those who have

been arrested and whose investigation has already been completed . . . but also those who had been exiled earlier.[28]

For everybody, the dramatic and disorienting social changes taking place in the country since 1929, the disastrous famine of the early 1930s, the incomprehensible economic system with its unpredictable "mistakes" and lurches back and forth all cried out for simplistic explanations. From peasant to Politburo member, the language about evil conspirators served a purpose. For the plebeians it provided a possible explanation for the daily chaos and misery of life. For the many committed enthusiasts it explained why their Herculean efforts to build socialism often produced bad results. For the nomenklatura member, it was an excuse to destroy their only challengers. For local party chiefs, it was a rationale for again expelling inconvenient people from the local machines. For the Politburo member, it provided a means to avoid self-questioning about party policy and a vehicle for closing ranks. The image of evil, conspiring Trotskyists was convenient for everybody.[29] The question, of course, was who was the evil force.

After receipt of the July letter and before the trial itself began, local secretaries ordered the party membership to be screened again for anyone who had had any connection in the past with Zinovievist or Trotskyist groups.[30] Over the next several months, thousands were expelled from the party for present and past suspicious activities. Meetings were held, files were scanned again, and memories wracked to uncover any possible former connection to the leftist opposition. In the climate following the trial, the definition of Trotskyism became quite fluid; it could include a careless remark decades before, an abstention in the early 1920s on some resolution against Trotsky, or a perceived lack of faith in the party line at any time.

Table 4 shows the quantitative dimension of these expulsions in comparison with those of the recently completed party screenings. Numerically, the attrition of this round of purges was smaller than the verification and exchange of documents; only about one half of one percent of the party was expelled. Although explicitly named Trotskyists and Zinovievists had constituted a small fraction of those expelled earlier, they made up nearly half of those removed in the new campaign. There was, however, one similarity between this round of expulsions and the previous operations. In both cases, local and regional party secretaries were again able to

Table 4

Expulsion of "Oppositionists," 1935–36

Time period	Number expelled from party	%age of party expelled	Trotskyists/ Zinovievists expelled	Trotskyists/ Zinovievists as %age of expelled
1935 *proverka*	263,885	11.1	7,504	2.8
1936 *obmen*	37,891	1.8	3,324	8.8
1936 after *obmen* to Feb. 1937	13,752	0.6	6,658	48.4

Source: RTsKhIDNI f. 17. op. 120, d. 278, ll. 2–3.

serve their own ends. They were again able to direct the fire downward; the vast majority of victims of these expulsions were again rank-and-file party members.

"Surely, Things Will Go Smoothly with Yezhov at the Helm"

The Kirov and Yenukidze cases had called NKVD chief Yagoda's competence into question. Although Yagoda said that he had always considered the followers of Zinoviev, Kamenev, and Trotsky to be guilty and had participated in the trials and repressions of them until the fall of 1936, since the attack on Yenukidze in mid-1935, it always seemed to be the party, not the NKVD, that uncovered the various plots and conspiracies.[31] Behind the scenes, Yagoda's credibility and leadership of the secret police became more questionable in 1936 as Yezhov, with Stalin's support, became curator of the NKVD's investigations of the opposition. Materials in Yezhov's archive show that he angled for Yagoda's job, never missing an opportunity to criticize the NKVD chief to Stalin. As a skilled bureaucratic player, Yezhov used bureaucratic "weapons of the weak" to manipulate his boss whenever possible.[32]

Moreover, when the former rightist Mikhail Tomsky committed suicide in August 1936, he left behind a letter hinting that Yagoda had been the one to recruit him into the Right Opposition back in 1928. Yezhov investigated the accusation, and while he reported to Stalin that Tomsky's charge against Yagoda lacked credibility, he nevertheless noted that "so many deficiencies have been uncovered in the work of the NKVD that it is impossible to tolerate them further."[33] Given Yezhov's relentless campaign, it is perhaps surprising that Yagoda held on as long as he did.

Yezhov used the middle months of 1936 to co-opt several of Yagoda's key deputies, including Frinovsky, Zakovsky, and the Berman brothers, against the Yagoda loyalists Molchanov and Prokofiev. Deputy NKVD Commissar Agranov seems to have tried to play each side against the other. In September 1936 the other shoe dropped and Yagoda was removed. From their vacation site at Sochi, Stalin and A. A. Zhdanov sent a telegram to the Politburo calling for Yagoda's replacement by Yezhov, claiming that under Yagoda the NKVD was "four years behind" in investigating the leftist opposition.[34]

It is difficult to know the immediate catalyst for this decision. Perhaps the dramatic explosions in the mines of Kemerovo three days earlier (which would soon be characterized as Trotskyist sabotage) cast further doubt on Yagoda's security measures. It is also possible that the arrest of G. Piatakov, deputy commissar for heavy industry, was related to Yagoda's fall. The arrest of Piatakov in mid-September raised the temperature considerably: Piatakov was an important, currently serving official whose arrest occasioned protests from Sergo Ordzhonikidze and perhaps others. The coincidence in time between Piatakov's arrest and Yagoda's removal may suggest that Yagoda had put his foot down against arrests within the office-holding bureaucracy. Or perhaps Yagoda's fall had been discussed by the Politburo in advance; we cannot know for certain. At any rate, Stalin's proposal was approved without a Politburo meeting (by polling the members [oprosom]), and not formally ratified until 11 October 1936. Even then, Yagoda's fate was not clear. Transferred to the "reserve list," he was appointed commissar of communications and remained a member of the Central Committee and at liberty for six months.

Yagoda had not been a popular figure, but Yezhov was regarded as a conscientious and loyal party worker, and his appointment did not cause any special alarm in party circles. Even Bukharin "got along very well" with Yezhov, considered him an "honest person," and welcomed the appointment.[35] Most Politburo members were on vacation at the time of Yezhov's appointment, and L. M. Kaganovich, who remained on duty for the Politburo in Moscow, wrote to his friend Ordzhonikidze (commissar for heavy industry) with the news. By this time, several of Orzhonikidze's assistants, department heads, and plant managers with "suspicious" pasts were already under investigation. Kaganovich's letter sought to reassure

Letter from Kaganovich to Ordzhonikidze applauding Yezhov's appointment as head of the NKVD. 30 September 1936

Ordzhonikidze that the appointment was a good one. "My dear, dear Sergo, how are you? First of all, I hope you are not angry with me for not writing to you for so long. The OGPU has been years behind schedule in this matter. It failed to forestall the vile murder of Kirov. Surely, things will go smoothly with Yezhov at the helm."[36]

2

дела пойдут хорошо. По моим
сведениям чв среде чекистов
за небольшим исключением
верхним смену руководства
хорошо. Сам Ягода, видимо,
тяжело переживает его
перемещение, но это нас трогать
не может когда дело идет об интересах
государства. Что касается Любова
то этот годе не на своем месте
как он оказался фид Союзного
наркомата.

2) В хозяйстве дела идут не плохо,
конечно в ряде районов недород
оказался большим чем вначале
предполагали.

Yezhov's new appointment occasioned several developments. First, he set about replacing Yagoda's people in the apparatus of the NKVD with "new men." These new recruits, brought in to "strengthen" and rebuild the staff of the NKVD, were largely taken from the party apparatus and from party political training schools; the Orgburo was kept busy processing these appointments.[37] In these weeks, the Politburo ratified numerous

Piatakov's telegram to Stalin voting to expel Sokolnikov from the party. 27 July 1936

lists of "mobilizations" of party workers for service in the NKVD. Yezhov would later brag that he had purged fourteen thousand chekists from the NKVD. Yagoda's fall and Yezhov's appointment at NKVD coincided with the extension of serious proceedings against ex-Trotskyists and other "suspicious persons" wherever they could be found. The July letter announcing the upcoming Zinoviev trial had claimed that terrorists had been able to embezzle state funds to support their activities. As early as summer 1936 G. I. Malenkov (head of the membership registration sector of the Central Committee and a close collaborator with Yezhov) had ordered his deputies to check the party files of several hundred responsible officials in economic administration for signs of suspicious activity in their pasts. In one such check, the files of 2,150 "leading personnel in industry and transport" turned up "compromising material" (defined not only as previous adherence to oppositional groups but also as party reprimands

Членам ЦК ВКП(б) №

<u>На голосование</u>

На основании неопровержимых улик установлено, что член ЦК Пятаков Ю.Л. поддерживал тесные связи с террористическими группами троцкистов и зиновьевцев. П.Б., считая, что такое поведение Пятакова несовместимо с пребыванием в составе ЦК и с принадлежностью ВКП(б), вносит на голосование членов ЦК предложение об исключении Пятакова из состава членов ЦК и из рядов ВКП(б)

За Л. Каганович

Kaganovich's first draft of Politburo resolution to expel G. Piatakov from the party. 10 September 1936

ЦЕНТРАЛЬНЫЙ КОМИТЕТ Всесоюзной Коммунистической Партии (большевиков)

ПЛЕНУМ

26.

Протокол № Пл 8/2 пункт Опросом членов ЦК ВКП(б) от 10-11.IX 1936 г.

СЛУШАЛИ:	ПОСТАНОВИЛИ:
О Пятакове Ю.Л.	На основании установленных неопровержимых данных о том, что член ЦК Пятаков Ю.Л. поддерживал тесные связи с террористическими группами троцкистов и зиновьевцев, ЦК ВКП(б), считая, что такое поведение Пятакова несовместимо с пребыванием в составе ЦК и с принадлежностью к ВКП(б), постановляет исключить Пятакова Ю.Л. из состава членов ЦК и из рядов ВКП(б).

Выписки т.т.
Ежову

Кем отправлены
(подпись)

Архив: Дело № 9 7 Ч-Л.

Politburo resolution expelling G. Piatakov from the party. 10–11 September 1936

or membership in other political parties) on 526 officials. At that time, though, only 50 of them were removed from their positions.[38]

From the fall of 1936 the NKVD began to arrest economic officials, mostly of low rank, ostensibly in connection with various incidents of industrial sabotage. By the beginning of 1937 nearly a thousand persons working in economic commissariats were under arrest.[39] The real bombshell, however, came in mid-September when Deputy Commissar of Heavy Industry Piatakov was arrested. Piatakov, a well-known former Trotskyist, had been under a cloud at least since July, when an NKVD raid on the

Telegram from Sergo Ordzhonikidze to Kaganovich voting to expel Ordzhonikidze's deputy G. Piatakov from the party. 11 September 1936

apartment of his ex-wife turned up compromising materials on his Trotskyist activities ten years earlier. In August, Yezhov interviewed him and told him that he was being transferred to a position as head of a construction project. Piatakov protested his innocence, claiming that his only sin was in not seeing the counterrevolutionary activities of his wife. He offered to testify against Zinoviev and Kamenev and even volunteered to execute them personally, along with his ex-wife. (Yezhov declined the offer as "absurd.") During August, Piatakov wrote both to Stalin and Ordzhonikidze, protesting his innocence and referring to Zinoviev, Kamenev, and Trotsky as "rotten" and "base."[40] None of this did him any good. He was expelled from the party on 11 September and arrested the next day.

As Sergo Ordzhonikidze's deputy at Heavy Industry, Piatakov was an important official with overall supervision over mining, chemicals, and other industrial operations. His arrest for sabotage and "terrorism" sent shock waves through the industrial establishment. Ordzhonikidze is said to have tried to intercede with Stalin to secure Piatakov's freedom, and he had been successful in protecting lower-level industrial cadres from NKVD harassment.[41] This time, though, Stalin and Yezhov forwarded to him transcripts of Piatakov's interrogations in which the latter gradually confessed to economic "wrecking," sabotage, and collaboration with Zinoviev and Trotsky in a monstrous plot to overthrow the Bolshevik regime.[42] According to Bukharin, who was present, Ordzhonikidze was invited to a "confrontation" with the arrested Piatakov, where he asked his deputy whether his confessions were coerced or voluntary. Piatako answered that they were completely voluntary.[43]

There are no documents attesting to Ordzhonikidze's protest. As from the account of his attendance at Piatakov's confrontation, we h only a couple of oblique references by Stalin and Molotov at the n plenum (February–March 1937) that Ordzhonikidze had been slow recognize the guilt of some enemies. But there is no evidence that his inte vention took the form of protest against the use of terror against party e emies; he was by no means a "liberal" in such matters. Ordzhonikidze, far as we know, never complained about the measures against Zinoviev Kamenev, Trotsky, Bukharin, Rykov, Tomsky, or any other oppositionist per se. His defense of "enemies" was a bureaucrat's defense of "his peo-ple," with whom he worked and whom he needed to make his organiza-tion function. From his point of view, Yezhov's depredations were improper only when they intruded into Ordzhonikidze's bailiwick, when they threat-ened the smooth fulfillment of the economic plans his organization an-swered for, and when they infringed on his circle of clients. As a card-carrying member of the upper nomenklatura, Ordzhonikidze was not against using terror against the elite's enemies, but he did fight to protect the patronage rights that he enjoyed as a member of that stratum.

In the case of another client, Ordzhonikidze had tried to shield the for-mer dissident Lominadze from arrest, telling Stalin that he (Ordzhoni-kidze) could bring Lominadze around to a loyal position. But when Ordzhonikidze became convinced that Lominadze was a lost cause, he proposed having him shot, a solution that was at the time too radical even for Stalin.[44]

The procedure by which Piatakov was expelled from the party illus-trates the themes of strong party discipline and nomenklatura solidarity. It also graphically shows the consequences of that solidarity when the elite began to commit suicide. Upon motions to expel a member of the Central Committee, members and candidates unanimously voted yes. (An occasional exception was Lenin's widow Krupskaia, who on occasion voted "agreed" to the expulsion motion, rather than the more positive "yes" [za].)[45] There were no dissidents, no arguments. Nomenklatura discipline overrode all other considerations. Piatakov voted to expel Sokolnikov, then was himself expelled. Zhukov voted (rather fiercely) to expel Piatakov, then was hi[mself] expelled a few months later.[46]

Even Or[dzhonikid]ze, who privately complained about Piatakov's detention, [accepted] the leadership's line and voted for his expulsion and subse[quent arrest].[47] Regardless of his doubts, he defended the notion of Piat[akov's guilt] to his deputies at Heavy Industry and chastised them for fai[ling to disco]ver the work of saboteurs.[48]

Personal Element

[In the a]utumn of 1936 the widening circle of arrests was claiming more [and mo]re victims. Those arrested or expelled from the party, or their rela[tives,] frequently appealed to high-ranking leaders for help and interces[sion]. Often these requests were ignored. Other times, however, a Politburo [me]mber would intercede and use his personal power to save an acquaintance. Such petitions for intercession were part of a long Russian tradition of appeal to tsars for help and are a special category of personal-political text. In this case, the author used apologetic discourse, paying his "symbolic taxes" by confessing his errors to a powerful figure. In so doing, despite his complaints about injustice, the author implicitly affirmed the terms and rules of the system. I. Moiseev-Yershistyi, who had been expelled from the party, wrote to Molotov:

> My dear and precious Viacheslav Mikhailovich! Having suffered an exceptionally grave tragedy in my Party life, I have taken the liberty to turn to you once again with a deep, heartfelt request to help me and my young children. Please don't let me sink into a life of shame and scorn.
>
> My dear, precious, beloved Viacheslav Mikhailovich, I know that our Party is so great, so mighty that the purity of its Leninist-Stalinist ideas is more exalted than anything else on earth, that it is the highest law of life. For that reason, my dear, beloved Viacheslav Mikhailovich, the greatest disciple of Lenin, who was a man of genius, I swear to you, the first and greatest assistant and

loyal Comrade in Arms of the Great Stalin, to You, my dear, beloved Viaches-lav Mikhailovich, I swear with all that's left of my life, I swear by the young lives of my beloved children that I will never violate this exalted law of the Party. I swear to you that I would gladly wipe away my crime with my own blood at the Party's call at any moment.

I. Moiseev (Yershistyi)

Two sets of instructions are appended to the letter:

To Comrade Yezhov: Moiseev-Yershistyi could hardly be troublesome to any-body in Leningrad. I doubt that he was justifiably expelled from the VKP(b). 9 September 1936. V. Molotov.

Inquire[d] with Shkiriatov. We have agreed to keep him in Leningrad and not to expel him from the Party. Let [the proper authorities in Leningrad] know about this.

Yezhov.[49]

The following letter was written by Mikhail Tomsky's widow to Yezhov following her husband's suicide. No record of an answer has been found in the archives.

Please help me find a job. I cannot live without work. Sometimes I feel that I am going crazy. I can no longer go on living cut off from life.

I have worked for a long time in the field of public catering and was a mem-ber of the Presidium of the Committee on Public Catering. I have also done administrative-economic work. I know how to work.

My eyes are hurting me now (the blood vessels in the pupils of both my eyes have burst), and I can read and write only for short periods of time. Perhaps it will all pass. . . .

I apologize for the length of this letter, but it's difficult to write more briefly. My greetings.

M. Tomskaia[50]

From the dock of the August 1936 show trial, Kamenev had mentioned in his testimony the names of former rightist leaders Bukharin, Rykov, and Tomsky. At the close of the court session, Procurator Vyshinsky an-nounced that he was opening an official investigation of the trio's possible complicity with the accused. Even before this, the denunciations of the leftists had begun to rub off on Bukharin. On the eve of the trial, in the wake of the Closed Letter of July, denunciations of Bukharin and other rightists had begun to flow in to the Central Committee. Thus I. Kuchkin wrote a note to Yezhov: "I would like to call your attention to the following: Comrade N. I. Bukharin has been traveling to Leningrad frequently. While there, he has been staying at the apartment of Busygin, a former Trotskyist and now a counter-revolutionary."[51]

Bukharin had been on vacation, mountain climbing in the Pamirs, when his name was mentioned at the Zinoviev trial. He rushed back to Moscow to defend himself, quickly writing a letter to Stalin protesting his innocence and demanding a confrontation with those arrested who had given evidence against him. Yezhov had meanwhile been busy trying to build a case against Bukharin. The key was G. I. Sokolnikov, a former oppositionist who had been arrested a month before the Zinoviev trial. In the course of his interrogation, Sokolnikov had apparently admitted not only his own close connections with the Zinovievists and Trotskyists but some complicity on Bukharin's part. Following Sokolnikov's testimony, Yezhov wrote to Stalin that in his opinion the rightists were involved in conspiracy, and asking permission to pursue the matter by reinterrogating several former Right Oppositionists. Stalin agreed. The results of these inquiries, combined with Sokolnikov's statement, were apparently the basis for the public mention of Bukharin at Zinoviev's trial.[52]

On 8 September, Bukharin and Rykov were granted a confrontation with the arrested Sokolnikov at Central Committee headquarters in the presence of a Politburo commission consisting of Kaganovich, Yezhov, and Vyshinsky. At that meeting Bukharin and Rykov denied any guilt and were permitted to question Sokolnikov. Sokolnikov stated that he had no personal knowledge of Bukharin's or Rykov's guilt. Sokolnikov's only information was that Kamenev had told him back in 1933 or 1934 that Bukharin and Rykov had known about the 1932 United Opposition bloc; he suggested that maybe that was not true and that Kamenev might only have been trying to recruit support by claiming the adherence of rightist leaders. Kaganovich immediately reported these results to Stalin, who ordered proceedings against Bukharin and Rykov stopped. Two days later, Vyshinsky's office issued a statement that there was insufficient evidence to proceed against the two rightist leaders.[53]

Yezhov went back to the drawing board. His arrests and interrogations of former rightists continued; over the next five months Yezhov would forward to Stalin some sixty transcripts of these interrogations. In October and November, Yezhov secured testimony about the complicity of Bukharin and Rykov from such people as Tomsky's personal secretary and from Old Bolshevik V. I. Nevsky.[54]

A Close Call for Bukharin: The December 1936 Plenum

Finally, by the first week in December, the stage was set for the arraign-ment of Bukharin and Rykov before the Central Committee's plenum. Yezhov gave the main speech against them. Citing testimony from a vari-ety of middle- and lower-level former oppositionists, he made the case that Bukharin, Rykov, and Tomsky were involved in the Zinoviev-Trotsky ter-rorist organization. As he would again and again, Bukharin refused to ad-mit his party guilt and attempted to refute the charges specifically and in detail.[55]

Prevailing party norms meant that one was supposed to perform a dis-cursive confession and implicate one's confederates as a matter of party duty. Otherwise, one's position was understood as an attack on the party and the Central Committee. Bukharin proposed a competing rhetoric, constative denial of guilt. If, as we have suggested, Bolshevik political re-ality was shaped by party discourse, Bukharin's position denied not only Yezhov's charges but his authority and, because Yezhov was a CC secre-tary, that of the party elite to shape that dominant narrative. For this he was denounced for "acting like a lawyer" instead of a Bolshevik and for being "antiparty." And, in terms of party understanding, he was. Bukha-rin must have known this, so one wonders what he could possibly have hoped to gain by so stridently denying not only the charges but the affirm-ing canons and group power assumptions that lay behind them.

Assuming that Bukharin was neither stupid nor suicidal, there is only one answer. At the June 1935 plenum on Yenukidze, Yezhov's antioppesi-tion proposal had not been authoritative. Then, in September, Stalin had saved Bukharin from the wolves by quashing the investigation against him. Now, in December, Bukharin was gambling that Stalin would again intervene to save him by contradicting Yezhov's line. It was a risky strat-egy, and an unsympathetic CC audience gave him a hard time.

> BUKHARIN: I am happy that this entire business has been brought to light be-fore a war and that our [NKVD] organs have been in a position to expose all of this rot before a war so that we can come out of war victorious. Because if all of this had not been revealed before the war but during it, it would have brought about absolutely extraordinary and grievous defeats for the cause of socialism. . . .[56] But I shall begin with the following. I was present at the death of Vladimir Ilich Lenin, and I swear by the last breath of Vladimir Ilich—and everyone knows how much I loved him—that everything that

has been spoken here today, that there is not a word of truth in it, that there is not a single word of truth in any of it. . . .

MOLOTOV: That's not the point. You are always acting as a lawyer, not just for others but also for yourself. You know how to make use of tears and sighs. But I personally do not believe these tears. These facts must all be verified, because Bukharin has so thoroughly lied through his teeth these past few years. . . .

BUKHARIN: I have the right to defend myself.

MOLOTOV: I agree, you have the right to defend yourself, a thousand times over. But I consider it my right not to believe your words. Because you are a political hypocrite. And we shall verify this juridically.

BUKHARIN: I am not a political hypocrite, not even for a second! (Noise in the room, voices of indignation). . . .

SARKISOV: . . . So here you are swearing by Lenin. Permit me to remind you all of one story. Here Bukharin is telling you that he swears by Lenin, but, together with the Left-SRs, he in fact wanted to arrest Lenin.

BUKHARIN: Rubbish!

SARKISOV: It's a historical fact. It's not rubbish. You yourself said so once.

BUKHARIN: I said that the SRs suggested this, but I reported this to Lenin. How shameless of you to juggle the facts!

SARKISOV: You are not denying it. That only confirms the fact.

BUKHARIN: I told this to Lenin, and now [ironically] I am guilty of having wanted to arrest Lenin?!!!

KAGANOVICH: What are all these facts? Beginning in 1928, Kamenev established ties with Tomsky. Moreover, Bukharin was present at their conversations. We know all this from Tomsky's statement. . . . And finally, in 1934 Zinoviev invited Tomsky to his dacha to drink tea. Tomsky went. Evidently, this tea party was preceded by something else, because after drinking tea Tomsky and Zinoviev went in Tomsky's car to pick out a dog for Zinoviev. You see what friendship, what help, they went together to pick out a dog.

STALIN: What about this dog? Was it a hunting dog or a guard dog?

KAGANOVICH: It was not possible to establish this. . . .

STALIN: Anyway, did they fetch the dog?

KAGANOVICH: They got it. They were searching for a four-legged companion not unlike themselves.

STALIN: Was it a good dog or a bad dog, anybody know? (Laughter in the hall). . . .

KAGANOVICH: [Their purpose was] to maintain their army, to carry out their plans pertaining to terrorist acts.

BUKHARIN: What, Comrade Kaganovich, have you gone out of your mind?!

STALIN: . . . We believed in you, we decorated you with the Order of Lenin, we moved you up the ladder and we were mistaken. Isn't it true, comrade Bukharin?

BUKHARIN: It's true, it's true, I have said the same myself.

STALIN: [Apparently paraphrasing and mocking Bukharin] "You can go ahead and shoot me, if you like. That's your business. But I don't want my honor to be besmirched." And what testimony does he give today? That's what happens, Comrade Bukharin.

BUKHARIN: But I cannot admit, either today or tomorrow or the day after tomorrow, anything which I am not guilty of. (Noise in the room).

STALIN: I'm not saying anything personal about you.[57] . . . It's been very hard on you. But, when you consider all these facts which I have talked about, and of which there are so many, we have no choice but to look more closely into this matter.[58]

These texts from the December 1936 plenum reveal a great deal about the nature of the attack on Bukharin and his response to it. Several speakers dismissed Bukharin's factual proofs that he could not have met with other accused at particular times. For Kosior, "Nothing is proven by that." Molotov said, "That's not the point. You are always acting as a lawyer." The specific facts and charges were not the point for this party audience; Bukharin's duty was to be politically and ritually useful.

Stalin even made jokes about Kaganovich's laborious factual reconstruction of the story of Tomsky, Zinoviev, and the dog. And in his final interchange with Bukharin, Stalin made the point perfectly clear: Bukharin's position now required him to provide the text that the party required, regardless of Bukharin's "personal honor" or, indeed, of his "legal" guilt or innocence. As an exasperated Kalinin told Bukharin at the plenum, "You must simply help the investigation." Otherwise, Bukharin would fall into the category of the party's enemies who struck a blow at the party by committing suicide (literally or figuratively) without cooperating with the party.

The distinction between juridical guilt and party guilt holds the key to this matter and, indeed, to much that happened in the party during the period of the terror. According to party thinking, Bukharin might well be innocent in a juridical sense of the specific charges made against him, but he nevertheless was guilty on a party sense for not supporting the party's line. That line, as was clear to all in the leading strata of the party, was the destruction of the former opposition, and as a good soldier of the party and nomenklatura, Bukharin was expected to cooperate in it.

Bukharin was obliged to do everything in his power to support that policy: to perform the denunciations of his former followers, to inform on any suspicious activities on their parts, and, if necessary, to confess and publicly associate himself with their crimes, all for the good of the party. If that meant his death, so be it. Since the Civil War, party members were in all cases supposed to be prepared to give their lives for the Revolution (which, as Bolsheviks, they believed to be synonymous with the party line). This was the price of that iron party discipline, a standard that Bukharin himself had helped to build and to which he had held others. For the Bolsheviks, personal existence was a subset of party existence, and the life of the party took precedence over physical life. As we saw from the documents above, even suicide—that most personal of acts—had only political meaning for the Bolsheviks.

Bukharin's personal agony did not elicit sympathy or pity from his former friends on the Central Committee. (Oddly enough, Stalin's remarks to and about Bukharin were the only conciliatory ones.) Quite the contrary, Bukharin's refusal to follow party discipline, his putting personal honor ahead of party (and group ritual) duty, infuriated the nomenklatura. It was an attack not only on the authority of the party leadership but also on its members, and they reacted with scorn, insults, and fury at one of their own who had broken the rules and who had jeopardized party unity for personal reasons, insulting them in the process. Following the Bolshevik tradition going back to Lenin's time, this put Bukharin outside the pale of the comrades. His speech produced a person—a reconstructed Bukharin—as an objective enemy, joining enemies that included tsarists, counterrevolutionaries, and fascists. Bukharin had spoken to the plenum as "we," but they already thought of him as "they." As we have seen, Bukharin's flat denial challenged the new Yezhov line on the rightists as enemies. By refusing ritually to confess, Bukharin was also denying the nomenklatura's right to establish the dominant narrative.

Nevertheless, the plenum did not expel Bukharin and Rykov from the party, nor did it order their arrest, despite specific proposals to that effect from some of the Central Committee members. This inconclusive result was not for want of trying on Yezhov's part. He was direct and unambiguously accusatory in his speech, repeating the charges he had been making against Bukharin for three months. Even while the plenum was meeting, he was sending to Stalin, Molotov, and Kaganovich records of the interrogation of rightist E. F. Kulilov, who testified that Bukharin had told him in 1932 of "directives" to kill Stalin.[59] The last day the plenum was meeting, Stalin apparently ordered another confrontation between the accused Kulikov and Piatakov on the one hand and Bukharin and Rykov on the other. The latter denied all the charges.

Then Stalin did a strange thing. Despite Yezhov's condemnatory report, the lack of any support for Bukharin and Rykov from the plenum, and the damning testimony of Kulikov and others, Stalin moved "to consider the matter of Bukharin and Rykov unfinished" and suggested postponing a decision until the next plenum.[60] Yezhov was again sent back to the drawing board; once again his proposals were not adopted.

We do not know the reasons for Stalin's procrastination with Bukharin. This was the second time (the first being the time of the Zinoviev trial) that Stalin had ordered proceedings against Bukharin quashed, suspended, or delayed. It is tempting to imagine the existence of some group within the Central Committee that was resisting the move against the rightists, forcing Stalin to retreat and prepare his position again. However, there is absolutely no evidence to support this. Unlike the case of the valuable Piatakov, neither Ordzhonikidze nor any other leader interceded for Bukharin. As far as we can tell from the documents, Bukharin and Rykov were met only with unrelenting hostility and even rude insults from those present at the plenum, many of whom were prepared to order his arrest on the spot. The only person dragging his feet was Stalin. As we shall see below, this would not be the last time Stalin would resist or delay a move against Bukharin. Even in 1937, after the death of Ordzhonikidze, Stalin would show little enthusiasm for a quick and final liquidation of the leading rightists.

Perhaps he felt some special sympathy for his former friend Bukharin. Perhaps he feared some reaction from the party or country should he destroy the rightist leader. Or perhaps he merely wished to keep his lieutenants uncertain of his plans. Perhaps he himself was not sure of his plans. It was clear that Bukharin had been expected to carry out the apology ritual and had pointedly refused to do so. But unlike Yenukidze in 1935, the refusal on Bukharin's part had resulted in leniency, not harsher punishment.

At any rate, one additional aspect of this mysterious meeting suggests hesitation or indecision on Stalin's part. The December plenum was a completely hidden transcript. Unlike virtually every other party plenum in Soviet history, it was kept completely secret. No announcement, however terse, appeared in the party press before or after the meeting. In fact, until very recently scholars were not sure that a plenum had taken place at that time, much less that Stalin had called off the attack at the last minute. Stalin hushed it up completely. The December 1936 plenum was somehow a bungled discourse, at least for Yezhov and the other lieutenants who had called for rightist blood.

On this question too, the December 1936 plenum leaves us with more questions than answers. Was Stalin afraid to announce the meeting beforehand for fear of allowing pro-Bukharin forces to prepare? Probably not. After all, such hypothetical forces could exist only in the Central Committee, and members of that body knew of the meeting beforehand; they had even received protocols of testimony against Bukharin before the meeting. And why maintain the secrecy for years after the meeting, even to the point that someone later went back into the archives and removed the text of Stalin's speech? Could it have been that once Bukharin's fate was decided in 1937, there was something embarrassing about wavering or indecision back in 1936?

We can suspect, from the documents we have, some of the motivations for the new policy to destroy the opposition in 1936 and can explain some of the actions of the political players. For Stalin, the discrediting and annihilation of alternative leaders, even has-beens of the defeated opposition, had a clear political advantage, whether or not personal malice or revenge for past slights played a part. It also allowed him, by implied threat, to secure the obedience of his bureaucracy.

For the party as a whole, there were also motives for cooperation in the destruction of the opposition. Fear certainly played a part. On a very basic level, once the policy became clear no one was prepared to defend those identified as the party's enemies for fear of joining in their punishment. No one wanted to die or lose his position and privileges. But fear alone cannot explain these events and the conduct of the political actors in them. Even though the autumn of 1936 had seen the arrest and condemnation of serving state leaders, no one in the nomenklatura could logically fear that *he* would become a target. They must have said to themselves: "Of course it is a serious thing to execute a Zinoviev or a Piatakov, but after all they had been dissidents and I never was anything but a loyal team player. Besides, they were clever and professional politicians and organizers, and probably were up to something unsavory." Zinoviev and Piatakov, like other party enemies (including in their time tsarist officers, Whites, and foreign powers) belonged to the category of *them,* not *us.* Repression was something *we* did to *them* (and vice versa), and it was inconceivable that *we* would repress *us.* "I was never one of *them,* why should I be afraid?"

Moreover, although the political weakness of their regime meant that any threatening "new situation" was likely to inspire *political* fear, paralyzing personal fear did not come easily to such people. Before the revolution, many of them had spent long years in prison or Siberian exile. Yan Rudzutak had spent ten years in chains in a tsarist jail. During the Civil War, nearly all of them had been combatants; they had killed, ordered deaths, and seen comrades fall beside them. Some of them had been captured by Whites, tortured, and sentenced to death. Prison and death were not strangers to them; these were hard men and it probably took a lot to frighten them. Indeed, the accounts we have of survivors of Stalinist camps are notable for the lack of personal terror they relate during their ordeals. We need not fall back on some concept of Russian courage or fatalism to explain their mentality. Ideological fanaticism, a wartime formative experience, and Bolshevik traditions, combined with a lifetime national experience of deprivation and hard living, more than account for it.

Aside from fear, there were other reasons for the nomenklatura to support the destruction of the opposition. First, one suspects that having read the voluminous confessions of former colleagues whom they knew well, most Central Committee members believed that Bukharin was actually guilty as charged. All of these veteran Bolsheviks were intensely political persons and professional conspirators who also functioned within a long-standing cultural matrix of patrons and clients. Their lives had largely consisted of forming blocs, conspiracies, and factions. It was impossible for them to believe that Bukharin and Rykov, who were practitioners from the same school, could have cut off all contact with their adherents and clients and given up all hope of regaining influence. It simply didn't ring true to the other members of the club who shared the same mentality. That Bukharin and Rykov did not know what their followers were doing or thinking was impossible to believe. Party circles in Moscow and Leningrad were not that large; everyone knew everyone. Conversations in kitchens and dachas, social meetings, and telephone contacts took place constantly. Who could believe that all this could have been without political content, as Bukharin and Rykov claimed? As Kosior said, "Do you

want us to believe now, after all that's happened, do you want us to believe
that Bukharin . . . knows nothing?"

Second, the destruction of its leaders and adherents was the final neu-
tralization of the alternative party nomenklatura. Although the threat
from the opposition seems to us negligible, the elite at the time obviously
felt a continuing crisis in the wake of collectivization and with the rise of
German fascism: a "new situation" in which economic and social stability
was still a hope and in which the final success of the Stalinist line was by
no means assured. After all, they themselves had come to power unex-
pectedly in the midst of a national crisis twenty years before, and even
Bukharin had mentioned the necessity of clearing the political decks before a war. The nomenklatura members of the Central Committee would
react hysterically at the accusation that the opposition had formed a
"shadow government" that awaited a crisis to seize power.

Third, those in the highest level of the elite in Stalin's immediate circle
must have felt a special urgency to destroy the former dissidents. As for
Stalin and the nomenklatura in general, the "liquidation" of the opposition and its leaders was a matter of preemptive self-preservation and political insurance. But the Molotovs, Kaganovichs, and Zhdanovs of the
Politburo had their own particular interests. To take the present case, as
long as Bukharin was alive, they lived under an implied threat. Not so long
ago Stalin had embraced Bukharin as the other of the two "Himalayas" of
the party, and throughout the 1920s the two of them had virtually been
corulers. Bukharin had been close to Stalin and a guest at the latter's family gatherings.[61] The fall of Bukharin and "his people" in 1929 had meant
the supremacy of the Molotovs and Kaganovichs (and "their people") in
the inner circle. But Stalin's maneuvers and sudden changes of political
line in the 1920s meant that anything could happen at the top. So while
Stalin's lieutenants probably never slept very well in the dictator's shadow,
as long as Bukharin and Rykov lived, an additional threat hung over them.
After their speeches to the plenum, Yezhov, Molotov, and the other senior
leaders who had led the charge against Bukharin could have derived no
pleasure from Stalin's sudden turn, which abandoned their positions.
Stalin's move put the new political line in doubt. Bukharin's denial had
been a risky gamble to challenge the nomenklatura, deny Yezhov's authority, and rely on Stalin for support. But, oddly enough, it worked.

Within the party leadership, therefore, there was an identifiable politics. It is possible to interpret the events of 1936–37 as a dynamic and con-

stantly changing constellation of political forces. If we set aside the notion of a grand plan of Stalin's to kill everyone (the evidence for which, aside from our knowing the end and reading backward, is quite weak), it is possible to understand the politics of the 1930s as an evolving history in which persons and groups jockeyed for position and self-interest. Stalin was desperate to achieve supreme power and to be able to discipline the apparatus. The lieutenants wanted to remain lieutenants. The nomenklatura wanted to eliminate rivals and control those beneath them. It may have been that at any given moment, all the players were maneuvering for advantage using the available political tools, issues, and discourses, without any of them, including Stalin, knowing where everything was headed. This fluid situation was described fifty years later by Molotov, who admitted his role in the terror and still believed it to have been necessary. For Molotov, the developing events were "not simply tactics. Gradually things came to light in a sharp struggle in various areas."[62]

CHAPTER SEVEN

The Sky Darkens

If you knew someone, you'd give him your full trust. Everything was based
on these connections and on trust. How can one do such things?!
—A. A. Andreev, 1937

I consider the criticism and the Party sanctions levied against me personally by
the Central Committee to be, in my opinion, very lenient,—because of the
enormous harm caused by me as a result of the activities of these Trotskyists.
—B. P. Sheboldaev, 1937

IN JANUARY 1937 Moscow decided to press the point about the dangers
of "carelessness" among the regional nomenklatura by making examples
of two of the most prominent regional leaders, Pavel Postyshev (first secretary in Ukraine) and Boris Sheboldaev (first secretary of the Azov–Black
Sea Territorial Party Committee). Recent arrests of alleged Trotskyist terrorists in both regions provided a setting for criticizing the practices of the
regional satraps without delving too much into the real workings of the
system and without weakening the regional party apparatus as an institu-
tion, both points which nobody wanted to discuss. The new Moscow political transcript went as follows: the arrests of terrorists under the noses
of trusted, veteran party leaders reveal deficiencies in leadership. The leading secretaries had been too trusting, too "politically blind," and too involved in economic administration to pay the necessary attention to "party
work." Their laxity had allowed the enemy to work unmolested, and the
bureaucratism and "familyness" of their machines made them deaf to
"signals from below" about enemies.

It is clear that this new line was carefully thought-out and presented by the Stalinist center. By criticizing the regional leaders and making examples of two of the most prominent, Stalin could have been serving several purposes. These actions first of all allowed Stalin to root out former oppositionists down to the local level. Local party leaders were no longer able to shield such people, regardless of their talents and usefulness to local economic and administrative agencies. The new policy thus weakened local patronage control and made it clear that Moscow would have a say in hirings and firings and would intrude itself into cadres policy. The new line also showed territorial party leaders who was boss and put them on notice that they must toe the current Moscow political line. By encouraging rank-and-file criticism, within limits, Stalin also attempted to open up new lines of information (or denunciation) that bypassed the middle-level leadership, which before this had been able to squelch discontent and filter information coming from below.

At the same time, the tsar could not govern without his nobles, or at least without a boyar class. The new critical line against the party apparatus was carefully circumscribed. While the leaders were criticized, they were not denounced as enemies, conscious protectors of enemies, corrupt, or even poor Bolsheviks. Stalin made this very clear in his speech to the February–March plenum, which was prominently published in party newspapers.[1] The two leading secretaries who lost their jobs were given new posts as heads of other provinces. Grassroots criticism was to be kept under control and channeled against particular leaders and their faults rather than against the regime itself.

These Stalinist tactics were risky for the nomenklatura, whose smooth functioning at all levels was based on patronage control, on maintaining control over the rank-and-file members (as well as the population at large), and on a unified narrative at all levels of the nomenklatura. Stalin's criticism from below–party democracy tactic risked a split in the party elite by turning the top against the middle and by inciting the rank and file against their heretofore legitimate leaders. Although at this time the regional leaders were not branded as enemies or their loyalty questioned, the new political transcript from the top represented the beginning of Stalin's offensive against the nomenklatura. Ironically, it had been this very idea—organizing the lower levels of the party against their leaders—that had so terrorized and infuriated the nomenklatura as a whole when Riutin had suggested it.

Making Examples of Some Provincial Chiefs

In the first week of January, the Stalinist emissary A. A. Andreev traveled to Rostov-on-Don to organize the removal of Boris Sheboldaev, the powerful first secretary of the Azov–Black Sea Territorial Party Organization, and thereby to promulgate the new line on careless regional secretaries. In the autumn of 1936 the spreading arrests of former Trotskyists had reached into Sheboldaev's province, and he had been summoned to the Politburo for a dressing down about the tolerance he had shown for them. On 2 January the Politburo passed a resolution removing him from his position, and it was this text that Andreev carried with him to Rostov-on-Don, the capital of the territory, to validate the new line. Convening first the narrow leadership circle and then the broader provincial elite, Andreev laid out the Politburo's decision, chastised the Sheboldaev team, and encouraged lower-level party members to help root out incompetent leaders and traitors. As usual, the procedure by which a party leader was disciplined was a kind of performance ritual with its own internal set of rules. An emissary from the "center" arrived and arraigned the local leader. Thus in Rostov, emissary Andreev told the regional party leaders that "The Trotskyist center carried out its activities in Rostov with impunity for a fairly long period of time. . . . The reason [for the enemy's success] is the extremely uncritical, credulous attitude—inadmissible for a Bolshevik—on the part of people such as Comrade Sheboldaev, a member of the CC."[2] That leader then provided the required apologetic "tax payment" by confessing his error and pointedly affirming the justice of the charges (usually by saying that they were "completely correct"). Then those in attendance affirmed the accusations by providing additional details and charges. Finally, a resolution was adopted that transformed the new discourse into a formal text.[3]

Unlike Yenukidze and Bukharin, Sheboldaev understood the need for an apologetic performance and recognized that he did not have the stature or influence to avoid it. Such a speech was necessary both to affirm the unity and "correctness" of the party leadership and to reinforce Sheboldaev's implicit claim to continued membership in the elite. Playing the role expected of him as a loyal member of the nomenklatura, Sheboldaev bowed before the Central Committee's will and took his medicine by performing a ritualized affirmation of the new dominant line: "Comrades, I have come up to the podium for only one reason, namely, to say that I consider the decision by the Central Committee of the VKP(b) concerning my mistakes and the work of the Territorial Committee of the VKP(b), of which I was the leader, to be absolutely right, absolutely just, because no other decision by the CC of the VKP(b) is possible. . . . Comrades, I consider it to be absolutely correct that the chief and main responsibility for this state of affairs should be placed on my shoulders."[4]

For loyally participating in the required apology ritual, Sheboldaev escaped severe punishment. Although he was removed from Rostov, he immediately received another important posting in another party organization. Encouraged by the new line and freed from Sheboldaev's control, party members then unleashed heretofore impossible criticism of the former provincial party leadership. No less than Sheboldaev himself, they were playing roles of contributing to party unity and affirming their status.

G. M. Malenkov, head of the personnel registration sector of the Central Committee, had accompanied Andreev to Rostov. Whereas Andreev had emphasized the theme of vigilance against enemies, Malenkov concentrated on the lack of democracy and input from below that had characterized Sheboldaev's leadership.[5]

In the discussion, there was criticism of several members of Sheboldaev's former leadership team. One special target was the territorial chief of the Party Control Commission (KPK), the party's disciplinary body that was supposed to have been more vigilant against the recently uncovered Trotskyists. Comrade Brike of the KPK was frequently denounced from the floor. Here we have an example of Moscow wanting to keep the criticism within manageable limits by carefully trying to shape the language. Brike, as KPK representative, answered to the party's KPK in Moscow, which was headed in early 1937 by N. I. Yezhov. As someone with such a powerful potential protector, Brike was rescued by Malenkov: "Comrades, the draft resolution includes an assessment of the activities of the Plenipotentiary of the KPK. The Central Committee shall concern itself with this matter, and this matter shall henceforth become the Central Committee's concern." The transcript next has a chorus of voices asking, "But may we ask about it?" followed by laughter.[6]

In the wake of Andreev's visit, district party meetings around the province removed members of the Sheboldaev team. In accordance with party tradition, larger meetings of party activists were organized to promulgate and discuss Moscow's decision to remove Sheboldaev.[7] These meetings

dutifully adopted resolutions in favor of the change and sent corresponding affirmations to the center.

These discursive rituals were the vehicles by which policies were implemented. Everyone played his part. But it is again important to remember
that these were not hollow or a priori invented events. They responded to
and at the same time influenced real political events in the localities. In the
present case, for example, the new rhetoric prompted calls in these party
organizations to speed up the reexamination of cases of rank-and-file
members who had been expelled in the previous year's verification and exchange of party documents. Sheboldaev's subordinates had carried out
these expulsions; the implication was that if they had so misread the danger of Trotskyism, they might well have expelled the wrong people. Stalin
had said as much at the June 1936 plenum.

Shortly after Sheboldaev's removal, Pavel Postyshev, who was second
secretary of the Ukrainian party organization and first secretary of the
Kiev Party Committee, was also reprimanded and deprived of one of his
posts. Seven weeks later, he was fired from his position as Ukrainian party
secretary and transferred to the position of first secretary of the Kuibyshev
Provincial Party Organization.[8]

The demotions of Sheboldaev and Postyshev were significant events.
These were powerful men who had acted practically as independent princes
of their territories. Their censures were accompanied by a visible political
campaign against "suppression of criticism" and "violations of party democracy." At the February–March 1937 plenum of the Central Committee, A. A. Zhdanov would give a fiery speech on these themes, decrying the
practice of "co-option" by which regional party leaders had refused to call
party elections, instead appointing their favorites to high positions in their
machines. Zhdanov called for mandatory party elections to be held in
May of 1937 in which party leaders at all levels were to face reelection in
unprecedented secret-ballot voting by the party rank and file. Several Central Committee members greeted Zhdanov's electoral proposal with luke-
warm enthusiasm; some even openly suggested postponing the voting for
various reasons.[9] But Stalin defended Zhdanov's proposal for new party
elections.[10]

The new emphasis on "party democracy" authorized lower-level party
members to criticize their superiors for poor work and suppression of criticism. Before the plenum, such criticism was dangerous; it almost always
led to retaliation by the regional machines that controlled the fates of

party members in their provinces. But the February–March plenum unleashed serious insurrections within the party by authorizing and protecting critics. In one district of the Western Region, for example, a membership meeting expelled the local district party secretary against the wishes of the regional committee. Representing the regional party machine, the local NKVD chief tried to defend the district secretary, to no avail. Protecting one of their own, the regional leadership gave the ejected leader a job in the regional party committee.[11]

The criticism of regional party chiefs in early 1937 also revisited the issue of who had been (and should not have been) expelled in the recently completed membership screenings of 1935–36, the verification and exchange of party documents. As we have seen, those operations had been under the control of the regional chiefs themselves and had resulted in mass expulsions of rank-and-file party members; only rarely were any full-time party officials expelled in these screenings. We saw that in June 1936 Stalin and others had complained about this practice and had ordered the territorial leaders to "correct mistakes" by speeding up appeals and readmissions of those who had been expelled for no good reason. In early March 1937 top-level Moscow leaders again denounced the "heartless and bureaucratic" repression of "little people." Malenkov noted that more than one hundred thousand of those expelled had been kicked out for little or no reason, while Trotskyists who occupied party leadership posts had passed through the screenings with little difficulty.[12]

Stalin echoed the theme in one of his speeches to the February–March 1937 plenum. According to him, by the most extravagant count the numbers of Trotskyists, Zinovievists, and rightists could be no more than thirty thousand persons. Yet in the membership screenings, more than three hundred thousand had been expelled; some factories now contained more ex-members than members. Stalin worried that this was creating large numbers of embittered former party members, and he blamed the territorial chiefs for the problem: "All these outrages that you have committed are water for the enemy's mill."[13] In the case of Postyshev's removal, Stalin and others had taken up the cause of one Nikolaenko, a party member expelled by Postyshev's wife Postolovskaia in Kiev. "Signals" from "little people" like Nikolaenko about enemies had been ignored by Postyshev, who had instead persecuted those sending the warnings.[14]

Certainly, much of this rhetoric was demagogic posturing. For Stalin and other central leaders it was good political policy to pose as the defenders of the rank and file against the depredations of evil boyars. Indeed, although appeals and reconsiderations continued throughout the 1930s, many of these little people were never readmitted. Moreover, it was time-honored practice for higher leaders to blame their subordinates for unpopular or mistaken policies and for the subordinates dutifully to admit their mistakes.

On the other hand, even in the darkest days of the hysterical hunt for enemies in 1937 and 1938, most of those expelled back in 1935 and 1936 who appealed to Moscow were reinstated. Virtually all those expelled for "passivity" were readmitted, and appellants charged with more serious party offenses who appealed to the Party Control Commission in Moscow (run by Yezhov and later by the equally fierce Shkiriatov) were usually readmitted, the proportion of successful appeals reaching 63 percent by 1938.[15]

Furthermore, a good bit of Stalin's criticism was hidden behind closed doors to the Central Committee and never intended for public consumption, thus reducing any demagogic impact. More important, statistical data presented by Malenkov and never released to the public showed vast differences between regional officials' and Moscow leaders' versions of membership verification. Table 5 shows that the screenings had targeted masses of rank-and-file party members in 1935 and 1936 when checking was done by territorial officials. However, after the screenings, verification of party members was under the direct control of the Central Committee, and the results were different. When "checking" was done by central, rather than territorial, authorities, the attrition was heavier at the top than at the bottom. Moscow was less interested in (and even hostile to) mass expulsions of the rank and file; its targets were former Trotskyists with rank. Clearly, Moscow and the regional secretaries had different ideas about what the screenings should have accomplished.

At the February–March 1937 plenum, Stalin criticized the undemocratic practices of party officials in the provinces but drew a sharp line between their "mistakes" and the "enemies" who needed to be "smashed." "Is it that our party comrades have become worse than they were before, have become less conscientious and disciplined? No, of course not. Is it that they have begun to degenerate? Again, no. Such a supposition is completely unfounded. Then what is the matter? . . . The fact is that our party comrades, carried away by economic campaigns and by enormous suc-

Table 5

Verification and Expulsion of Party Cadres, 1935–37

	Total checked by CC	Expelled	%age expelled of total checked
Obkom department heads	398	35	8.8
Gorkom department heads	2,031	111	5.5
Instructors	1,620	63	3.9
Gorkom/raikom secretaries	5,275	184	3.5
Cell secretaries	94,145	3,212	3.4
Totals	103,469	3,605	3.5

Source: Malenkov speech to February–March plenum, *Voprosy istorii,* no. 10, 1995, 7–8.

cesses on the front of economic construction, simply forgot some very important facts."[16]

The Politburo was at pains to show that Sheboldaev and Postyshev were not to be considered enemies themselves; they had simply been negligent, even though Sheboldaev's personal secretary and most of Postyshev's lieutenants in Kiev had been arrested as Trotskyists. While criticizing Sheboldaev, Postyshev, and others, several speakers at the plenum cited mitigating circumstances: such leaders were, in fact, burdened with economic work and were not completely at fault. Significantly, both secretaries were transferred to lesser but significant posts: Postyshev became first secretary of Kuibyshev Region, and Sheboldaev was sent to head the Kursk party organization. A. A. Andreev, who had led the sacking of Sheboldaev, had prepared a resolution for the February–March plenum linking Sheboldaev and Postyshev and denouncing them in rather strong language.[17] Apparently, though, it was Stalin's decision not to promulgate such a strong statement, and the resolution was never introduced.

Similarly, in the weeks that followed the transfers of these two, the Central Committee intervened on several occasions to protect them from those who sought to characterize their demotions more negatively. In one case, a newspaper editor in the Azov–Black Sea Territory was reprimanded after allowing publication of an article saying that Sheboldaev had been fired. In another instance, Stalin intervened personally as late as July 1937 to order a "campaign against Comrade Postyshev" stopped. As always, precise conventions of language had to be followed precisely.[18]

Party Discipline and the Fall of Bukharin

Although there was a critical but generally conciliatory attitude toward the regional secretaries at the February–March plenum, the official rhetoric on former oppositionists was increasingly severe. Two months earlier, at Stalin's suggestion, the previous plenum had not condemned Bukharin and Rykov and had postponed consideration to the next meeting. In the interim, Yezhov had been busy. He continued to interrogate former oppositionists in order to get "evidence" incriminating the rightist leaders. On 13 January 1937 Bukharin participated in a "confrontation" with V. N. Astrov, a former pupil of Bukharin now arrested for treason. In the presence of Stalin and other Politburo members, Astrov angrily accused Bukharin of active participation in subversive conspiracies. Allegedly, Bukharin had used his former students in the Institute of Red Professors (the "Bukharin School") as the basis for an underground organization. Bukharin denied everything.[19]

Between 23 and 30 January, Moscow was the site of the second of the famous show trials. This time, Deputy Commissar of Heavy Industry Piatakov, the journalist Karl Radek, the former diplomat G. Sokolnikov, and fourteen other defendants were charged with industrial wrecking and espionage at the behest of Trotsky and the German government. As before, all the defendants confessed to the charges.

The Fall of Bukharin: The February–March Plenum of the Central Committee

The stage was now set for Bukharin's next arraignment at the upcoming plenum of the Central Committee, scheduled for 19 February 1937. The meeting had to be postponed, however, because of the sudden death of Heavy Industry Commissar Sergo Ordzhonikidze on the eighteenth. Officially announced as heart failure, his death now seems clearly to have been a suicide. Subsequent testimony from those around him suggests that he had been despondent for some time, and there is information that he had had arguments with Stalin, perhaps about those from his agency who had been arrested.[20]

The plenum was rescheduled to open 23 February, but the drama began three days earlier, when Bukharin sent two documents to the Central Committee. The first was a letter again protesting his innocence and announcing that he was beginning a hunger strike on the twenty-first to protest the accusations against him. He wrote on the twentieth, "I cannot live like this any more. I have written an answer to the slanderers. I am in no physical or moral condition to come to the plenum, my legs will not go, I cannot endure the existing atmosphere, I am in no condition to speak. . . . In this extraordinary situation, from tomorrow I will begin a total hunger strike until the accusations of betrayal, wrecking, and terrorism are dropped."[21]

Along with this letter, which he asked the Politburo not to circulate to the full Central Committee, Bukharin forwarded a statement to that body of more than one hundred pages in which he attempted to refute, point by point, the charges made against him.[22] With careful detail, he showed the inconsistencies among the various confessions and statements implicating him and in many cases proved that he could not have been in the places indicated by his accusers. He maintained his complete loyalty to Stalin's party line since 1930, again denied charges of terrorism and treason, and expressed outrage that such accusations could even have been made. Moreover, in a subtle way, he questioned the honesty of the secret police by alluding to the fact that confessions could be supplied by defendants according to the demands of the police.

It would seem that Bukharin's only chance to survive, and it was a slim one, was to agree with the charges, to "come clean," confess to everything, and throw himself on the mercy of the Central Committee. Only in this way could he "disarm" completely before the party, "clean himself of the filth he had fallen into," as Stalin was to say, and provide the service—as a public counterexample—that the party demanded. After all, that was the standard Bukharin had demanded of the Trotskyists back in the 1920s, and for him to deny it now with a legalistic defense was bound to make him look self-serving and hypocritical to his comrades.

His hunger strike and initial refusal to attend the plenum (both of which he retracted almost immediately) were taken as vivid examples of an anti-party stance, or, as Mikoian would call it, a "demonstration" against the party no less insulting or threatening than an actual street rally against the Bolsheviks. In this light, how could Bukharin have hoped to prevail or even survive by continuing to deny the charges? Perhaps he based his position on the ambiguous outcome of the previous plenum, when he had challenged Yezhov's sally and Stalin had blocked Bukharin's demise. If he counted on a reprise in February, however, he was wrong.

The plenum opened on 23 February with the formal report by Yezhov on the charges against Bukharin and Rykov. In the days before the plenum, members of the Central Committee had received voluminous materials on these charges, including lengthy transcripts of the confessions of Bukharin's former associates. Yezhov's speech, therefore, contained few specifics but rather summarized the accusations. Beginning with a long survey of the history of the Right Opposition, he said that the former rightists, like the Trotskyists, had formed underground terrorist cells with the goal of carrying out espionage and assassinations against the Soviet government. This conspiracy had as its founding document the Riutin Platform, the dangerous competing discourse of 1932, which Yezhov now said that Bukharin had at least commissioned, if not written.

Yezhov went on to say that on the basis of "incontrovertible documentary materials" there was no question that Bukharin and Rykov had at least known of preparations for the Kirov assassination and had conspired to kill other party leaders as part of a planned "palace revolution" to overthrow the party. "It seems to me that all this raises, in connection with Bukharin and Rykov, people who are fully responsible for the whole activity of the right opposition in general and for their anti-soviet activity in particular,—raises the question of their continuation not only in the Central Committee but also as members of the party." Voices from the plenum responded, "Right," and "It is too little."[23]

Yezhov was followed by A. I. Mikoian, who was no less severe in his castigation of Bukharin and Rykov as traitors and assassins. Mikoian noted that Trotsky's tactics since the late 1920s had been to organize various declarations, protests, and demonstrations against the party leadership: "Bukharin, following in enemy of the people Trotsky's footsteps, turned his arms against the Central Committee. It was Trotsky who was always putting forth ultimatums, Trotsky always hurled written statements at us. . . . Trotsky even organized demonstrations against the party on the street, but Bukharin does not have the possibility to organize a demonstration, now he has no masses, it is another time. . . . When there are no masses, no other means of protest, then Bukharin resorts to a hunger strike as a form of protest."[24]

Even if for the sake of argument one accepted Bukharin's claim that he did not order any assassinations, Mikoian continued, it was clear from the testimonies of his former associates that Bukharin must have at least known the things they were planning. In Mikoian's words, "One thing nobody can argue with. To know of terror against the leadership of the party, of wrecking in our factories, of espionage, of Gestapo agents, and to say nothing about it to the party—what is this?! . . . The rightist terroristic activities were known to Bukharin, he knew that they were preparing terrorist acts against the leadership of the party, he knew and he did not tell the Central Committee. Is this permissible for a member of the Central Committee and a member of the party?! It is proved and clear even to a blind man."[25] Finally, it was Bukharin's turn to speak. He was not to have an easy time of it.

> BUKHARIN: If you think that [my accusers] told the truth, that I issued terroristic instructions while out hunting, then I won't be able to change your mind. I consider this a monstrous lie, which I can't take seriously.
> STALIN: You babbled on and on, and then you forgot.
> BUKHARIN: I didn't say a word. Really!
> STALIN: You really babble a lot.
> BUKHARIN: I agree, I babble a lot, but I do not agree that I babbled about terrorism. That's absolute nonsense. Just think, comrades, how could you ascribe to me a plan for a palace coup?![26]

Bukharin was followed to the podium by his fellow rightist leader Aleksei Rykov, who was also grilled by the CC.[27] After Bukharin and Rykov spoke, the plenum saw one Central Committee member after another go to the podium and denounce the two in the strongest possible terms. This arraignment lasted more than two days.

> SHKIRIATOV: Enough, we must put an end to this, we must make a decision. Not only is there no place for these people in the CC and in the Party. Their place is at a court of law, their place, i.e. the place of these state criminals is in the dock.
> [KOSIOR: Let them prove it at a court of law.]
> SHKIRIATOV: Yes, at a court of law. What makes you think, Bukharin and Rykov, that leniency will be shown to you? Why? When such feverish work is carried out against our Party, when these people are organizing conspiratorial, terroristic cells against the Party in order, by their terroristic actions, "to put the members of the Politburo out of their way." We cannot limit ourselves to merely expelling them [Bukharin and Rykov] from the Party. This must not be! The law established by the socialist state must be applied to the enemy. They must not only be expelled from the CC and from the Party. They must be prosecuted. . . .
> VOROSHILOV: Bukharin is a very peculiar person. He is capable of many

things. Vile, you know, as a mischievous cat and at once he starts covering his tracks, he starts confusing things, he starts carrying out all kinds of pranks, in order to come out of this filthy business clean, and he had succeeded in this often thanks to the kindness of the Central Committee. . . . He must not get away with it. The Central Committee is not a tribunal. We do not represent a court of law. The Central Committee is a political organ. . . .

I believe that the guilt of this group, of Bukharin, of Rykov and especially of Tomsky, has been completely proven.[28]

A. A. Andreev noted Stalin's "patience" in the matter of prosecuting Bukharin and the others:

No, no, as far as you are concerned, the Party and the Central Committee have given you sufficient time, more than enough time and means to disarm yourselves and prove yourself innocent. No one else from the ranks of the oppositionists and enemies has been afforded such a period of time, the Party has not afforded such a period of time to anyone other than you. The Party did the maximum to keep you in its ranks. How much effort has been expended, how much patience has been shown to you by the Party, and especially, I must say, by Comrade Stalin. Yes, precisely, by Comrade Stalin, who always urged us, who constantly warned us, whenever comrades here or there, whenever local organizations here or there raised the issue "pointblank," as is said, in reference to the rightists and whenever the question would arise in the CC, Comrade Stalin would caution them against excessive haste, he always warned us. Nevertheless, you abused the Party's trust.[29]

At this point, Komsomol leader Kosarev tried to summarize and end the discussion.

KOSAREV: It seems to me that the time has come for us to stop calling Rykov, Bukharin and other rightists comrades. People who have laid their hands on our Party, on the leadership of our Party, people who have lifted their hands against Comrade Stalin, cannot be our comrades. They are enemies, and we must deal with them as we would with any enemy. Bukharin and Rykov must be expelled from the register of the Central Committee and from the Party. They must be arrested at once and brought to trial for working as enemies against our socialist country.
Exclamations from many sides: Right! Right![30]

Molotov noted that the real point was Bukharin's and Rykov's duty to set an example to others by "disarming." By refuting the charges, they were giving aid and comfort to the enemy and sending dangerous signals to others:

But we must consider the fact that there are enemies in our midst. When they give a signal such as: "Hold on, keep on struggling, don't give up, deny the truth, deny the evidence, dodge, duck,"—this still leaves some people in the position of enemies, of people who have not disarmed themselves. It's not Rykov and Bukharin,—they have other people, they have been in our Party and they are still in it now. We cannot close our eyes to this. They call out not only to their supporters in our Party, but also to those who are outside the Party. They give them their signal. It is clear from the policies of Bukharin and Rykov at the present time that they have strayed much further along the path of doubts and errors, that they have strayed far, that they are straying more and more, that they are continuing their worse traditions of struggling against the Party. . . .

Already at the last Plenum we had sufficient evidence, and yet we postponed this case once again. We decided to give this man the opportunity to extricate himself if he is in trouble. If he is guilty, we'll give him time to admit his mistakes, to turn aside from it, to repent of it, to put an end to it. We have sought to bring this about in every way possible.[31]

Mikhail Kalinin made a point that everyone in the room understood; that there was a difference between judicial guilt and political guilt. It was the latter that mattered:

And when some people shouted at Bukharin during his speech that, namely, you are acting like a lawyer, Bukharin replied: "Well, what of it? My situation is such that I must defend myself." I think, and those comrades who shouted at him also probably think, when they speak of "acting like a lawyer," that it doesn't mean that Bukharin should not defend himself. That's not the point. What it means, instead, is that, in defending himself, he is employing the methods of a lawyer who wants, at whatever cost, to defend the accused, even when the latter's case is completely hopeless. . . . It means that he assumed a priori that there were two camps here, namely the CC and Bukharin.[32]

For Kalinin and the other CC members, the matter was clear: There were young hotheads prepared to use violence to change the system. There was talk about palace coups in groups that practiced conspiratorial secrecy behind a facade of loyalty. Yes, Bukharin and Rykov had confessed their previous political mistakes and publicly associated themselves with the party majority. But they had done it without enthusiasm, without commitment. They knew, or at least must have heard about, the incendiary sentiments of their former followers; how could they not? They saw each other in meetings, on the street, in kitchens, at dachas. Bukharin's legalistic and logical-factual attempts ("like a lawyer") to prove that he could not have been a member of any conspiracy were entirely beside the point and insulting to his comrades on the CC. To lifelong professional politicians and conspirators, it was simply inconceivable that Bukharin had not known about his followers' subversive and potentially violent subculture. Not to report that was tantamount to participating in it. Those were the rules, rules that Bukharin had helped craft and apply to others, and everybody understood them.

After this litany of denunciations from Central Committee members, Bukharin was given another chance to speak. Allowing those accused of party crimes to speak a second time in rebuttal was a fairly unusual procedure, and was cited by some speakers as proof that the Central Committee was willing to give him every fair chance to defend himself. As before, however, he was not allowed to speak unmolested.

BUKHARIN: Comrades, first and foremost, I must tell you that I shall disregard all sorts of attacks bearing, to a significant extent, on my personal character, attacks which depicted me either as a buffoon or as a subtle hypocrite. I cannot dwell on the unworthy aspect of these speeches and I consider this entirely superfluous. . . . But that is not at all my main argument. I have compared facts, many chronological dates. Armed with this comparison, I've refuted everything.

MOLOTOV: Nothing of the sort. Your refutation is not worth a farthing, because we have enough facts.

BUKHARIN: I would be grateful if someone, anyone were to mention it, but not a single person has mentioned it, no one has said a word about it.

MOLOTOV: My God! Everybody is talking about it. . . .

BUKHARIN: In spite of the fact that I cannot explain a host of things, fair questions posed to me, [in spite of the fact that] I cannot explain fully or even half-fully many questions posed to me concerning the conduct of people testifying against me. However, this circumstance, namely, that I cannot explain everything is not in my eyes an argument for my guilt. I repeat, I've been guilty of many things, but I protest with all the strength of my soul against being charged with such things as treason to my homeland, sabotage, terrorism and so on, because any person possessing such qualities would be my deadly enemy. I am ready and willing to do anything against such a person. (Noise, voices.) . . .

KHLOPLIANKIN: It's time to throw you in prison!

BUKHARIN: What?

KHLOPLIANKIN: You should have been thrown in prison a long time ago!

BUKHARIN: Well, go on, throw me in prison. So you think the fact that you are yelling: "Throw him in prison!" will make me talk differently? No, it won't.[33]

In accordance with party traditions, the reporter on the agenda question was given a chance to give a concluding speech. In this case, Yezhov summed up the case against Bukharin and Rykov. Although his original report had called only for expelling them from the party, his concluding remarks suggested that they should be arrested.[34]

From the speeches to the plenum, it seemed that there was little disagreement on the question. None of the speakers even came close to defending Bukharin or opposing arrests of the traitors. They were furious with Bukharin and Rykov not only for their alleged "treason" to the party but for their refusal to serve the party and the ritual by playing the prescribed roles. Regardless of Bukharin's intent, his speech in ritual context transformed him into an enemy. Once again, the senior nomenklatura had closed ranks against those perceived as violating their rules. However, even though we have a version of the entire text concerning Bukharin and Rykov, the plenum's proceedings to a great extent remain mysterious. Indeed, the documents themselves raise strange questions.

Since Lenin's time, it had always been a party tradition that the main reporter on an agenda question offered a draft resolution beforehand. More recently, it had become the responsibility of the Politburo (that is, of Stalin himself) to prepare such a preliminary resolution in advance of the plenum. These drafts were circulated to the Central Committee members before the report, and speeches were given. In the present case, there was a draft resolution to be adopted on the basis of Yezhov's main report. The draft has not been located in the archives; presumably it followed the outlines of Yezhov's recommendation and called for expelling Bukharin and Rykov from the party.

In the vast majority of cases in the 1930s, discussion of the main report was perfunctory, and although minor corrections and amendments might be offered and even accepted from the floor, the Central Committee almost always voted unanimously to adopt the draft resolution. In rare cases when there was disagreement or when the drift of the meeting went beyond the draft proposals, an ad hoc commission of Central Committee members would retire during the meeting to work out a new text for the final resolution. (This had happened at the 17th Party Congress in 1934, when Ordzhonikidze and Molotov had proposed different industrial targets for the second Five Year Plan.)[35]

In this case, several of the speakers had gone beyond Yezhov's formal recommendation for expulsion. No doubt sensing the winds, some of them —including Yezhov—had called for arresting Bukharin and Rykov. Others had flatly suggested that they be shot. Formally, then, it was necessary for a commission to edit the draft resolution in favor of stronger measures. But the matter was more complicated than that. There is evidence that some, perhaps including Stalin himself, may have argued for a different approach altogether. The resolution subsequently produced by the commission and approved by the plenum did, in fact, consign Bukharin and Rykov to the not-so-tender mercies of the NKVD. However, it contained language indicating indecision at the top.[36] The ambiguity arises from Stalin's report to the plenum on the deliberations of the ad hoc commission. Stalin told the plenum,

> There were differences of opinion as to whether they should be handed over for trial or not handed over for trial, and if not, then as to what we should confine ourselves to. Part of the commission expressed itself in favor of handing them over to a Military Tribunal and having them executed. Another part of the commission expressed itself in favor of handing them over for trial and having them receive a sentence of 10 years in prison. A third part expressed itself in favor of having them handed over for trial without a preliminary decision as to what should be their sentence. And, finally, a fourth part of the commission expressed itself in favor of not handing them over for trial but instead referring the matter of Bukharin and Rykov to the NKVD. The last-named proposal won out. . . .
>
> There were some on the commission, a rather substantial number, as well as here at the CC Plenum, who felt that there was apparently no difference between Bukharin and Rykov, on the one hand, and those Trotskyists and Zinovievists, on the other hand, who were brought to trial and punished accordingly. The commission does not agree with such a position and believes that one ought not to lump Bukharin and Rykov in with the group of Trotskyists and Zinovievists, since there is a difference between them, a difference that speaks in favor of Bukharin and Rykov.
>
> If we look at the Trotskyists and Zinovievists, we see that they were expelled from the Party, then restored, then expelled again. If we look at Bukharin and Rykov, we see that they had never been expelled. We should not equate the Trotskyists and Zinovievists, who had once, as you well know, staged an anti-Soviet demonstration in 1927, with Rykov and Bukharin. There are no such sins in their past. The commission could not fail but take into account that there are no such sins in the past actions of Bukharin and Rykov and that, until very recently, they gave no cause or grounds for expelling them from the Party.[37]

It was quite unusual for Stalin himself to give such reports; this is the first and only time in party history that he did so. This text was truly a hidden transcript: it was never published with any of the versions of the stenographic report and was never transferred to the party archives with other materials of the plenum. The transcript of this ambiguous and contradictory decision on Bukharin never even found its way into the heavily edited and limited-circulation stenographic report, which showed the plenum beginning on 27 February—four days after it actually started.[38]

We have two versions of the skeletal protocol of the commission's deliberations on which Stalin reported. Apparently one of them was made during the meeting; the other seems to have been edited immediately thereafter. The alterations made to this document raise more questions than they answer.

First, in the original protocol, Yezhov was the main reporter who proposed handing Bukharin and Rykov over to the courts and executing them. However, because this was not the final result and because party discursive tradition prohibited even a private admission that a formal report was rejected, the document was doctored to make it appear that there had been no proposal from Yezhov, but rather a round table with numbered "exchange of opinions" among the members of the commission.

But although expulsion from the party was a foregone conclusion, in the original polling not a single member proposed or voted for what would become the final decision: turning the matter of Bukharin and Rykov over to the NKVD for further investigation. In the initial polling of thirty-six members of the commission, six (Yezhov, Budennyi, Manuilsky, Shvernik, Kosarev, and Yakir) spoke for executing Bukharin and Rykov. Eight (Postyshev, Shkiriatov, Antipov, Khrushchev, Nikolaeva, Kosior, Petrovsky, and Litvinov) were for arresting and trying Bukharin and Rykov but for sentencing them to prison rather than to death. Sixteen members expressed no opinion, or perhaps their votes were not recorded.

It is the remaining group of six voters that is especially intriguing. In the original protocol, five members were "for the suggestion of Comrade Stalin." But what was that suggestion? In the original document, Stalin spoke against the death penalty, a prison sentence, or even a trial, and in favor of the relatively lenient punishment of internal exile. But in the final version, Stalin's "suggestion" had become the final decision not to send them to trial but to turn the matter of Bukharin and Rykov over to the

NKVD for further investigation. These documents make it clear that there really was indecision and a discussion that changed Stalin's mind. The result was a compromise of all the suggestions.

Once again Stalin was resisting application of either a prison or death sentence. Why? It may have been that he was lying back, proposing a light punishment in order to see what the others said, thereby identifying those with "soft" views on the opposition and marking them for later retaliation. In this way, he would be able to test the level of support for his plan to kill off the former opposition. This could explain why some, aware of the game, simply expressed themselves in favor of Stalin's proposal while others kept silent. Mitigating against this explanation, however, is the lack of any correlation between the penalties proposed by those present and their fates. Thus Shkiriatov, Khrushchev, Nikolaeva, Petrovsky, and Litvinov voted against the sternest punishment, execution, but all survived the purges. Kosarev, Yakir, and Yezhov voted for execution and were themselves arrested and shot.

It is far more likely that Stalin had not decided exactly how far to proceed against Bukharin and Rykov. As the final resolution showed, it had not been "proved" that they had in fact joined the Trotskyist "terror organization." Rather, "at a minimum" they knew about the Trotskyists' plans, which is not the same thing. Yezhov had been the one closest to the investigations and interrogations of the rightists. Back in the fall of 1936, he had written to Stalin to express "doubt[s] that the rightists had concluded a direct organizational bloc with the Trotskyists and Zinovievists." At that time, Yezhov recommended a "minimum punishment" of exile to a far region for Bukharin and Rykov.[39] Yezhov's 1936 formulation was precisely the one voiced by Stalin at the February–March 1937 plenum: that "at a minimum" Bukharin and Rykov had known about the terrorist plans of others and failed to report them. A distinction was made between them and the Trotskyists, and Stalin's first proposed punishment was exile. He used the same word (*vysylka*) that Yezhov had used in his letter the previous autumn. When Stalin reported the several contending points of view at the meeting and related how a compromise had been reached, he was telling the truth.

More than a year would pass before Bukharin's trial. As late as June of 1937, after Bukharin had been in prison three months, Stalin told a meeting of military officers that although Bukharin and Rykov had "connections" to enemies, "we have no information [*dannye*] that he himself was an informer."[40] Even later in June, after Bukharin began to "confess" to

П р о т о к о л

заседания комиссии Пленума ЦК ВКП(б) по делу

Бухарина и Рыкова

27 февраля 1937 года.

ПРИСУТСТВОВАЛИ:

тов.МИКОЯН - председатель.

Члены комиссии: т.т. Андреев,Сталин,Молотов,Каганович Л.М., Ворошилов,Калинин,Ежов,Шкирятов,Крупская Косиор,Ярославский,Жданов,Хрущев,Улья- нова,Мануильский,Литвинов, Якир, Каба- ков,Берия,Мирзоян,Эйхе,Багиров,Икрамов, Варейкис,Буденный,Яковлев Я., Чубарь, Косарев,Постышев,Петровский,Николаева, Шверник,Угаров,Антипов,Гамарник.

_Слушали_предложения членов Комиссии:

Предложения _т_. Ежова об исключении Бухарина и Рыкова из состава кандидатов ЦК ВКП(б) и членов ВКП(б) и предании их суду Военного Трибунала с применением высшей меры наказания - расстрела.

Членами комиссии были внесены следующие предложения:

2. т.Постышева - исключить из состава кандидатов ЦК ВКП(б) и членов ВКП(б) и предать суду, без примене- ния расстрела.

3. т.Буденный - исключить из состава кандидатов ЦК ВКП(б) и членов ВКП(б) и предать суду с применением расстрела.

4. т.Сталина - исключить из состава кандидатов ЦК ВКП(б) и членов ВКП(б), суду не предавать, а выслать.

5. т.Мануильский - исключить из состава кандидатов ЦК ВКП(б) и членов ВКП(б), предать суду и расстрелять.

5. т.Шкирятов - исключить из состава кандидатов ЦК ВКП(б) и членов ВКП(б), предать суду, без применения расстрела.

6. т.Антипов - То же.

7. т.Хрущев - То же.

8. т.Николаев - То же.

9. т.Ульянова М. - За предложение т.Сталина.

10. т.Шверник - Исключить из состава кандидатов ЦК ВКП(б) и членов ВКП(б), предать суду и расстрелять.

11. т.Косиор С. - Исключить из состава кандидатов ЦК ВКП(б) и членов ВКП(б), предать суду, без применения расстрела.

Two-page protocol of the Central Committee Commission on the fates of Bukharin and Rykov, with edits and variations from Stalin's proposal. 27 February 1937

206 *33*

– 2 –

12. т.Петровский – Исключить из состава кандидатов ЦК ВКП(б) и
членов ВКП(б), предать суду, без применения
расстрела.

13. т.Литвинов – Т о ж е.

14. т.Крупская – За предложение т.Сталина.

15. Косарев – Исключить из состава кандидатов ЦК ВКП(б) и
членов ВКП(б), предать суду и расстрелять.

16. т.Якир – Т о ж е.

17. т.Варейкис – за предложение т.Сталина.

18. т.Молотов – за предложение т.Сталина.

19. т.Ворошилов – за предложение т.Сталина.

П о с т а н о в и л и :

1) Исключить из состава кандидатов ЦК ВКП(б) и членов ВКП(б)
Бухарина и Рыкова; суду их не предавать, а ~~передать НКВД~~ *направить дело будет*
и род.
(Принято единогласно). *в НКВД*

2) Поручить комиссии в составе т.т.Сталина, Молотова, Воро-
шилова, Кагановича, Микояна и Ежова выработать на основе принятого
решения проект мотивированной резолюции.

ПРЕДСЕДАТЕЛЬ

the charges against him, it would be half a year before Stalin brought him
to the dock.

Could it have been that Stalin put off destroying him for personal reasons? Although personal affection seems unlikely from such a calculating
political monster, certainly treatment of no other repressed oppositionist
was moderated so many times at Stalin's initiative. Even after Bukharin's
arrest, his wife was allowed to live in her apartment in the Kremlin for several months. Stalin personally intervened to prevent her eviction. About
the time Bukharin began to confess in the summer of 1937, she was given
the option to live in any of five cities outside Moscow; she picked As-

trakhan. Although according to Beria, Yezhov wanted to have her shot along with other "wives of enemies of the people," Stalin refused.[41] Ultimately, however, she spent many years in exile. There is no doubt that Stalin had instigated or authorized Yezhov's campaign against the rightists. It could never have gone so far without Stalin's continued support. But when and to what degree would Bukharin be destroyed? It is entirely possible that Stalin himself had not decided exactly what to do with Bukharin and Rykov. As we noted earlier, as long as these former lieutenants lived, Stalin's political options remained open and the futures of his present lieutenants remained in doubt. By once again postponing a final decision on Bukharin, Stalin maintained the mystery about his true intentions, or even whether he had himself decided them.

Stalin's position also maintained maximum flexibility. He had not publicly or wholeheartedly associated himself with Yezhov's charges and had taken an almost neutral stance at the plenum; he gave Bukharin and Rykov unprecedented time to answer the charges, and in comparison with the other speakers, his demeanor seemed balanced and evenhanded. The minutes of the plenum's deliberations on Bukharin and Rykov were never circulated even to senior regional party officials. Only those present knew what had been said, and given Stalin's reticence and ambiguous stance, not even they were sure what he wanted. Even now, his proposal implied that the matter was not proved and needed to be checked further.

As in December 1936, his move to postpone implicitly cast doubt on Yezhov's investigation to date, and it was not inconceivable that he could change course at any time. Indeed, at the end of 1938, Stalin would remove Yezhov, disavow his excesses, order the arrest of the purgers, and release a number of those "falsely arrested." As long as Bukharin's death did not have Stalin's official stamp, as long as he postponed a decision, such a reversal was possible. Bukharin could be released and Yezhov and the purgers arrested. Stranger things could and did happen in this period.

Bukharin and Rykov were arrested at the plenum and sent to prison, yet it would be more than a year, March 1938, before they were brought to trial. For whatever reason, the Bukharin affair resembled the Yenukidze and Postyshev cases. In all three instances, the victims were personal friends of Stalin's who were ultimately executed. But in each of these cases, the road to the execution cellar was characterized by hesitation and false starts directly attributable to Stalin. Even today, when we have a mass of revealing documents, the story remains unclear. As with any highly skilled politician, his maneuvers, his personal and political motives, remain hidden.

CHAPTER EIGHT

The Storm of 1937:
The Party Commits Suicide

All kulaks, criminals and other anti-Soviet elements subject to punitive measures are broken down into two categories: a) To the first category belong all the most active of the above-mentioned elements. They are subject to immediate arrest and, after consideration of their case by the troikas, to be shot.—NKVD Operational Order, 1937

We did not trust; that's the thing.—V. M. Molotov

THE FEBRUARY–MARCH 1937 plenum also marked the beginnings of a purge of the police. Although Yezhov had taken over leadership of the NKVD from Yagoda the previous September, most of Yagoda's senior deputies and appointees were still in place. These NKVD officials were professionals, having served in the police since the Civil War, and removing such people unceremoniously would be disruptive and politically difficult. Not only were they entrenched political players of the nomenklatura, but their removal could raise inconvenient questions: if Yagoda and company were to be directly branded as longtime incompetents (or worse), as was becoming the fashion, the long series of political persecutions and prosecutions (against Mensheviks, Trotskyists, kulaks, and other opponents) could be called into question. When Yagoda had been replaced, therefore, his political loyalty had not been disputed, and he had been given the position of Commissar of Communications. Removing such people was a delicate and high-level political decision requiring considerable preparation and "political education."

"Strengthening" the NKVD, Again

Yezhov chose the February–March plenum as the venue for attack. The agenda contained the item "Lessons of the Wrecking, Diversion, and Espionage of the Japanese-German-Trotskyist Agents," for which Yezhov was slated to give the main report, a denunciation of Yagoda's management of the NKVD. Since the middle of 1936, when Yezhov had summoned NKVD Deputy Commissar Yakov Agranov to a "conspiratorial meeting," Yezhov had been trying to turn Yagoda's deputies against him.[1] By early 1937 he had succeeded in "turning" several central and regional NKVD officials. In preparation for the attack he was to give at the plenum, this new "Yezhov group" within the police received special invitations to attend.[2]

Yezhov's report attacked Yagoda's leadership indirectly by focusing on the sins of his Deputy Molchanov, former chief of the Secret Political Department of the NKVD. The plenum unanimously approved a resolution closely based on Yezhov's report.[3] Yagoda attempted to defend himself by refuting the charges of lax leadership and by claiming that he had in fact taken the lead in investigating and arresting Trotskyists. One of Yezhov's new followers, Leningrad NKVD chief Leonid Zakovsky, took the lead in attacking Yagoda and Molchanov: "We heard what I would consider a very incoherent speech by Comrade Yagoda, our former Commissar for Internal Affairs and I believe that the Plenum of the Central Committee of the Party cannot be satisfied with it. First of all, Comrade Yagoda's speech contained many errors, very incorrect, inexact [assertions], and I would add, no political [assessment]. It is not true that Yagoda's hands were tied and that he could not manage the apparat of state security."[4]

Yakov Agranov had been named Yezhov's deputy commissar of the NKVD in the same 1936 Politburo resolution appointing Yezhov, and Yezhov had used Agranov to undermine Yagoda for some time. Agranov had tried to work both sides of the street by implementing Yezhov's directives in such a way so as not to offend Yagoda. He now came under attack for this ambiguity and did his best to defend himself.[5]

> Comrades! It is absolutely clear that the old leadership of the NKVD has turned out to be incapable of managing state security.
>
> The Central Committee of our Party acted wisely in placing Comrade Yezhov, Secretary of the CC of our Party, at the head of the NKVD.
>
> The person to head the militant organ of the proletarian dictatorship ought to be someone invested with the full trust of the Party of Lenin and Stalin.

The appointment of Comrade Yezhov has cleared the air with its strong, bracing Party spirit.[6]

The attack on Yagoda had been strong, but inexplicable delays surround his downfall. At the end of the discussion, an especially aggressive member, I. P. Zhukov, called directly for Yagoda's arrest. Zhukov was always trying to display his vigilance, and his attacks on Bukharin had been so wild as to elicit laughter from the plenum. Now he went beyond the script and had to be restrained:

> ZHUKOV: Because this business needs to be investigated, and in order to investigate it, it is necessary to give instructions to the NKVD, to Comrade Yezhov. He will conduct the matter perfectly—(noise in the hall)
> VOICE: I don't understand. What is the proposal?
> YEZHOV: Everybody is arrested.
> ZHUKOV: Why not arrest Yagoda? (noise in the hall) Yes, yes. I am convinced that the matter will come to that.
> KOSIOR: What is your proposal? (movement and noise in the hall)
> VOICE: What is the proposal? It's not necessary to agree to anything.[7]

Yagoda was neither expelled from the party nor arrested by the plenum. Yet one month later, the Politburo ordered this very thing. When that order was produced, the text contained a note of unusual urgency about arresting the former NKVD chief that seemed to contradict the plenum's hesitation to take the step just a few weeks before. It is likely that in the intervening weeks, Molchanov and others from Yagoda's circle had been arrested and forced to give testimony implicating their former boss in "criminal activities."

Even after the decision was taken to expel and arrest Yagoda, there seems to have been some indecision. The expulsion order exists in two variants, the first a routine dismissal but the second (signed by Stalin) expressing the urgent need for his arrest: "The Politburo of the CC of the VKP(b) undertakes to inform the members of the CC of the VKP that, in view of the danger of leaving Yagoda at liberty for so much as one day, it is compelled to order his immediate arrest."[8] Even then, he was not dismissed from his position as commissar for communications for another week.[9]

In the days following Yagoda's arrest, Yezhov began shifting around regional and central NKVD personnel in order to put his loyal followers into key positions. He also began a series of "mobilizations" of dependable cadres to staff the NKVD, drawing them from the ideological party schools.

Cadres in Trouble: After the February–March Plenum

The February–March plenum had written a new political transcript for the party. It had raised the level of "vigilance" against oppositionists and enemies to new heights and established the principle that the enemy was everywhere. It had also criticized the regional nomenklatura for not being vigilant enough to prevent infiltration by those enemies. These regional bosses were taken to task for bureaucratism, suppression of criticism, undemocratic practices, and paying too much attention to economic management.

In the precise texts of the plenum, these themes were discrete: the opposition was the enemy, but the cadres were just careless. The enemy had to be destroyed, but poor cadres should be retrained and indoctrinated. In the wake of the plenum, however, these themes began to blur together. Partly as a result of the new campaign of "criticism from below," incompetent, abusive, or unpopular party leaders in the provinces were more and more often branded as enemies themselves. Carelessly tolerating the enemy became protecting the enemy. Suppression of the rank and file gradually became Trotskyist sabotage of party norms. Not catching a wrecker became wrecking. Reports on the February–March 1937 plenum to local organizations show the increasing paranoia and vigilance. The stated differences between Trotskyists and rightists and among various foreign enemies ran together in the popular mind, and there was now talk of "Japanese-German-Rightist-Trotskyists."

That the regional party leaders were coming more and more under a cloud following the February–March 1937 plenum is clear from several events. On the basis of a speech by A. A. Zhdanov, the Central Committee ordered regional party leaders to stand for reelection in May. Heretofore, such elections had been purely a formality; balloting was not secret, and the regional leaders were able to keep their people in power because no one below was willing to oppose their candidates openly. This time, though, the rules were different. The elections were to be held by secret ballot, and it seems to have been the intention of the Moscow leaders to take advantage of rank-and-file party hostility to their local chiefs in order to control those chiefs "from below" with an election. If the party elections of May 1937 were meant to dethrone territorial party leaders, they were a failure. Although there was significant turnover in district and cell committees, the upper reaches of the regional party elite remained in office through the spring of 1937.[10]

A second, less publicized event was just as important. Another of the mechanisms that regional "family circles" had used to protect themselves was the inclusion of the local NKVD chief in the machine. Although nominally the provincial NKVD reported to Moscow, it was more often than not part of the local party group. As long as the long-serving NKVD chiefs remained in place, they tended to defend party leaders who were being criticized from below.[11] There were few arrests of prominent local party machine members, and police persecution fell on ordinary people for minor offenses. In the spring of 1937 this began to change as Yezhov quietly replaced and transferred the existing provincial NKVD leaders. At the same time, party organizations inside the security services were transferred from the control of the territorial party committees to that of the police themselves, thereby detaching local NKVD officials from those committees.[12]

The Explosion

On 11 June 1937 the world was shocked by the Soviet press announcement that eight of the most senior officers of the Red Army had been arrested and indicted for treason and espionage on behalf of the Germans and Japanese. The list included the most well-known field commanders in the Soviet military: Marshal M. N. Tukhachevsky (deputy commissar of defense) and Generals S. I. Kork (commandant of the Frunze Military Academy), I. E. Yakir (commander of the Kiev Military District), and I. P. Uborevich (commander of the Belorussian Military District), among others. Arrested the last week of May, the generals were brutally interrogated by the NKVD and had "confessed" by the beginning of June. On 2 June a meeting of 116 high-ranking officers heard reports by Defense Commissar K. I. Voroshilov and Stalin on the case. At that meeting, Stalin said that "without a doubt a military-political conspiracy against Soviet power had taken place, stimulated and financed by German fascists."[13] On 12 June, at an expanded session of the Military Collegium of the Supreme Court, all were convicted. They were shot on the same day.[14] Yan Gamarnik, chief of the Political Administration of the Red Army, had committed suicide before he could be arrested.

We do not know why Stalin decided to decapitate the Red Army in 1937. Several possible elements may have contributed to the decision. First, Tukhachevsky and the other accused had frequently disagreed with Stalin's loyal but incompetent minister of defense, Voroshilov, and on at least one occasion had openly insulted him. Second, rumors had reached Stalin from Europe (apparently along with disinformation documents from the German secret police) to the effect that Tukhachevsky and his group were disloyal. Third, relations between party and army in the Soviet system had always been rocky. From time to time, the party had appointed "political commissars" to watch over the officer corps; such political watchdogs had been installed just before the arrest of the generals.[15] Members of the Tukhachevsky group were not "party first, army second" personalities like Voroshilov, Semen Budenny, and others who had fought alongside Stalin in the Civil War. Finally, of course, the army was an armed, organized force that could conceivably challenge Stalin and the party regime for control of the country.

The officers had been under suspicion for some time. Both Stalin and Molotov had mentioned at the February–March plenum that it would be necessary to verify [*proverit'*] the military to weed out any enemies. The previous year, Yezhov had arrested and had questioned for months a few military officers who had been active Trotskyists at some time in the past. In the spring of 1937 the investigators had focused on securing testimony against Tukhachevsky and his circle. It seems that several things came together in April–May 1937: the possible receipt of the disinformation documents from Germany and the confessions of V. M. Primakov and other Trotskyist officers directly implicating Tukhachevsky.

There is reason to believe that military commanders doubted at first that the military plot was real. In early June, Stalin addressed a meeting of top military men and rather convincingly made the case for Tukhachevsky's treason. In the course of his argument, he implied that there had been some doubts among military men that had to be cleared up: "Comrades, I hope that now nobody doubts that there was a military-political conspiracy against Soviet power."[16] In 1971 and 1975 V. M. Molotov admitted that many "mistakes" had been made in the repressions of the 1930s. But he doggedly insisted that of all the cases, that of Tukhachevsky and the generals had been clear: they were guilty of preparing a coup against Stalin. "Beginning in the second half of 1936 or maybe from the end of 1936 he was hurrying with a coup. . . . And it is understandable. He was

afraid that he would be arrested. . . . We even knew the date of the coup."[17]
Both in public and in private, Stalin certainly acted as if he believed the
military plot was real. In 1937, in private conversation with Georgi Dimitrov, head of the Communist International, Stalin said of the oppositionists, "We were aware of certain facts as early as last year and were preparing to deal with them, but first we wanted to seize as many threads as
possible. They were planning an action for the beginning of this year.
Their resolve failed. *They were preparing in July to attack the Politburo at
the Kremlin.* But they lost their nerve—they said: 'Stalin will start shooting and there will be a scandal.' I would tell our people—they will never
make up their minds to act, and I would laugh at their plans."[18]

Given the discipline of the nomenklatura behind Stalin, the army had
been the last force capable of stopping the arrests. Bukharin, under arrest
since March, may have realized this. Just before his arrest, he apparently
told his wife that the current leadership wanted to destroy the Old Bolshevik oppositionists for fear that if they came to power, they would destroy
the Stalinist faction. He advised her that in the event of his arrest, she
should flee the country with the help of the American diplomat William C.
Bullit, who had promised to help.[19] Later his wife was taunted by an
NKVD interrogator: "You thought that Yakir and Tukhachevsky would
save your Bukharin. But we work well. That's why it didn't happen."[20]
Nine days after the arrest of Tukhachevsky and Yakir, Bukharin wrote to
Yezhov from prison and began to confess.[21]

May 1937, when the generals and several powerful civilian figures were
arrested, represents a major watershed in the 1930s. This was the first
time that large numbers of people were repressed who had never been
overt oppositionists, and who had always sided with Stalin in the various
party disputes. The new policy in the second half of 1937 was, essentially,
to destroy anyone suspected of present or possible future disloyalty to the
ruling Stalin group. As Molotov put it,

> 1937 was necessary. . . . We were obligated in 1937 [to ensure] that in time of
> war there would be no fifth column. . . . I don't think that the rehabilitation
> [by Khrushchev] of many military men, repressed in 1937, was correct. The
> documents are hidden now, but with time there will be clarity. It is doubtful
> that these people were spies, but they were connected with spies, and the main
> thing is that in the decisive moment there was no relying on them. . . . If
> Tukhachevsky and Yakir and Rykov and Zinoviev in time of war went into op-
> position, it would cause such a sharp struggle, there would be a colossal num-

ber of victims. Colossal. And on the other hand, it would mean doom. It would be impossible to surrender, it [the internal struggle] would go to the end. We would begin to destroy everyone mercilessly. Somebody would, of course, win in the end, but on both sides there would be huge casualties.[22]

There is no evidence that the accused officers were involved in any plot against Stalin, despite rumors to the contrary.[23] Yet the regime acted as if leaders believed that there was a plot, or at least as if they feared retaliation from some corner. All the officers were arrested in transit, secretly, away from their commands. Tolerating no delay, Yezhov's investigators tortured the officers mercilessly until they confessed. Analysis many years later showed that there were bloodstains on the confession signed by Tukhachevsky.[24] On the day of the trial investigators were still beating confessions out of the accused, who were shot immediately after sentencing. Unlike the long delays with Bukharin and some others, this was a Stalin-Yezhov coup that was presented to the country as a fait accompli.

The laconic party documents marking their party expulsion do not capture the drama and brutality of the event: "The Central Committee has received information implicating CC Member Rudzutak and CC Candidate Member Tukhachevsky in participation in an anti-Soviet Trotskyist-Rightist conspiratorial bloc and in espionage work against the USSR on behalf of fascist Germany. In connection with this, the Politburo of the CC VKP(b) puts to a vote to members and candidate members of the CC VKP(b) the proposal to expel Rudzutak and Tukhachevsky from the party and transfer their cases to the NKVD."[25]

The archives are filled with such documents, each legally required in order to expel a Central Committee member from the party before arrest. Clearly, though, it is legalism at work here and not legality. First, Rudzutak and Tukhachevsky were no longer referred to as "comrade" in the document proposing their expulsion. Procedures required referring to them as "comrades" up to the time of their official expulsion from the party. Second, this action was taken before any trial or formal accusation, or even before the "information" could be evaluated. In the atmosphere of 1937, simply "receiving information" was enough for the Politburo to seal one's fate. As was always the case in 1937, every member and candidate member of the Central Committee once again held to nomenklatura discipline and voted in favor of the resolution. Even Lenin's widow, Krupskaia, who sometimes qualified her vote by answering "agreed" rather than "for," voted "for" in this case.[26]

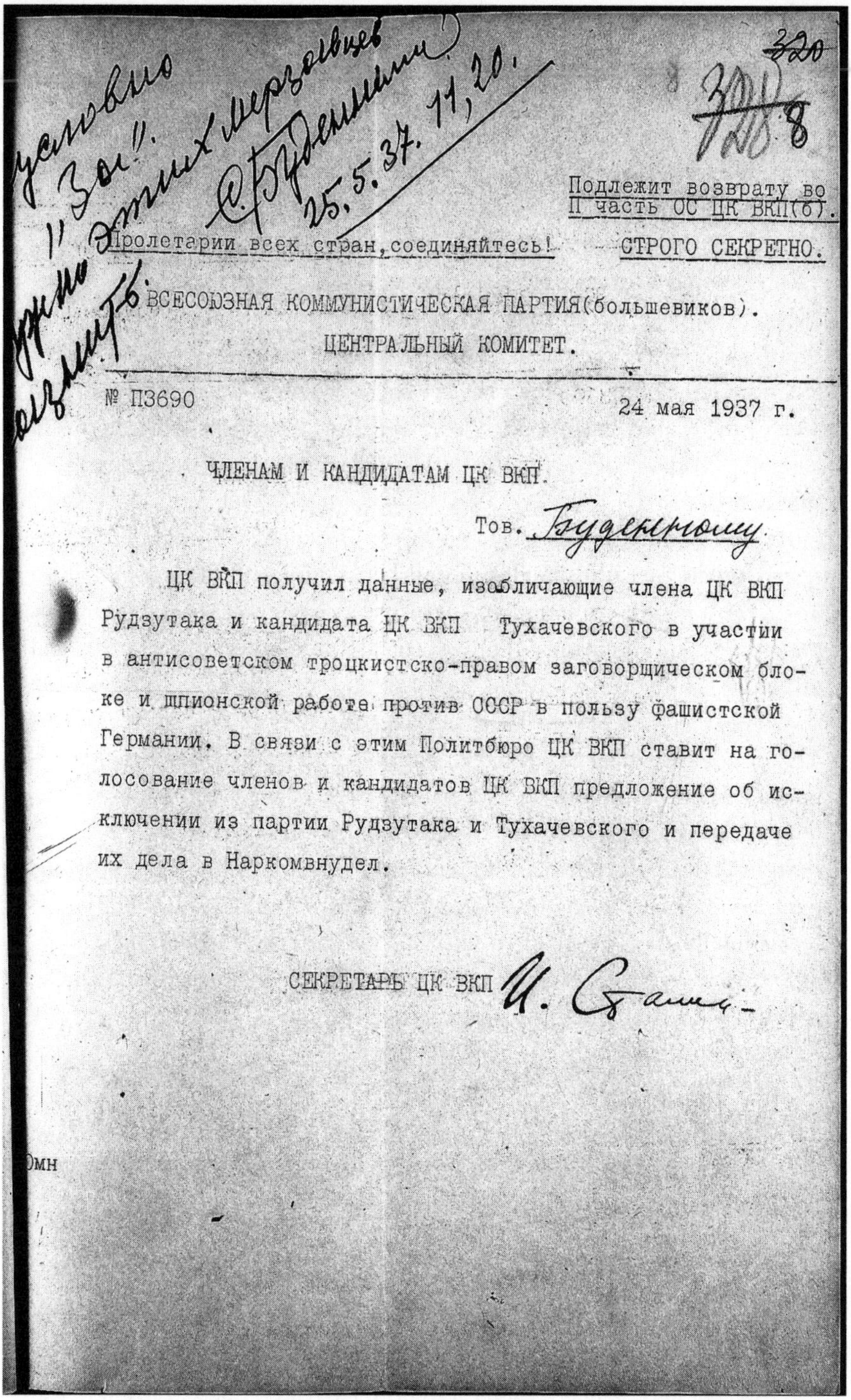

Note: handwritten marginal notes

[Handwritten note in top left margin:] условно "За"! Только этих мерзавцев нужно казнить

[Handwritten signature:] С. Будённый 25.5.37. 11,20.

Подлежит возврату во
II часть ОС ЦК ВКП(б).

Пролетарии всех стран, соединяйтесь! — СТРОГО СЕКРЕТНО.

ВСЕСОЮЗНАЯ КОММУНИСТИЧЕСКАЯ ПАРТИЯ(большевиков).

ЦЕНТРАЛЬНЫЙ КОМИТЕТ.

№ П3690   24 мая 1937 г.

ЧЛЕНАМ И КАНДИДАТАМ ЦК ВКП.

Тов. *Будённому.*

     ЦК ВКП получил данные, изобличающие члена ЦК ВКП Рудзутака и кандидата ЦК ВКП Тухачевского в участии в антисоветском троцкистско-правом заговорщическом блоке и шпионской работе против СССР в пользу фашистской Германии. В связи с этим Политбюро ЦК ВКП ставит на голосование членов и кандидатов ЦК ВКП предложение об исключении из партии Рудзутака и Тухачевского и передаче их дела в Наркомвнудел.

            СЕКРЕТАРЬ ЦК ВКП *И. Стали—*

Омн

Politburo ballot to expel Tukhachevsky and Rudzutak from the party and send their cases to the police. Semen Budenny's copy with his marginal note: "Unconditionally yes. It is necessary to finish off this scum." 24 May 1937

In the ten days following the death of Tukhachevsky, 980 senior commanders were arrested. Many were tortured and shot. In the coming months the Soviet military establishment was devastated by arrests and executions. In 1937, 7.7 percent of the officer corps were dismissed for political reasons and never reinstated; in 1938 another 3.7 percent were removed. In 1937 and 1938, according to the latest estimates, more than 34,000 military officers were discharged for political reasons. Of these, 11,596 were reinstated by 1940, leaving the fate of more than 22,000 officers unknown; they either were arrested or retired.[27] In the wake of Stalin's coup against the military, special service was duly rewarded, and on 24 July, Yezhov received the Order of Lenin "for outstanding success in leading the organs of the NKVD in the implementation of government assignments."[28]

The fall of the generals triggered an explosion of terror nationwide directed at leading cadres in all fields and at all levels. In the second half of 1937, most people's commissars (ministers), nearly all regional first party secretaries, and thousands of other officials were branded as traitors and arrested. The majority of these high-ranking officials seem to have been shot in 1937–40.[29] Several times per week throughout 1937, NKVD chief Yezhov forwarded to Stalin interrogation transcripts in which senior officials confessed to treason and named their fellow "conspirators." In nearly all cases, Stalin ordered the arrest of those named.[30]

Stalin had finally decided. If there had been indecision in the previous period about repression of some leaders, there was none now. If Stalin had seemed neutral or less than enthusiastic about repressing certain people, after the fall of the generals his name is all over the documents authorizing the terror. As usual, the remaining members of the CC voted unanimously for the proposed expulsions from the party:

> The CC of the VKP(b) declares its lack of political confidence in Comrades Alekseev, Liubimov, Sulimov, members of the CC of the VKP(b), and in Comrades Kuritsyn, Musabekov, Osinsky and Sedelnikov, candidate members of the CC of the VKP(b), and hereby decrees:
>
> That Comrades P. Alekseev, Liubimov and Sulimov be expelled from membership in the CC of the VKP(b) and that Comrades Kuritsyn, Musabekov, Osinsky and Sedelnikov be expelled from candidate membership in the CC of the VKP(b).
>
> Re: Antipov, Balitsky, Zhukov, Knorin, Lavrentev, Lobov, Razumov, Rumiantsev, Sheboldaev, Blagonravov, Veger, Goloded, Kalmanovich, Koma-

Карточка учета рассылки и возврата протокола ПБ №

От ___ из 124 голосовало 128. ___

КОМУ ПОСЛАН	Расписка в получении	Отметка о возврате	№№ экземп.	КОМУ ПОСЛАН	Расписка в получении	Отметка о возврате
Чл. ЦК ВКП(б)			45	Носову	за. т-ма 729/ш	
Алексееву	за. т-ма 811/ш		46	Орджоникидзе		
Андрееву	за. т-ма 791/ш		47	Петровскому	за. т-ма 825/ш	
Антипову	за. Выл.		48	Постышеву	за. т-ма 805/ш	
Бадаеву	за. Выл.		49	Пятакову		
Балицкому	за. Выл.		50	Пятницкому	за. Выт.	
Бауману	за. Выл.		51	Разумову	за. т-ма 800/ш.	
Берия	за. т-ма 787/ш		52	Рудзутаку	за. Выл.	
Бубнову	за. Выл.		53	Румянцеву	за. Выл. 784/ш	
Варейкису	за. т-ма 813/ш		54	Рухимовичу	за. Выт.	
Ворошилову	за. Выт.		55	Рындину	за. т-ма 819/ш	
Гамарнику	за. Выл.		56	Сталину	за. См. ориг. голос	
Евдокимову	за. т-ма 802/ш		57	Стецкому	за. Выл.	
Ежову	за. Выл.		58	Сулимову	за. Выл.	
Енукидзе			59	Уханову		
Жданову	за. См. ориг. голос.		60	Хатаевичу	за. т-ма 817/ш	
Жукову	за. Выл.		61	Хрущеву	за. Выл.	
Зеленскому	за. Выт.		62	Чернову	за. Выл.	
Иванову	за. Выт.		63	Чубарю	за. Выт.	
Икрамову	за. Выт.		64	Чувырину	за. т-ма 811/ш	
Кабанову			65	Чудову	за. Выт.	
Кагановичу Л.	за. Выл.		66	Швернику	за. Выл.	
Кагановичу М.	за. Выл.		67	Шеболдаеву	за. т-ма 801/ш	
Калинину	за. См. ориг. голос		68	Эйхе	за. т-ма 793/ш	
Кирову			69	Ягода		
Кнорину	за. Выл.		70	Якиру	за. Выл.	
Кодацкому	за. Выл.		71	Яковлеву Я.	за. Выл.	
Косареву	за. Выл.					
Косиору Ст.	за. т-ма 794/ш			**Кандидатам в ЦК**		
Косиору И.	не посылалось		72	Багирову	за. т-ма 814/ш	
Кржижановскому	за. Выл.		73	Благонравову	за. Выл.	
Криницкому	за. т-ма 790/ш		74	Блюхеру	за. т-ма 813/ш	
Крупской	Согласна. Выл.		75	Буденному	за. Выл.	
Куйбышеву			76	Булганину	за. Выл.	
Лаврентьеву	за. т-ма 785/ш		77	Булину	за. Выт.	
Лебедю	за. Выл.		78	Бухарину Н. И.		
Литвинову	за. Выл.		79	Бройдо	за. Выл.	
Лобову	за. Выл.		80	Быкину	за. т-ма 786/ш	
Любимову	за. Выл.		81	Вегеру	за. т-ма 796/ш	
Мануильскому	за. Выл.		82	Вейнбергу	за. Выт.	
Межлауку В.	за. Выл.		83	Гикало	за. т-ма 812/ш	
Микояну	за. Выл.		84	Голодеду	за. т-ма 806/ш	
Мирзояну	за. т-ма 804/ш		85	Гринько	за. Выл.	
Молотову	за. Выл.		86	Грядинскому	за. т-ма 793/ш	
Николаевой	за. Выл.		87	Демченко	за. Выт.	

Politburo ballot tally on expulsion of K. Ukhanov, with Lenin's widow voting "agreed" instead of "for." 20 May 1937 rov, Kubiak, V. Mikhailov, Polonsky, N. N. Popov, Unshlikht, Aronshtam, Krutov.

The following motion by the Politburo of the CC is to be confirmed.

The following persons are to be expelled for treason to the Party and motherland and for active counter-revolutionary activities:

[a] Antipov, Balitsky, Zhukov, Knorin, Lavrentev, Lobov, Razumov, Rumiantsev and Sheboldaev are to be expelled from membership in the CC of the VKP(b) and from the Party;

[b] Blagonravov, Veger, Goloded, Kalmanovich, Komarov, Kubiak, V. Mikhailov, Polonsky, N. N. Popov and Unshlikht are to be expelled from candidate membership in the CC of the VKP(b) and from the Party;

[c] Aronshtam and Krutov are to be expelled from membership in the Central Inspection Commission and from the Party.

[d] The cases of the above-mentioned persons are to be referred to the NKVD.

In view of incontrovertible facts concerning their belonging to a counter-revolutionary group, Chudov and Kodatsky are to be expelled from membership in the CC of the VKP(b) and from the Party, and Pavlunovsky and Struppe are to be expelled from candidate membership in the CC of the VKP(b) and from the Party.[31]

This first list of Central Committee expulsions in June had included several leading regional party secretaries, including Rumiantsev from Smolensk, Sheboldaev from Kursk, and Chudov and Kodatsky from Leningrad. By the end of 1937 nearly all of the eighty regional party leaders had been replaced, including those of the union republics. Frequently they were blamed for economic and agricultural failures that occurred in 1936–37.[32]

Because expelling and removing a regional party secretary formally required a vote from his party organization, and because Stalin wished to mobilize rank-and-file party members against the midlevel leadership, these removals were conducted in a specific way. A high-ranking Politburo emissary was dispatched from Moscow to the provincial capital with instructions to "verify" the party leadership. A plenum of the regional party committee was called, with the emissary putting forward the charges against the regional leader and "his people." Typically, the local first secretary would speak (if he was still at liberty), then members of the local party committee would be unleashed to denounce their leader (which was now safe, in the presence of a big Moscow man), and finally the local leader would then be removed.[33]

For example, between June and September 1937, A. A. Andreev traveled to Voronezh, Cheliabinsk, Sverdlovsk, Kursk, Saratov, Kuibyshev, Tashkent, Rostov, and Krasnodar to remove the territorial leaderships.[34] At each stop, he was in telegraphic communication with Stalin, relaying to him the results of the plenums and the opinions of the local party members. Frequently Andreev recommended expelling and arresting the local leadership, and Stalin always approved these requests:

> Telegram from I. V. Stalin to A. A. Andreev in Saratov
>   The Central Committee agrees with your proposal to bring to court and shoot the former workers of the Machine Tractor Stations.
>   Stalin
>   28 July 1937[35]

The language used in both the reports and the replies indicates that both Andreev and Stalin actually believed they were uprooting real treason. In some cases, the matter was more doubtful, and Stalin proposed simply removing the regional secretary and sending him to Moscow, where, in almost all cases, he would be arrested.[36]

On several occasions, Andreev was accompanied by a central NKVD official to carry out the necessary arrests. In several places, Andreev told Stalin that the former local party leadership, through its control of the local NKVD, had arrested large numbers of innocent people. In Saratov, Andreev reported that the former ruling group had dictated false testimony for the signatures of those arrested; he blamed it on the "Agranov gang" within the NKVD. In Voronezh, Andreev complained that "masses" of innocent people had been expelled and arrested. With Stalin's approval, Andreev organized special troikas to review these cases—six hundred in Voronezh alone—and release those arrested by the now-condemned former leadership.[37]

The campaign for vigilance was now out of control, with officials at all levels denouncing each other and encouraging arrests to protect themselves. At the June 1937 plenum of the Central Committee, Yezhov gave an amazing speech in which he announced the discovery of a grand conspiracy that united leftists, rightists, Trotskyists, members of former socialist parties, army officers, NKVD officers, and foreign communists. This "center of centers," he said, consisted of thirteen discrete "anti-Soviet organizations" that had seized control of the army, military intelligence, the Comintern, and the commissariats of Foreign Affairs, Transport, and Agriculture. He claimed that the conspiracy had representatives in every provincial party administration and was thoroughly saturated with Polish and German spies. The Soviet government was said to be hanging by a thread.[38]

The archives currently available to us provide little in the way of personal correspondence between key leaders. Such private, hidden transcripts would provide important clues about the correlation between what the Stalinists said in public and what they confided to each other. The examples we do have, however, strongly suggest that there was little difference between the Stalinist leaders' private thoughts and public positions. It is, of course, difficult to know the inner thoughts of the top leaders about the degree of guilt of those they destroyed. But if their private correspondence is any gauge, they seem really to have believed in the existence of a far-flung conspiracy.

Stalin and Molotov took a personal hand in whipping up the hysteria. On several occasions they not only signed long lists of people to be shot but also encouraged terror in the provinces. Stalin wrote a series of circular letters containing passages like the following:

> I consider it absolutely necessary to politically mobilize members of the kolkhozy for a campaign aimed at inflicting a crushing defeat on enemies of the people in agriculture. The CC of the VKP(b) orders the provincial committees, the territorial committees and the CCs of the national Communist parties to organize, in each district of each province, two or three public show trials of enemies of the people/agricultural saboteurs who have wormed their way into district Party, Soviet and agricultural. These trials should be covered in their entirety by the local press.[39]

> With the aim of protecting the kolkhozy and sovkhozy from the sabotage of enemies of the people, the Council of People's Commissars of the USSR and the CC of the VKP(b) have decided to crush and annihilate the cadres of wreckers in the field of animal husbandry. . . .
>
> With this aim in mind, the Council of People's Commissars of the USSR and the CC of the VKP(b) propose that 3 to 6 open show trials be organized in each republic, region and province, that the broad masses of peasants be involved in them and that the trials be widely covered in the press.
>
> All persons convicted of sabotage are to be sentenced to death by execution, and reports of these executions are to be published in the local press.[40]

In the fall of 1937 the decimation of the Central Committee continued, with Stalin showing no hesitation or indecision:

Plenary Session of the Central Committee

11–12 October 1937

Comrade Stalin has the floor.

STALIN: The first question concerns membership in the CC. During the period between the June Plenum and the present Plenum several members of
   the CC were removed from the CC and arrested: Zelensky, who turned
   out to be a Tsarist secret police agent [okhrannik], Lebed', Nosov, Piatnitsky, Khataevich, Ikramov, Krinitsky, Vareikis—all together 8 persons.
   Examination and verification of all available materials have shown that
   these people are all enemies.

   If there are no questions [from the floor], I would like the Plenum to
   take this information under advisement.

VOICES: That's right. We have taken it under advisement.

STALIN: In addition, during this same period 16 persons were removed from
   the CC as candidate members and arrested: Grinko, Liubchenko,—who
   shot himself to death, Yeremin, Deribas,—who turned out to be a Japanese spy, Demchenko, Kalygina, Semenov, Serebrovsky,—who turned
   out to be a spy, Shubrikov, Griadinsky, Sarkisov, Bykin, Rozengol'ts,—
   who turned out to be a German-English-Japanese spy.

VOICES: Wow!

STALIN: Lepa, Gikalo and Ptukha—all together 16 persons. An investigation and verification of materials available showed that these people [the
   16 persons above] were also enemies of the people. If there are no questions or objections [from the floor], I would like for the Plenum to take
   this information also under advisement.

VOICES: Let's approve it.

ANDREEV: There is a motion on the floor to approve the Politburo's proposal. Any objections?

VOICES: None.

ANDREEV: (voting) Adopted unanimously.[41]

As had always been the case, the members of the Central Committee
quickly and, as a group, suicidally voted unanimously each time to expel
those designated as enemies.[42] These arrests of Central Committee members proceeded over more than a year's time. At no point was it clear to
anyone how far the process would go; each member at a given moment
probably thought that despite the spreading arrests, he was not an enemy
and was therefore safe. As the episode was recalled in 1975,

MOLOTOV: In the first place, on democratic centralism . . . Listen, it did not
   happen that a minority expelled a majority. It happened gradually. 70 ex-

pelled 10–15 people, then 60 expelled another 15. All in line with majority
and minority.

CHUEV: This indicates an excellent tactic but it doesn't indicate rectitude.

MOLOTOV: But permit me to say that it corresponds with the factual development of events, and not simply tactics. Gradually things were disclosed in a
sharp struggle in various areas. Someplace it was possible to tolerate: to be
restrained even though we didn't trust [someone]. Someplace it was impossible to wait. And gradually, all was done in the order of democratic
centralism, without formal violation. Essentially, it happened that a minority of the composition of the TsK remained of this majority, but without formal violation. Thus there was no violation of democratic centralism, it happened gradually although in a fairly rapid process of clearing the
road.[43]

Finally, there was the strong pull of party tradition and democratic centralism, the feeling that the nomenklatura had to remain unified, to hang
together even as they were hanging separately. In the name of party unity
and with a desperate feeling of corporate self-preservation, the nomenklatura committed suicide. They also contributed to their own destruction
by pushing things in the direction of mass terror.

A Blind, Mass Terror

We have seen that various leaders had tried to protect themselves by ordering mass expulsions and arrests of rank-and-file party members. In
turn, the rank and file denounced their bosses as enemies. It was a war of
all against all, with intraparty class and status overtones. As an unrepentant Molotov later recalled, "In our system, if you conducted some kind of
campaign, you conducted it to the end. And all kinds of things can happen
when everything is on such a scale."[44]

From mid-1937 to nearly the end of 1938, the Soviet secret police carried out a mass terror against ordinary citizens. These "mass operations,"
as they were called, accounted for about half of all executions during the
"Great Purges" of 1937–38. By the time it ended in November 1938,
767,397 persons had been sentenced by summary troikas; 386,798 of
them to death and the remainder to terms in GULAG camps.[45] Other
"mass operations" in 1937–38 targeted persons of non-Soviet citizenship
or national heritage, including Poles, Germans, Latvians, Koreans, Chinese, and others, accounting for an additional 335,513 sentences (includ-

ing 247,157 executions).[46] The process included systematic, physical tortures of a savage nature and scale, fabricated conspiracies, false charges, and mass executions. As such, the operations of 1937–38 must be counted among the major massacres of a bloody twentieth century.

Since the 8 May 1933 decree discussed above, the trend had been to reduce mass campaigns of political repression, and a variety of official statements by Stalin and Yezhov denounced mass operations. Such mass campaigns were unleashed rather than administered, heavy-handed and blunt instruments that frequently damaged rational policy planning (and Stalin's power) as much as they accomplished his goals. For Stalin, operating in campaign mode meant ceding central control, inviting chaos, and trusting the fate and reputation of the regime to far-off local authorities. When sufficient progress had been made, or when things had gone too far, it was necessary to restore order and rein in the chaos, and much of prewar Stalinist history is told in the flow and ebb, the launching and restraining of campaigns. Thus, for example, cleaning up the "campaign justice" of the collectivization period and restoring centralized order required checking the power of local political officials.[47]

Mass operations in 1933–36 were on a dramatically reduced scale, not comparable with those of the preceding period. According to secret police data, arrests for "counterrevolutionary insurrection" (a common charge in mass operations, including the subsequent kulak operation) fell from 135,000 in 1933 to 2,517 in 1936.[48] Despite the continuation of certain restricted mass operations, the era of mass repression seemed clearly on the wane. If Stalin had been trying to curb inefficient "mass operations," why then did he suddenly resort to them in the middle of 1937?

At that time, the Moscow leadership became afraid of threats in the countryside. In 1936 the USSR had adopted a new constitution that authorized the election of a new legislature, the Supreme Soviet. In June 1937 the Central Committee prescribed electoral procedures to enfranchise the entire adult population—including previously disenfranchised groups like former White officers, tsarist policemen, and kulaks—in a system of secret-ballot elections. These elections, according to the June 1937 decree, would be for contested seats, with multiple candidates campaigning. Local party leaders were horrified at Stalin's democratic experiment and complained to Moscow that the proposed Supreme Soviet elections were giving new hope and life to various anti-Bolshevik "class enemies" who sought to use the electoral campaign to organize legally.[49] Regional

party and NKVD leaders bombarded Moscow with stories of counterrevolutionary and "insurrectionary" groups taking shape in the countryside:
returning kulaks and other "anti-Soviet elements" encouraged by the possibility of free elections.[50]

At the February 1937 CC plenum, regional party secretaries made a
careful protest. Breaking with tradition, none of them signed up to speak
in the discussion of A. A. Zhdanov's report on democratic elections. Nor-
mally, at the conclusion of a main report to a Central Committee plenum,
speakers would register with the presidium to speak in the "discussion."
Typically, that discussion repeated the main points of the report and
praised the speaker for proposing "absolutely correct" solutions. But
when Zhdanov finished speaking about "party democracy," nobody registered or rose to speak. This had not happened in many years. A. A. Andreev, chairing the meeting, announced in despair, "I don't have anyone
registered. Somebody has to register." Regional secretary Robert Eikhe, of
Western Siberia, whined, "I can't; I'm not ready. I will speak tomorrow."
M. F. Shkiriatov wryly noted, "The orators have to prepare themselves."
Stalin pressed for someone to say something: "We need [at least] a provi-
sional conclusion." Finally, E. M. Yaroslavsky spoke up, "I ask to be registered." A delighted and relieved Stalin said, "There! Yaroslavsky!"[51]

Head of the League of the Militant Atheists, Yaroslavsky then held
forth on religion. Zhdanov's speech had mentioned the weakness of anti-
religious propaganda only in passing, as a typical failure of party work.
But Yaroslavsky's remarks gave the party secretaries a chance to complain
about their problems in the countryside and to warn of the danger of the
new electoral system, all in the context of "discussing" Zhdanov's speech
(which, according to accepted formula, they nevertheless praised). Party
secretaries had already blamed shortcomings in their regions on "contam-
ination" (zasorenie) by anti-Soviet elements.[52] They now warned that the
new electoral system gave anti-Soviet elements—religious and political—
"new possibilities to harm us" and would encourage attempts by enemies
to "conduct attacks against us, to organize a struggle against us."[53] S. V.
Kosior complained that thousands of religious believers were attending
religious-political "events" to cynically praise Stalin for their new rights.
Kosior went on to complain of "awful wildness, conservatism . . . fanatical religious sentiments that feed undisguised hatred of Soviet power."[54]

One noted that "We have a series of facts that harmful elements from
the remnants of the former kulaks and clergy, especially mullahs, are con-

ducting work among remnant groups and preparing for the elections. . . . It is clear that it is necessary to carry out a decisive struggle against these elements."[55] Another observed that "kulak elements, priests, sons of priests, sons of [tsarist] policemen . . . according to the new Constitution received electoral rights. They can vote. It seems to me that here we have to pay particular attention to the changes arising in the population which have gone on in each province."[56]

At CC plenums and in private correspondence, regional party leaders made plain their fear of and opposition to contested elections in the countryside. The dangerous idea of contested elections remained in force. But two weeks after the fall of the military leaders, as the arrests began to consume the middle and upper ranks of the party leadership, Stalin began grudgingly to hear the regional arguments about losing whatever control of the countryside they enjoyed to mysterious, hidden, "anti-Soviet elements."

Stalin needed local officials, even annoying and disobedient ones, to represent the regime and implement its policies out in the country. He needed to give them enough autonomy to do this, but without enough leeway to escape his authority or to go out of control and discredit the regime as a whole.[57] Implicitly or explicitly, he had to negotiate with them. Despite his elevation to semidivine status, he had to listen to their views and take their needs into account. These regional "feudal princes" or "red princes," as one scholar has called them, formed a cohesive interest group whose interests often contradicted Stalin's.[58]

After a series of disturbing reports from the provinces about "insurrectionary" organizations, on 28 June, Stalin and the Politburo finally approved a request from Robert Eikhe, the first secretary of the Western Siberian Territory (and the one who had pointedly refused to speak in support of Zhdanov's electoral ideas), to form an emergency troika with the right to pass death sentences.[59] In what would become a model for future troikas, it consisted of the heads of the provincial NKVD, party, and procuracy.[60] Four days later, eager to regularize, systematize, and control the procedure, Stalin sent a telegram to all provincial party and police agencies ordering the formation of troikas in each province with systematic reporting to him in Moscow.[61]

But Stalin was not yet willing to retreat from contested elections. He and his lieutenants continued to exhort regional party chiefs to campaign, to use propaganda to win the elections. And on 2 July 1937 *Pravda* no doubt disappointed the regional secretaries by publishing the first installment of the new electoral rules, officially enacting and enforcing contested, universal, secret-ballot elections.[62]

But Stalin now offered a compromise. The day the electoral law that so disturbed the regional leaders was published, the Politburo approved the launching of a mass operation against precisely the elements the local leaders had complained about, and hours later Stalin sent his telegram to provincial party leaders approving the formation of the lethal troikas.[63] It is hard to avoid the conclusion that in return for forcing the local party leaders to conduct an election, Stalin chose to help them win it by giving them license to kill or deport hundreds of thousands of "dangerous elements."[64]

Contemporaries immediately saw the link between the elections and the mass operations. Jailhouse informers in Tataria reported that those arrested in the mass operations thought that the Bolsheviks were afraid of the elections and had launched a preemptive strike out of concern that enemies would seize control of the voting in the districts.[65] Nikolai Bukharin, who was better placed to judge such things, praised mass terror in a letter to Stalin, noting that a general purge was in part connected with "the transition to democracy."[66] Three months later, in October, speakers at a Central Committee plenum would respond to Molotov's report on electoral preparations with comments on the mass operations. First Secretary Kontorin of Arkhangelsk said, "We asked and will continue to ask the Central Committee to increase our limits for the first category [executions] in connection with preparations for the elections."[67]

The Politburo therefore launched the "mass operations" of 1937–38 under pressure from regional party secretaries who feared the open elections. Many local officials may have been at least as quick to turn to repression as their boss in Moscow. It is not difficult to imagine that in 1937, local party leaders, fearful that they might be accused as "enemies of the people" in the spiraling terror of that year, would have found it convenient to launch repressive campaigns against others in order to deflect the witch hunt's heat away from themselves. Provincial party secretaries faced the brunt of anti-Bolshevik resistance on the ground, while trying to respond to unmeetable demands from Moscow on everything from agricultural deliveries to industrial production to construction to dissemination of propaganda. In the political space they inhabited, some of them may have found it easier to crush categories of people with "administrative-chekist" methods than to convince them with "political work," regardless of Moscow's current policy. For local leaders persecution was "a tool of rural administration."[68] In the Stalinist system, regional officials were not timid or liberal politicians, with the population's interests always at heart.[69]

Although it is clear that before June 1937 Stalin was not promoting mass operations, once he approved them he was determined to control them. A few days after his telegram, NKVD order no. 447 prescribed the summary execution of more than fifty-five thousand people who had committed no capital crime and were to be "swiftly" judged by extralegal organs without benefit of counsel or even formal charge. Their "trials" were to be purely formal; these victims were "after consideration of their case by the troikas, to be shot." An extract of the troika's minutes would form the only "legal" basis for the execution. Limits were established for each regional quota, and increases had to be approved by the Politburo. Although Stalin and Yezhov would approve almost all regional requests for increased execution limits, it is significant that these were in fact limits and not quotas. Not trusting the local party leaders to avoid hysterical massacres, Stalin was most determined to retain control over the operation.

Almost anyone could fall under one of the categories of victims: those committing "anti-Soviet activities," those in camps and prisons carrying out "sabotage," criminals, people whose cases were "not yet considered by the judicial organs," family members "capable of active anti-Soviet actions." It is also significant that round-number limits were established, with victims to be chosen by local party, police, and judicial officials according to their own lights. These limits do not correlate exactly with population; they rather seem to reflect a focus on sensitive economic areas where the regime believed the concentration of "enemies" to be the greatest, or where in previous trials and campaigns the greatest number of oppositionists had been unmasked. The regime was lashing out blindly at suspected concentrations of enemies.

This "operation," which would be extended into the next year, represented a reversion to the combative methods of the Civil War, when groups of hostages were taken and shot prophylactically or in blind retaliation. It also recalled the storm of dekulakization in 1929, when the regime was also unable to specify exactly who was the enemy and lashed out with mass deportation.[70] The new Red Terror of 1937, like its predecessors, reflected a deep-seated insecurity and fear of enemies on the part of the regime as well as an inability to say exactly who was the enemy, hence the round-number limits. Stalin and his associates knew there was opposition to the regime, feared that opposition (as well as their own inability to concretely identify or specify it), and decided to lash out brutally and wholesale. In this sense, the new Red Terror was an admission of the regime's inability to govern the countryside efficiently or predictably, or even to control it with anything other than periodic bursts of unfocused violence.

At first glance, it is perhaps surprising that the authors of this massacre would commit their plans to writing and would preserve the document in archives for future historians to find. On the other hand, the Bolshevik leadership believed they were right to "clean" the country of "alien elements." Although, as in the similarly worded documents on the mass executions of Polish officers in 1940, they never publicly stated what they had done, they were not afraid to create a text about their decision. They were not ashamed of what they were doing. In true bureaucratic fashion, a text, albeit a secret one, was produced: personnel, budgetary appropriations, and transportation were specified. The supplement to this document shows how this terror was administered according to the Bolsheviks' vision of economic rationality, and the text that follows is surely one of the most chilling documents in modern history:

OPERATIONAL ORDER
of the People's Commissar for Internal Affairs of the USSR. No. 00447 Concerning the punishment of former kulaks, criminals and other anti-Soviet elements.
30 July 1937. City of Moscow
It has been established by investigative materials relative to the cases of anti-Soviet formations that a significant number of former kulaks who had earlier been subjected to punitive measures and who had evaded them, who had escaped from camps, exile and labor settlements have settled in the countryside. This also includes many church officials and sectarians who had been formerly put down, former active participants of anti-Soviet armed campaigns. Significant cadres of anti-Soviet political parties (SR's, Georgian Mensheviks, Dashnaks, Mussavatists, Ittihadists, etc.) as well as cadres of former active members of bandit uprisings, Whites, members of punitive expeditions, repatriates and so on remain nearly untouched in the countryside. Some of the above-mentioned elements, leaving the countryside for the cities, have infiltrated enterprises of industry, transport and construction. Besides, significant cadres of criminals are still entrenched in both countryside and city. These include horse and cattle thieves, recidivist thieves, robbers and others who had been serving their sentences and who had escaped and are now in hiding. Inadequate efforts

to combat these criminal bands have created a state of impunity promoting their criminal activities. As has been established, all of these anti-Soviet elements constitute the chief instigators of every kind of anti-Soviet crimes and sabotage in the kolkhozy and sovkhozy as well as in the field of transport and in certain spheres of industry. The organs of state security are faced with the task of mercilessly crushing this entire gang of anti-Soviet elements, of defending the working Soviet people from their counter-revolutionary machinations and, finally, of putting an end, once and for all, to their base undermining of the foundations of the Soviet state. Accordingly, I therefore ORDER THAT AS OF 5 AUGUST 1937, ALL REPUBLICS, REGIONS AND PROVINCES LAUNCH A CAMPAIGN OF PUNITIVE MEASURES AGAINST FORMER KULAKS, ACTIVE ANTI-SOVIET ELEMENTS AND CRIMINALS. . . .

II. CONCERNING THE PUNISHMENT TO BE IMPOSED ON THOSE SUBJECT TO PUNITIVE MEASURES AND THE NUMBER OF PERSONS SUBJECT TO PUNITIVE MEASURES.

1. All kulaks, criminals and other anti-Soviet elements subject to punitive measures are broken down into two categories:

a) To the first category belong all the most active of the above-mentioned elements. They are subject to immediate arrest and, after consideration of their case by the troikas, to be shot.

b) To the second category belong all the remaining less active but nonetheless hostile elements. They are subject to arrest and to confinement in concentration camps for a term ranging from 8 to 10 years, while the most vicious and socially dangerous among them are subject to confinement for similar terms in prisons as determined by the troikas. . . .

IV. ORDER FOR CONDUCTING THE INVESTIGATION.

1. Investigation shall be conducted into the case of each person or group of persons arrested. The investigation shall be carried out in a swift and simplified manner. During the course of the trial, all criminal connections of persons arrested are to be disclosed.[71]

Unlike previous identifications of enemies, which often took the form of filling various symbols (Trotskyist, rightist) with new content, this operation was simply a mass killing not of categories (however attributed or defined) but of vague opponents. Without negotiating or defining who was to be involved, the operation sought to remove clumsy statistical slices of the population of each province. It was not targeting of enemies, but blind rage and panic. It reflected not control of events but a recognition that the regime lacked regularized control mechanisms. It was not policy but the failure of policy. It was a sign of failure to rule with anything but force.

Based on the sources now available (which are probably incomplete) we can say that with order no. 447 plus subsequent known limit increases, Moscow gave permission to shoot about 236,000 victims. We are fairly certain that some 386,798 persons were actually shot, leaving more than 150,000 shot without currently documented central sanction either from the NKVD or the Politburo.[72] The possibility exists that local authorities went far beyond the permitted limits, especially when it came to shooting victims. In Turkmenistan, for example, where we happen to have full data on all approvals, we know that the Politburo approved 3,225 executions, but local authorities shot 4,037, an excess of 25 percent over approved limits.[73] In Smolensk, archival research shows an approved limit of 4,000, but local authorities are known to have shot 4,500 and continued shooting victims even after a November 1938 decision ordering them to stop. They simply backdated the paperwork and continued shooting.[74] Some regional party chiefs were enthusiastic about the mass operations. First Secretary Simochkin in Ivanovo liked to watch the shootings and was curious about why some of his subordinates chose not to.[75] In Turkmenistan, First Secretary Chubin was so involved with the mass killings that in 1938 he tried to secure the recall of a new NKVD chief sent to stop them.[76]

All in all, the kulak operation of 1937–38 was hardly a model of planned efficiency, and the center's detailed orders were often disregarded. Soon after the operation began, it was necessary for Moscow NKVD chiefs to issue more telegrams clarifying procedures.[77] According to order no. 447, the operation was to begin with those to be executed, followed by a second stage encompassing those to be sent to camps. In the event, regional troikas sentenced victims to both categories simultaneously.[78] Order no. 447 had forbidden the persecution of families of those arrested; in the event, troikas did this frequently.[79] In fact, almost every restriction order no. 447 had placed on local conduct of the operation was violated in its implementation. Given that local authorities decided how many would be repressed, who would live, and who would die, it is difficult to agree that everything was "administered" from Moscow. Senior NKVD official Stanislav Redens said at a January 1938 NKVD conference, perhaps with some resignation, that the Moscow NKVD was able to give only "general directions" because regional secret police organizations acted "independently."[80]

The operation lasted not the mandated four months but fifteen, and in some places the shootings continued after the 17 November 1938 orders halting them and insisting on procuratorial sanction for all arrests.[81] More than a week after that, Yezhov's successor L. P. Beria was still issuing decrees to local NKVD offices to "immediately stop all mass operations" and repeating the strictures of the 17 November 1938 orders limiting the NKVD to individual arrests with procuratorial sanction.[82] Fully six months after that, USSR Procurator Vyshinsky complained to Stalin and Molotov that the NKVD still made arrests without that sanction.[83]

This was certainly a blind terror. Like a psychotic mass killer who begins shooting in all directions, the Stalinist center had little idea who would be killed. It opened fire on vague targets, giving local officials license to kill whomever they saw fit. The opposite of controlled, planned, directed fire, the mass operations were more like blind shooting into a crowd. The Stalinist regime resembled not so much a disciplined army as a poorly trained and irregular force of Red Cavalry, and the aftermath resembled the chaos of a battlefield, where the casualties bore only accidental resemblance to the originally intended victims both in number and type.

It is tempting to see the mass operations as part of a Stalinist plan for population policy or social engineering on a vast scale. Going beyond the modernist state's usual efforts to map, standardize, and enumerate society in order to control it, "authoritarian high-modernist states," to use James Scott's terminology, take the next step and use large-scale, concerted force to impose "legibility, appropriation, and centralization of control."[84] Seen this way, the mass operations would be a deliberate "modernist" attempt to cultivate society by weeding out or excising alien or infected elements by killing them or removing them permanently from the body social.

On the other hand, as we have seen, the mass operations were unplanned, ad hoc reactions to a perceived immediate political threat. Rather than a thought-out policy, modernist or otherwise, they recalled instead the Civil War reflex: a violent recourse to terror—hostage taking and mass shootings—in the face of an enemy offensive. Indeed, they interrupted the ongoing policy of judicial reengineering. Despite the detailed operational plan (which was, of course, drawn up at the last minute and promptly ignored), the mass operations were more spasm than policy, and too imprecise and locally arbitrary in their targets to constitute centralized social engineering.

Derailing existing policy on judicial reform and modernization that the regime had cultivated since 1933, the operations illustrate the unpredictability and incoherence of the Stalinist system. Unable to plan or to efficiently carry out any kind of operation, the Stalinists quickly issued detailed instructions that just as quickly became meaningless in the chaos of the campaign.[85] This was an operation in which central directives were violated or ignored and which left local officials in control. An anticipated four-month operation against escaped kulaks became a fifteen-month massacre of a wide variety of locally and randomly identified targets. The final result bore almost no relation to Stalin's original directive, and descriptions like "centralization" and "planning" seem inappropriate to characterize such a system.

We can only speculate about the ultimate reasons for the mass terror of 1937. Scholars have long thought that it flowed from Stalin's desire to preempt any possible "fifth column" behind the lines of the coming war.[86] However, the major steps in the terror do not chronologically match escalations in foreign policy or war scares in the 1930s, and as we have also seen, fear that opposition in the countryside was reaching dangerous levels played a role. It was a purely domestic event (the 1937 electoral campaign) that sparked the mass terror. Much of Bolshevik policy was governed by their fears of opposition large and small.[87] It is not difficult to imagine that their paranoia could lead them to launch mass terror from fear of losing control of the countryside, as various anti-Soviet elements used the electoral campaign to organize themselves, spread their views, and spawn dangerous rumors. The foreign and domestic explanations are not mutually exclusive, and Stalin may well have seen the threatening opposition in the countryside as the seeds of wartime opposition.

Moreover, the genesis and development of these operations point to the importance of the structure of the system to an understanding of events. These terror campaigns had constituencies behind them outside of Moscow that saw them as suitable tools of Bolshevik administration. The documents we now have indicate a kind of dialectical relation between Stalin and peripheral officials in the mass terror operations. It is clear that to understand that system as a whole we must include the regional politicians' (in this case suicidal) role, which, in this case, seems to have been more than simple obedience or posing as more royalist than the king. Local authorities had their own interests that did not always coincide with Moscow's, and the relationship between center and periphery is crucial to the functioning (and dysfunction) of the system. It seems important "to examine the dictatorship as well as the Dictator."[88]

We have seen that there is good reason to believe that the nomen-klatura, the regional party officials, turned to violence sooner than Stalin did when it came to mass operations. Accordingly, they bear much of the responsibility for the general escalation of violence in the unfolding terror that would consume them. In this sense, therefore, the leadership of the Bolshevik party committed suicide. It was a grim irony that first secretaries were thus deploying unprecedented powers of life and death over their subjects at the very moment their own fates were being decided in Moscow.

1937: The Personal Element

The terror of 1937 destroyed countless lives of victims and their families. Many of those victimized wrote letters to people in positions of authority asking them to intercede on their behalf to correct injustices or otherwise alleviate their situations. Such letters were in a long Russian peasant tradition of appealing to powerful persons for help. Sometimes they were addressed to official bodies, particularly to the Presidium of the Central Executive Committee of Soviets. More often, they were directed to particular persons: to Stalin or to M. I. Kalinin (chairman of the Presidium of the CEC and titular head of state). As the only one in the top leadership of peasant origins, Kalinin was nicknamed the "All-Union village elder" and as such received a huge number of letters of appeal. As far as we can tell, the vast majority of these letters went unanswered during the 1937–38 terror.

Part of the human tragedy of this terror was its effect on families. Not only did fathers and mothers who were branded as enemies disappear, but frequently (as in the case of Alexander Tivel that began this book) the relatives of those repressed were themselves arrested. We know, for example, that Stalin, Molotov, and the other Politburo members routinely approved lists of wives and/or children of "enemies of the people" who were to be arrested. As a person from the Caucasus, where traditions of vendetta and family vengeance were culturally rooted, Stalin perhaps naturally thought in terms of punishing kin groups as much as individuals. At a dinner on the anniversary of the October Revolution in 1937, Stalin mentioned this in a lengthy toast that was transcribed by Georgi Dimitrov:

> Whoever attempts to destroy that unity of the socialist state, whoever seeks
> the separation of any of its parts or nationalities—that man is an enemy, a

sworn enemy of the state and of the peoples of the USSR. And we will destroy each and every such enemy, even if he was an old Bolshevik; we will destroy all his kin, his family. We will mercilessly destroy anyone who, by his deeds or his thoughts—yes, his thoughts—threatens the unity of the socialist state. To the complete destruction of all enemies, themselves and their kin![89]

On the other hand, possible retribution against family members also had more calculating political utility. The threat of retribution against one's relatives would have a discouraging effect on possible traitors. In this atmosphere, promises that one's family would not be repressed may also have encouraged those under arrest to provide the required confessions. Finally, as Molotov noted, it was necessary to remove arrested persons' family members from society to avoid the spread of negative political sentiments. Indeed, when asked by Feliks Chuev in 1986, "Why did repression fall on wives, children?" Molotov at first did not even seem to understand why there was a question about it: "What does it mean, 'why?' They had to be isolated to some degree. Otherwise, they would have spread all kinds of complaints . . . and degeneration [*razlozhenia*: corruption, infection] to a certain degree. Factually, yes [they were repressed]."[90] Once again, innocent people were victimized because of what they *might* do.

Why?

We will probably never know all the reasons for the eruption of wild terror in the middle of 1937. Nomenklatura fear of opposition, Stalin's personal vengeance and fear of alternative leaders, the top leadership's mistrust of those around them, and preparations for war all played a part.

By the middle of 1937, coinciding with Stalin's coup against the "military plot," suspicions hardened, political transcripts changed again, and the careful texts separating this and that group into enemies, comrades, and those making mistakes blurred together. There were now two distinct representations of reality. For the public, the enemy could be a party leader who had been a German-Japanese spy and assassin for years—even as far back as Lenin's time—betraying socialism and carrying out secret conspiracies against the party. This construction of reality was the one found in the press and in the proceedings of the show trials. It masked personal and policy conflicts within the elite and attempted to rally the population by giving it negative examples and stark, simple depictions of common enemies. As Stalin explained to Dimitrov in a particularly revealing moment, it was necessary to blacken the reputations of those repressed as much as possible for the consumption of "workers [who] think that everything is happening because of some quarrel between me and Tr[otsky], because of St[alin]'s bad character. It must be pointed out that these people fought against Lenin, against the party during Lenin's lifetime."[91] From the minutes of closed Central Committee meetings that we have seen, it is also more than likely that many members of the nomenklatura believed in the guilt of those arrested, although perhaps not in the accusation that they had been foreign spies for twenty years.

The construction of reality in the innermost circle was a bit different. Here, in the Politburo, it was a matter of personal trust and loyalty. The level of fear and paranoia among Stalinist leaders had reached such proportions that it led them to strike even against longtime friends and comrades, people who had supported the Stalin line without fail for years, if there was the slightest reason to believe that they had been or would in the future be disloyal. Possible future reality became present danger. Suspicion became guilt. Based on what someone might do in the future, he became the same as a spy today. A party leader could be arrested for having uttered "a liberal phrase somewhere."[92] For this insider's view of reality, we once again rely on the unrepentant Molotov of the 1970s and 1980s, in this case remembering the interrogation of Yan Rudzutak:

> MOLOTOV: Rudzutak—he never confessed! He was shot. Member of the Politburo. I think that consciously he was not a participant [in a conspiracy] but he was liberal with that fraternity [of conspirators] and thought that everything about it [the investigation] was a trifle. But it was impossible to excuse it. He did not understand the danger of it. Up to a certain time he was not a bad comrade. . . .
>
> He complained about the secret police, that they applied to him intolerable methods. But he never gave any confession.
>
> "I don't admit to anything that they write about me." It was at the NKVD. . . . They worked him over pretty hard. Evidently they tortured him severely.
>
> QUESTION: Couldn't you intercede for him, if you knew him well?
>
> MOLOTOV: It is impossible to do anything according to personal impressions. We had evidence.
>
> QUESTION: If you believed it . . .

MOLOTOV: I was not 100% convinced. How could you be 100% convinced if they say that. . . . I was not that close to him. . . . He said "No, all this is wrong. I strongly deny it. They are tormenting me here. They are forcing me. I will not sign anything."

QUESTION: And you reported this to Stalin?

MOLOTOV: We reported it. It was impossible to acquit him. Stalin said, "Do whatever you decide to do there."

QUESTION: And he was shot?

MOLOTOV: He was shot.[93]

Molotov had a similar recollection about the Politburo member Vlas Chubar:

MOLOTOV: I was in Beria's office, we were questioning Chubar. . . . He was with the rightists, we all knew it, we sensed it, was personally connected with Rykov. . . . Antipov testified against him. . . .

QUESTION: You believed Antipov?

MOLOTOV: Not so much and not in everything, I already sensed that he could be lying. . . . Stalin could not rely on Chubar, none of us could.

QUESTION: Thus, it happened that Stalin did not pity anyone?

MOLOTOV: What does it mean, to pity? He received information and had to verify it.

QUESTION: People denounced each other . . .

MOLOTOV: If we did not understand that, we would have been idiots. We were not idiots. [But] we could not entrust these people with such work. At any moment they could turn. . . .

There were mistakes here. But we could have had a great number more victims in time of war and even come to defeat if the leadership had trembled, if in it had been cracks and fissures, the appearance of disagreement. If the top leadership had broken in the 30s, we would be in a more difficult position, many times more difficult, than it turned out. . . .

If we did not take stern measures, the devil knows, how these troubles would have ended up. Cadres, people in the state apparatus . . . such a leading composition—how it conducts itself, not firmly, staggering, doubting. Many very difficult questions which one had to solve, to take on oneself. In this I am confident. And we did not trust; that's the thing.[94]

These events mark a drastic change in the pattern of Stalinist discourse. This period, that of "blind terror," really marks the temporary eclipse of the discursive strategy altogether. It is as if the Stalinists, prisoners of their fears and iron discipline, had decided that they could not rule any longer by rhetorical means.

The texts on mass shootings were completely hidden transcripts; they were kept top secret and were not designed for circulation, discussion, or compliance in the party, state, or society. Unlike other party documents, they were not normative and did not prescribe forms of behavior. They were in no sense an implicit conversation designed to negotiate compliance. They involved no variant texts or emphases tailored to specific groups. Unlike with other discursive texts, there was no affirmation involved, either of unanimity or power relations. Nor were there suggestions of, or invitations to, established rituals or similar linguistic practices. Aside from those directly charged with the killings, no one was to know. In one sense, the outbreak of this blind terror was not the culmination of previous rhetoric; it was the end or negation of discourse altogether.

CHAPTER NINE

Ending the Terror, 1938

There were deficiencies. . . . I am not saying that Yezhov was spotless, but he was a good party worker. There should have been more supervision. . . . There was some, but not enough.—V. M. Molotov, 1991

It is interesting that before the events of the thirties, we lived all the time with oppositionists, with oppositionist groups. All around—one against another, what good is that?—V. M. Molotov, 1991

THE WILD AND VICIOUS terror of 1937 is sometimes known as the *Yezhovshchina:* the "time of Yezhov." This is a misnomer for several reasons. First, it puts excessive emphasis on N. I. Yezhov, who, although he was the head of the secret police that carried out much of the terror, was only one of the important political actors and forces involved. While he had a certain amount of freedom in identifying and arresting various "enemies," he almost certainly took his orders from Stalin and the Politburo.

Second, *Yezhovshchina* is a misleading epithet because that terror consisted of a number of discrete movements, offensives, measures, and countermeasures. Party membership screenings were not the same as police arrests. Various groups and constituencies played changing roles; one group might be sponsoring the persecution of another at one moment, but a few months later their roles might be reversed. Regional party secretaries, midlevel officials of the party apparatus, rank-and-file party members, economic managers, former members of the left and right oppositions, Politburo and Central Committee members, and ordinary citizens interacted with and against one another in the 1930s in a bewildering series of combinations and alliances.

Because all of these groups were in some measure and at some time victims of the terror, it is tempting to see these events as part of a single event or grand plan directed by Stalin. Although there is no doubt that he was the author and organizer of much of what we call the Great Terror of the 1930s (another inexact shorthand for the disparate events of that decade), we have seen that on many occasions his policies were marked by contradiction and vacillation. More than once, documents reflecting his private remarks to the elite had to be altered or sanitized because they did not fit the prevailing policies or because they sharply contradicted subsequent events.

Under whatever name one chooses, terror continued throughout 1938. More than 638,000 people were arrested in that year (compared with over 936,000 in 1937), the vast majority being accused of "counterrevolutionary" crimes. At least 328,000 persons were executed in 1938, and the population of the GULAG labor camps increased that year by roughly the same number.[1] Moreover, that year the Moscow show trials returned, this time for Bukharin, Rykov, Yagoda, and others, and arrests of Central Committee and Politburo members continued.

Huge as it was, the terror of 1938 hit some groups much harder than others. Indeed, unlike the wholesale slaughter of 1937, the victims and processes of 1938 lend themselves to more discrete analysis and breakdown. Unlike the maelstrom of the second half of 1937, the terror of 1938 can be broken down into identifiable targets, beneficiaries, and initiatives. Consistent with the emphasis of our study, we focus first on the party apparatus.

Cadres and Purges: The January 1938 Resolution

In January 1938 a Central Committee plenum produced a published resolution that criticized mass expulsions from the party based on "false" or excessive "vigilance." This document has been interpreted in two radically different ways, both of them wrong. On the one hand, it has been seen as an early signal that the terror was to be slowed down or stopped, or at least that some in the leadership were pushing such a relaxation.[2] Others have seen the document as another bit of Stalinist misdirection, as some kind of attempt by Stalin and his circle to pose cynically as the saviors of people from a terrible and unjust phenomenon.[3]

Actually, this document had little to do directly with the mass terror that was sweeping the country. It was rather part of the continuing rene-gotiation of the status of the nomenklatura party secretaries that had been ongoing since at least 1934. Rather than some kind of signal (false or oth-erwise) about terror in general, it was really part of the multifaceted and multigroup politics that we have seen in the Stalinist 1930s.

The ongoing conflict between the Politburo and the regional nomen-klatura had been discursively played out in terms of a constantly shifting attempt by various groups to identify scapegoats and to divert attention from real problems and real culprits: "Who was the enemy?" or "Who was to blame?" Since 1934 Stalin had criticized the regional secretaries as "feudal princes" who had tried to make their territorial machines inde-pendent of Moscow. When the enemy had been redefined in August 1936 as has-beens of the Zinoviev and Trotskyist oppositions, the nomenkla-tura jumped onto this bandwagon—not a peep was raised in defense of their old revolutionary comrades—as long as suspicion did not fall on members of their own regional machines with suspicious pasts. But in the fall of 1936 that identification was made and party machines were combed for disloyal officials, now labeled with the flexible Trotskyist epithet. The situation took yet another course at the February–March plenum, when the focus returned to former oppositionist leaders like Bu-kharin and Rykov. Although Stalin's and Zhdanov's remarks at the plenum served notice that the nomenklatura must be obedient, the focus was else-where, and the secretaries quickly backed the new line on enemies.

This dynamic between the Politburo and the nomenklatura was not a simple one. In a larger sense, the tension had to do with the very founda-tions of the regime. For Stalin to attack the nomenklatura head-on risked discrediting the entire regime: the nomenklatura was the Bolshevik Party, and to smash it—as he did in mid-1937—risked smashing the legitimacy of Bolshevik rule. On the other hand, unconditional Politburo support of the nomenklatura also risked discrediting the regime by endorsing elite pretensions and thereby alienating the rank-and-file party membership and ordinary citizens who were the targets of the secretaries' control and arbitrary rule. This dilemma helps to explain the Aesopian language of of-ficial proclamations, the need to manufacture different Central Commit-tee texts for different audiences, the abstract Kabuki plays with images of traitorous Trotskyists, and the high-level waffling on the fates of Yenu-kidze, Bukharin, and Yagoda. Each of these contradictory maneuvers, texts, and pronouncements carried strong symbolic content.

This long-standing game came to an abrupt end in the second half of 1937 when Stalin used the power of the NKVD to destroy the regional sec-retaries both politically and physically. Stalin tried to have it both ways: to destroy the independent-minded officials without casting doubt on the in-stitutions they represented. Stalin's annihilation of the regional secretaries was publicly characterized as the removal of "Trotskyist-Bukharinist" traitors, not as a calling to account of misbehaving or high-handed offi-cials. Although the administrative "mistakes" of the arrested secretaries were discussed (now as treason), the main public lesson their fall was sup-posed to teach had to do with traitors and conspirators. Thus the central leadership sought to destroy office holders without weakening the institu-tion of office holding.

This, however, was a difficult job. The mass removal of regional secre-taries and their leadership machines could not but weaken the authority of leadership in general. Memoir accounts testify to the breakdown of au-thority in factories and other institutions in this period, as bosses were afraid to issue any orders that might later be interpreted as sabotage, and as their underlings took advantage of the situation to disobey, threaten, and denounce their chiefs. Factory workers defied managers amid a gen-eral breakdown of authority.[4]

The terror was destroying the party. The documents of the January 1938 plenum show that the Politburo, and Stalin personally, were now concerned about the decomposition and discrediting of the party. The party now had to be "rehabilitated": mass expulsions had to be stopped; admissions of new members and readmissions of those expelled had to be speeded up. The Moscow leadership realized that it could not govern without a nomenklatura. The party, now cured of disease, had to be given a clean bill of health. The trick was finding a symbolic formula by which to do that.

In the course of the terror and in the wake of the removal of party offi-cials, newly promoted secretaries were being installed. The new nomen-klatura now needed protection, reassurance, and authority. The new, younger party officials had to have the authority to govern. At the same time, however, Stalin and his circle wanted to continue weeding out offi-cials they considered disloyal. They wanted to continue the "mass opera-tions" against kulaks, criminals, and others in the general population. It was necessary to find a formulation that would consolidate and restore the party: to stop the terror in the party without weakening it elsewhere.

Formulating such a text meant taking a position against certain kinds of "excesses" and not others.

The Central Committee resolution of January 1938 provided such a formulation. It attacked the "false vigilance" of "certain careerist Communists who are striving to . . . insure themselves against possible charges of inadequate vigilance through the indiscriminate repression of party members." Such a leader "indiscriminately spreads panic about enemies of the people" and "is willing to expel dozens of members from the party on false grounds just to appear vigilant himself. It is time to understand that Bolshevik vigilance consists essentially in the ability to unmask an enemy regardless of how clever and artful he may be, regardless of how he decks himself out, and not in indiscriminate or 'on the off-chance' expulsions, by the tens and thousands, of everyone who comes within reach."[5]

Thus the mass depredations in the party were to be blamed (not without some justification) on former party secretaries who for the most part had already been removed. The "serious mistakes" and "false vigilance" of certain party leaders, however, were not to be taken as signs of a slackening of the hunt for enemies. "On the contrary," the resolution said, vigilance against enemies was not to weaken. (The upcoming show trial of Bukharin and Rykov proved that.) In fact, the NKVD was in no way criticized in the January 1938 resolution. The police—the archetypal agents of vigilance—were given credit for righting various wrongs: "Large numbers of communists have been expelled from the party on the grounds that they are enemies of the people. But the organs of the NKVD found no grounds for arrest." Indeed, the January resolution called on the party to increase vigilance against enemies of the people.

Although the resolution had identified certain party secretaries as the cause for the crisis in the party, it nevertheless had the effect of stabilizing the party nomenklatura as a group. By locating the problem with "certain" secretaries of the previous period, it implicitly gave approval to the actions of the new regional officials in general. In its final passages, the resolution gave responsibility for rectifying the situation (admitting more members, dramatically speeding up appeals and readmissions, and halting the expulsion of rank-and-file members) to party secretaries themselves. That is, the sins of the past were relegated to certain discredited members of the secretarial nomenklatura, but the group as a whole was not only exonerated but given the job of rebuilding the party, with the authority and credibility to do it. In the months that followed, mass expulsions from the party ceased, large numbers of expelled members were readmitted, and re-cruitment of new members began for the first time since 1933.[6]

As usual, the means chosen was the symbolism of a Central Committee plenum and resulting carefully worded texts. Symbolic policy messages were conveyed to the party and public through examples, case studies, or scapegoats on the agenda for discussion; it was government by metaphor. Everyone in the Bolshevik leadership implicitly understood this practice, and party discipline required all to cooperate, even the person singled out as the symbol of the negative. The nomenklatura became especially furi-ous when one of its members refused to play the role assigned to him for the corporate good, Bukharin's recalcitrance at the February–March 1937 plenum being the case in point.

The Fall of Postyshev

In early 1938 the needs of the Politburo and the nomenklatura in general also included a scapegoat upon whom the sins of the preceding period could be heaped and whose admission of mistakes and downfall could thus put a final punctuation mark on the preceding period. Postyshev was to play this role.

Pavel Postyshev had long been known as a territorial party secretary who favored mass expulsions of party members. Since 1935 there had been numerous complaints against him from those expelled. At the June 1936 plenum he had been criticized for a "light-minded" attitude toward the rank and file. On those occasions, however, even though he had been called on the carpet, the matter was hushed up from the party generally. In January 1937 Postyshev had been fired from his position in Kiev and transferred to Kuibyshev; even then the Politburo had gone out of its way to shield Postyshev from any serious attacks. Postyshev was tough. He had recently requested the arrest of his own regional NKVD chief for ex-pressing even oblique private doubts about the terror.[7] Even though he had his detractors, he enjoyed high-level protection through 1937.

But given the need for a new party discourse at the beginning of 1938, Postyshev became the requisite negative symbol. Sometime around the be-ginning of the year, the Politburo member A. A. Andreev was assigned the task of gathering compromising material on Postyshev's party expulsions in Kuibyshev.[8] These documents, which became the basis for the January 1938 plenum attack on Postyshev and the resolution of the plenum, included documentation of mass party expulsions from the Kuibyshev soviet, from the ranks of party raikom secretaries, and from other organizations.[9] One report from Bazarno-Syzgansky district noted that large numbers had been expelled as enemies by order of Postyshev's men, although the NKVD subsequently found reason to arrest very few of them.[10] Entire district party organizations had been disbanded because everyone had been expelled on Postyshev's order.

As with other events we have studied, the decision to call a plenum of the Central Committee (and to make an example of Postyshev) showed few signs of long-range planning. Indeed, the documents Andreev compiled were procured only days before the plenum opened, and the Politburo decided only on 7 January to call a plenum for the eleventh. By 9 January, G. M. Malenkov had drafted a resolution for approval at the plenum, as well as a "Secret Letter" to all party organizations explaining the new line. But no Secret Letter was sent. Upon Stalin's suggestion at the subsequent plenum, it was redrafted into a published resolution.[11]

In Malenkov's original draft resolution, which he wrote after discussing the matter with Stalin, he recommended only a censure for Postyshev. Nevertheless, at the last minute Stalin changed the recommendation to include removing Postyshev from his Kuibyshev post and the Politburo and placing him "at the disposal of the Central Committee."[12] Although Postyshev was to be sacked from his Kuibyshev position, he was not expelled from the party, nor was he denounced as an enemy.

At the plenum the traditional forms were followed. Evidence was presented showing how Postyshev had ignored "signals." A decision was taken in the form of a draft resolution to be formally adopted in a plenum ritual, at which the accused leader was to confirm the charges as "completely correct" and pay his symbolic taxes by confession. Thus lessons would be taught, new signals sent, and unanimity affirmed. As had been the case with Smirnov, Yenukidze, Bukharin, and Rykov, speaker after speaker rose to attack the accused in a self-affirming ceremony of the nomenklatura elite. They closed ranks against one of their own who was now to become a symbol. They also implicitly served as vehicles for corporate construction of elite identity through the prescribed ceremony.

In this case, however, Postyshev seems at first either not to have understood or to have rejected what was required of him. From his point of view, he had not done anything wrong. He evidently forgot that right and wrong, correct and incorrect policy were what the party defined them to be at a given moment. So important was the ritual that Kaganovich and other speakers even prompted Postyshev when he misspoke. Postyshev protested that he was speaking sincerely, but Kaganovich captured the essence of the matter by replying, "Not every act of sincerity is correct." Only in the course of the meeting itself did Postyshev come to understand that correct and useful performative ritual speech, not constative right and wrong, was required.

A) Session of 14 January (day session).

POSTYSHEV: And now concerning the disbanding of the 30 Party district committees. I must say something, Comrades, concerning my mistake. My situation at the time was also a very grave one. In what sense? The Soviet and Party leaderships were in enemy hands, from the Provincial leadership at the top to the district leadership at the bottom.

MIKOYAN: All of it? From top to bottom?

POSTYSHEV: The entire district leadership. What's so amazing about it? . . .

KAGANOVICH: But there were errors. Why do you keep talking only about objective conditions?

POSTYSHEV: I shall talk about my personal mistakes.

KAGANOVICH: You shouldn't justify yourself by saying that they were all scoundrels.

POSTYSHEV: I never said all of them, I'm not so completely insane as to call everyone an enemy of the people. I never said that, I spoke only of the leadership of many of the district committees. . . .

MOLOTOV: Not a single honest man remained in the leadership?

POSTYSHEV: Viacheslav Mikhailovich [Molotov], I'll be glad to enumerate them to you [formal *vy*].

MOLOTOV: I'm [only] asking a question. I have doubts about what you are saying. . . .

POSTYSHEV: What do you want?

YEZHOV: And so it turns out that you [informal *ty*] only committed a formal mistake. But you know that the CC has characterized your mistake as not a formal one, but as a major political error in substance. So, are you trying to say that the decision of the CC is not correct?

POSTYSHEV: Why should I reduce the whole affair to a formal mistake? Please permit me to finish and explain this whole business to the best of my ability.

KAGANOVICH: You are not very good at explaining it—that's the whole point.

POSTYSHEV: Whether I explain it well or poorly, I am speaking sincerely, my thoughts are sincere.

KAGANOVICH: Not every act of sincerity is correct.

POSTYSHEV: In any case, I'm speaking sincerely.

MOLOTOV: And we too are criticizing you sincerely.

KAGANOVICH: You are speaking mistakenly. If you got confused at first, then at least, correct your mistake by the time you finish your speech.

Session of 14 January (evening session).

ANDREEV (CHAIRMAN): Comrade Postyshev, take your seat. This is no place for strolling about. . . .

POSTYSHEV: I ask you to please give me the floor.

ANDREEV: I will put your name down on the list of speakers.

POSTYSHEV: Comrade Stalin, I ask that I be given the floor.

STALIN: Why should we let you speak out of turn?

POSTYSHEV: I ask you just once to make an exception for me.

ANDREEV: We'll ask the Plenum right now.

POSTYSHEV: Comrades, please permit me to speak right now. Otherwise, I'll forget everything.

VOICE: Wait your turn.

POSTYSHEV: Please, please let me speak.

ANDREEV: Take your seat! I'll put it to a vote right now. Who is for letting Comrade Postyshev speak out of turn? One, two. Who is opposed to putting Comrade Postyshev's name on the list ahead of everybody else? A majority— . . .

ANDREEV: There is a motion on the floor to give Comrade Postyshev the floor so that he can make a statement, after which discussions will cease and Comrade Malenkov will deliver the concluding speech. Any objections to this motion? None. Comrade Postyshev has the floor and he will make a statement.

POSTYSHEV: I can only say one thing, Comrades, and that is that I recognize the speech which I gave earlier to be fully and totally incorrect and incompatible with the Party spirit. I do not understand myself how I could have made that speech. I ask the CC Plenum to forgive me. Not only have I never associated with enemies, but I have always fought against them. I have always fought on the side of the Party against enemies of the people with all my Bolshevik soul, and I shall fight the enemies of the people with all my Bolshevik soul.

I have made many mistakes. I did not understand them. Perhaps even now I have not fully understood them. I shall say only one thing, that is, that the speech I gave was incorrect and un-Party in spirit and I ask the Plenum of the CC to forgive me for making this speech. . . .

POSTYSHEV: I consider the decision of the Central Committee concerning me to be correct. I simply underestimated the situation. Do you really think I did this deliberately?

MALENKOV: You did not say this when you were speaking from the podium, when you were given the right to make a statement, and the shorthand record contains only your purely formal statement.

POSTYSHEV: I shall correct my speech and shall record in it admission of my mistake.[13]

At the January 1938 plenum, Stalin had proposed removing Postyshev from the Politburo but leaving him on the Central Committee. But a month later this decision was changed and Postyshev was now charged not only with party malfeasance and "principled mistakes" but with knowing of the enemy's machinations. His refusal to carry out the apology ritual immediately hurt him in the end.

The documents show that Postyshev had enemies and critics in the party for years. Shkiriatov had assembled a file on him in early 1936. Postyshev had been attacked at the June 1936 plenum and fired from his Kiev job in January 1937. But it is hard to avoid the impression that Stalin was not among Postyshev's longtime enemies. Shkiriatov's 1936 complaint file was never pursued. The sharp personal attack on Postyshev at the June 1936 plenum was edited out of the final version of the minutes, and when Postyshev was removed from Kiev, he was given a new job running the Kuibyshev party organization. Stalin condemned Postyshev's critics in 1937. Even in January 1938 Stalin proposed that Postyshev remain in the party and even on the Central Committee. Yet it seems that Postyshev's enemies finally won the war when a month later Postyshev was expelled from the party on the basis of charges not mentioned at the previous plenum. (The dates of this and the preceding document are curious. Postyshev was expelled from the party by vote between 17 and 20 February, but the date on the document sending his case to the Control Commission [for expulsion] is 23 February.)[14] The final chapter of Postyshev's career saw the renaming of Postyshevsky District in Donetsk region.[15]

The sacking of Postyshev was accompanied by a large-scale reshuffling of the NKVD in Ukraine. It is possible to see in this a sorting-out of Ukrainian NKVD chiefs according to their membership in Postyshev's circle. Some of the replaced officials were probably removed ("put at the disposal of the NKVD") for their closeness to Postyshev. Others, however, were given equivalent or higher-ranking posts; perhaps they had helped gather evidence against him.[16]

The Violence Continues

Even as the overvigilant Postyshev was being sacrificed for the sake of ending mass expulsions in the party, the terror continued unabated on other fronts. The same week that Postyshev was expelled from the party for his excess zeal, the Politburo formally extended the time period for work of the murderous troikas; they were supposed to have finished their "mass operations" by the end of 1937. At the same time, the Politburo raised the execution and exile limits established in the original order. The Politburo considered and approved higher limits for various provinces on a weekly basis, and sometimes more often. These decisions would eventually prolong troika operations until nearly the end of 1938. In Ukraine alone, an additional forty-eight thousand people ("First Category") were to be shot.[17]

The mass operations were particularly violent in the Far East, where they were influenced by the regime's paranoia about sealing the country's borders.[18] The limit for the Far Eastern Territory would be increased again to twenty thousand (fifteen thousand to be shot; five thousand to the camps) in July 1938.[19]

As these large-scale repressions continued, so did the removals and arrests of high-level officials whom Stalin and the Politburo decided they could not trust. In 1938 there was a second purge of the military high command, as those officers who had sat on Marshal M. N. Tukhachevsky's court-martial were themselves purged. In the fall, the Far Eastern Red Army was purged. Its commander, Marshal Bliukher, was arrested and beaten to death without confessing.[20]

At the same time, there are signs in the first half of 1938 that the terror was getting out of the control of the center. In February and March 1938 a series of decrees sought to reestablish centralized direction of the violence. As with the January 1938 plenum, the goal seems to have been to restore order and centralized control of parts of the terror without sending signals that might restrain "vigilance" altogether. Lower-level party secretaries and procurators had to be restrained from excessive purging. Whether from conviction or from a self-defensive desire to display their vigilance, their zeal had exceeded their authority. Texts were produced restricting repression of Red Army officers and restraining zealous local prosecutors. Once again, the emphasis was on limiting uncontrolled repression "from below."[21]

On 2 March 1938 the third and last of the Moscow show trials opened. In the dock were Bukharin, Rykov, Yagoda, four former USSR commissars, and several other former officials, sixteen in all. The first show trial (of Zinoviev, Kamenev, and others in 1936) had centered around accusations of political assassination. The second (of Piatakov, Sokolnikov, Radek, and others in January 1937) had incorporated the former Trotskyist opposition and broadened the accusations to include industrial sabotage. This third spectacle tied together the previous sets of charges and associated the former Right Opposition with what was now called a Right-Trotskyist Bloc. According to this final scenario, the Trotskyists and rightists had since 1932 organized a series of underground cells for the purpose of assassinating Soviet leaders, sabotaging the economy, and carrying out espionage at the behest of German, Japan, and Poland. They were accused of conspiring with foreign powers to cede to them parts of the USSR, should they come to power. The inclusion of Yagoda allegedly showed that the secret police had been implicated in the plot, thereby explaining why it had taken so long to uncover the plot.

As with the two previous trials, the event received wide publicity in the press, and a lengthy transcript of the proceedings was published in a large press run.[22] The intended lessons of the event are clear: that all oppositionists are traitors, that one must be constantly on guard against all kinds of sabotage, and that foreign enemies were everywhere.

Although one defendant (Krestinsky) initially balked, eventually all the accused pleaded guilty. Given that Radek and Sokolnikov in the previous trial had not received the death sentence, it is possible that the accused in the third trial may have believed that cooperation could save their lives. On the other hand, Molotov later said that they could have entertained no such hopes: "What, do you think they were fools?" he said in reply to a question on the subject.[23]

This "Bukharin Trial" has been analyzed numerous times in scholarly studies.[24] One of the more interesting aspects of it was Bukharin's testimony: he again contested the ritual. While pleading guilty and admitting to the overall validity of the fantastic charges made against him, he nevertheless refused to confirm specific details of the supposed conspiracy and argued with prosecutor Vyshinsky over numerous details. Although Bukharin's real purpose will probably never be known, he may have been trying to fulfill his party duty (and perhaps preventing retaliation against his family) by confessing, while at the same time defending his personal honor.[25] As he had done at the December 1936 and February 1937 Central Committee plenums, he refused to sully his reputation by admitting to monstrous accusations. In this way, he may have been trying to send a rhetorical "Aesopian message" to the party, the country, and the world: the accusations behind these trials are completely false, and we are being made to confess.

On the other hand, he may have been making a subtle attempt to save his life. It was possible for him to believe that his tactics could have led to a commutation of the inevitable death sentence. Bukharin in the weeks preceding the trial seems to have believed in the possibility in a letter he wrote to Stalin. Had he confessed fully and without reservation, there would have been no grounds to spare him; he would have been a confessed spy. But by suggesting that at least some of the charges were not true, he may have believed that he was leaving the door open for Stalin to spare his life. Whatever his thinking, the decision had already been made, and Bukharin, Rykov, and the others were executed the day after the trial.

Bukharin's trial demonstrates what Karl Radek had once called the "algebra" of confession.[26] According to Stalin's formula, criticism was the same as opposition; opposition inevitably implied conspiracy; conspiracy meant treason. Algebraically, therefore, the slightest opposition to the regime or failure to report such opposition was tantamount to terrorism. This was the a priori formula behind the show trials, one of whose purposes was to fill in the facts—to assign values to the equation's variables—with the desired concrete testimony. Although Bukharin refused to provide the details, he admitted to the logic and truth of the algebra.

His attitude received an odd resonance years later in Molotov's reminiscences. When asked about Bukharin's guilt in 1973, he said, "I do not admit that Rykov agreed, that Bukharin agreed, even that Trotsky agreed—to give away the Far East, Ukraine, the Caucasus—I do not exclude that some conversations about that took place and then the [NKVD] investigators simplified it." But just a few pages later, in response to a question about the lack of any concrete evidence except the testimony of the accused, Molotov retorted, "What more proof do you need of their guilt, when we knew that they were guilty, that they were enemies!" When asked, "Then there can be no question that they were guilty?" Molotov replied, "Absolutely."[27] The algebra was compelling.

Ending the Terror

Our knowledge of events in 1938 is limited. We know that arrests and executions continued, although perhaps not at the hysterical pace of 1937. In 1938, according to NKVD archives, 593,326 people were arrested for "counterrevolutionary crimes," compared with 779,056 in 1937. In 1938, 205,509 people were sentenced to labor camps, compared with 429,311 in 1937. Although the numbers executed in the "mass operations" in 1938 were roughly comparable to those in 1937 (353,074 in 1937; 328,618 in 1938), many of those shot in 1938 had doubtless been arrested the year before.[28]

There are signs that by the middle of 1938 the winds were shifting in the high leadership. In April, Yezhov was named commissar of water transport while retaining his leadership of the NKVD and the Party Control Commission. On the face of it, the appointment seems to have been a promotion; he now headed three important agencies: NKVD, the Commissariat of Water Transport, and the Party Control Commission. Moreover, the appointment to Water Transport was not an illogical post for a chief of the secret police. The NKVD (and OGPU before it) had always been heavily involved in purging transport agencies and building canals with forced labor, and Yezhov brought a number of NKVD officials with him to Water Transport.[29] Still, it could not have escaped notice that Yezhov's predecessor Yagoda had been eased out of his police position via the same post.

It is possible that several members of the Politburo (the names A. A. Zhdanov, A. A. Andreev, and K. E. Voroshilov are sometimes mentioned) began to complain that the arrests were weakening the state by promoting too many new and inexperienced leaders into high positions. It seems also that some officials of the NKVD complained to party officials about Yezhov's administration of the police. These complaints are said to relate to misuse of government funds and Yezhov-authorized executions of some officials without investigation or trial.[30]

In the summer of 1938 several signals pointed to a decline in Yezhov's status. In August, G. Liushkov, NKVD chief in the Far East Territory, fled across the Manchurian border and defected to Japan. A close Yezhov intimate and assistant, Liushkov had participated in key police investigations from the Kirov assassination through the purge trials. His defection represented not only a serious security breach but a black mark against his chief. Second, at the end of August, L. P. Beria was brought from Georgia to be Yezhov's deputy at NKVD. Like Yezhov's handpicked assistants, Beria was a career police official, but he was an outsider to the central NKVD circles. His appointment gave Stalin his own man inside Yezhov's administration.[31] Third, in the summer of 1938 Yezhov had had a violent disagreement with V. M. Molotov in a cabinet meeting, apparently threatening him with arrest. Stalin had forced Yezhov to apologize.[32] However, Yezhov's fall and the ending of the terror were gradual processes. Even as Yezhov's personal prestige was falling, executions and arrests continued under his direction. In July a large number of arrested officials, including Yan Rudzutak, were shot. In the summer, the Politburo candidate members Kosior, Chubar, and Eikhe were arrested.

By the fall of 1938, however, the Politburo was changing course. A Politburo resolution of 8 October formed a special commission to study arrest procedures and the apparent lack of judicial supervision over police activities.[33] Although Yezhov chaired the commission, it is significant that the other members were from outside his circle: Beria was an outside appointment as Yezhov's deputy; Rychkov was from the office of the state procurator, and Malenkov was from the Central Committee personnel department. To have a committee looking into arrest procedures was bad enough for Yezhov, but to have it staffed by high-ranking people from other agencies was a real danger to him.

The threat was real. The following month, the Politburo approved and distributed a decree on arrest procedures and judicial supervision. On 15 November the Politburo suspended "until further notice" the work on the murderous NKVD troikas.[34] Two days later the Politburo issued a more comprehensive decree, sharply criticizing the work on the NKVD and completely "liquidating" the troikas. The 17 November decree was characteristic of Stalinist shifts in the 1930s. Discursive rules in the party forbade any admission that previous policy had been in error, so one blamed the executors, not the policy makers, and praised the preceding policy while abolishing it. As we have seen, there is clear documentary evidence that the sins now attributed to the NKVD were encouraged, if not ordered, by Stalin himself. The "mass operations," slipshod procuratorial controls, forced confessions, and the rest were part of high policy that did not originate with the NKVD.

More than cynical scapegoating was at work here, although there was plenty of that in the new discourse. As had been the case in the decrees of May 1933, June 1935, and March 1937 (which the 17 November decree referenced explicitly), the present order went out of its way to applaud repression while apparently seeming to limit it. As with those earlier decrees, the point was to centralize administration in fewer hands. The 1933 and 1935 decrees had not ended arrests; they had simply limited the number of people and agencies authorized to carry them out. The clear meaning of this decree, without saying so openly, was that the NKVD (and Yezhov) were responsible for *disorderly* repression. Yezhov and the NKVD were not blamed for terror; they were blamed for disorder. Procuratorial sanction before arrest, which had fallen into disuse over the past two years, was reasserted. The new texts thus offered a political transcript to the readers of the decree that enemies were still dangerous, but they were to be destroyed carefully and selectively.[35]

Two days later the Politburo again discussed the work of the NKVD, based on a report from Ivanovo NKVD chief Zhuravlev.[36] Clearly, the Zhuravlev report was instigated by Beria in an attempt to finally discredit Yezhov.[37] That report was an attack on Yezhov and several of his lieutenants, and Yezhov was blamed for not "unmasking" them himself. One expert on Yezhov long ago concluded that "Yezhov's primary crime, however, consisted in the fact that he had not informed Stalin of his actions."[38] Just as Yezhov had done to discredit his predecessor Yagoda, Beria now claimed that Yezhov had been hiding investigations from Stalin.[39] When Stalin demanded an explanation, Yezhov sent him a list of more than one hundred pending investigations, all of which Yezhov had reported on to him.[40] But it was too late for Yezhov. Four days later, after a four-hour meeting with Stalin, Molotov, and Voroshilov, Yezhov sent a letter to Stalin resigning from his post at NKVD.[41] His text was formulaic, recognizing and taking the blame for the "mistakes" of the NKVD in espionage and investigatory work. In this and another explanatory letter, Yezhov cited overwork in trying to excuse his sloppy work and excessive drinking. The Politburo accepted his resignation the same day, then two days later named Beria to head the NKVD. The removal of Yezhov's deputies proceeded quickly. Yezhov last appeared in public on 21 January 1939, atop Lenin's mausoleum with the rest of the Politburo.[42] His name was in good repute at least until April 1939, when Sverdlovsk Obkom "requested" that one of their districts be renamed from Yezhovsk to Molotovsk.[43]

Stalin removed Yezhov for a variety of reasons. The terror had to be ended, and the only text that could do that without discrediting Bolshevism, the party, or Stalin was one in which there had been "excesses" in the work of its executors. Postyshev became the evil "other" in party affairs; now it was Yezhov's turn to take the blame for the police. Another reason for Yezhov's fall was his chronic drinking. We know from various testimonies that during his tenure at NKVD he drank huge quantities every day. He himself mentioned this problem in one of his letters to Stalin and at his own trial. He was drunk at work, at home, at his dacha, and he presided over group drinking bouts with cronies. Stalin and others complained that Yezhov was often absent from his various jobs and was falling behind in his work. Moreover, given the political secrets in Yezhov's head, it was inconceivable for Stalin to allow him to babble them to all and sundry at drunken parties. As far as we can tell, before and after Yezhov's own arrest, all of his professional, personal, and family drinking buddies were rounded up and shot.

It may seem odd that Yezhov's letters to Stalin did not refer to the "excesses" or failures in control over the NKVD that had been spelled out in the 17 November resolution. First, at his trial more than a year later, Yezhov did not admit to any excesses, seeming, rather, genuinely to believe that his only sin was in not purging his own apparatus. Second, to discuss this was to defend himself by pointing out that he was only following Stalin's orders. This was impossible. Clearly, the new text was to blame those who had carried out the repression, thereby protecting the reputations of those—especially Stalin—who had ordered it. To deviate from that text would mean separating oneself from or "taking up arms" against the party, precisely the crimes Bukharin, Zinoviev, and Trotsky had been accused of. As always, protecting Stalin and the party was the main thing.

The texts of November 1938 not only ordered an end to the wild terror. They signaled a return to politics as usual. In this particular regard, it is less important to ascertain the degree to which procuratorial sanction would be rigorously enforced (although it seems to have been) than to recognize the return of a system of discursive politics aimed at achieving central control over politics and society. November 1938 thus represented not only an end to the terror but a return to the attempt to control events with "legal" hegemony and a systemic/systematic governing narrative.

Yezhov's removal thus again presented the question of variant "transcripts" for different audiences. The question then, as it always was with the Bolsheviks, was finding the best way to use the decision (and information about it) in the service of the party leadership. The question of truth was always subservient to rhetorical control; more precisely, discourse control became truth. The real reasons for policy changes never had any-thing to do with the subsequent utility of information that was released to various audiences.

The general public could read only the terse *Pravda* announcement that Yezhov had resigned for reasons of health and had been replaced by Beria. It was not useful to tell them more: the mass operations had been secret (or at any rate never mentioned publicly), and in the interests of maintaining the facade of party/state unity, it was inexpedient to discuss "mistakes" of the NKVD and failures of the judicial system, or to hint at conflicts in the leadership. Any criticism of excessive vigilance or NKVD mistakes would have cast doubt on the entire vigilance campaign, as well as on party con-trol over the police, and could lead (as it would in 1956) to questions about whether victims had been unjustly condemned.

The broader party and bureaucratic audience (down to the level of district party secretary) was told something different; according to their transcript, the problem was one of "excesses" in the terror. Whatever the real reasons for Yezhov's fall, it was at that moment useful to the leadership to reassure the new nomenklatura that although things had been out of control, all was now in hand and there would be no more excesses. For example, in Decem-ber 1938, Stalin piously replied to a letter from Orel First Secretary Boitsov: "I received your letter about false testimony from the six arrested. There are analogous communications from various places and also complaints against former Commissar Yezhov that, as a rule, he ignored such things. These complaints served as one reason for Yezhov's removal."[44]

For this broader elite, it was necessary for the Politburo to portray the problem as a rogue NKVD that had somehow escaped party supervision. In this version of reality, it would have been inconvenient to discuss the specific crimes of Yezhov's deputies, since to the nomenklatura audience it would have been clear that those deputies had in fact been vetted by the Politburo in the first place.

The more restricted privileged circle of the top leadership, however, read from yet another script, that of Zhuravlev's report and Yezhov's resulting letter. Here the reasons for the replacement were different. Yezhov's letter mentioned only in passing the defects in the work of the NKVD (underesti-mating intelligence work) and never referred to the problems of excesses, lack of judicial supervision, forced confession, faked interrogation proto-cols, and the like. For Yezhov, his mistakes consisted only in the fact that his deputies turned out to be enemies. It might seem ironic that this least believable version was the most secret. On the other hand, as we have seen, the information power of those on high consisted largely in knowing the transcripts of those below them, not in a particular version prepared for them. They knew the real story, or at least the possible stories about Yezhov's removal. They understood the dangers of telling the masses too much and the necessity of reassuring the new nomenklatura about the previous excesses.

In 1973 Molotov was vague about Yezhov's relations with Stalin and his fall from power. In some places, Molotov seemed to be trying to disassociate Stalin from Yezhov:

> MOLOTOV: Yezhov was accused because he began to name quantities [of arrests] by provinces, and in the provinces numbers by district. In some provinces they had to liquidate not less than two thousand, in some district not less than 50 people. . . . That is what he was shot for. There was no monitoring over it. . . .
>
> QUESTION: Was it the Politburo's mistake that they trusted the organs [of the NKVD] too much?
>
> MOLOTOV: No. There were deficiencies. . . . I am not saying that Yezhov was spotless, but he was a good party worker. There should have been more supervision. . . . There was some, but not enough.[45]

Of course, Yezhov was not shot for establishing limits by province. We have seen that these limits were in each case approved by Stalin and the Politburo.[46] The question of Stalin's "supervision" is more ambiguous. Above, Molotov suggested that there had not been enough supervision over Yezhov. In other places Molotov gave a different evaluation, and his attempts to shield Stalin from criminal responsibility were hopelessly contradictory. Finally, he admitted that whatever Stalin's role, in the final analysis the terror had been justified:

> QUESTION: If Stalin knew everything, if he did not rely on stupid advice, then it means that he bears direct responsibility for the repression of innocent people.
>
> MOLOTOV: Not quite. It is one thing to put forward an idea, and another thing to carry it out. It was necessary to beat the rights, necessary to beat the Trotskyists, to give the order to punish them decisively. For this [repression of innocent people], Yezhov was shot.[47]

> QUESTION: Did even Stalin have doubts in 1937 that things had gone too far?
>
> MOLOTOV: Of course, not only doubts. Yezhov, the chief of security, was shot.

QUESTION: But didn't Stalin make him a scapegoat in order to blame everything on him?

MOLOTOV: It is an oversimplification. Those who think so don't understand
the situation in the country at that time. Of course, demands came from
Stalin, of course things went too far, but I think that everything was permitted thanks to one thing: only to hold on to power![48]

The Aftermath

Yezhov's fall meant an end to the mass operations and executions, but not
to the terror or its effects. Mass arrests hit the Komsomol at the end of
1938 as that organization's leadership was purged. In early 1939 several
leading officials who had been arrested in 1938 were shot, including Kosior, Chubar, and Postyshev. Moreover, the new NKVD chief Beria purged
the NKVD and arrested all of Yezhov's deputies and department heads. In
the short period September–December 1938, 140 NKVD officials from the
central apparatus and 192 from the provinces were arrested, including 18
NKVD chiefs of union republics. Thus was the Yezhov patronage group
removed.[49]

The 17 November 1938 resolution about judicial controls and procuratorial supervision over the NKVD represented a victory for USSR Procurator Vyshinsky. For a long time he had favored maintaining procedural
norms: procurators had to agree to arrests, specific charges had to be lev-
eled, and some semblance of procedural regularity was to be followed.
This approach did not necessarily mean less terror; it meant rather that the
bureaucratic t's were to be crossed and the i's dotted. After Yezhov's fall,
Vyshinsky became more visible in Politburo documents. While never criticizing the terror administration, he did make suggestions aimed at controlling, regularizing, and even limiting it. Vyshinsky wrote to Stalin,

> Recently a great number of cases have been heard by the Special Board at-
> tached to the People's Commissar for Internal Affairs of the USSR. 200 to 300
> cases have been reviewed at each session of the Special Board. Under such cir-
> cumstances it is not to be ruled out that wrong decisions may have been made.
> For this reason I presented my observations on the matter to Comrade Beria
> with a proposal to establish procedures for the work of the Special Board
> which would allow its sessions to be held more often, making it possible for
> fewer cases to be heard at each session.[50]

From the end of 1938, numerous NKVD cases were reopened. We have
little evidence on the scale of these reconsiderations; rumor places the

number of people released in the tens of thousands. Anecdotal evidence suggests that if one had not signed a confession, one's chances to be freed were increased in the post-Yezhov period. Still, the numbers exonerated were small compared with the numbers repressed, executed, and sent to camps in the preceding two years. Releasing large numbers of the falsely accused would have raised inconvenient questions about the honesty and competence of the party and police, Stalin's role, and the need for repression in the first place. And many in the leadership really believed that huge numbers were guilty. In response to a question in 1971 about why many innocent people had not been freed, Molotov answered, "But many were correctly arrested. They checked it out, some were freed."[51]

Although some were freed and "mistakes" were admitted, at least within the party circles, the fall of Yezhov did not mean a significant relaxation in state repression. In the long run, the numbers of camp victims continued to increase (although with ups and downs) until Stalin's death.[52] In the short run, a series of memorandums in 1939 shows that the mechanism of repression was still in good repair and that the leadership had no intention of relaxing it. The camp regime was not to be modified, releases on probation were prohibited, and legal barriers to rehabilitation were strengthened.[53]

After the fall of Yezhov and the turn toward legality, Chairman of the USSR Supreme Court I. T. Goliakov took the lead in the legal rectification of the "mistakes" of the terror. Joined by Procurator General Pankrat'ev and Commissar of Justice Rychkov, Goliakov attempted to streamline the procedure whereby procuratorial protests could result in successful appeals of those wrongly convicted. On 3 December 1939 Goliakov wrote to Stalin and Molotov proposing such an expedited procedure. Stalin referred the matter to Beria, who disagreed. Molotov concurred, and the idea was dropped.[54] We conclude with another remarkable passage from Molotov in 1982 about the salutary effects of the terror on the subsequent period:

> It is interesting that before the events of the 30s, we lived all the time with oppositionists, with oppositionist groups. After the war, there were no opposition groups, it was such a relief that made it easier to give a correct, better direction, but if a majority of these people had remained alive, I don't know if we would be standing solidly on our feet. Here Stalin took upon himself chiefly all this difficult business, but we helped properly. Correctly. And without such a person as Stalin, it would have been very difficult. Very. Especially in the period of the war. All around—one against another, what good is that?[55]

CHAPTER TEN

Two Bolsheviks

I know all too well that great plans, great ideas and great interests take precedence over everything, and I know that it would be petty for me to place the question of my own person on a par with the universal-historical tasks resting, first and foremost, on your shoulders.—N. I. Bukharin, 1937

I request that Stalin be informed that I am a victim of circumstances and nothing more, yet here enemies I have overlooked may have also had a hand in this. Tell Stalin that I shall die with his name on my lips.—N. I. Yezhov, 1940

NIKOLAI IVANOVICH BUKHARIN and Nikolai Ivanovich Yezhov had both joined the party before the 1917 revolutions and therefore belonged to the exclusive group of "Old Bolsheviks."

Bukharin was of the Lenin type: a highly educated intellectual who spoke and wrote several languages. Like Lenin, Bukharin was a theoretician who produced an impressive corpus of published works within the Marxist tradition. Even as he languished in a Stalinist prison awaiting trial, he wrote several extensive philosophical and economic works as well as a novel.[1] His theoretical writings had been cornerstones of Bolshevik politics. They were widely read and discussed by the leadership and in the 1920s had formed the theoretical basis for the New Economic Policy.

Yezhov, on the other hand, belonged to the Stalin type of practical Bolshevik organizer and administrator. A factory worker by profession, Yezhov never finished primary school. (Bukharin graduated from Moscow University.) In the Civil War and through the 1920s, while Bukharin edited newspapers, Yezhov served on party committees in the provinces, working his way up the ladder to a post in a provincial party administration. Bukharin, like Lenin, was an *intelligent*. Yezhov, like Stalin, was an organizer and committeeman.

Both had sided with Stalin in the 1920s in the struggle against Trotsky, Zinoviev, and the "left opposition." Bukharin, from his lofty seat in the Politburo, brought the weight of his wit (and the controlled press) to bear on Stalin's enemies, while in the provinces numerous Yezhovs organized and purged the party committees. Their paths diverged in 1929, when Stalin veered to the left and launched the collectivization and industrialization campaigns. Bukharin protested and defended the mixed, gradualist approach of the New Economic Policy. Yezhov supported Stalin and was assigned to vet party personnel in the radical new USSR Commissariat of Agriculture, then in industry, and finally in the party personnel department itself. Yezhov thus helped to remove Bukharin's supporters from key positions.

The two knew each other. Back in 1936 Bukharin had greeted Yezhov's appointment as head of the NKVD with relief. Bukharin had blamed Yagoda for various frame-ups against the opposition, and told his wife that Yezhov was an "honest person" who "won't falsify things."[2] For his part, Yezhov had at first taken a soft line on Bukharin when the latter was under suspicion for "organizing terror." Yezhov wrote to Stalin in 1936 that the Bukharinists were not as guilty as the Trotskyists. The latter, he thought, should be shot, but he recommended milder punishment for the rightists.[3]

The two had much in common. As Old Bolsheviks, both believed absolutely in the party dictatorship. Both believed that dangerous enemies existed, that they had to be "mercilessly crushed." Both believed in the discipline of democratic centralism and, as Trotsky had said, that it was impossible to be right against the party. Both believed that the truth was whatever the party said it was. Both, in their separate ways, were ready to die for the party and for the Revolution. Ultimately, both had occasion to do so.

We present below the last known appeals of each of them to Stalin. These texts are so important and interesting, especially juxtaposed with each other, that we offer rather long quotations from them. These two documents are surrounded with irony. Bukharin had been glad when Yezhov came to head the NKVD in 1936, believing him to be an honest man. But soon Yezhov became Bukharin's chief tormentor at the December 1936 and February 1937 plenums of the Central Committee. Although they became bitter enemies, both praised Stalin and invoked his name even while both must have known that Stalin was the author of their downfalls. For both Bukharin and Yezhov, as their statements show, it was desperately important that Stalin know of their innocence and loyalty.

The two texts are vastly different in style. Bukharin's letter, although rambling, is full of theoretical, historical, and literary references. Yezhov's statement, reflecting his different background, is direct and angry. But both texts suggest a similar psychological twist in their attitudes toward Stalin. On one level, of course, each man knew that Stalin had ordered his arrest and would decide his fate. At the same time, in their texts both maintained a kind of separation between the process and its author. For Bukharin, his "case" was impersonally "moving" as if pushed along by some machine or process. For Yezhov, the fault was hidden enemies within the NKVD who had done him in. Neither blamed Stalin, even indirectly or implicitly. Was this simple etiquette or perhaps a deliberately false and flattering exoneration aimed at winning Stalin's pardon? Or could they really have believed on some level that the process and Stalin were two different things?

Bukharin had been arrested immediately after his expulsion from the party in March 1937. He had begun to confess to the charges made against him in June, and by December of 1937 his participation in the scenario of the third show trial was confirmed. It was at that time that he wrote personally to Stalin in the following document.

Bukharin's Letter to Stalin, 10 December 1937[4]

Very Secret [ves'ma sekretno]

Personal

Request no one be allowed to read this letter without the express permission of I. V. Stalin.

To: I. V. Stalin 7 pages + 7 pages of memoranda.[5]

Iosif Vissarionovich:

This is perhaps the last letter I shall write to you before my death. That's why, though I am a prisoner, I ask you to permit me to write this letter without resorting to officialese, all the more so since I am writing this letter to you alone: the very fact of its existence or non-existence will remain entirely in your hands.

I've come to the last page of my drama and perhaps of my very life. I agonized over whether I should pick up pen and paper,—as I write this, I am shuddering all over from disquiet and from a thousand emotions stirring within me, and I can hardly control myself. But precisely because I have so little time left, I want to *take my leave* of you in advance, before it's too late, before my hand ceases to write, before my eyes close, while my brain somehow still functions.

In order to avoid any misunderstandings, I will say to you from the outset that, as far as the *world at large* (society) is concerned: a) I have no intention of recanting anything I've written down [confessed]; b) In this sense (or in connection with this), I have no intention of asking you or of pleading with you for anything that might derail my case from the direction in which it is heading. But I am writing to you for your personal information. I cannot leave this life without writing to you these last lines because I am in the grip of torments which you should know about.

1) Standing on the edge of a precipice, from which there is no return, I tell you on my word of honor, as I await my death, that I am innocent of those crimes which I admitted to at the investigation.

2) Reviewing everything in my mind—insofar as I can—I can only add the following observations to what I have already said at the Plenum:

a) I once heard someone say that someone had yelled out something. It seems to me that it was Kuz'min, but I had never ascribed any real significance to it—it had never even entered my mind;

b) Aikhenval'd told me in passing, *post factum* as we walked on the street about the conference which I *knew nothing* about (nor did I know anything about the Riutin platform) ("the gang has met, and a report was read")—or something of the sort. And, yes, I concealed this fact, feeling pity for the "gang."

c) I was also guilty of engaging in duplicity in 1932 in my relations with my "followers," believing sincerely that I would thereby *win them back wholly to the Party.* Otherwise, I'd have alienated them from the Party. That was all there was to it. In saying this, I am clearing my conscience *totally. All the rest either never took place or, if it did, then I had no inkling of it whatsoever.*

So, at the Plenum I spoke the truth and *nothing but the truth,* but no one believed me. And here and now I speak the absolute truth: All these past years, I have been honestly and sincerely carrying out the Party line and have learned to cherish and love you wisely.

3) I had no "way out" other than that of confirming the accusations and testimonies of others and of elaborating on them. Otherwise, it would have turned out that I had not "disarmed."

4) Apart from extraneous factors and apart from argument #3 above, I have formed, more or less, the following conception of what is going on in our country:

There is something *great and bold about the political idea* of a general purge. It is a) connected with the pre-war situation and b) connected with the transition to democracy. This purge encompasses 1) the guilty; 2) persons under suspicion; and 3) persons potentially under suspicion. This business could not have been managed without me. Some are neutralized one way, others in another way, and a third group in yet another way. What serves as a guarantee for all this is the fact that people inescapably talk about each other and *in doing so* arouse an everlasting distrust in each other. (I'm judging from my own experience. How I raged against Radek, who had smeared me, and then I myself followed in his wake . . . [ellipsis Bukharin's]) In this way, the leadership is bringing about a *full guarantee* for itself.

For God's sake, don't think that I am engaging here in reproaches, even in my inner thoughts. I wasn't born yesterday. I know all too well that *great* plans, *great* ideas and *great* interests take precedence over everything, and I know that it would be petty for me to place the question of my own person *on a par with the universal-historical tasks* resting, first and foremost, on your shoulders. But it is here that I feel my deepest agony and find myself facing my chief, agonizing paradox.

5) *If* I were absolutely sure that your thoughts ran precisely along this path, then I would feel so much more at peace with myself. Well, so what! If it must be so, then so be it! But believe me, my heart boils over when I think that you might *believe* that I am guilty of these crimes and that in your heart of hearts you yourself think that I am really guilty of all of these horrors. *In that case,* what would it mean? Would it turn out that I have been helping to deprive [the Party] of many people (beginning with myself!), that is, that I am wittingly committing an *evil?!* *In that case,* such action could never be justified. My head is giddy with confusion, and I feel like yelling at the top of my voice. I feel like pounding my head against the wall: For, *in that case,* I have become a cause for the death of others. What am I to do? What am I to do?

6) I bear not one iota of malice towards anyone, nor am I bitter. I am not a Christian. But I do have my quirks. I believe that I am suffering retribution for those years when I really waged a campaign [against the Party line?]. And if you really want to know, more than anything else I am oppressed by one fact, which you have perhaps forgotten: Once, most likely during the summer of 1928, I was at your place, and you said to me: "Do you know why I consider you my friend? After all, you are not capable of intrigues, are you?" And I said: "No, I am not." At that time, I was hanging around with Kamenev ("first encounter").[6] Believe it or not, but it is *this* fact that stands out in my mind as original sin does for a Jew [*sic*]. Oh, God, what a child I was! What a fool! And now I'm paying for this with my honor and with my life. For *this* forgive me, Koba. I weep as I write. I no longer need anything, and you yourself know that I am probably making my situation worse by allowing myself to write all this.

But I just can't, I simply can't keep silent. I must give you my final "farewell." It is for this reason that I bear no malice towards anyone, not towards the [party-state] leadership nor the investigators nor anyone in between. I ask you for forgiveness although I have already been punished to such an extent that everything has grown dim around me, and darkness has descended upon me.

7) When I was hallucinating, I saw you several times and once I saw Nadezhda Sergeevna.[7] She approached me and said: "What have they done with you, Nikolai Ivanovich? I'll tell Iosif to bail you out." This was so real that I was about to jump and write a letter to you and ask you to . . . bail me out! [Ellipsis Bukharin's.] Reality had become totally mixed up in my mind with delusion. I know that Nadezhda Sergeevna would never believe that I had harbored any evil thoughts against you, and not for nothing did the subconscious of my wretched self cause this delusion in me. We talked for hours, you and me. . . . Oh, Lord, if only there were some device which would have made it possible for you to see my soul flayed and ripped open! If only you could see how I am attached to you, body and soul, quite unlike certain people like Stetsky or Tal'. Well, so much for "psychology,"—forgive me. No angel will appear now to snatch Abraham's sword from his hand. My fatal destiny shall be fulfilled.

8) Permit me, finally, to move on to my last, minor, requests.

a) It would be a thousand times easier for me *to die* than to go through the coming trial: I simply don't know how I'll be able to control myself—you know my nature: I am not an enemy either of the Party or of the USSR, and I'll do all within my powers [to serve the party's cause], but, under such circumstances, my powers are minimal, and heavy emotions rise up in my soul. I'd get on my knees, forgetting shame and pride, and plead with you not to make me go through with it [the trial]. But this is probably already impossible. I'd ask you, if it were possible, to let me die before the trial. Of course, I know how harshly you look upon such matters.

b) If I'm to receive the death sentence, then I implore you beforehand, I entreat you, by all that you hold dear, not to have me shot. Let me drink poison in my cell instead (let me have morphine so that I can fall asleep and never wake up). For me, this point is extremely important. I don't know what words I should summon up in order to entreat you to grant me this as an act of charity. After all, politically, it won't really matter, and, besides, no one will know a thing about it. But let me spend my last moments as I wish. Have pity on me! Surely you'll understand,—knowing me as well as you do. Sometimes, I look death openly in the face, just as I know very well that I am capable of brave deeds. At other times, I, ever the same person, find myself in such disarray that I am drained of all strength. So if the verdict is death, let me have a cup of morphine. I *implore* you. . . .

c) I ask you to allow me to bid farewell to my wife and son. No need for me to say good-bye to my daughter. I feel sorry for her. It will be too painful for her. It will also be too painful to Nadya and my father. Anyuta, on the other hand, is young.[8] She will survive. I would like to exchange a few last words with her. I would like permission to meet her before the trial. My argument is as follows: If my family sees what I *confessed* to, they might commit suicide from sheer unexpectedness. I must somehow prepare them for it. It seems to me that this is in the interests of the case and its official interpretation.

d) If, contrary to expectation, my life is to be spared, I would like to request (though I would first have to discuss it with my wife) the following:[9]

*) that I be exiled to America for x number of years. My arguments are: I would *myself* wage a campaign [in favor] of the trials, I would wage a mortal war against Trotsky, I would win over large segments of the wavering intelligentsia, I would in effect become Anti-Trotsky and would carry out this mission in a big way and, indeed, with much zeal. You could send an expert security officer [chekist] with me and, as added insurance, you could detain my wife here for six months until I have proven that I am really punching Trotsky and Company in the nose, etc.

**) But if there is the slightest doubt in your mind, then exile me to a camp in Pechora or Kolyma, even for 25 years. I could set up there the following: a university, a museum of local culture, technical stations and so on, institutes, a painting gallery, an ethnographic museum, a zoological and botanical museum, a camp newspaper and journal.

In short, settling there with my family to the end of my days, I would carry out pioneering, enterprising, cultural work.

In any case, I declare that I would work like a dynamo wherever I am sent.

However, to tell the truth, I do not place much hope in this since the very fact of a change in the directive of the February Plenum speaks for itself (and I see all too well that things point to a trial taking place any day now).

And so these, it seems, are my last requests (one more thing: my *philosophical work,* remaining after me,—I have done a lot of useful work in it).

Iosif Vissarionovich! In me you have lost one of your most capable generals, one who is genuinely devoted to you. But that is all past. I remember that Marx wrote that Alexander the First lost a great helper to no purpose in Barclay de Tolly after the latter was charged with treason. It is bitter to reflect on all this. But I am preparing myself mentally to departing from this vale of tears, and there is nothing in me towards all of you, towards the Party and the cause but a great and boundless love. I am doing everything that is humanly possible and impossible. I have written to you about all this. I have crossed all the t's and dotted all the i's. I have done all this in advance, since I have no idea at all what condition I shall be in tomorrow and the day after tomorrow, etc. Being a neurasthenic, I shall perhaps feel such universal apathy that I won't be able even so much as to move my finger.

But now, in spite of a headache and with tears in my eyes, I am writing [this letter]. My conscience is clear before you now, Koba. I ask you one final time for your forgiveness (only in your heart, not otherwise). For that reason I embrace you in my mind. Farewell forever and remember kindly your wretched N. Bukharin 10 December 1937.

Yezhov fell from power at the end of 1938 and was arrested early in 1939. After a lengthy interrogation at which he was accused of being a spy for Poland and England, he was confessing by the middle of 1939. It is not known whether he wrote personally to Stalin, as Bukharin had. The document below represents part of his final statement at his secret trial in February 1940.

A Statement Made Before a Secret Judicial Session of the Military Collegium of the Supreme Court of the USSR. 3 February 1940.[10]

For a long time I have thought about what it will feel like to go to trial, how I should behave at the trial, and I have come to the conclusion that the only way I could hang on to life is by telling everything honestly and truthfully. Only yesterday, in a conversation with me, Beria said to me: "Don't assume that you will necessarily be executed. If you will confess and tell everything honestly, your life will be spared." After this conversation with Beria I decided: It is better to die, it is better to leave this earth as an honorable man and to tell nothing but the truth at the trial. At the preliminary investigation I said that I was not a spy, that I was not a terrorist, but they didn't believe me and beat me up horribly. During the 25 years of my Party work I have fought honorably against enemies and have exterminated them. I have committed crimes for which I might well be executed. I will talk about them later. But I have not committed and am innocent of the crimes which have been imputed to me by the prosecution in its bill of indictment. . . .

I did not organize any conspiracy against the Party and the government. On the contrary, I used everything at my disposal to expose conspiracies. In 1934, when I began conducting the case of the "Kirov affair," I was not afraid to report Yagoda and other traitors on the Extraordinary Commission (ChK) [the Extraordinary Commission for Combating Counterrevolution and Sabotage, or Cheka] to the Central Committee. Sitting on the Cheka, enemies such as Agranov and others led us by the nose, claiming that this was the work of the Latvian Intelligence Service. We did not believe these Chekists and forced them to reveal to us the truth [about] the participation of the rightist-Trotskyist organization. Having been in Leningrad at the time of the investigation into the murder of S. M. Kirov, I saw how the Chekists tried to mess up the whole case. Upon my arrival in Moscow, I wrote a detailed report concerning all this in the name of Stalin, who immediately after this called for a meeting. . . .

One may wonder why I would repeatedly place the question of the Cheka's sloppy work before Stalin if I was a part of an anti-Soviet conspiracy. . . .

Coming to the NKVD, I found myself at first alone. I didn't have an assistant. At first, I acquainted myself with the work, and only then did I begin my work by crushing the Polish spies who had infiltrated all departments of the organs of the Cheka. Soviet Intelligence was in their hands. In this way, I, "a Polish spy," began my work by crushing Polish spies. After crushing the Polish spies, I immediately set out to purge the group of turncoats. That's how I began my work for the NKVD. I personally exposed Molchanov, and, along with him, also other enemies of the people, who had infiltrated the organs of the NKVD and who had occupied important positions in it. I had intended to arrest Lyushkov but he slipped out of my hands and fled abroad. I purged 14,000 Chekists.[11] But my great guilt lies in the fact that I purged so few of them. My practice was as follows: I would hand over the task of interrogating the person under arrest to one or another department head while thinking to myself: "Go on, interrogate him today,—Tomorrow I will arrest you." All around me were enemies of the people, my enemies. I purged Chekists everywhere. It was only in Moscow, Leningrad and the Northern Caucasus that I did not purge them. I thought they were honest, but it turned out, in fact, that I had been harboring under my wing saboteurs, wreckers, spies and enemies of the people of other stripes. . . .

I have never taken part in an anti-Soviet conspiracy. If all the testimonies of the members of the conspiracy are carefully read, it will become apparent that they were slandering not only me but also the CC and the government. . . .

I am charged with corruption as pertaining to my morals and my private life [moral'no-bytovoe razlozhenie]. But where are the facts? I have been in the public eye of the Party for 25 years. During these 25 years everyone saw me, everyone loved me for my modesty and honesty. I do not deny that I drank heavily, but I worked like a horse. Where is my corruption? I understand and honestly declare that the only cause for sparing my life would be for me to admit that I am guilty of the charges brought against me, to repent before the Party and to implore it to spare my life. Perhaps the Party will spare my life when taking my services into account. But the Party has never had any need of lies, and I am once again declaring to you, that I was not a Polish spy, and I do not want to admit guilt to that charge because such an admission would only be a gift to the Polish landowners, just as admitting guilt to espionage activity for England and Japan would only be a gift to the English lords and Japanese samurai. I refuse to give such gifts to those gentlemen. . . .

I'll now finish my final address. I ask the Military Collegium to grant me the following requests: 1. My fate is obvious. My life, naturally, will not be spared since I myself have contributed to this at my preliminary investigation. I ask only one thing: Shoot me quietly, without putting me through any agony. 2. Neither the Court nor the CC will believe in my innocence. If my mother is alive, I ask that she be provided for in her old age, and that my daughter be taken care of. 3. I ask that my nephews not be subjected to punitive measures because they are not guilty of anything. 4. I ask that the Court investigate thoroughly the case of Zhurbenko, whom I considered and still consider to be an honest man devoted to the Leninist-Stalinist cause.[12] 5. I request that Stalin be informed that I have never in my political life deceived the Party, a fact known to thousands of persons, who know my honesty and modesty. I request that Stalin be informed that I am a victim of circumstances and nothing more, yet here enemies I have overlooked may have also had a hand in this. Tell Stalin that I shall die with his name on my lips.

Both Yezhov and Bukharin defended their personal honor. Bukharin, as he had done at his trial, made it clear that while he was prepared to admit to the overall charges against him, he was innocent of the specifics and had always been a loyal Bolshevik. Yezhov took a stronger line in his statement by repudiating the confession he had given to the NKVD interrogators and finally insisting on his complete innocence and constant loyalty to the cause.

Here there is a significant difference, and that difference tells us a great deal about two Bolshevik attitudes toward the party and terror. Yezhov admitted to nothing in connection with the charges against him. In his statement, however, Bukharin admitted to a bit more than he had at the February 1937 Central Committee plenum. There he had denied any knowledge of the activities, conspiratorial or otherwise, of his former followers after 1930. In this letter, however, he admitted to having known that they were up to something as late as 1932 and to not having told Stalin about it out of pity or a belief that he could reform them: "Aikhenval'd told me in passing . . . 'the gang has met, and a report was read'—or something of the sort. And, yes, I concealed this fact."

Knowing of underground activities of others and not reporting them was precisely what Bukharin had been accused of. It is difficult to see how such an admission could have done anything other than destroy any credibility he may still have had. Stalin might thus have legitimately wondered at what point Bukharin was telling (or would tell) the whole truth about his connections and knowledge of others' activities.

Both Yezhov and Bukharin knew that they would almost certainly be shot. Yet both pleaded for their lives on the bases of a lack of major sin in the past and of potential usefulness in the future. Each thought, or wanted to think, that there was some chance that Stalin would spare him. Bukharin in particular displayed an amazing naïveté when he suggested that Stalin exile him to America but warned that he would have to discuss it first with his wife. Bukharin and Yezhov pursued different discursive strategies to try to save their lives. Each, while intimating that his death was probably politically necessary, in different ways tried to give Stalin a reason to spare him. Each offered to Stalin a possible public narrative and construction of reality that could explain saving his life. The documents can therefore be seen as dialogues, although their interlocutor, Stalin, remained silent.

Bukharin's letter was that of one insider and longtime comrade writing to another. By surmising Stalin's "great and bold" idea for a purge, Bukharin spoke to Stalin as a fellow senior leader, as one of the top group that since before 1917 had originated and implemented great and bold ideas. Bukharin assured Stalin that he would confess at his trial and participate in the required apology/scapegoating ritual, but by drawing a distinction between that performance and the real truth, Bukharin's text explicitly recognized that the campaign against enemies was constructed and not reflective of political reality.

By alluding to Stalin's late wife, drawing on the long personal relationship between Stalin and Bukharin, and mentioning his physical ailments, Bukharin was also trying to evoke personal intimacy as well as political loyalty. Essentially, Bukharin was saying to Stalin, "You and I have been insiders together for a long time, and I want you to know that I understand the symbolic rituals and am willing to play along to show my loyalty. But we have been friends for so long; can't you help me in my misery and at the same time find some use for me?" Because of Stalin's history of saving Bukharin at the last minute, Bukharin must have thought he had a reasonable chance to save himself.

Yezhov took a different tack, and although he recognized the likelihood of his own death, he may have also been pursuing a strategy to save his life. Even though his text was technically a statement to the court, it was clear that it was addressed to Stalin. Because of his different relationship to Stalin, as subordinate rather than onetime equal and friend, Yezhov's position was more complicated, and he could not draw on the same discursive strategies as Bukharin; he did not have the long personal connection to Stalin that Bukharin, as a fellow member of Lenin's guard, had.

Because he really believed that spies were everywhere, Yezhov could not "nod and wink" at the invention and political construction of the hunt for enemies as Bukharin had. Nor could he follow what might have seemed an obvious strategy to the court: to argue that he was innocent of everything because "Stalin told me to do it" would have been not only suicidal but disloyal to Stalin and the party.

Unlike Bukharin, Yezhov calculated that to confess to the espionage charges against him at his trial not only would help the enemy but would deprive Stalin of a reason to save him. So Yezhov's text followed what was really the only potentially saving rhetorical strategy available to him: he did not make any distinction between true/false constative speech and useful performance, as Bukharin had done. The performative was, in fact, the real. He was saying to Stalin, "Unlike others, I accept as truth the basic premise that enemies are everywhere. See? They even smeared me. It's not necessary to scapegoat me for excesses. One could say that what happened was not false and there were no excesses; I [we] did what was necessary and it is defensible. I do not and will not refer to your role in this in any way, and as a loyal executor of a correct policy I could still be useful to you."

Both Bukharin and Yezhov were shaped by the texts and language of Stalinism, but in different ways. Yezhov, the comparatively simple party man, really believed that the victims of the terror were enemies and that they were guilty. He bragged about the number of enemies he had destroyed and said that his mistake consisted in not destroying more of them. He accepted at face value that all his assistants had turned out to be spies. The idea that the country had been riddled with literally millions of traitors and agents did not seem outlandish or absurd to him. He believed it to the end. At his trial Yezhov refused to confess to the scenario provided him. Instead, he told the "truth" as he understood it. He was not lying or being coy when he expressed fear that confessing to being a Polish spy would give comfort to the enemy. In Yezhov's black-and-white mentality, the enemy without really consisted of Polish pans, English lords, and Japanese samurai. For the Yezhovs, with no knowledge of the outside world, these were not shorthands or caricatures but real foes: the master public narrative was true on the face of it. For him, discourse merely described reality.

Bukharin, on the other hand, because he had sat in the highest councils for so long and understood the Bolshevik utilitarian attitude toward the "truth," could understand "something great and bold about the political idea of a general purge" of the guilty, the potentially guilty, and the merely suspicious. Truth, guilt, and innocence were defined by the party as whatever furthered the cause. Bukharin was prepared to give his life for that cause, telling Stalin, "If I were absolutely sure that your thoughts ran precisely along this path, then I would feel so much more at peace with myself." For Bukharin, the official public narrative and accompanying ritual were instruments. For him, discourse was an artifice to create a reality for the masses, and he understood that his death was to be a symbolic act to further the party's goals of unity. For Yezhov, on the other hand, party discourse *was* objective reality.

Which was the more authentic Stalinist? On one level, Bukharin was. He understood what was being asked of him; in his time he had demanded similar sacrifices from other Bolsheviks. He believed in the party's need for his ritual confession as part of its "universal-historical tasks," understood his party duty, and, within his personal limits, did it. Like Arthur Koestler's protagonist Rubashov in the novel *Darkness at Noon,* Bukharin was caught in a kind of Bolshevik intellectual trap. His education and Western logic told him that he was innocent and that he did not deserve to die. But his whole political life in the Bolshevik milieu told him otherwise and forced him to play out the political sequence he himself had helped to create: everything is justified for the party. As for Rubashov, part of Bukharin's tragedy was that he had devoted his life to the Revolution, and now the Revolution was destroying him.

On another level, however, Yezhov's statement also reflected genuine Bolshevism. Its uncompromising tone, lack of personal emotion, and true belief in the need to crush all enemies spoke more to the traditional iron-willed Bolshevik than Bukharin's intensely personal pleading. There is no reason to think that Yezhov understood anything of Bukharin's dilemma. For him, things were much simpler, and political utility or epistemological relativism did not enter into the matter. His situation was as clear-cut as a battlefield. Enemies were numerous and dangerous; his Civil War experience, social background, and party leadership told him so. The counter-revolutionaries had to be destroyed. He just did not happen to be one of them.

Part of the difference between the two was, of course, class background.

Workers like Yezhov had never been part of the theoretical world of Bolshevik politics, and intellectuals like Bukharin could relate to their plebeian followers only with great difficulty. But another difference had to do
with their different positions in the party. Yezhov's belief in the "correctness" of the leadership was absolute. He was a soldier who marched, understood, and indeed shot when, what, and whom the party dictated.
Bukharin, on the other hand, had long been a general, accustomed to interpreting the world for the party (and population) and presenting various
layers of the party with texts, transcripts, and discourses deemed suitable
for them.

Yezhov, although vicious and probably unbalanced, died simply, even
honestly. One is certain that he saw his end as a martyr's death, believing
that what he had done was right and that he had been dragged down by
the omnipresent evil enemies he had tried to destroy. Bukharin also understood his execution as a martyr's fate. But he died the death of an intellectual plagued at the end by self-doubt, whose death was the result of a web
of defensive political language, symbols, and rituals self-consciously built
up to keep a certain idea (and group) in power, even if it meant the members of the group volunteering to die one by one. Conditioned as it was by
elite party discipline, the constructed reality that the Bukharins had built
eventually facilitated their deaths. Bukharin died in a complex reality he
helped create. Yezhov died in a simple reality he believed.

Conclusion: Quicksand Politics

THE ROAD TO TERROR was a crooked and winding track. It doubled back on itself, ran into dead ends, and sometimes washed out altogether in unexpected political weather. In fact, there were many roads crisscrossing this strange political terrain, and they had many possible destinations. We single out this one because we know the starting point and the end point, but there is no reason to believe that terror was the only or inevitable outcome of these events.

We used to perceive only one road, and it was straight and simple. The main causal element for the terror has always been Stalin's personality and culpability. In most accounts there were no other authoritative actors, no limits on his power, no politics, no discussion of society or social climate, no confusion or indecision. Given the narrow focus, it was difficult to say more than "At this time Stalin decided to destroy . . . " (Western variant) or "On this date I. V. Stalin signed an order . . . " (Soviet/post-Soviet variant).

But even with Stalin in the role of master conductor, orchestrating from a prepared script (which, we have shown, was not the case), a more complete explanation of the terror must include other factors, and it is these factors that we have tried to add to the equation. That other powerful persons and groups had an interest in repression, that the social and political climate may have facilitated terror, and that the road to terror may have

231

been crooked and roundabout are premises too long ignored. It is our contention that the environment was as important as the agent in explaining the phenomenon as a whole. Straight roads do not run through broken and rocky terrain. Put another way, many people and groups contributed to a terror that would destroy them in the long run.

In schematic terms, we can now describe some of the features of the road. The Bolshevik elite, including Stalin, reacted with fear and anxiety to a disorderly and confused situation produced by the "Stalin Revolution" of the early 1930s. Even though the Stalinists had "won," by implementing their revolution, theirs was an unsatisfying victory. The regime had little doubt that despite its brave proclamations of victory and party unity, there was desperate opposition to it at many levels. Peasants sang about Stalin chewing bones on top of a coffin. Student groups cranked out incendiary pamphlets, and well-known party members gathered in the night to write platforms calling for the overthrow of the leadership. Even within that leadership, some Central Committee members knew about and sympathized with these nefarious activities and didn't report them. Stalinists were worried about personal meetings and conversations, not only among former oppositionists, but even among themselves. As they had been at the end of the Civil War, the Bolsheviks were insecure at precisely the time of their apparent ascendancy.

Their fears of losing control, even of losing power, led them into a series of steps to protect their position and consolidate the situation: sanctioning and building a unifying cult around Stalin, stifling even the hint of dissent within the elite by closing ranks around a rigid form of party discipline, and embarking on a program of centralization in everything from administration to culture. State building, with uniform laws, alternated with mobilizing terror, but both had the same goal: asserting the control of Stalin and the Moscow elite.

They tried to micromanage their entire political environment. They realized, even subconsciously, how little real day-to-day influence they had out in the countryside. Aware that they had failed to create a predictable and obedient administration, the Stalinists tried to govern by campaign, by creating ideological discourse and rituals, by the use of special plenipotentiaries, by creating parallel bureaucratic channels of information and control, by various "extraordinary situations." Whether we call it soft versus hard, moderate versus radical, or legalistic versus repressive, there seemed to be two policies, two currents that alternated in rapid sequence.

But these were not factions: the alternating and contending policy discourses often came from the same people, including Stalin, and were really two sides of the same coin. That coin was ending chaos, getting control and centralizing authority. They wanted to control printed discourse: sometimes that meant restraining locals, and sometimes it meant purging libraries. They wanted to control the judiciary: sometimes they chose to reinforce procuratorial sanction, and sometimes they pushed the extralegal Special Board. Sometimes the Politburo called for more arrests; other times it seemed to be narrowly circumscribing them. In either case, the point was that such decisions were to be made centrally, and Moscow, not local authorities, was to decide what was criminal and who should be arrested. Thus the dichotomy was not really "hard" versus "soft," but rather hard or soft roads to centralization of decision making and enforcing "fulfillment of decisions." Both the terror and its opposite, the Stalin Constitution, were thus about the same thing.

But despite what appear to be successes in these steps, Stalin and the elite were not able to overcome their insecurity. Stalin's suspicious nature and the elite's fears for their position combined to form a natural partnership in favor of centralization. His drive for personal power and the elite's drive for corporate status and authority made them natural allies for several years. They supported and endorsed each other to the outside world, including not only the Soviet population but also the party rank and file. Although his suspicion and their corporate anxiety fed upon each other, their joint action from 1932 to 1937 ultimately satisfied neither.

Although Stalin and the nomenklatura elite were generally united until 1937, as early as 1934 cracks had begun to appear in their alliance. Stalin's speech to the 17th Party Congress that year complained about the "feudal princes" of the party apparatus who thought that party directives "were not written for them but for fools." The nomenklatura's members were for discipline and obedience—among those below them. They were for using terror to excise opposition—but not in their own machines. They were for legality—as long as they controlled the courts and decided who would be arrested in their territories. Stalin and the Politburo insisted that *everyone* obey, follow discipline, and bow to central controls.

Stalin and his Moscow intimates tried a variety of tactics in the 1930s to control their own far-flung system. Membership purges, political jawboning about "fulfillment of decisions," delicate manipulation of texts to form or adjust alliances, investigations by police and control commissions, and various other tactics all failed to produce the results Stalin wanted.[1] As we have suggested, it was a delicate game in which Stalin and the other political actors jockeyed for power and advantage. The game had rules: nothing could be allowed to jeopardize the public image of Bolshevik unity or the regime's control over the country.

The use and content of language also played a delicate and subtle role in crystallizing and changing politics. Thus the evolution from "class enemy" to "the enemy with a party card" transformed a party united against the bourgeoisie into a party whose rank and file were suspicious of highly placed enemies within the elite. Manipulating language ended in the disaster of 1937, when language slipped from anyone's control, and anyone could be labeled a "Trotskyist" or "Bukharinist" simply in order to be isolated and destroyed. When in July 1937 Yezhov seriously posited the existence of a "left-right, Trotskyist-Bukharinist, German-Japanese-British-Polish espionage ring," it was clear that language was finished as a tool. The overtuning of language led to the destruction of the entire political system. Stalin and his closest associates, in a panic about loss of control of the country in time of war that still echoes in Molotov's and Kaganovich's memoirs, threw the entire political system into the air.

Everything came apart in the summer of 1937. After a series of failed attempts to control the nomenklatura elite and bend them to his will, Stalin turned against that elite; that elite turned against itself; and both struck out at a variety of "enemies" in the population. Characteristically, those enemies could not be identified very precisely. Alliances fractured and reformed; in 1937 and 1938 normal politics was replaced by a hysterical and paranoiac war of all against all.

Terror Without Planning

The road to centralized power was not necessarily a road to terror, and in any case, this road had no map. There were many twists and turns, and it would be a mistake to see in this some sort of grand plan for terror.[2] Without a doubt, at every juncture Stalin acted in ways that would increase his personal power; in this, at least, he seems to have had a clear goal. A careful look at events gives us several reasons to believe that the terror unfolded in an unplanned, ad hoc, even reactive way.

Actually, Stalin and his cronies were never very good at planning in general, as if anyone could be in the dramatically changing decades after the Russian revolutions of 1917. In the 1920s they planned for NEP to solve the economic balances. Then they scrapped it and decreed a planned economy without knowing what that meant. Beginning in 1928, they stumbled blindly from restricting wealthy peasants, to deporting them, to full collectivization, to semicollective cartels, all the while lurching back and forth without knowing where they were going with agriculture. In literally every area of domestic or foreign policy, as Politburo decisions and other documents now show, they spent most of their time putting out fires: reacting to crises (some totally unexpected, some that their own policies produced), improvising, mobilizing, and "storming" rather than governing. The Stalinists chronically made bad decisions based on bad information. Even though they were professional ideologists, they could not even produce a coherent ideological explanation for what they were doing—or had already done—that could survive more than a couple of years without drastic modification. There was no planning anywhere, so we should not expect it when it comes to repression.

First, we saw in a multitude of cases that repression moved in fits and starts and circles. The cases of Zinoviev, Kamenev, Smirnov, Yenukidze, Postyshev, Yagoda, and especially Bukharin were hardly handled in such a way as to suggest a plan. In each of these cases, there were false starts and abrupt "soft" but apparently "final" decisions that had to be contradicted later when other decisions were made. Had there been a plan, it would have been much easier and more convincing *not* to have let them off the hook so repeatedly and publicly.

Accordingly, final and fatal private and, more significantly, public texts had to explain previous and now embarrassing contrary decisions. An authoritative 1935 text exonerated Zinoviev and Kamenev of Kirov's murder, but the next year's discourse maintained that, after all, they were guilty. Yenukidze was expelled and then readmitted, both apparently on Stalin's initiative and amid considerable confusion, and then finally arrested a year later. The Politburo criticized Postyshev, fired him, rehired him, denounced his critics, fired him again. In January 1938 it decided to keep him in the party and then days later expelled him. Bukharin was denounced at the 1936 trial, then publicly cleared in the press, then denounced again in December, but saved by Stalin at a plenum that remained secret for decades. Finally, in February 1937 he was expelled and arrested in a flurry of puzzling paperwork that raises serious doubts about who wanted what. He was brought to trial an entire year later, fully six months after he began to confess to the charges brought against him.

Between 1935 and 1938 Stalin's assistant Yezhov drafted and redrafted a book, "From Fractionalism to Open Counterrevolution," which was a history of the opposition's allegedly inevitable turn to terror. During these years, the book had to be constantly rewritten to reflect the contradictory reversals in official discourse on "enemies." In early drafts, for example, Zinoviev and Kamenev were only morally culpable. In later drafts of the book, this section was rewritten to portray Zinoviev and Kamenev as the direct organizers of the Kirov murder. Later drafts had to make them spies and wreckers as well. Obviously, this interpretation had not been foreseen in 1935. Yezhov's book was never published.[3]

We might imagine that Stalin would have had a more convincing and less contradictory plan. He would have gotten his story straight from the beginning, saving himself the awkwardness of having to reverse and revise published decisions. Stalin's early interventions to defer or delay repression were embarrassing later when the official line praised the complete destruction of the "traitors." This may explain why several of Stalin's speeches to the Central Committee in 1935–37 either were not transcribed or were later removed from the archives, and could account for the fact that the plenum where he displayed his most ambiguous attitude (December 1936) was hushed up completely during his lifetime.

Actually, the false starts, contradictions, and reversals have been evident for a long time. But they have been inconsistent with our image of Stalin as not only evil but omniscient, omnipotent, almost supernatural. We have somehow needed to make him a leader who could lay murderous plans years ahead of time, could predict opposition and obstacles, and could successfully execute the scheme. Therefore in order to explain some of these zigzags it was sometimes suggested that Stalin liked to play a sadistic cat-and-mouse game with his victims: he swatted them about, trapped and released them for play. Aside from the fact that there are no sources supporting this idea, the notion is nonsense. No one can read the discourse of the Stalinists throughout the 1930s without sensing their nervousness, indecision, and even frequent panic. Nobody, including Stalin, had the leisure for games; these were serious matters in which lives were sacrificed to save a regime whose leaders felt it was hanging by a thread. Stalin distrusted the NKVD until late 1936 and the army until mid-1937. It would have been insufferably stupid of him to play games with armed elites in such circumstances, and no one has ever accused him of being stupid. Besides, he didn't need games; nobody would block him.

We see one clue to explaining the zigzags when, at several key junctures, Central Committee members advocated repressive measures that defied and went beyond those prescribed by Stalin's closest henchmen.[4] In one of the concrete glimpses we have of actual discussions in the Politburo, Stalin in 1930 had been outvoted by a Politburo majority that took a more aggressive stance than he did on punishment of oppositionists.[5] It may have been about this time, as Kaganovich later recalled, that younger members of the Central Committee asked Stalin why he was not tougher on the opposition.[6] We have seen other instances in which Stalin did not seem to have had the most radical or harsh attitude toward persecuting oppositionists. Stalin's immediate lieutenants had as much or more to gain by the final elimination of the Old Bolshevik opposition as he did: as the alternative leadership they were more of a threat to his lieutenants than to him. The opposition was the *former* elite, and as long as its members survived, the positions of the current Politburo and Central Committee members seemed even more insecure. It would not have taken much for the Molotovs and Kaganovichs to take implacable and cruel positions toward the opposition, regardless of Stalin's plans or lack of them. Everyone had his own interests.

The politics of the 1930s—and there *was* a politics—cannot be understood in terms of Stalin alone. Below him were Politburo members, Central Committee members, powerful chiefs and secretaries of central and territorial organizations, district and city party secretaries, full-time party activists, and ordinary party members. There were disagreements between Stalin and the nomenklatura—and among the nomenklatura—on power, planning, who was an enemy, elections, and a variety of other issues. Each of these groups had its own fears and its own interests to defend vis-à-vis those above them and those below. Everyone was maneuvering. Each of them grabbed as much autonomy as he could from above and used discursive, political, and/or repressive strategies to defend that autonomy and ensure obedience from those below. Everyone imagined that everyone else was trying to overthrow him. Each of them participated in and contributed to a suicidal violence that would eventually consume them.

If politics is defined as the deployment of power and influence through language, among other things, there was politics everywhere in the 1930s, as shifting issues and contingencies produced changing alignments between and among all these groups. This is the way bureaucratic politics works in other times and places, and indeed in all complex organizations. There is every reason to believe that this situation also existed in the Soviet 1930s.

Why the delay and confusion in the unfolding of the terror? The answer is that politics everywhere and always produces a fluid situation. Multi-player political maneuvering, even in conditions of growing personal dictatorship, is always messy, contradictory, and inconsistent with straight lines. The answer is that no one, including Stalin, knew where things would lead in the end. Although Stalin was a master of tactics, it may be only hindsight that makes us see a long-term Byzantine strategy in his actions. Following the principle of Occam's Razor, the simplest explanation is usually the best: Stalin's policies were confused and contradictory because he was confused and contradictory. If "quicksand society" aptly describes a situation of constant change and shifting where it was impossible to get one's footing, this was surely "quicksand politics."[7]

Given what we now know, it is ironic to read, as we still can, that the political events and documents of 1932–37 were some kind of preparation, a building crescendo of repression. In fact, the recourse to blind terror from the summer of 1937 was the opposite of the politics that had gone before. It was an abandonment not only of the varying hard/soft, moderate/radical, legalist/repressive discourse, but of policy discourse itself. In the preceding period, even the repressive trend had always implied a Moscow-directed repression and had been aimed at securing obedience and central control. The 1937–38 terror was different. Although it specified centrally planned quotas and procedures, it did not specify targets and left the selection of victims to local troikas and other bodies. Unlike the competing discourses about control and centralization in 1932–37, the 1937–38 terror was centrally authorized chaos. It was the negation of politics, speech, and language.

Legacies of the Terror

The terror left human disaster and titanic social change. Alexander Tivel's relatives were not alone in the 1950s as they tried to win legal and moral rehabilitation for their persecuted kin. Those who had survived the Stalinist camps would never be the same; even those who maintained their health were scarred forever. A generation of Soviet citizens never found out what happened to their friends and family; a generation of children wondered forever about their parents. Huge numbers of lives had been destroyed in one of the greatest human and personal tragedies of modern times.

People of the former Soviet Union still live with the social and political consequences of the 1930s terror. In our days, the victims, ghosts, and heirs of the terror still walk the earth. Stalin has been in his grave for more than half a century, but his victims are still being counted and remembered, and even today not many months go by without the discovery of hidden mass graves or nameless human bones washing up on some river bank. Stalin, his last henchmen Molotov and Kaganovich, and their countless victims have all now gone to their rewards. But in social and political terms, something survives from that time.

Stalin wanted an orderly and predictably functioning state to fulfill economic and military plans and policies. This required a professionally competent bureaucracy with some kind of career security, functioning within a rule-based system. But the heritage of Bolshevik revolutionary mobilization and energy made him fear a bureaucratic class outside party control. Social opposition, dissidence, and alternative discourses of all kinds constantly encouraged the resort to terror and lawlessness to maintain Bolshevik control. In the long run, the problem of "two models in one," as one scholar described it, would be a basic contradiction of the Stalinist system.[8]

In the long run, there would be steady and growing tension between statism and radicalism. Stalin and his circle would use (or threaten to use) a number of tools to prevent the solidification of an independent bureaucratic class, including membership screenings, party interventions that circumvented laws, and terror. The population of the GULAG camps continued to rise steadily up to the time of Stalin's death.[9] As long as Stalin lived, and to a lesser extent as long as his closest lieutenants remained in power, the state could not "normalize." As a result, the nomenklatura bureaucracy could not finally consolidate its hold on power. After Stalin's death in 1953, however, it was gradually freed. Terror was renounced, the rule of law was solidified, and a multipolar politics took shape in which a number of bureaucratic constituencies outside the Politburo became players in a system that did not constantly threaten their lives and interests. Rationalization and bureaucratic interests replaced high-level dictatorship and control. The fall of Khrushchev in 1964 was another significant landmark in the nomenklatura's freeing itself from Bolshevik political control and the power of a single leader.

Even though Stalin killed huge numbers of them in the 1930s, and even though the Communist Party and Soviet Union were dismantled in the early 1990s, the nomenklatura elite lives on. It survived Stalin and Stalinism. Although Stalin managed to destroy the elite of the 1930s, he did not and could not destroy the nomenklatura as a component of the regime. Back in the 1930s, Trotsky had predicted that the growing power of the nomenklatura could have one of two results. Either the workers would rise up and overthrow the elite, or that elite would ultimately be successful in converting itself into a true ruling class that not only wielded political power but owned the means of production outright.[10] As we know, there was no workers' revolution. Instead, the nomenklatura survived socialism and did in fact inherit the country. Its cohesion, connections, and experience were sufficient to allow its members to become not only the "new" governing elite, but the legal owners of the country's assets and property.

Numbers of Victims of the Terror

Scholars have long debated the precise numbers of victims of the terror of the 1930s. Their efforts have produced a wide gap, often of several millions, between high and low estimates. Using census and other data, they have put forward conflicting computations of birth, mortality, and arrests in order to calculate levels of famine deaths due to agricultural collectivization (1932–33), victims of the Great Terror (1936–39), and total "unnatural" population loss in the Stalin period. Some have posited relatively high estimates while others working from the same sources have put forth lower totals.[1] Each side has accused the other of sloppy or incompetent scholarship, and the conversation has often been marked by an unseemly and harsh tone.

Soviet secret police documents are now available that permit us to narrow the range of estimates. These materials are from the archival records of the Secretariat of GULAG, the Main Camp Administration of the NKVD/MVD (the USSR Ministry of the Interior), housed in the formerly "special" (closed) sections of the State Archive of the Russian Federation (GARF). The data are summarized in table 1, page 67.[2]

Archival data show that the total camp and exile population seems to have been slightly below 4 million before the war. Were we to extrapolate from the fragmentary prison data we do have, we might reasonably add a figure of 300,000–500,000 for each year as well as an additional contingent of about 200,000 exiles other than "kulaks," to put the maximum total detained population at around 4.5 million in the period of the Great Purges.[3]

Mainstream published estimates of the total numbers of arrests in the late 1930s have ranged from Dmitri Volkogonov's 3.5 million to Robert Conquest's 5–8 million to Olga Shatunovskaia's nearly 20 million.[4] The new archival materials suggests that Volkogonov was closest to the mark. A 1953 NKVD statistical report shows that 1,575,259 people were arrested by the security police in the course of 1937–38, 87.1 percent of them on political grounds. Of those arrested by the secret police, 1,344,923, or 85.4 percent, were convicted. (The contrast is striking with the period 1930–36, when 61.2 percent were arrested for political reasons and 61.7 percent of those arrested were eventually convicted, and especially with the years 1920–29, when 58.7 percent of security police arrests were for political reasons but only 20.8 percent of those arrested were convicted.)[5]

To be sure, the 1,575,259 people in the 1953 report do not include all 1937–38 arrests. Court statistics put the number of prosecutions unrelated to "counterrevolutionary" charges at 1,566,185, but it is unlikely that all persons in this cohort count in the *arrest* figures.[6] Especially if their sentences were noncustodial, such persons were often not formally arrested. 53.1 percent of all court decisions involved noncustodial sentences in 1937 and 58.7 percent in 1938, so the total of those who were executed or incarcerated gives 647,438 persons in categories other than "counterrevolution."[7] It therefore seems likely that the total number of arrests in 1937–38 is not too far from 2.5 million.

Although we do not have exact figures for arrests in 1937–38, we do know that the population of the GULAG camps increased by 175,487 in 1937 and by 320,828 in 1938 (it had declined in 1936). The population of all labor camps, labor colonies, and prisons on 1 January 1939, near the end of the Great Purges, was 2,022,976. This gives us a total increase in the camp and prison population in 1937–38 of 1,006,030. One must add to this figure the number of those who had been arrested but not sent to camps either because they were released sometime later, or because they were executed.

Popular estimates of executions in the Great Purges of 1937–38 vary from 500,000 to 7 million.[8] We do not have exact figures for the numbers of executions in these years, but we can now narrow the range considerably. According to a Gorbachev-era press release of the KGB, 786,098 persons were sentenced to death "for counterrevolutionary and state crimes" by various courts and extrajudicial bodies between 1930 and 1953.[9] According to the NKVD archival material currently available, 681,692 people were shot in 1937–38 (compared with 1,118 persons in 1936).[10] These archival figures, coming from a statistical report "on the quantity of people convicted upon cases of NKVD bodies," include victims who had not been arrested for political reasons, whereas the KGB press release concerns only persons persecuted for "counterrevolutionary offenses."[11] In any event, the data available at this point make it clear that the number shot in the two worst purge years was more likely a question of hundreds of thousands than of millions. The only period between 1930 and the outbreak of the war when the number of death sentences for non-political crimes outstripped those meted out to "counterrevolutionaries" was from August 1932 to the last quarter of 1933.[12]

Aside from executions in the terror of 1937–38, many others died in the regime's custody during the 1930s. If we add the figure we have for executions up to 1940 to the number of persons who died in GULAG camps and the few figures we have found so far on mortality in prisons and labor colonies, then add to this the number of peasants known to have died in exile, we reach a figure of 1,473,424 deaths directly due to repression in the 1930s.[13] If we put at hundreds of thousands the casualties of the most chaotic period of collectivization (deaths in exile, rather than from starvation in the 1932 famine), plus later victims of different categories for which we have no data, it is likely that "custodial mortality" figures of the 1930s would reach 2 million: a huge number of "excess deaths." The figures we can document for deaths due to repression are inexact, but the available sources suggest that we are now in the right ballpark, at least for the prewar period.

Accurate overall estimates of numbers of victims are difficult to make because of the fragmentary and dispersed nature of recordkeeping. Generally speaking, we have runs of quantitative data of several types: on arrests, formal charges and accusations, sentences, and camp populations. But these "events" could have taken place under the jurisdiction of a bewildering variety of institutions, each with its own statistical compilations and reports. These agencies included the several organizations of the secret police (NKVD troikas, special collegia, or special conferences (*osobye soveshchaniia*), the procuracy, the regular police, and various types of courts and tribunals. No single agency kept a master list reflecting the totality of repression, and great care is necessary to untangle the disparate events and actors in the penal process.

Further research is needed to locate the origins of inconsistencies and possible errors, especially when differences are significant. One must note, however, that the accuracy of Soviet records on much less mobile populations does not seem to give much hope that we can ever clarify each problem. For example, the Central Committee gave quite different figures in two documents that were compiled about the same time for the total party membership and its composition as of 1 January 1937.[14] Yet another number was given in published party statistics.[15] The conditions of perpetual movement in the camp system created even greater difficulties than those posed by keeping track of supposedly disciplined party members who had just seen two major attempts to improve the bookkeeping practices of the party.[16]

At times tens of thousands of inmates were listed in the category of "under way" in hard regime camp records, though the likelihood that some of them would die before leaving jail or during the long and torturous transportation made their departure and especially their arrival uncertain.[17] The situation is even more complicated with labor colonies, where, at any given moment, a considerable proportion of prisoners were being sent or taken to other places of detention, where a large number of convicts served rather short terms, and where many people had been held pending investigation, trial, or appeal of their sentences.[18]

Moreover, we do not yet know whether camp commandants, in an effort to receive higher budgetary allocations, inflated their reports on camp populations to include people slated for transfer to other places, prisoners who were only expected to arrive, and even the dead. Conversely, though, they may have been equally well advised to report as low a figure as possible in order to secure easily attainable production targets.

Because of these uncertainties, there is still controversy about the accuracy of these data, and no reason to believe them to be final or exact.[19] One cannot stress enough that with our current documentation, we can posit little more than general ranges (although narrow ones). Still, these are the only data currently available from police archives. Moreover, there are good reasons for assuming that they are not wildly wrong because of the consistent way numbers from different sources compare with one another.[20] These figures are analogous to those presented in secret reports to the Soviet Politburo in 1963 and 1988.[21] Figures produced by researchers using other archival collections of different agencies show close similarities in scale. Documents of the People's Commissariat of Finance discuss a custodial population whose size is not different from the one we have established.[22] Similarly, the labor force envisioned by the economic plans of the GULAG, found in the files of the Council of People's Commissars, does not imply figures in excess of our documentation.[23] Last but not least, the "NKVD contingent" of the 1937 and 1939 censuses is also consistent with the data we have for detainees and exiles.[24]

APPENDIX TWO

Biographical Notes

The following biographical notes were compiled from archival materials at RGASPI and mainly encompass the period covered in this study.

Agranov, Ya. S. (1893–1938). From 1934 to 1937, first deputy people's commissar for internal affairs of the USSR. From May 1937, head of the NKVD for Saratov Province. Repressed.

Akulov, I. A. (1888–1937). From 1929 to 1930, secretary and member of the Presidium of the All-Union Central Council of Trade Unions (VTsSPS). From 1929, deputy people's commissar of the Workers' and Peasants' Inspectorate (RKI). From 1931 to 1933, deputy chairman of the OGPU. From 1933 to 1935, procurator of the USSR. From 1935 to 1937, secretary of the Central Executive Committee (TsIK) of the USSR. Repressed.

Andreev, A. A. (1895–1971). From 1930, chairman of the Central Control Commission (CCC) of the VKP(b), people's commissar of the Workers' and Peasants' Inspectorate (RKI), and deputy chairman of the Council of People's Commissars (SNK) of the USSR. From 1931 to 1935, USSR people's commissar for railway transport. From 1935 to 1946, secretary of the CC of the VKP(b).

Beria, L. P. (1899–1953). From 1931, first secretary of the CC of the KP(b) of Georgia, first secretary of the Trans-Caucasus Regional Committee, and first secretary of the Tbilisi City Committee of the Party. From 1938 to 1945, USSR people's commissar for Internal Affairs. In 1953, arrested and shot.

Bliukher, V. K. (1890–1938). From 1929 to 1938, commander of the Special Red Banner Far Eastern Army. Repressed.

Budenny, S. M. (1883–1973). From 1924 to 1937, inspector of the cavalry of the Workers' and Peasants' Red Army (RKKA). From 1937 to 1938, commander of the troops of the Moscow Military District and member of the Chief Military Council of the USSR People's Commissariat for Defense.

Bukharin, N. I. (1888–1938). In the 1920s, Politburo member and leader of the Right Opposition. From 1929, head of a section of the Supreme Council for the National Economy of the USSR (VSNKh). From 1932, a member of the Collegium of the People's Commissariat for Heavy Industry (NKTP). From 1934 to 1937, editor in chief of the newspaper *Izvestia*, published by the Central Executive Committee (TsIK) of the USSR. In 1928–30, he headed the rightist opposition in the VKP(b). Repressed.

Bulganin, N. A. (1895–1975). From 1931, chairman of the Executive Committee of the Moscow Soviet. From 1937 to 1938, chairman of the Council of People's Commissars (SNK) of the RSFSR. From 1938 to 1941, deputy chairman of the Council of People's Commissars of the USSR.

Chubar, V. Ya. (1891–1939). From 1923 to 1934, chairman of the Council of People's Commissars (SNK) of the Ukrainian SSR. From 1934 to 1938, deputy chairman of the Council of People's Commissars and of the Council for Labor and Defense (STO) of the USSR, and USSR people's commissar for finance. Repressed.

Chudov, M. S. (1893–1937). From 1928 to 1936, second secretary of the Leningrad Provincial Committee of the VKP(b). Repressed.

Eikhe, R. I. (1890–1940). From 1929 to 1937, first secretary of the Siberian and Western Siberian Regional Committees and first secretary of the Novosibirsk City Committee of the VKP(b). From 1937 to 1938, USSR people's commissar of agriculture. Repressed.

Eismont, N. B. (1891–1935). From 1926 to 1932, RSFSR people's commissar for trade, deputy USSR people's commissar for internal and foreign trade, and RSFSR people's commissar for supplies. Arrested in 1932, released in February 1935, and continued working as a free laborer in the Novy Tambov camp of the NKVD. Died in an automobile accident.

Frinovsky, M. P. (1898–1940). From 1930 to 1933, chairman of the OGPU of the Azerbaijan SSR. In 1933, head of the Chief Directorate for Border Troops of the OGPU of the USSR. From 1936 to 1938, deputy, then first deputy USSR People's Commissar for Internal Affairs. Repressed.

Gamarnik, Ya. B. (1894–1937). From 1929 to 1937, head of the Political Directorate of the Workers' and Peasants' Red Army (RKKA). During this time, also deputy USSR people's commissar for military and naval affairs and deputy chairman of the Revolutionary Military Council of the USSR. Committed suicide.

Kaganovich, L. M. (1893–1991). From 1930 to 1935, first secretary of the Moscow Committee of the VKP(b). From 1934 to 1935, chairman of the Commission for Party Control (KPK) attached to the CC of the VKP(b). From 1935 to 1937 and from 1938 to 1942, USSR people's commissar for railway transport. From 1937 to 1939, USSR people's commissar for heavy industry. From 1928 to 1939, secretary of the CC of the Party.

Kalinin, M. I. (1875–1946). From 1922 to 1938, chairman of the Central Executive Committee (TsIK) of the USSR. From 1938 to 1946, chairman of the Presidium of the Supreme Soviet of the USSR.

Kamenev, L. B. (1883–1936). From 1922, deputy chairman of the Council of People's Commissars (SNK) of the RSFSR. From 1924 to 1925, chairman of the Council for Labor and Defense (STO). From January 1926, USSR people's commissar for trade. From 1926 to 1927, plenipotentiary representative of the USSR in Italy. From 1929, chairman of the Main Concessionary Committee. Repressed.

Khrushchev, N. S. (1894–1971). From 1932 to 1934, second secretary of the Moscow City Committee. From 1935 to 1938, first secretary of the Moscow Provincial and City Committees of the VKP(b).

Kirov, S. M. (1886–1934). From 1926 to 1934, first secretary of the Leningrad Provincial Committee of the VKP(b). In 1934, elected secretary of the CC of the VKP(b). Assassinated in Leningrad.

Kodatsky (Kadatsky), I. F. (1893–1937). From 1932, chairman of the Executive Committee of the Leningrad Soviet. In 1937, appointed head of the Main Directorate for the Construction of Light Machinery of the People's Commissariat for Heavy Industry. Repressed.

Kosarev, A. V. (1903–39). From 1929 to 1939, secretary-general (first secretary) of the CC of the All-Union Leninist-Communist Youth League (VLKSM). Repressed.

Kosior, S. V. (1889–1939). From 1928 to 1937, secretary of the CC of the KP(b) of the Ukraine. In 1938, both deputy chairman of the Council of People's Commissars (SNK) of the USSR and chairman of the Commission for Soviet Control attached to the Council of People's Commissars of the USSR. Repressed.

Krupskaia, N. K. (1869–1939). From 1929, RSFSR deputy people's commissar for education. Lenin's wife.

Krylenko, N. V. (1885–1938). From 1931, RSFSR people's commissar for justice. From 1936, USSR people's commissar for justice. Repressed.

Kuibyshev, V. V. (1888–1935). From 1930 to 1934, chairman of the State Planning Commission (Gosplan) of the USSR and deputy chairman of the Council of People's Commissars (SNK) of the USSR and of the Council for Labor and Defense (STO) of the USSR. From 1934, chairman of the Commission for Soviet Control attached to the Council of People's Commissars of the USSR and first deputy chairman of the Council of People's Commissars of the USSR and of the Council for Labor and Defense (STO) of the USSR.

Lominadze, V. V. (1897–1935). In 1930, first secretary of the Trans-Caucasus Regional Committee of the VKP(b). From August 1933, secretary of the Magnitogorsk City Committee of the VKP(b). Committed suicide.

Malenkov, G. M. (1902–88). From 1930, director of the Department of the Moscow Committee of the Party. From 1934 to 1939, director of the Department of Leading Party Organs of the CC of the VKP(b).

Molchanov, G. A. (1897–1937). From 1930 to 1936, head of the Secret-Political Department of the Main Administration for State Security (GUGB) of the NKVD of the USSR. From 1936 to 1937, people's commissar of Belorussia for internal affairs. Repressed.

Molotov (Skriabin), V. M. (1890–1986). From 1921 to 1957, a member of the CC of the Party. In 1921, candidate member, then from 1926 to 1957, member of the Politburo (Presidium) of the CC. From 1930 to 1941, chairman of the Council of People's Commissars (SNK) of the USSR.

Ordzhonikidze, G. K. (1886–1937). From 1930, chairman of the Supreme Council for the National Economy of the USSR (VSNKh), then USSR people's commissar for heavy industry. Committed suicide.

Osinsky, N. (V. V. Obolenskii) (1887–1938). From 1929, deputy chairman of the Supreme Council for the National Economy of the USSR (VSNKh) and deputy chairman of the State Planning Commission (Gosplan) of the USSR. In 1933, Chairman of the State Commission for Determining Crop Productivity attached to the Council of People's Commissars (SNK) of the USSR. Repressed.

Petrovsky, G. I. (1878–1958). From 1919 to 1938, chairman of the All-Ukrainian Central Executive Committee (TsIK) of the Ukrainian SSR and one of the chairmen of the Central Executive Committee of the USSR.

Piatakov, G. L. (1890–1937). From 1931 to 1936, deputy people's commissar of the USSR for heavy industry. Repressed.

Piatnitsky, I. A. (1882–1938). From 1922 to 1935, secretary of the Executive Committee of the Communist International (IKKI). From 1935 director of the Administrative-Political Department of the CC of the VKP(b). Repressed.

Postyshev, P. P. (1887–1939). From 1930 to 1934, secretary of the CC of the VKP(b). From 1930 to 1933, director of departments of the CC of the VKP(b). From 1933 to 1937, second secretary of the CC of the KP(b) of the Ukraine, first secretary of the Kiev Provincial Committee of the KP(b) of the Ukraine, then first secretary of the Kharkov Provincial and City Committees. From 1937 to 1938, first secretary of the Kuibyshev Provincial Committee of the VKP(b). Repressed.

Radek, K. B. (1885–1939). From 1925 to 1927, rector of the Chinese Workers' University of Moscow. Member of the editorial board of the newspaper *Izvestia*. In 1935, a member of the Constitutional Commission of the Central Executive Committee (TsIK) of the USSR. Convicted in 1937 and murdered in prison.

Riutin, M. N. (1890–1937). In 1930, member of the Presidium of the Supreme Council for the National Economy (VSNKh) of the USSR. Subsequently, from March to October 1930, chairman of the Board of the Photographic and Film Industry Association. Repressed.

Rudzutak, Ya. E. (1887–1938). From 1926 to 1937, deputy chairman of the Council of People's Commissars (SNK) and of the Council for Labor and Defense (STO) of the USSR. Simultaneously, from 1931 to 1934, chairman of the Central Control Commission (CCC) and people's commissar of the Workers' and Peasants' Inspectorate (RKI) of the USSR. Repressed.

Rumiantsev, I. P. (1886–1937). From 1929 to 1937, first secretary of the Western (Smolensk) Provincial Committee of the VKP(b). Repressed.

Rykov, A. I. (1881–1938). From 1924 to 1930, chairman of the Council of People's Commissars (SNK) of the USSR, chairman of the RSFSR Council of People's Commissars, and chairman of the Council for Labor and Defense (STO) of the USSR. A leader of the Right Opposition. From 1931 to 1936, USSR people's commissar for communications. Repressed.

Sheboldaev, B. P. (1895–1937). From 1931 to 1934, secretary of the Northern Caucasus Regional Committee of the VKP(b). From 1934 to 1937, secretary of the Azov–Black Sea Regional Committee of the VKP(b). From 1937, secretary of the Kursk Provincial Committee of the VKP(b). Repressed.

Shkiriatov, M. F. (1883–1954). From 1922 to 1934, member of the Central Control Commission (CCC) of the VKP(b). From 1927 to 1934, member of the Collegium of the People's Commissariat of the Workers' and Peasants' Inspectorate (RKI) of the USSR. From 1934 to 1939, secretary of the Party Collegium of the Commission for Party Control (KPK) attached to the CC of the VKP(b).

Shliapnikov, A. G. (1885–1937). People's commissar for labor in the first Soviet government. From 1920 to 1922, one of the leaders of the "Workers' Opposition." From 1923 to 1932, member of the Collegium of the State Publishing House (Gosizdat) and a councillor to the Plenipotentiary Bureau of the USSR in France. From 1932, member of the Presidium of the State Planning Commission (Gosplan). In 1933, expelled from the party. Repressed.

Smirnov, A. P. (1878–1938). From 1928 to 1930, deputy chairman of the Council of People's Commissars (SNK) of the RSFSR and secretary of the CC of the VKP(b). From 1931 to 1933, chairman of the All-Union Council for Utilities and Maintenance Enterprises attached to the Central Executive Committee (TsIK) of the USSR. In 1934, expelled from the party. Repressed.

Smirnov, I. N. (1881–1936). From 1923 to 1927, people's commissar of the USSR for communications. Member of the Trotskyist opposition. In 1933, convicted and sentenced to five years in prison. In 1936, sentenced to be shot as a member of the Trotskyist-Zinovievist Center.

Sokolnikov, G. Ya. (1888–1939). From 1929 to 1932, plenipotentiary representative of the USSR in Great Britain. Subsequently, USSR deputy people's commissar for foreign affairs. From 1935 to 1936, first deputy USSR people's commissar for light industry. Arrested in July 1936. Murdered in prison by his cellmates.

Stalin (Dzhugashvili), I. V. (1878–1953). Secretary of the CC of the Communist Party of the Soviet Union (KPSS) from 1922 to 1953.

Stetsky, A. I. (1896–1938). From 1930 to 1938, director of the Culture and Propaganda Department of the CC of the VKP(b). Also chief editor of the journal *Bolshevik*. Repressed.

Tomsky (Yefremov), M. P. (1880–1936). In the 1920s, chairman of Central Council of Trade Unions and a leader of the Right Opposition. From 1929, chairman of the All-Union Association of the Chemical Industry and deputy chairman of the Supreme Council for the National Economy (VSNKh). From 1932 to 1936, director of the Association of State Publishing Houses (OGIZ). Committed suicide.

Trotsky (Bronshtein), L. D. (1879–1940). From 1918 to 1925, chairman of the Revolutionary Military Council (RVS) of the Soviet Republic. Member of the Politburo of the CC of the VKP(b) in 1917 and from 1919 to 1926. Deported from the USSR in 1929 and assassinated in 1940.

Tukhachevsky, M. N. (1893–1937). From 1931, deputy chairman of the Revolutionary Military Council (RVS) of the USSR and head of armaments and munitions of the Workers' and Peasants' Red Army (RKKA). From 1934, USSR deputy people's commissar of defense. From 1936, first deputy USSR people's commissar for defense and head of the Directorate for Military Preparedness of the Workers' and Peasants' Red Army. Repressed.

Uglanov, N. A. (1886–1937). From 1928 to 1930, USSR people's commissar for labor. From 1930 to 1932, engaged in economic work in Astrakhan. From 1932 to 1933, worked in the People's Commissariat for Heavy Machinery Construction. Imprisoned in 1933. Repeatedly expelled from the party. Repressed.

Voroshilov, K. Ye. (1881–1969). From 1925 to 1934, chairman of the Revolutionary Military Council (RVS) of the USSR. From 1934 to 1940, USSR people's commissar of defense.

Vyshinsky, A. Ya. (1883–1954). From 1931 to 1935, procurator of the RSFSR and deputy people's commissar of the RSFSR for justice. From 1935 to 1939, procurator of the USSR.

Yagoda, G. G. (1891–1938). From 1924, deputy chairman of the OGPU. From 1934 to 1936, USSR people's commissar for internal affairs. From 1936 to 1937, USSR people's commissar of communications. Repressed.

Yakir, I. E. (1896–1937). From 1925 to 1935, commander of the Ukrainian Military District. From 1935 to 1937, commander of the Kiev, Leningrad, and Trans-Caucasus Military Districts. Repressed.

Yaroslavsky, E. M. (1878–1943). From 1923 to 1939, member of the Central Control Commission (CCC) and of the Commission for Party Control (KPK) attached to the CC of the VKP(b). From 1931 to 1935, chairman of the All-Union Society of Old Bolsheviks.

Yenukidze, A. S. (1877–1937). From 1922 to 1935, secretary of the Central Executive Committee (TsIK) of the USSR. Repressed.

Yezhov, N. I. (1895–1940). From 1929, USSR deputy people's commissar of agriculture. From 1930, chief of the Distribution Section, then chief of the Department of Cadres and chief of the Industrial Department of the CC of the VKP(b). From 1934 to 1935, deputy chairman of the Commission for Party Control (KPK). From 1935, chairman of the KPK. From 1936 to 1938, people's commissar of the USSR for internal affairs. From 1935 to 1939, secretary of the CC of the VKP(b). Executed on 4 February 1940.

Zhdanov, A. A. (1896–1948). From 1934 to 1944, secretary of the CC of the VKP(b) and first secretary of the Leningrad Provincial and City Committees of the VKP(b).

Zhukov, I. P. (1889–1937). In 1932, USSR deputy people's commissar for heavy industry. From 1933 to 1936, USSR deputy people's commissar for communications. From 1936 to 1937, RSFSR people's commissar for local industry. Repressed.

Zhuravlev, V. P. (1902–46). From 1937 to 1938, head of the NKVD for Kuibyshev Province. In 1938, head of the NKVD for Ivanovo Province. From December 1938, head of the NKVD for Moscow Province.

Zinoviev, G. E. (1883–1936). From 1919 to 1926, chairman of the Executive Committee of the Communist International (IKKI). From 1919 to 1926, one of the organizers of the United Opposition and one of the leaders of the Trotskyist-Zinovievist bloc. Expelled in 1927 from the VKP(b). Repressed.

Notes

Introduction

1. Feliks Chuev, *Sto sorok besed s Molotovym* (Moscow, 1991), 410–12.

2. Memo from V. Abakumov to Stalin, 17 July 1947, Rossiiskii gosudarstvennyi arkhiv noveishei istorii (hereafter RGANI), fond 89, opis' 18, delo 12.

3. Tivel's story is contained in his party file in RGASPI, f. 589, op. 3, d. 1466.

4. See, for example, Robert C. Tucker, *Stalin in Power: The Revolution from Above, 1928–1941* (New York, 1990), chapter 17.

5. For examples see Robert Conquest, *The Great Terror: A Reassessment* (Oxford, 1990), and two books by Oleg V. Khlevniuk, *1937: Stalin, NKVD i sovetskoe obshchestvo* (Moscow, 1992), and *Politbiuro: Mekhanizmy politicheskoi vlasti v 1930-e gody* (Moscow, 1996).

6. H. R. Trevor-Roper, *The European Witch-Craze of the Sixteenth and Seventeenth Centuries and Other Essays* (New York, 1968), 114–15.

7. The best work on this subject is Robert C. Tucker, *Stalin as Revolutionary, 1879–1929: A Study in History and Personality* (New York, 1973).

8. Technically, the word *nomenklatura* refers to the list of positions, appointment to which requires confirmation by a superior party body. Thus the nomenklatura of the Central Committee was the list of high positions reserved for Central Committee confirmation. With time, however, the word became a collective noun referring to the ruling stratum of the party itself.

9. James Hughes, "Patrimonialism and the Stalinist System: The Case of S. I. Syrtsov," *Europe-Asia Studies* 48 (1996), 551. See also Tucker, *Stalin as Revolutionary,* 303–4.

10. Inside the party, this was considered to have been the ultimate and unforgivable sin of the Trotskyist opposition of the 1920s.

11. To take only one local example, in See *Rabochii put'* (Smolensk), October 30, 1936, 1.

12. For a discussion of "transcripts" see James C. Scott, *Domination and the Arts of Resistance* (New Haven, 1990).

13. Ibid., 18.

14. Stephen Kotkin, *Magnetic Mountain: Stalinism as a Civilization* (Berkeley, 1995).

15. Pierre Bourdieu, *Outline of a Theory of Practice* (Cambridge, 1977), 193–94.

16. For such considerations see Veronique Garros, Natalia Korenevskaya, and Thomas Lahusen, *Intimacy and Terror* (New York, 1995), and Jochen Hellbeck, "Fashioning the Stalinist Soul: The Diary of Stepan Polubnyi (1831–1939)," *Jahrbucher fur Geschichte Osteuropas* 44 (1996), 344–73. See also Hellbeck's review of Kotkin's book ibid., 456–63.

17. Alexei Yurchak, *Everything Was Forever Until It Was No More: The Last Soviet Generation* (Princeton, 2006), 19. The preceding two paragraphs rely upon and condense Yurchak's excellent survey of John Austin's and Judith Butler's theoretical considerations about the nature of speech.

18. For a discussion of breakdowns in the party chain of command, see J. Arch Getty, *Origins of the Great Purges: The Soviet Communist Party Reconsidered, 1933–1938* (New York, 1985).

19. Bourdieu, *Outline of a Theory of Practice,* 190.

20. J. Arch Getty, "Afraid of Their Shadows: The Bolshevik Recourse to Terror, 1932–1938," in *Stalinismus vor dem Zweiten Weltkrieg. Neue Wege der Forschung,* ed. Manfred Hildermeier and Elisabeth Mueller-Luckner (Munich, 1998).

21. For an analysis of this literature and its limitations see Getty, *Origins,* 211–21.

22. See Walter G. Krivitsky, *In Stalin's Secret Service* (New York, 1939), 181, 183, 241, 242, and Alexander Orlov, *The Secret History of Stalin's Crimes* (New York, 1953), 178, 310.

1. The New Situation, 1930–32

1. On the Civil War see Diane P. Koenker, William G. Rosenberg, and Ronald G. Suny, eds., *Party, State, and Society in the Russian Civil War: Explorations in Social History* (Bloomington, Ind., 1989); Peter Kenez, *Civil War in South Russia, 1919–1920* (Berkeley, 1977). An unsurpassed early work is William Chamberlin, *The Russian Revolution,* vol. 2 (London, 1935).

2. See Orlando Figes, *Peasant Russia, Civil War: The Volga Countryside in Revolution, 1917–1921* (Oxford, 1989); Silvana Malle, *The Economic Organization of War Communism, 1918–1921* (New York, 1985).

3. Stephen F. Cohen, *Bukharin and the Bolshevik Revolution: A Political Biography, 1888–1938* (New York, 1975); Lewis H. Siegelbaum, *Soviet State and Society Between Revolutions, 1918–1929* (New York, 1992); Sheila Fitzpatrick, Alexander Rabinowitch, and Richard Stites, eds., *Russia in the Era of NEP: Explorations in Soviet Society and Culture* (Bloomington, Ind., 1991).

4. Robert H. McNeal, *Stalin: Man and Ruler* (Oxford, 1988).

5. See Graeme Gill, *The Origins of the Stalinist Political System* (Cambridge, 1990), for the development of party organization.

6. The classic work on Trotsky is still Isaac Deutscher, *The Prophet,* 3 vols. (Oxford, 1959).

7. Robert V. Daniels, *The Conscience of the Revolution: Communist Opposition in Soviet Russia* (New York, 1969).

8. See the memoirs of Stalin's daughter: "Nikolai Bukharin, whom everyone adored, often came for the summer"; Svetlana Alliluyeva, *Twenty Letters to a Friend* (New York, 1967), 31.

9. See Cohen, *Bukharin,* and Michal Reiman, *The Birth of Stalinism: The USSR on the Eve of the Second Revolution,* trans. George Saunders (Bloomington, Ind., 1987).

10. Rykov told this to the American newspaper reporter William Reswick; W. Reswick, *I Dreamt Revolution* (Chicago, 1956), 254.

11. Moshe Lewin, *Russian Peasants and Soviet Power: A Study of Collectivization* (London, 1968); R. W. Davies, *The Socialist Offensive: The Collectivization of Soviet Agriculture, 1929–1930* (Cambridge, Mass., 1980); Sheila Fitzpatrick, *Stalin's Peasants: Resistance and Survival in the Russian Village After Collectivization* (Oxford, 1994).

12. Sheila Fitzpatrick, *Education and Social Mobility in the Soviet Union, 1921–1934* (New York, 1979).

13. James C. Scott, *Domination and the Arts of Resistance* (New Haven, 1990), 57. See also Pierre Bourdieu, *Outline of a Theory of Practice* (Cambridge, 1977), chapter 4, for a discussion of "symbolic capital."

14. RGASPI, f. 17, op. 2, d. 453, ll. 53–61, 70–74, 77–78, 87–92. Two puns are involved here: 1) a pun on Kamenev's name: *kamen'* means "stone"; and 2) the expression: *derzhat' kamen' za pazukhoi,* that is, "to nurse a grievance, to harbor a grudge."

15. Scott, *Domination,* 49, 58.

16. RGASPI, f. 17, op. 2, d. 453, ll. 169–71, 175–86.

17. RGASPI, f. 17, op. 163, d. 1002, l. 218 (from the "special folders" of the Politburo).

18. For information on Riutin, see Boris A. Starkov, *Martem'ian Riutin: Na koleni ne vstanu* (Moscow, 1992). See also *Izvestiia TsK KPSS,* 1989, no. 6, 103–15, and 1990, no. 3, 150–62.

19. "Ko vsem chlenam VKP(b)," in Starkov, *Martem'ian Riutin,* 252–59.

20. The committee, which was also the central leadership group of the Union, consisted of Old Bolsheviks M. S. Ivanov, V. N. Kaiurov, P. A. Galkin, and P. P. Fedorov. *Izvestiia TsK KPSS,* 1990, no. 8, 200.

21. For this rumor, which appears to have originated in Paris, see Boris I. Nicolaevsky, *Power and the Soviet Elite: The Letter of an Old Bolshevik and Other Essays* (New York, 1965). Although this story is unsubstantiated, we do know of another incident eighteen months earlier, when a Politburo majority "strongly opposed" and overruled a Stalin motion for lenient punishments of Central Committee dissidents. The majority were for harsher punishments. See RGASPI, f. 17, op. 163, ll. 199, 218.

22. Published in I. V. Kurilova, N. N. Mikhailov, and V. P. Naumov, eds., *Reabilitatsia: Politicheskie protsessy 30–50-x godov* (Moscow, 1991), 334–443.

23. Michel Foucault, *The Archaeology of Knowledge and the Discourse on Language,* trans. A. M. Sheridan Smith (New York, 1972), 217.

24. In 1934 Stalin quoted from Trotsky's *Biulleten* at the 17th Party Congress; *XVII s"ezd Vsesoiuznoi Kommunisticheskoi Partii(b). 26 ianvaria–10 fevralia 1934g. Stenografichesky otchet* (Moscow, 1934), 32. In 1935 N. I. Yezhov quoted extensively from it to a closed meeting of the Central Committee; RGASPI, f. 17, op. 2, d. 542, ll. 73–76.

25. For Trotsky's analysis of the Stalin regime see Robert H. McNeal, "Trotskyist Interpretations of Stalinism," in *Stalinism: Essays in Historical Interpretation,* ed. Robert C. Tucker (New York, 1977), 30–52.

26. Trotsky Papers (Exile Correspondence), Houghton Library, Harvard University, 15821. The contents of these letters have not been preserved; Trotsky's archive contains only the postal receipts.

27. Ibid., 8114 (emphases in the original).

28. Ibid., 13095. See also J. Arch Getty, "Trotsky in Exile: The Founding of the Fourth International," *Soviet Studies* 38 (1986), 24–35.

29. Trotsky Papers; excision in the original document.

30. George Breitman and Bev Scott, eds., *Writing of Leon Trotsky [1932–1933]* (New York, 1972), 34.

31. Trotsky Papers, 4782.

32. Ibid., T-3522.

33. RGASPI, f. 17, op. 2, d. 577, l. 14.

34. See Sarah Davies, "'Us Against Them': Social Identities in Soviet Russia, 1934–41," *Russian Review* 56 (1997), 70–89.

35. RGALI (Russian State Archive of Literature and Art), f. 1518, op. 4, d. 22, ll. 27, 28; ANSPb (St. Petersburg Archive of the Academy of Sciences), f. 717, op. 1, d. 16, l. 48. We are indebted to Gábor Rittersporn for these citations.

36. There is a copy in RGASPI, f. 17, op. 120, d. 68.

37. RGASPI, f. 17, op. 120, d. 106, ll. 56, 560b, 58–59.

38. See Fitzpatrick, *Stalin's Peasants,* for a discussion of peasant hostility to Stalin and the regime.

39. RGASPI, f. 17, op. 120, d. 106, l. 17; op. 42, d. 90, ll. 10–11.

40. See Merle Fainsod, *Smolensk Under Soviet Rule* (Cambridge, Mass., 1958), chapter 19, "Censorship: A Documented Record."

41. RGASPI, f. 17, op. 120, d. 272, ll. 10–16.

42. RGASPI, f. 17, op. 3, d. 965, ll. 30, 63–64. See also high-level concern with libraries in *Gosudarstvennyi arkhiv Rossiskoi Federatsii* (GARF), f. 5446, op. 22a, d. 339, ll. 5–12.

2. Party Discipline in 1932

1. T. H. Rigby, *Communist Party Membership in the USSR, 1917–1967* (Princeton, 1968), 52.

2. For a discussion of this problem, see Sheila Fitzpatrick, *Stalin's Peasants: Resistance and Survival in the Russian Village After Collectivization* (New York, 1994), chapter 3.

3. For the best analysis of these developments, see Nabuo Shimotomai, "Springtime for the Politotdel: Local Party Organizations in Crisis," *Acta Slavica Iaponica* 4 (1986), 1034; see also J. Arch Getty, *Origins of the Great Purges: The Soviet Communist Party Reconsidered, 1933–1938* (New York, 1985), chapter 2.

4. See the documentary account in *Neizvestnaia Rossiia,* no. 1, 1992, 56–128.

5. Smirnov's arraignment before the Politburo was transcribed: L. P. Koshelova, L. A. Rogovaia, and O. V. Khlevniuk, *Stenogrammy zasedanii Politbiuro TsK RKP(b) 1923–1938. Tom 3, 1928–1938* (Moscow, 2007), 551–676.

6. RGASPI, f. 17, op. 2, d. 511, ll. 137–39. Typescript with Smirnov's corrections.

7. Sean Wilentz, *Rites of Power: Symbolism, Ritual, and Politics Since the Middle Ages* (Philadelphia, 1985), 6.

8. See Nina Tumarkin, *Lenin Lives! The Lenin Cult in Soviet Russia* (Cambridge, Mass., 1983); Nina Tumarkin, *The Living and the Dead: The Rise and Fall of the Cult of World War II in Russia* (New York, 1994). On the Stalin cult, see Graeme Gill, "Personality Cult, Political Culture, and Party Structure," *Studies in Comparative Communism* 17 (1984), 111–21; J. Arch Getty, "The Politics of Stalinism," in *The Stalin Phenomenon,* ed. Alec Nove (New York, 1992), 104–63.

9. Clifford Geertz, "Centers, Kings, and Charisma: Reflections on the Symbolics of Power," in *Local Knowledge* (New York: Basic, 1991), 124. For Geertz, "the easy distinction between the trappings of rule and its substance becomes less sharp, even less real" the closer they are examined.

10. James C. Scott, *Domination and the Arts of Resistance* (New Haven, 1990), 57. For a treatment of the function of apology as a "remedial ritual" or "remedial interchange," see Erving Goffman, *Relations in Public: Microstudies of the Public Order* (New York, 1971), 113–16.

11. See Michel Foucault, *The Archaeology of Knowledge and the Discourse on Language,* trans. A. M. Sheridan Smith (New York, 1972), 226.

12. RGASPI, f. 17, op. 2, d. 511, ll. 205–14. Typescript with Akulov's corrections.

13. RGASPI, f. 17, op. 2, d. 511, ll. 168–78. Typescript with Shkiriatov's corrections.

14. RGASPI, f. 17, op. 120, d. 70, l. 58.

15. RGASPI, f. 17, op. 2, d. 511, ll. 12–22. Typescript with Rudzutak's corrections.

16. RGASPI, f. 17, op. 2, d. 511, ll. 215–20. Typescript with Bukharin's corrections.

17. RGASPI, f. 17, op. 2, d. 511, ll. 117–19. Typescript.

18. RGASPI, f. 17, op. 2, d. 511, ll. 260–66. Typescript with Voroshilov's corrections.

19. For this view see Robert Conquest, *The Great Terror: A Reassessment* (Oxford, 1990); Robert C. Tucker, *Stalin in Power: The Revolution from Above, 1928–1941* (New York, 1990); A. A. Antonov-Ovseenko, *The Time of Stalin: Portrait of Tyranny* (New York, 1980).

20. For this argument see J. Arch Getty, *Origins of the Great Purges: The Soviet Communist Party Reconsidered, 1933–1938* (New York, 1985); J. Arch Getty and Roberta T. Manning, eds., *Stalinist Terror: New Perspectives* (New York, 1993); Gábor T. Rittersporn, *Stalinist Simplifications and Soviet Complications: Social Tensions and Political Conflicts in the USSR, 1933–1953* (Reading, 1991); Robert Weinberg, "Purge and Politics in the Periphery: Birobidzhan in 1937," *Slavic Review* 52 (1993), 13–27.

3. Repression and Legality

1. Stalin had personally nominated Bukharin to the *Izvestia* position in 1934. See RGASPI, f. 17, op. 3, d. 939, l. 2.

2. See John Barber, "Stalin's Letter to Proletarskaya Revolyutsiya," *Soviet Studies* 28 (1976), 21–41, and George M. Enteen, "Writing Party History in the USSR: The Case of E. M. Yaroslavsky," *Journal of Contemporary History* 21 (1986), 321–39. On the activities of Soviet censors both locally and nationally, see Merle Fainsod, *Smolensk Under Soviet Rule* (Cambridge, Mass., 1958), 365–77, and Marianna Tax Choldin and Maurice Friedberg, *The Red Pencil: Artists, Scholars, and Censors in the USSR* (Boston, 1989).

3. RGASPI, f. 17, op. 2, d. 453, ll. 169–71, 175–86.

4. RGASPI, f. 17, op. 3, d. 874, l. 15.

5. Clifford Geertz, *The Interpretation of Cultures* (New York, 1973), 219–20.

6. RGASPI, f. 17, op. 120, d. 87, ll. 27–28.

7. For copies of these letters and orders, see *Istochnik*, no. 4, 1996, 137–44.

8. RGASPI, f. 17, op. 3, d. 961, l. 16.

9. For background, see Peter H. Solomon, Jr., *Soviet Criminal Justice Under Stalin* (Cambridge, 1996); Robert Sharlet, "Stalinism and Soviet Legal Culture," in *Stalinism: Essays in Historical Interpretation,* ed. Robert C. Tucker (New York, 1977), 155–79; Gábor T. Rittersporn, "Soviet Officialdom and Political Evolution: Judiciary Apparatus and Penal Policy in the 1930s," *Theory and Society* 13 (1984), 211–37; and Eugene Huskey, "Vyshinsky, Krylenko, and the Shaping of the Soviet Legal Order," *Slavic Review* 46 (1987), 414–28.

10. See Solomon, *Soviet Criminal Justice,* chapters 3 and 4.

11. *Pravda,* 2 March 1930. See also Stalin's "Reply to Kolkhoz Comrades," *Pravda,* 3 April 1930.

12. I. V. Stalin, *Sochninenia* (Moscow, 1951), 13: 72.

13. RGASPI, f. 17, op. 3, d. 840, l. 9.

14. RGASPI, f. 17, op. 162, d. 13, ll. 99–100.

15. Solomon, *Soviet Criminal Justice,* 117.

16. L. A. Paparde, *Novoi etap klassovoi bor'by i revoliutsionnaia zakonnost'* (Novosibirsk, 1933), 4–26.

17. Solomon, *Soviet Criminal Justice,* 223, 225.

18. See GARF, f. 3316, op. 2, d. 1534, ll. 87, 112; d. 1754, ll. 21, 26; f. 9474, op. 16, d. 48, ll. 15, 17, 35–36, 42; d. 79, ll. 6, 16. See also the discussions in V. P. Danilov and N. A. Ivnitsky, eds., *Dokumenty svidetel'stvuiut, 1927–32: Iz istorii derevni nakanune i v khode kollektivizatsii 1927–1932 gg.* (Moscow, 1989), 40–46, and J. Arch Getty, Gábor T. Rittersporn, and V. N. Zemskov, "Victims of the Soviet Penal System in the Pre-war Years: A First Approach on the Basis of Archival Evidence," *American Historical Review* 98 (1993), 1017–49.

19. See Robert Conquest, *The Great Terror: A Reassessment* (Oxford, 1990), appendix.

20. Gordon W. Morrell, *Britain Confronts the Stalin Revolution: Anglo-Soviet Relations and the Metro-Vickers Crisis* (Waterloo, Ontario, 1995), 150.

21. RGASPI, f. 17, op. 3, d. 922, l. 16. Some exceptions were made. Troikas in the Far Eastern Territory could continue passing death sentences. Moreover, in the following period, the Politburo continued to authorize death sentences by troikas

on a case-by-case period during specified periods. See, for example, RGASPI, f. 17, op. 162, d. 15, ll. 2, 27.

22. RGASPI, f. 17, op. 3, d. 922, ll. 50–55. Printed. This document was first described by Merle Fainsod in *Smolensk Under Soviet Rule* (Cambridge, Mass., 1958), 185–88, from one of the circular copies found in the Smolensk Archive. Two months earlier, in March 1933, the Politburo had ordered a reduction in prison populations and normalization of rations for prisoners. V. N. Khaustov et al., eds. *Lubianka. Stalin i VChK-GPU-OGPU-NKVD. Ianvar' 1922–dekabr' 1936* (Moscow, 2003), 410–13.

23. GARF, f. 5446, op. 15a, d. 1073, l. 35.

24. See Glenn G. Morgan, *Soviet Administrative Legality: The Role of the Attorney General's Office* (Stanford, 1962).

25. RGASPI, f. 17, op. 3, d. 939, l. 2; *Izvestiia,* 11 July 11 1934.

26. See the documents in the Politburo's "special folders," RGASPI, f. 17, op. 163, d. 1043, ll. 33–39.

27. *Izvestiia,* 22 December 1934.

28. RGASPI, f. 17, op. 162, d. 16, ll. 88–89.

29. B. A. Viktorov, *Bez grifa "sekretno." Zapiski voennogo prokurora* (Moscow, 1990), 139–40.

30. Khaustov et al., *Lubianka,* 814.

31. RGASPI, f. 17, op. 3, d. 943, l. 10; op. 3, d. 954, l. 38.

32. See J. Arch Getty, *Origins of the Great Purges: The Soviet Communist Party Reconsidered, 1933–1938* (New York, 1985), chapter 2, for a description of party purges. See also T. H. Rigby, *Communist Party Membership in the USSR, 1917–1967* (Princeton, 1968), 204, for a discussion of these nonpolitical targets.

33. RGASPI, f. 17, op. 3, d. 922, ll. 50–55.

34. P. N. Pospelov et al., *Istoriia Kommunisticheskoi Partii Sovetskogo Soiuza,* tom. 4, chast' 2 (Moscow, 1971), 283.

35. *XVII s"ezd, Vsesoiuznoi Kommunisticheskoi Partii(b). 26 ianvaria–10 fevralia 1934g. Stenograficheskly otchet* (Moscow, 1934), 33–34.

36. Ibid., 32–34.

37. See, for example, Boris I. Nicolaevsky, *Power and the Soviet Elite: The Letter of an Old Bolshevik and Other Essays* (New York, 1965), 43, 48–50.

38. See, for example, Conquest, *Great Terror.*

39. J. Arch Getty, "State and Society Under Stalin: Constitutions and Elections in the 1930s," *Slavic Review* 50 (1991), 18–36.

40. Solomon, *Soviet Criminal Justice,* chapter 5. For a discussion of Stalinist state building, see J. Arch Getty, "Les bureaucrats bolcheviques et l'État stalinien," *Revue des Études Slaves* 64 (1991), 1–25.

41. Moshe Lewin, *The Making of the Soviet System* (New York, 1985), 281–84.

42. RGASPI, f. 17, op. 163, d. 1033, ll. 61–62.

43. RGASPI, f. 17, op. 165, d. 47, l. 3.

44. Solomon, *Soviet Criminal Justice,* 166.

45. RGASPI, f. 17, op. 163, d. 1052, l. 153.

46. See Getty, "State and Society." For another view, see Sheila Fitzpatrick, *Stalin's Peasants: Resistance and Survival in the Russian Village After Collectivization* (New York, 1994), 281.

4. Growing Tension in 1935

1. Robert Conquest, *Stalin and the Kirov Murder* (New York, 1989), 4.

2. Ibid. See also Robert C. Tucker, *Stalin in Power: The Revolution from Above, 1928–1941* (New York, 1990), chapter 12. Anastas Mikoian, writing years later, wondered whether Stalin's relatively lenient treatment of NKVD chief Genrikh Yagoda after the assassination meant that Stalin and Yagoda had conspired to kill Kirov. A. I. Mikoian, *Tak bylo: razmyshleniia o minuvshem* (Moscow, 1999), 316–17. On the other hand, Yagoda probably avoided taking major blame because two months before the assassination he had complained about the Leningrad NKVD's incompetence and had tried to shake up its leadership. V. N. Khaustov et al., eds., *Lubianka. Stalin i VChK-GPU-OGPU-NKVD. Ianvar' 1922–dekabr' 1936* (Moscow, 2003), 569–71.

3. "Vokrug ubistva Kirova," *Pravda,* 4 November 1991, and A. Yakovlev, "O dekabr'skoi tragedii 1934 goda," *Pravda,* 28 January 1991.

4. See, for example, the accounts of persecution of the opposition in *Izvestiia TsK KPSS,* nos. 7 and 9, 1989.

5. Adam Ulam, *Stalin: The Man and His Era* (New York, 1973), 375–88.

6. In 1956 Khrushchev formed a commission chaired by N. Shvernik to investigate the Kirov murder. It "found nothing against Stalin. . . . Khrushchev refused to publish it—it was of no use to him." Feliks Chuev, *Sto sorok besed s Molotovym* (Moscow 1991), 353.

7. Francesco Benvenuti, "Kirov in Soviet Politics, 1933–1934," Soviet Industrialization Project Series no. 8, University of Birmingham (England), 1977. See also Oleg V. Khlevniuk, *Politbiuro: Mekhanizmy politicheskoi vlasti v 1930-e gody* (Moscow, 1996), 118–25.

8. *Izvestiia TsK KPSS,* no. 7, 1989, 114–21.

9. See the analysis ibid., and in J. Arch Getty and Roberta T. Manning, eds., *Stalinist Terror: New Perspectives* (New York, 1993), 44–46.

10. "Vokrug ubistva Kirova," *Pravda,* 4 November 1991.

11. J. Arch Getty and Oleg V. Naumov, *Yezhov: The Rise of Stalin's "Iron Fist"* (New Haven, 2008), chapter 7.

12. See J. Arch Getty, *Origins of the Great Purges: The Soviet Communist Party Reconsidered, 1933–1938* (New York, 1985), appendix; J. Arch Getty, "The Politics of Repression Revisited," in Getty and Manning, *Stalinist Terror,* 40–62.

13. S. V. Kulashov, O. V. Volobuev, E. I. Pivovar, et al., *Nashe otechestvo. chast' II.* (Moscow, 1991), 310; Boris Starkov, "Ar'ergardnye boi staroi partiinoi gvardii," in *Oni ne molchali,* ed. A. V. Afanas'ev (Moscow, 1991), 215; Oleg V. Khlevniuk, *1937: Stalin, NKVD i sovetskoe obshchestvo* (Moscow, 1992), 46.

14. Anna Kirilina, *Rikoshet, ili skol'ko chelovek bylo ubito vystrelom v Smol'nom* (Saint Petersburg, 1993).

15. Matthew E. Lenoe, *The Kirov Murder and Soviet History* (New Haven, forthcoming, 2010).

16. *Izvestiia TsK KPSS,* no. 7, 1989, 69, and no. 1, 1990, 39.

17. RGASPI, f. 17, op. 3, d. 955, l. 24; *Izvestiia TsK KPSS,* no. 7, 1989, 75. When the Politburo announced NKVD staff changes after the Kirov assassination, it included an unusual formulation "obligating" Yagoda to report back to the Politburo in three days on fulfillment of the orders. See RGASPI, f. 17, op. 3, d. 955, l. 24.

18. *Pravda*, 23 December 1934 and 16 January 1935; *Izvestiia TsK KPSS*, no. 7, 1989, 70.

19. See *Leningradskaia pravda*, 6, 8, 11, 12, 18 December 1934, for reports.

20. *Leningradskaia pravda*, 20 March 1935.

21. Getty and Naumov, *Yezhov*, 139–40; Khaustov et al., *Lubianka*, 670–71, 821.

22. Khaustov et al., *Lubianka*, 592–93.

23. V. N. Khaustov, "Deiatel'nost' organov bezopasnosti NKVD SSSR (1934–1942)," Ph.D. diss., Akademiia FSB, Moscow, 1997, 38.

24. RGASPI, f. 617, op. 1, d. 118, ll. 25, 34. Yezhov's letter to Stalin was his own idea. Typically, reports and memos written to Stalin *in response* to his request or order contain phrases like "in response to your order" or something similar, wording that is absent in Yezhov's letter. Yezhov's campaign against Yagoda is treated in detail in Getty and Naumov, *Yezhov*.

25. Yagoda deeply resented Yezhov's meddling in his bureaucratic bailiwick. He complained to his subordinates about it and told them not to talk business with Yezhov without his, Yagoda's, permission. When one of them did so anyway, Yagoda exploded: "He screamed at me, demanding to know why I had not sought permission from him" before talking to Yezhov. "He told me that Yezhov was not the Central Committee, that his orders were not directives, and that only he—Yagoda—had the right to deal with the Central Committee on questions of the NKVD's work." When Agranov told his boss Yagoda that a certain measure should be coordinated with Yezhov, Yagoda exploded at him too, "If you are not the boss in your own house, then go ahead and coordinate your work with him." See RGASPI, f. 17, op, 2, d. 598, ll. 2–4, 12–18, ll. 23–26, 29–35, 41–42. See also I. V. Kurilova, N. N. Mikhailov, and V. P. Naumov, eds., *Reabilitatsiia: Politicheskie protsessy 30–50-x godov* (Moscow, 1991), 153–54, and Yezhov's statement at his own trial in *Moskovskie novosti*, no. 5, 1994.

26. *Izvestiia TsK KPSS*, no. 8, 1989, 95–115. Printed.

27. RGASPI, f. 17, op. 120, d. 174, ll. 11–14, 74–75; d. 175, ll. 73, 76; d. 176, ll. 13, 125, 127, 128, 133, 135.

28. "Anti-Soviet agitation" could include anything from printing subversive leaflets to telling dangerous political jokes.

29. *Izvestiia TsK KPSS*, no. 1, 1990, 38–58.

30. *Izvestiia TsK KPSS*, no. 7, 1989, 85, no. 1, 1990, 39.

31. *Izvestiia TsK KPSS*, no. 1, 1990, 54.

32. This, at least, was Molotov's memory of him. Chuev, *Sto sorok besed*, 438.

33. RGASPI, f. 17, op. 3, d. 805, l. 16. For Yezhov's early career, see Getty and Naumov, *Yezhov*.

34. The verifications operations had to do with interagency economic agreements and investigation of customs fraud. See RGASPI, f. 17, op. 3, d. 916, l. 6; d. 913, l. 1.

35. Kaganovich, his apparent patron, was chairman of the KPK.

36. RGASPI, f. 17, op. 3, d. 948, l. 36; d. 951, l. 1.

37. *Izvestiia TsK KPSS*, no. 7, 1989, 65–93. See also Khaustov, et al., *Lubianka*, 599–669.

38. For background on the Yenukidze affair, see Iurii Zhukov, *Inoi Stalin. Politicheskie reformy v SSSR v 1933–1937 gg.* (Moscow, 2003), chapter 6.

39. RGASPI, f. 17, op. 2, d. 542, ll. 55–86. Typed.

40. RGASPI, f. 17, op. 2, d. 542, ll. 125–41.

41. Yezhov's remarks and implied criticism of Yagoda's NKVD were part of his long-term campaign to discredit Yagoda.

42. RGASPI, f. 17, op. 2, d. 542, ll. 175–78.

43. RGASPI, f. 17, op. 2, d. 542, ll. 158–59.

44. RGASPI, f. 17, op. 2, d. 547, l. 69.

45. RGASPI, f. 17, op. 2, d. 544, l. 22. Printed stenographic report.

46. Khaustov et al., *Lubianka,* 663–69.

47. RGASPI, f. 17, op. 42, d. 136, l. 87.

48. RGASPI, f. 17, op. 3, d. 965, l. 30. For the list, see ll. 63–64.

49. RGASPI, f. 17, op. 3, d. 970, l. 50.

50. RGASPI, f. 17, op. 3, d. 374, l. 108; d. 974, l. 137.

51. RGASPI, f. 17, op. 3, d. 965, l. 75.

52. See reports of Party Control Commission inspectors in RGANI, f. 6, op. 1, d. 5, ll. 90, 95, 98–99, 165–66; and d. 59, l. 186.

53. RGASPI, f. 17, op. 120, d. 179, ll. 34–77, 253–68. Note: syntax in original is incoherent.

54. RGASPI, f. 17, op. 120, d. 171, ll. 62–670b.

55. Smolensk Archive file 499, ll. 308–9.

56. See Getty, *Origins,* chapters 2 and 3, for background on this and other purges. These new data on NKVD participation in the proverka revise the earlier conclusions there, based on other archives, that the police played little role in the operation.

57. RGASPI, f. 17, op. 120, d. 177, ll. 20–22. This number is almost certainly incomplete. A subsequent internal Central Committee memo of February 1937 inexplicably gave a figure of 263,885 proverka expulsions (RGASPI, f. 17, op. 120, d. 278, l. 2). It was not uncommon in this period for the same agencies to give wildly varying figures for party membership.

58. RGASPI, f. 17, op. 120, d. 184, ll. 60–66.

59. RGASPI, f. 17, op. 120, d. 179, ll. 34–77.

60. See Stalin's speech on "fulfillment of decisions" at the 17th Party Congress in early 1934: *XVII s"ezd Vsesoiuznoi Kommunisticheskoi Partii(b). 26 ianvaria–10 fevralia 1934g. Stenografichesky otchet* (Moscow, 1934), 23–35.

61. For example, see RGASPI, f. 17, op. 71, d. 34, ll. 114–15.

62. Yezhov frequently noted, in 1935 but not later, that allowing party committees to purge themselves was a good idea. See RGASPI, f. 17, op. 120, d. 77, ll. 4 ff.

63. The most publicized case was the Central Committee's rebuke of the Saratov party organization. See RGASPI, f. 17, op. 114, d. 585, ll. 1–2 for the Orgburo meeting on Saratov. The resulting press campaign is in *Pravda,* 12 July 1935; *Partiinoe stroitel'stvo,* no. 13, July 1935, 44–45; and A. A. Zhdanov, *Uroki politicheskikh oshibok Saratovskogo kraikoma* (Moscow, 1935). The subject would come up again the following year.

64. See Yezhov's and Stalin's remarks to the June 1936 plenum of the Central Committee; RGASPI, f. 17, op. 2, d. 572, ll. 67–75.

65. RGASPI, f. 17, op. 120, d. 278, l. 7.

66. Several thousand persons who had been expelled for oppositional activities were deported from Moscow. See Khaustov et al., *Lubianka,* 724–35. Oleg V.

Khlevniuk has written that eventually more than two hundred thousand expelled party members were placed under NKVD surveillance: *1937: Stalin, NKVD i sovetskoe obshchestvo* (Moscow, 1992), 57. It is difficult to imagine how this could have been possible.

67. For the report, see RGASPI, f. 17, op. 120, d. 181, ll. 102–5.

68. RGASPI, f. 17, op. 120, d. 182, ll. 93–94; d. 183, l. 166.

69. RGASPI, f. 17, op. 2, d. 576, ll. 67–70. Ellipses in the original.

70. For examples, see RGASPI, f. 17, op. 120, d. 183, l. 166; d. 181, ll. 102–5, and GARF, f. 9415, op. 5, d. 487, ll. 90–91.

5. The Fork in the Road

1. "O kolichestve osuzhdennykh po delam organov NKVD za 1930–1936 gody," GARF, f. 9401, op. 1, d. 4157, ll. 201–5. For analysis of these data, see J. Arch Getty, Gábor T. Rittersporn, and V. N. Zemskov, "Victims of the Soviet Penal System in the Pre-War Years: A First Approach on the Basis of Archival Evidence," *American Historical Review* 98 (1993), 1017–49. See also Robert Thurston, *Life and Terror in Stalin's Russia, 1934–1941* (New Haven, 1996), 9–12.

2. See Eugene Huskey, "Vyshinsky, Krylenko, and the Shaping of the Soviet Legal Order," *Slavic Review* 46 (1987), 414–28; J. Arch Getty, *Origins of the Great Purges: The Soviet Communist Party Reconsidered, 1933–1938* (New York, 1985), 199–201; Robert H. McNeal, "The Decisions of the CPSU and the Great Purge," *Soviet Studies* 23 (1971), 177–85. See also Peter H. Solomon, Jr., *Soviet Criminal Justice Under Stalin* (Cambridge, 1996), part 3.

3. RGASPI, f. 17, op. 3, d. 976, l. 17.

4. RGASPI, f. 17, op. 3, d. 980, l. 9.

5. For examples, see RGASPI, f. 17, op. 21, d. 2206, ll. 228–29.

6. James C. Scott, *Domination and the Arts of Resistance* (New Haven, 1990), 50.

7. *Pravda*, 5 June 1936. For security reasons, it was customary for Pravda to announce Central Committee plenums only after they had been completed.

8. See, for example, *Pravda*, 7–10 June 1936.

9. RGASPI, f. 17, op. 2, d. 568, ll. 135–36.

10. RGASPI, f. 17, op. 2, d. 572, l. 67.

11. It seems that the plenum did in fact produce a resolution criticizing the regional secretaries for mass expulsions, although none was published at the time and none can be located in the archives. It was only quoted in part two years later: *Pravda*, 19 June 1938.

12. RGASPI, f. 17, op. 2, d. 572, ll. 73–75.

13. RGASPI, f. 17, op. 2, d. 568, ll. 13, 141, 154–55.

14. Here Stalin seems to have changed his mind once again on Yenukidze. The previous September he had written to Kaganovich that NKVD materials suggested that Yenukidze was "not one of us," *chuzhdyi nam chelovek*. RGASPI, f. 81, op. 3, d. 100, ll. 92–93.

15. RGASPI, f. 17, op. 2, d. 572, ll. 67–73.

16. RGASPI, f. 17, op. 2, d. 568, ll. 165–68.

17. *Voprosy istorii*, no. 2, 1995, 9 (stenographic report of the February–March 1937 plenum). At the time of this writing, no archival version of the full steno-

graphic report of this plenum is available to researchers. It is serialized in the journal *Voprosy istorii;* subsequent references to that journal are to this published plenum transcript, unless otherwise indicated.

18. RGASPI, f. 17, op. 2, d. 562, l. 2; f. 17, op. 2, d. 598, l. 34; *Voprosy istorii,* no. 2, 1995, 18.

19. Scott, *Domination,* 55–56.

6. The Face of the Enemy, 1936

1. Olberg may have been a double agent or a police informer, secretly spying on the Trotskyist organizations on behalf of the NKVD. To date, no documents have been found to support or disprove this theory.

2. *Voprosy istorii,* no. 10, 1994, 21, 26 (stenographic report of the February–March 1937 plenum).

3. *Voprosy istorii,* no. 2, 1995, 17 (stenographic report of the February–March 1937 plenum); *Izvestiia TsK KPSS,* no. 8, 1989, 85.

4. *Izvestiia TsK KPSS,* no. 9, 1989, 35. The so-called Kirov Law of 1 December 1934 was passed immediately after Kirov's assassination and mandated abbreviated legal proceedings and immediate application of death sentences, without appeal, to those convicted of terrorism.

5. *Izvestiia TsK KPSS,* no. 8, 1989, 83.

6. Molotov dismissed this idea out of hand because the accused would have correctly found such an offer preposterous: "They were not fools, after all." Feliks Chuev, *Sto sorok besed s Molotovym* (Moscow 1991), 404.

7. See Arthur Koestler, *Darkness at Noon* (New York, 1941).

8. "Zasluzhennyi prigovor," 4 August 1936; RGASPI, f. 671, op. 1, d. 172, ll. 497, 525.

9. *Izvestiia TsK KPSS,* no. 8, 1989, 91–92, 102.

10. *Izvestiia TsK KPSS,* no. 8, 1989, 100–115; printed.

11. This first show trial was hardly a "bolt from the blue," as some émigré commentators, far from the events they described, wrote. See Robert Conquest, *The Great Terror: A Reassessment* (Oxford, 1990), p. 150, citing the apocryphal "Letter of an Old Bolshevik."

12. Trotsky Papers (Exile Correspondence), Houghton Library, Harvard University, 13095.

13. *Izvestiia TsK KPSS,* no. 8, 1989, 92; no. 9, 1989, 42.

14. The transcript of the trial was published as *Sudebnyi otchet po delu Trotskistko-Zinov'evskogo terroristicheskogo tsentra* (Moscow, 1936), and was translated into English as *The Case of the Trotskyist-Zinovievite Center* (New York, 1936). For examples of other such sentences from the "special folders" (*osobye papki*) of the Politburo, see RGASPI, f. 17, op. 162, d. 16, ll. 1, 62, 64.

15. *Izvestiia TsK KPSS,* no. 8, 1989, 93.

16. RTsKhIDNI, f. 17, op. 120, d. 271, l. 21. For other examples, see op. 21, d. 2195, ll. 114, 1140b.

17. See Roberta T. Manning, "The Soviet Economic Crisis of 1936–1940 and the Great Purges," in *Stalinist Terror: New Perspectives,* ed. J. Arch Getty and Roberta T. Manning (New York, 1993), 116–41.

18. *Voprosy istorii,* no. 10, 1995, 8.

19. *Voprosy istorii,* no. 3, 1995, 3–15.

20. For examples, see speeches by Malenkov, Mekhlis, Beria, and Kudriavtsev to the February–March 1937 plenum. *Voprosy istorii,* nos. 5–6, 1995, 10; no. 7, 1995, 19–21; no. 10, 1995, 10–15.

21. Smolensk Archive file 116/154e, l. 88.

22. See Malenkov's speech to the February–March 1937 Plenum of the Central Committee. *Voprosy istorii,* no. 10, 1995, 7.

23. See J. Arch Getty, "Pragmatists and Puritans: The Rise and Fall of the Party Control Commission in the 1930s," *Carl Beck Papers in Russian and East European Studies* 1208 (1997), 1–45.

24. See Stalin's concluding speech in *Voprosy istorii,* no. 3, 1995, 3–15, nos. 11–12, 1995, 11–22. His remarks were published as a pamphlet called *Mastering Bolshevism* (New York, 1937).

25. For a fuller discussion of this problem, see Gábor T. Rittersporn, *Stalinist Simplifications and Soviet Complications: Social Tensions and Political Conflicts in the USSR, 1933–1953* (Reading, 1991).

26. *Voprosy istorii,* nos. 5–6, 1995, 4.

27. Quoted in V. N. Khaustov et al., eds. *Lubianka. Stalin i glavnoe upravlenie gosbezopasnosti NKVD, 1937–1938* (Moscow, 2004), 92.

28. RGASPI, f. 17, op. 3, d. 981, l. 58. The Politburo did not meet to approve this resolution. Drafted by Kaganovich and later signed by Stalin (who was on vacation at the time), the Politburo resolution was approved by polling the members. See *Izvestiia TsK KPSS,* no. 5, 1989, 72.

29. See Gábor T. Rittersporn, "The Omnipresent Conspiracy: On Soviet Imagery of Politics and Social Relations in the 1930s," in Getty and Manning, *Stalinist Terror,* 99–115.

30. For examples of such far-fetched accusations from this era, see RGASPI, f. 17, op. 71, d. 35, ll. 6–15, and d. 74, ll. 2–3.

31. For Yagoda's claims see RGASPI, f. 17, op. 2, d. 598, ll. 1–18.

32. J. Arch Getty and Oleg V. Naumov, *Yezhov: The Rise of Stalin's "Iron Fist"* (New Haven, 2008), chapter 9, uses materials, including rough drafts of letters to Stalin from Yezhov's archive, to show his psychology and techniques of manipulation.

33. RGASPI, f. 558, op. 11, d. 729, ll. 81–84.

34. Nikita Khrushchev, *The Secret Speech Delivered to the Closed Session of the 20th Congress of the CPSU* (London, 1956), 35–36. The "four years behind" referred to the formation of the Zinoviev-Trotsky bloc and the simultaneous appearance of the Riutin Platform in late 1932. See also the discussion of Yagoda's fall in J. Arch Getty, *Origins of the Great Purges: The Soviet Communist Party Reconsidered, 1933–1938* (New York, 1985), 119–26.

35. A. M. Larina, *Nezabyvaemoe* (Moscow, 1989), 269–70.

36. RGASPI, f. 85, op. 27, d. 93, ll. 12–13. Handwritten.

37. See *Pravda,* 20 December 1937, and *20 let VchK-OGPU-NKVD* (Moscow, 1938).

38. RGASPI, f. 17, op. 71, d. 42, ll. 1–8.

39. *Voprosy istorii,* no. 2, 1994, 22.

40. *Izvestiia TsK KPSS,* no. 9, 1989, 36–37; RGASPI, f. 85, op. 1, d. 136, ll. 47–48.

41. Oleg V. Khlevniuk, *Stalin i Ordzhonikidze: Konflikty v Politbiuro v 30-e gody* (Moscow, 1993).

42. RGASPI, f. 17, op. 85, d. 186.

43. Larina, *Nezabyvaemoe*, 327–28.

44. *Voprosy istorii*, nos. 11–12, 1995, 14–16.

45. For an example, see RGASPI, f. 17, op. 2 d. 614, l. 2140b.

46. RGASPI, f. 17, op. 2, d. 573, ll. 23, 26, 35, 36.

47. RGASPI, f. 17, op. 2, d. 573, l. 33.

48. RGASPI, f. 85, op. 29, d. 156, ll. 5–12. Typed text without corrections.

49. RGASPI, f. 17, op. 120, d. 272, ll. 54–55.

50. RGASPI, f. 17, op. 120, d. 272, ll. 76–78.

51. Letter by I. Kuchkin to N. I. Yezhov, 11 August 1936. RGASPI, f. 17, op. 120, d. 272, l. 41.

52. *Izvestiia TsK KPSS,* no. 5, 1989, 72–73. Those to be reinterrogated included Nikolai Uglanov, former district party secretary in Moscow, and M. Riutin.

53. Ibid., 71.

54. Ibid., 74, 84.

55. RGASPI, f. 17, op. 2, d. 575, ll. 11–19, 40–45, 49–53, 57–60, 66–67. From the uncorrected shorthand minutes.

56. In the 1970s an unrepentant Molotov defended the terror in precisely the same prewar terms. See Chuev, *Sto sorok besed,* 390, 413, 432.

57. Using the informal *ty.*

58. Bukharin's Speech to the December 1936 CC Plenum, 4 December 1936. RGASPI, f. 17, op. 2, d. 575, ll. 69–74, 82–86, 122–26, 144, 159–62, 165–67, 169–72, from the uncorrected shorthand minutes; RGASPI, f. 17, op. 2, d. 576, ll. 67–70, from uncorrected "excerpts" pages of the minutes.

59. *Izvestiia TsK KPSS,* no. 5, 1989, 75–76.

60. Ibid., 76. In the versions of the plenum available to researchers in RGASPI, this part of the transcript has been removed.

61. Svetlana Alliluyeva, *Twenty Letters to a Friend* (New York, 1967), 31.

62. Chuev, *Sto sorok besed,* 463.

7. The Sky Darkens

1. *Pravda,* 29 March and 1 April 1937.

2. For Andreev's speech to the plenum of the Azov–Black Sea Territorial Committee, 6 January 1937, see RGASPI, f. 17, op. 21, d. 2196, ll. 10–13, 16–17, 22–23, 32–40. Typed, without corrections.

3. Resolution of the Azov–Black Sea Territorial Committee on Removal of Comrade Sheboldaev, 5 January 1937. RGASPI, f. 17, op. 21, d. 2214, l. 5.

4. B. P. Sheboldaev's speech to the Plenum of the Azov–Black Sea Territorial Committee, January 6, 1937. RGASPI, f. 17, op. 21, d. 2196, ll. 5–9. Typed text, unsigned and uncorrected.

5. RGASPI, f. 17, op. 21, d. 2196, ll. 266–70.

6. RGASPI, f. 17, op. 21, d. 2196, l. 279.

7. RGASPI, f. 17, op. 21, d. 2214, l. 9.

8. RGASPI, f. 558, op 1, d. 5023, ll. 1–17. Manuscript, apparently in Stalin's hand.

9. *Pravda,* 6 March 1937. For the stenographic report of Zhdanov's speech and the discussion of it, see RGASPI, f. 17, op. 2, d. 612, ll. 3–42. For less than enthusiastic comments from CC members, see the remarks of Kosior (l. 19), Khataevich (l. 21), and Mirzoian (ll. 27–29). See also *Voprosy istorii,* no. 10, 1995, 21.

10. RGASPI, f. 17, op. 2, d. 612, l. 42.

11. Smolensk Archive, f. 111, ll. 2–66; f. 321, ll. 87–96. See also the discussion in J. Arch Getty, *Origins of the Great Purges: The Soviet Communist Party Reconsidered, 1933–1938* (New York, 1985), 151–53.

12. *Voprosy istorii,* no. 10, 1995, 3–4.

13. *Voprosy istorii,* nos. 11–12, 1995, 21.

14. For a discussion of the Nikolaenko affair, see Oleg V. Khlevniuk, *1937: Stalin, NKVD i sovetskoe obshchestvo* (Moscow, 1992), 102–9.

15. RGANI, f. 6, op. 6, d. 23, ll. 1–2, files of the Party Control Commission.

16. *Pravda,* 1 April 1937; *Voprosy istorii,* no. 3, 1995, 5.

17. RGASPI, f. 73, op. 2, d. 4.

18. RGASPI, f. 17, op. 21, d. 2214, ll. 16–18, 26; op. 3. d. 989 (Protocol no. 51 of the Politburo, 20 June–31 July 1937, no. 39).

19. *Izvestiia TsK KPSS,* no. 4, 1989, 76, 84. Six months later, at Stalin's order, Astrov was released from prison and given an apartment and a job in historical research. Later, in the Khrushchev period, Astrov stated that Yezhov himself had "confirmed" to Astrov that the rightists were in fact terrorists. As Astrov said in 1957, "This confirmation removed my moral impetus to resist the demands of the investigators." I. V. Kurilova, N. N. Mikhailov, and V. P. Naumov, eds., *Reabilitatsia: Politicheskie protsessy 30–50-x godov* (Moscow, 1991), 259.

20. See the account in Oleg V. Khlevniuk, *Stalin i Ordzhonikidze: Konflikty v Politbiuro v 30-e gody* (Moscow, 1993), 111–29.

21. *Voprosy istorii,* nos. 2–3, 1992, 6.

22. Ibid., 43.

23. *Voprosy istorii,* nos. 4–5, 1992, 16.

24. Ibid.

25. Ibid., 22.

26. Ibid., 24, 32–34.

27. *Voprosy istorii,* nos. 6–7, 1992, 4, 16–17.

28. Ibid., 1992, 23–24, 30.

29. *Voprosy istorii,* nos. 8–9, 1992, 3, 8–9.

30. Ibid., 1992, 17–19.

31. Ibid., 1992, 20, 25, 29.

32. *Voprosy istorii,* no. 10, 1992, 6–7.

33. *Voprosy istorii,* no. 2, 1993, 3–10, 17.

34. Ibid., 26, 27, 33.

35. See *XVII s"ezd Vsesoiuznoi Kommunisticheskoi Partii(b). 26 ianvaria–10 fevralia 1934g. Stenografichesky otchet* (Moscow, 1934), 435–36, 648–50, and the accounts in Kendall E. Bailes, *Technology and Society Under Lenin and Stalin: Origins of the Soviet Technical Intelligentsia, 1917–1941* (Princeton, 1978), 302, and Eugene Zaleski, *Stalinist Planning for Economic Growth, 1933–1953* (Chapel Hill, 1980), 115–29.

36. RGASPI, f. 17, op. 2, d. 577, l. 4.

37. *Voprosy istorii,* no. 1, 1994, 12–13.

38. RGASPI, f. 17, op. 2, d. 612, vols. 1 and 2.

39. Oleg V. Khlevniuk, *Politbiuro: Mekhanizmy politicheskoi vlasti v 1930-e gody* (Moscow, 1996), 210.

40. *Istochnik*, no. 3, 1994, 75.

41. Beria told this to Bukharin's widow. A. Larina, *Nezabyvaemoe* (Moscow, 1989), 178.

8. The Storm of 1937

1. *Izvestiia TsK KPSS*, no. 9, 1989, 36. See also Robert Conquest, *Inside Stalin's Secret Police: NKVD Politics, 1936–39* (Stanford, 1985).

2. RGASPI, f. 17, op. 114, d. 622, l. 13.

3. RGASPI, f. 17, op. 2, d. 577, ll. 9–10. From the printed stenographic report.

4. RGASPI, f. 17, op. 2, d. 598, ll. 2–4, 12–15, 17–18. Typed, corrected minutes.

5. Agranov was not arrested until mid-1937. Three weeks after the plenum, he addressed an NKVD conference on the sins of Molchanov. See *Izvestiia TsK KPSS*, no. 8, 1989, 84.

6. RGASPI, f. 17, op. 2, d. 598, ll. 23–26, 29–35, 41, 42. Typed, corrected minutes.

7. *Voprosy istorii*, no. 2, 1995, 21.

8. RGASPI, f. 17, op. 2, d. 614, ll. 103, 119.

9. RGASPI, f. 17, op. 3, d. 985, ll. 3, 34.

10. See J. Arch Getty, *Origins of the Great Purges: The Soviet Communist Party Reconsidered, 1933–1938* (New York, 1985), chapter 6, for an analysis of the 1937 party elections.

11. See, for example, Roberta T. Manning, "The Great Purges in a Rural District: Belyi Raion Revisited," in *Stalinist Terror: New Perspectives*, ed. J. Arch Getty and Roberta T. Manning (New York, 1993), 168–97.

12. RGASPI, f. 17, op. 114, d. 623, l. 5.

13. *Istochnik*, no. 3, 1994, 73.

14. The most authoritative account of the "military conspiracy" based on still secret archives is in *Izvestiia TsK KPSS*, no. 4, 1989, 42–80.

15. See V. A. Zolotarev, ed., *Prikazy narodnogo komissara oborony SSSR, 1937–21 iiunia 1941g.* (Moscow, 1994), 11–13.

16. See V. N. Khaustov et al., eds., *Lubianka. Stalin i glavnoe upravlenie gosbezopasnosti NKVD, 1937–1938* (Moscow, 2004), 202–9.

17. Feliks Chuev, *Sto sorok besed s Molotovym* (Moscow, 1991), 418, 442.

18. Ivo Banac, ed., *The Diary of Georgi Dimitrov, 1933–1949* (New Haven, 2003), 11 November 1937, 70.

19. RGASPI, f. 39, op. 2, d. 45, ll. 105–7. This was relayed to Stalin in March 1937 from the NKVD.

20. A. Larina, *Nezabyvaemoe* (Moscow, 1989), 27.

21. Boris A. Starkov, "Narkom Yezhov," in Getty and Manning, *Stalinist Terror*, 35, based on documents in the KGB archive.

22. Chuev, *Sto sorok besed*, 390, 413.

23. See, for example, A. Svetlanin (pseud. V. Likhachev), *Dal'nevostochnyi zagovor* (Frankfurt, 1953); Walter Krivitsky, *I Was Stalin's Agent* (New York, 1939).

24. *Izvestiia TsK KPSS*, no. 4, 1989, 50.

25. RGASPI, f. 17, op. 2, d. 615, l. 68.

26. Ibid., ll. 79–790b.

27. Roger Reese, "The Red Army and the Great Purges," in Getty and Manning, *Stalinist Terror*, 198–214.

28. RGASPI, f. 17, op. 3, d. 989, l. 60.

29. See RGASPI, f. 17, op. 2, d. 614, for numerous Politburo orders to arrest Central Committee members and other high-ranking party leaders.

30. See Khaustov et al., *Lubianka*, for many of these.

31. RGASPI, f. 17, op. 2, d. 614, ll. 1–4.

32. See Roberta T. Manning, "The Soviet Economic Crisis of 1936–1940 and the Great Purges," in Getty and Manning, *Stalinist Terror*, 116–41.

33. For an example of such an incident when Kaganovich visited Smolensk, based on transcripts of local party documents, see RGASPI, f. 17, op. 21, dd. 3966–4092.

34. RGASPI, f. 73, op. 2, d. 19, ll. 1–106.

35. RGANI, f. 89, op. 48, d. 9, l. 1.

36. RGASPI, f. 73, op. 2, d. 19, ll. 6, 44.

37. RGASPI, f. 73, op. 2, d. 19, ll. 6–7, 27, 106.

38. V. Danilov, R. Manning, and L. Viola, eds., *Tragediia sovetskoi derevni. Kollektivizatsiia i raskulachivanie. Dokumenty i materialy v 5 tomax, 1927–1939*, vol. 5 (Moscow, 2004), 306–8.

39. RGANI, f. 89, op. 48, d. 12, l. 1–2. For local press coverage see *Rabochii put'* (Smolensk), 29 August, 6–8, 20–24, 25–27 September, 2, 27 October, 17–18 November. See also Sheila Fitzpatrick, "How the Mice Buried the Cat: Scenes from the Great Purges of 1937 in the Russian Provinces," *Russian Review* 52 (1993), 299–320.

40. RGANI, f. 89, op. 48, d. 20, ll. 1–2.

41. RGASPI, f. 17, op. 2, d. 628, ll. 115–19.

42. The only two members said to have protested were G. Kamensky and O. Pi-atnitsky, either at the June 1937 or June 1938 Central Committee plenums. See V. I. Piatnitskii, *Zagovor protiv Stalina* (Moscow, 1998). Unfortunately, no record of their remarks can be found in available archives.

43. Chuev, *Sto sorok besed*, 463.

44. Ibid., 393.

45. TsA FSB collection of documents, and published in A. I. Kokurin and N. V. Petrov, *GULAG (Glavnoe upravlenie lagerei), 1917–1960* (Moscow, 2000), 433. Although many people who were not kulaks fell victim to this operation, we shall here retain the title "kulak operation." This was the contemporary usage in party and police documents and serves to distinguish it from other mass terror campaigns.

46. For space considerations, and because these "national operations" had different targets, causes, and procedures, they are not treated here. See Terry Martin, "The Origins of Soviet Ethnic Cleansing," *Journal of Modern History* 70 (1998), 22; A. E. Gur'ianov, ed., *Repressii protiv poliakov i pol'skikh grazhdan* (Moscow, 1997), 33; I. L. Shcherbakova, ed., *Nakazannyi narod: Repressii protiv rossiiskikh nemtsev* (Moscow, 1999), 44.

47. The quoted phrase is from Peter H. Solomon, Jr., *Soviet Criminal Justice Under Stalin* (Cambridge, 1996), chapter 3.

48. TsA FSB, collection of documents.

49. See J. Arch Getty, "State and Society Under Stalin: Constitutions and Elections in the 1930s," *Slavic Review* 50 (1991), 18–36; Sheila Fitzpatrick, *Stalin's Peasants: Resistance and Survival in the Russian Village After Collectivization* (Oxford, 1994), 212–13, 282–85.

50. See Danilov, Manning, and Viola, *Tragediia,* 79–86, 90–91, 114–16, 172–73, 240–41, 521–26.

51. *Voprosy istorii,* no. 5, 1993, 14.

52. See Steven Merritt, "The Great Purges in the Soviet Far East, 1937–1938," Ph.D. diss., University of California, Riverside, 2000.

53. *Voprosy istorii,* no. 5, 1993, 18 (Vareikis); no. 6, 1993, 5, 6 (Eikhe).

54. *Voprosi istorii,* no. 6, 1993, 8.

55. Ibid., 23–24 (Mirzoian).

56. Ibid., 27 (Kabakov).

57. See Gábor T. Rittersporn, *Stalinist Simplifications and Soviet Complications: Social Tensions and Political Conflicts in the USSR, 1933–1953* (Reading, 1991), for this argument in detail.

58. Aleksandr Eliseev, *Pravda o 1937 gode. Kto razviazal "bol'shoi terror"?* (Moscow, 2008).

59. Troikas, or three-person tribunals, had existed during the Civil War to provide drumhead justice to enemies of the regime on an expedited basis without usual judicial procedure. They had been revived during collectivization to deal out mass sentences of exile or death to opponents of the collective farms. Their reestablishment in 1937 reflected what the regime thought was a crisis atmosphere in the country. For a survey of the history of extrajudicial organs, including troikas, in Soviet history see *Izvestiia TsK KPSS,* no. 10, 1989, 80–82.

60. Danilov, Manning, and Viola, *Tragediia,* 258; Khaustov et al., *Lubianka,* 230.

61. Danilov, Manning, and Viola, *Tragediia,* 319.

62. Stalin gave up on contested elections only in the autumn of 1937. See Getty, "State and Society," 31–32.

63. "Polozhenie o vyborakh Verkhovnyi Sovet SSSR," *Pravda,* 2 July 1937, 1; "Ob antisovetskikh elementakh," Politburo resolution, 2 July 1937; *Trud,* 4 June 1992, 1.

64. This account of the mass operations is presented in greater detail in J. Arch Getty, "'Excesses Are Not Permitted': Mass Terror Operations in the Late 1930s and Stalinist Governance," *Russian Review* 16 (2002), 112–37. I am grateful to the *Russian Review* for permission to quote from that article. For details of the execution of the mass operations, see also Mark Iunge and Rolf Binner, *Kak terror stal "bol'shim." Sekretnyi prikaz No. 00447 i tekhnologiia ego ispolneniia* (Moscow, 2003).

65. A. F. Stepanov, *Rasstrel po limitu. Iz istorii politicheskikh repressii v TASSR v gody "ezhovshchiny"* (Kazan, 1999), 14.

66. For Bukharin's letter, see *Istochnik,* 1993/0, 23–25, and an English version in J. Arch Getty and Oleg V. Naumov, *The Road to Terror: Stalin and the Self-Destruction of the Bolsheviks, 1932–1939* (New Haven, 1999), 556–60.

67. Plenum of the Central Committee, VKP(b) 11–12 October 1937, stenogram, RGASPI, f. 17, op. 2, d. 625, ll. 1–10, 38, 49, 55, 63, 70.

68. Solomon, *Soviet Criminal Justice,* 127.

69. Lynne Viola, "The Campaign to Eliminate the Kulak as a Class, Winter, 1929–1930: A Reevaluation of the Legislation," *Slavic Review* 45 (1986), 503–24, was the first to document the inclination of local leaders to use force in the countryside regardless of Moscow's current policy.

70. Fitzpatrick, *Stalin's Peasants,* 55.

71. *Trud,* no. 88, 4 June 1992, 1, 4.

72. Calculated from Politburo protocols (special folders): RGASPI, f. 17, op. 162, dd. 21–23; TsA FSB, collection of documents; Kokurin and Petrov, *GULAG,* 97–104; V. M. Samosudov, *Bol'shoi terror v Omskom Priirtyshe, 1937–1938* (Omsk, 1998), 160–61, 241; Nikolai Il'kevich, "Rasstreliany v Viaz'me: novoe o M. N. Goretskom," *Krai Smolenskii* 1–2 (1994), 129–44; David Shearer, "Crime and Social Disorder in Stalin's Russia: A Reassessment of the Great Retreat and the Origins of Mass Repression," *Cahiers du Monde Russe* 39 (1998), 139–41; *Moskovskie novosti,* no. 25, 21 June 1992, 18–19; *Izvestiia,* 3 April 1996; O. V. Khlevniuk, "Les mechanismes de la 'Grande Terreur': Des années 1937–1938 au Turkmenistan," *Cahiers du Monde Russe* 39 (1998), 204–6. Nikita Petrov believes that additional permissions were given orally or by telegrams and puts the excess shooting figure at about thirty thousand (personal communication). Such evidence is not currently available to researchers.

73. See Khlevniuk, "Les mechanismes," 204.

74. See Roberta T. Manning, "Massovaia operatsiia protiv 'kulakov i prestupnykh' elementov: apogei Velikoi Chistki na Smolenshchine," in *Stalinizm v Rossiiskoi provintsii: Smolenskie arkhivnye dokumenty v prochtenii zarubezhnykh i Rossiiskikh istorikov,* ed. E. V. Kodin (Smolensk, 1999), 239–41; Il'kevich, "Rasstreliany v Viaz'me," 138.

75. Mikhail Shreider, *NKVD iznutri: zapiski chekista* (Moscow, 1995), 80.

76. Khlevniuk, "Les mechanismes," 203.

77. Thus in another telegram "Supplementing Operational Order No. 447," deputy NKVD chief Frinovskii warned local police: "Sentences of condemned persons can be announced [to them] only for the second category [sentences to camp]. Do not announce [death sentences] of the first category [to the accused]. I repeat, do not announce." Memorandum no. 247 of the Secretariat, Narkom NKVD, TsA FSB, f. 100, op. 1, por. 5, l. 275.

78. See, for example, the breakdowns for Omsk in Samosudov, *Bol'shoi terror,* 160–61, 241, and in Stepanov, *Rasstrel po limitu,* 51–55, 71–74.

79. The Politburo had authorized persecution of families of oppositionists and of "enemies of the people" convicted by military tribunals and military collegia, but not under the kulak operation of order no. 447. See Politburo resolution "Vopros NKVD" of 24 May 1937, RGASPI, f. 17, op. 162, d. 21, l. 45; "Operativnyi prikaz No. 486: Ob operatsii po repressirovaniiu zhen i detei izmenikov rodiny," 15 August 1937, TsA FSB, f. 100, op. 1, por. 1, ll. 224–35. These harsh regulations had been softened already by 1938. See "Tsirkuliar NKVD SSSR No. 106: O detiakh repressirovannykh roditelei," 20 May 1938, TsA FSB, f. 100, op. 1, por. 1, ll. 248, and "Prikaz NKVD SSSR No. 689: O poriadke aresta zhen izmennikov rodinii," 17 October 1938, TsA FSB, f. 100, op. 1, por. 1, ll. 258–59.

80. TsA FSB, collection of documents.

81. The mass operations were formally halted on 17 November 1938 by a joint

order of the Politburo and the Council of People's Commissars, signed by Stalin and Molotov: "O prokurature SSSR," *Moskovskie novosti,* 21 June 1992, 19. Accompanying directives restored procuratorial sanction for all arrests: "Iz protokola No. 65 zasedaniia Politbiuro TsK VKP(b): Postanovlenie Soveta Narodnykh Komissarov SSSR i Tsentral'nogo Komiteta VKP(b)," RGASPI, f. 17, op. 3, d. 1003, ll. 85–87. The Politburo decision halting all troika cases and "other simplified procedures" had been taken in a 15 November 1938 secret resolution: RGASPI, f. 17, op. 162, d. 24, l. 62.

82. "Prikaz No. 762: O poriadke osushchestvleniia postanovleniia SNK SSSR I TsK VKP(b) ot 17 noiabria 1938 goda," 26 November 1938, TsA FSB, f. 100, op. 1, por. 1, ll. 260–64.

83. Vyshinskii to Stalin and Molotov, 21 May 1939, RGASPI, f. 82, op. 2, d. 897, l. 28.

84. James C. Scott, *Seeing Like a State: How Certain Schemes to Improve the Human Condition Have Failed* (New Haven, 1998). Scott discusses Stalinist collectivization in these terms, arguing that it failed because as a "centralized high modernist solution," it could not encompass the complexities and peculiarities of agriculture and thus failed either to achieve the state's goal of scientifically advanced farming or to put food on the table (see 193–222). Scott notes that other goals such as space exploration, transportation planning, flood control, or aircraft manufacturing were more susceptible to centralized high modernist treatments. On the other hand, it is not at all clear that these efforts differed from collectivization in degree of complexity. Collectivization *was* different from them insofar as it was implemented by a quasi-military and violent campaign that produced more chaos than centralization or legibility in the end. It may be that efforts to achieve standardization, centralization, control or concerted national effort are doomed to failure if implemented by their antithesis, a wild and uncontrollable military offensive whose wounds and arbitrariness last forever.

85. For a similar example of detailed instructions followed by chaos in an earlier mass operation, see Lynne Viola, "A Tale of Two Men: Bergavinov, Tolmachev, and the Bergavinov Commission," *Europe-Asia Studies* 52 (2000), 149–66.

86. See Khlevniuk, Politbiuro, 194–98; Isaac Deutscher, *Stalin: A Political Biography* (London, 1968), 373; Joseph Edward Davies, *Mission to Moscow: A Record of Confidential Dispatches to the State Department, Official and Personal Correspondence, Current Diary and Journal Entries, Including Notes and Comment up to October, 1941* (New York, 1941). Molotov made this point in his conversations with Feliks Chuev: Chuev, *Sto sorok besed,* 390, 393, 413–14. Bukharin also connected the terror "with the pre-war situation," *Istochnik,* 1993/0, 23–25. Rumors among those arrested in the mass operations included the thought that war had started and the regime was neutralizing suspicious elements: Stepanov, *Rasstrel po limitu,* 14. On the other hand, the first steps were taken to stop the terror in autumn 1938, precisely when the Munich conference, the German occupation of Czechoslovakia, and the Polish crisis produced the most direct security threat to the USSR.

87. J. Arch Getty, "Afraid of Their Shadows: The Bolshevik Recourse to Terror, 1932–1938," in *Stalinismus vor dem Zweiten Weltkrieg. Neue Wege der Forschung,* ed. Manfred Hildermeier and Elisabeth Mueller-Luckner (Munich, 1998), 169–92.

88. Ian Kershaw, *Hitler, 1889–1936: Hubris* (New York, 1998), xxviii.

89. Banac, *Diary of Dimitrov,* 7 November 1937, 65.

90. Chuev, *Sto sorok besed,* 415.

91. Banac, *Diary of Dimitrov,* 11 February 1937, 52.

92. According to Molotov: Chuev, *Sto sorok besed,* 423.

93. Ibid., 410–12.

94. Ibid., 413–14, 393.

9. Ending the Terror, 1938

1. J. Arch Getty, Gábor T. Rittersporn, and V. N. Zemskov, "Victims of the Soviet Penal System in the Pre-war Years: A First Approach on the Basis of Archival Evidence," *American Historical Review* 98 (1993), 1022–23, based on NKVD archives found in GARF.

2. Robert H. McNeal, *Stalin: Man and Ruler* (New York, 1988), 210–11.

3. Robert Conquest, *The Great Terror: A Reassessment* (New York, 1990), 248–49.

4. See Sheila Fitzpatrick, "Workers Against Bosses: The Impact of the Great Purges on Labor-Management Relations," in *Making Workers Soviet: Power, Class, and Identity*, ed. Lewis H. Siegelbaum and Ronald Grigor Suny (Ithaca, N.Y., 1994), 311–40.

5. *Pravda,* 19 January 1938. A partial English version can be found in Robert H. McNeal, *Resolutions and Decisions of the CPSU* (Toronto, 1974), 3: 188–95. This resolution quoted the June 1936 CC resolution on excessive expulsions.

6. *Pravda,* 7 August 1938. See also T. H. Rigby, *Communist Party Membership in the USSR, 1917–1967* (Princeton, 1968), 214–18. Rigby called the January 1938 plenum "the turning of the tide" in party expulsions.

7. RGANI, f. 89, op. 48, d. 19, l. 1.

8. See the files in RGASPI, f. 17, op. 120, dd. 327–29 on Postyshev, which bear Andreev's name.

9. RGASPI, f. 17, op. 120, d. 327, ll. 1, 2, 23–27; d. 329, ll. 31–36.

10. RGASPI, f. 17, op. 120, d. 329, ll. 43–45; d. 327, l. 27.

11. RGASPI, f. 17, op. 2, d. 782, l. 3.

12. RGASPI, f. 17, op. 163, d. 1180, l. 57–59.

13. RGASPI, f. 17, op. 2, d. 639, ll. 14–16, 20–22, 32–33. From the printed stenographic report.

14. RGASPI, f. 17, op. 2, d. 640, ll. 1–2, and f. 17, op. 3, d. 996, l. 4.

15. RGASPI, f. 17, op. 114, d. 642, ll. 10.

16. RGASPI, f. 17, op. 3, d. 996, ll. 34–35.

17. See RGANI, f. 89, op 73, d. 41, ll. 4–11; *Moskovskie novosti,* no. 25, 21 June 1992, 19.

18. RGANI, f. 89, op. 73, d. 124, ll. 1–2.

19. RGANI, f. 89, op. 73, d. 149, l. 1.

20. *Izvestiia TsK KPSS,* no. 12, 1989, 100.

21. RGASPI, f. 17, op. 3, d. 996, l. 60; op. 114, d. 642, l. 3.

22. An English edition appeared as *Report of the Court Proceedings in the Case of the Anti-Soviet "Bloc of Rights and Trotskyists"* (Moscow, 1938).

23. Feliks Chuev, *Sto sorok besed s Molotovym* (Moscow, 1991), 404.

24. See Conquest, *Great Terror,* chapter 11; Robert C. Tucker and Stephen F. Cohen, eds., *The Great Purge Trial* (New York, 1965).

25. After a lengthy delay, Bukharin's wife was arrested. She spent years in exile and in labor camps.

26. For a discussion of Radek's interesting testimony, see Robert C. Tucker, *Stalin in Power: The Revolution from Above, 1928–1941* (New York, 1990), 394–409.

27. Chuev, *Sto sorok besed,* 401, 404.

28. GARF, f. 9401, op. 1, d. 4157, ll. 201–5.

29. RGASPI, f. 17, op. 3, d. 998, ll. 21, 37, 40–41.

30. Boris A. Starkov, "Narkom Yezhov," in *Stalinist Terror: New Perspectives,* ed. J. Arch Getty and Roberta T. Manning (New York, 1993), 36, based on NKVD documents not currently available to researchers. For an earlier view of Zhdanov as a Yezhov opponent, see J. Arch Getty, *Origins of the Great Purges: The Soviet Communist Party Reconsidered, 1933–1938* (New York, 1985), 119–21, 199–201.

31. For the preceding few years Beria had been first secretary of the Transcaucasus Party Committee, but in the Civil War and 1920s he was a professional chekist.

32. Starkov, "Narkom Yezhov," 37–38.

33. RGASPI, f. 17, op. 3, d. 1002, l. 37.

34. Although they continued in the Far East. *Moskovskie novosti,* 21 June 1992, 19.

35. Ibid.; RGASPI, f. 17, op. 3, d. 1003, ll. 85–87.

36. Zhuravlev's report has not been found in the archives.

37. V. N. Khaustov et al., eds., *Lubianka. Stalin i glavnoe upravlenie gosbezopasnosti NKVD, 1937–1938* (Moscow, 2004), 662–63.

38. Starkov, "Narkom Yezhov," 38.

39. Khaustov et al., *Lubianka,* 662–63.

40. RGASPI, f. 671, op. 1, d. 265, ll. 29–41.

41. See *Istoricheskii arkhiv,* 1995, nos. 5–6, 25, for Stalin's calendar showing the meeting with Yezhov.

42. *Pravda,* 22 January 1939.

43. RGASPI, f. 17, op. 3, d. 1003, ll. 34–35, 82–84; d. 1004, l. 11; d. 1008, l. 59.

44. Quoted in Khaustov et al., *Lubianka,* 629.

45. Chuev, *Sto sorok besed,* 399.

46. A copy of a memorandum in Stalin's hand approving an increase in limits for execution appeared in *Moskovskie novosti,* 21 June 1992, 19.

47. Chuev, *Sto sorok besed,* 437.

48. Ibid., 401.

49. Khaustov et al., *Lubianka,* 663–64.

50. RGANI, f. 89, op. 18, d. 2, l. 1.

51. Chuev, *Sto sorok besed,* 437.

52. Getty, Rittersporn, and Zemskov, "Victims of the Soviet Penal System," 1048–49, based on NKVD archives.

53. RGANI, f. 89, op. 73, d. 3, ll. 1–4. No answer has been found in the archives.

54. Peter H. Solomon, Jr., *Soviet Criminal Justice Under Stalin* (Cambridge, 1996), 261–63.

55. Chuev, *Sto sorok besed,* 395.

10. Two Bolsheviks

1. Gennadii Bordiugov, ed., *Tiuremnye rukopisi N. I. Bukharina,* 2 vols. (Moscow, 1966).

2. A. M. Larina, *Nezabyvaemoe* (Moscow, 1989), 269–70.

3. Oleg V. Khlevniuk, *Politbiuro: Mekhanizmy politicheskoi vlasti v 1930-e gody* (Moscow, 1993), 206, quoting uncited text from Yezhov's archive.

4. *Istochnik,* 1993/0, 23–25. All emphases in the text are by Bukharin himself. Bukharin addresses Stalin throughout by the familiar "ty."

5. The memoranda have not been found in the archives.

6. Alluding metaphorically to a political romance.

7. Stalin's late wife.

8. Nadya was Bukharin's first wife, Anyuta his current wife.

9. According to Yu. Murin's accompanying notes, after the introductory "If," Bukharin has crossed out the words "You have decided in advance."

10. *Moskovskie novosti,* no. 5, 30 January 1994.

11. Even though the data are inexact, Yezhov is wildly exaggerating here. According to one calculation, Yezhov arrested 1,220 NKVD officials through 1937, the height of his purge of Yagoda's people. V. N. Khaustov et al., eds., *Lubianka. Stalin i glavnoe upravlenie gosbezopasnosti NKVD, 1937–1938* (Moscow, 2004), 664. According to another source, the number of NKVD security personnel arrested from mid-1937 to August 1938 was 2,274.

12. A. S. Zhurbenko was one of Yezhov's department heads at NKVD who was also head of the Moscow province NKVD at the time of his arrest in November 1938. He was shot ten days after Yezhov's statement.

Conclusion

1. For the use of the Party Control Commission, see J. Arch Getty, "Pragmatists and Puritans: The Rise and Fall of the Party Control Commission in the 1930s," *The Carl Beck Papers in Russian and East European Studies* 1208 (1997), 1–45.

2. A. Eliseev, *Pravda o 1937 gode. Kto razviazal 'bol'shoi terror'?* (Moscow, 2008).

3. The various contradictory versions of Yezhov's draft are in RGASPI, f. 671, op. 1, d. 273.

4. See RGASPI, f. 17, op. 2, d. 547, l. 69, and d. 544, l. 22 (on Yenukidze); *Voprosy istorii,* no. 2, 1995, 21 (on Yagoda); RGASPI, f. 17, op. 2, d. 577, ll. 30–33, and *Voprosy istorii,* no. 1, 1994, 12–13 (Stalin's remarks on Bukharin).

5. RGASPI, f. 17, op. 163, d. 1002, l. 218.

6. Lazar M. Kaganovich, *Pamiatnye zapiski* (Moscow, 1996), 557.

7. See Moshe Lewin, *The Making of the Soviet System* (New York, 1985), 44, 265.

8. Ibid., 281–85.

9. J. Arch Getty, Gábor T. Rittersporn, and V. N. Zemskov, "Victims of the Soviet Penal System in the Pre-war Years: A First Approach on the Basis of Archival Evidence," *American Historical Review* 98 (1993), 1017–49.

10. Leon Trotsky, *The Revolution Betrayed* (New York, 1972), 248–49, 252–54, 284–85.

Appendix One

1. For the most significant high estimates see S. Rosefielde, "An Assessment of the Sources and Uses of Gulag Forced Labour, 1929–56," *Soviet Studies* 33 (1981), 51–87, and "Excess Mortality in the Soviet Union: A Reconstruction of Demographic Consequences of Forced Industrialization, 1929–1949," *Soviet Studies* 35 (1983), 385–409; Robert Conquest, "Forced Labour Statistics: Some Comments," *Soviet Studies* 34 (1982), 434–39, and *The Great Terror: A Reassessment* (Oxford, 1990), 484–89.

Lower estimates can be found in R. W. Davies and S. G. Wheatcroft, "Steven Rosefielde's 'Kliuvka,'" *Slavic Review* 39 (1980), 603; S. G. Wheatcroft, "On Assessing the Size of Forced Concentration Camp Labour in the Soviet Union, 1929–56," *Soviet Studies* 33 (1981), 265–95, and "Towards a Thorough Analysis of Soviet Forced Labour Statistics," *Soviet Studies* 35 (1983), 223–37; Jerry Hough and Merle Fainsod, *How the Soviet Union Is Governed* (Cambridge, Mass., 1979), 176–77; Barbara Anderson and Brian Silver, "Demographic Analysis and Population Catastrophes in the USSR," *Slavic Review* 44 (1985), 513–36.

2. The data discussed here and presented in the text of this book are analyzed in depth in J. Arch Getty, Gábor T. Rittersporn, and V. N. Zemskov, "Victims of the Soviet Penal System in the Prewar Years: A First Approach on the Basis of Archival Evidence," *American Historical Review* 98 (1993), 1017–49.

3. See GARF, f. 9414, op. 1, d. 1139, l. 88, for what is likely to be the record number of prison inmates at the beginning of 1938 and GARF, f. 9401, op. 1, d. 4157, ll., 202, 203–5, for figures on exile, which may nevertheless contain a certain number of people banished in the wake of collectivization.

4. A. Antonov-Ovseenko, *The Time of Stalin: Portrait of a Tyranny* (New York, 1980), 212; Roy Medvedev, *Let History Judge: The Origins and Consequences of Stalinism*, rev. ed. (New York, 1989), 455; *Moskovskie novosti*, 27 November 1988; O. Shatunovskaia, "Fal'sifikatsiia," *Argumenty i fakty*, no. 22, 1990; Conquest, *Great Terror*, 485–86.

5. GARF, f. 9401, op. 1, d. 4157, ll. 203, 205. A handwritten note on this document tells us that 30 percent of those sentenced between 1921 and 1938 "upon cases of the security police" were "common criminals," and their number is given as 1,062,000. As the report mentions 2,944,879 convicts, this figure constitutes 36 percent; 30 percent would amount to about 883,000 persons (l. 202).

6. GARF, f. 9492, op. 6, d. 14, l. 14.

7. This is calculated on the basis of GARF, f. 9492, op. 6, d. 14, l. 29, by subtracting the number of "counterrevolutionaries" indicated on l. 14. The actual figure is nevertheless somewhat smaller, since the data on death sentences include "political" cases.

8. Medvedev, *Let History Judge*, 455; *Moskovskie novosti*, November 27, 1988; O. Shatunovskaia, "Fal'sifikatsiia."

9. *Pravda*, 14 February 1990, 2.

10. *Pravda*, 22 June 1989, 3; *Kommunist*, 1990, no. 8, 103; GARF, f. 9401, op. 1, d. 4157, l. 202.

11. "Spravka o kolichestve osuzhdennykh po delam organov NKVD" (GARF, f. 9401, op. 1, d. 4157, l. 202). Judiciary statistics mention 4,387 death sentences pronounced by ordinary courts in 1937–38, but this figure includes also a certain number of "political" cases (GARF, f. 9492, op. 6, d. 14, l. 29).

12. This was the year of a heavy-handed application of a particularly harsh decree against the theft of public property (the "Law of August 7, 1932"), and 5,338 people were condemned to death under its terms in 1932 and a further 11,463 in 1933 (GARF, f. 9474, op. 1, d. 76, l, 118; d. 83, l. 5). Not all these people were executed (d. 97, ll. 8, 61).

13. At least 69,566 deaths were recorded in prisons and colonies between January 1935 and the beginning of 1940 (GARF, f. 9414, op. 1, d. 2740, ll. 52, 60, 74). The other data are 288,307 for strict regime camps and 726,030 for people executed "upon cases of the political police."

14. RGASPI, f. 17, op. 120, d. 278, ll. 8, 10; RGANI (the Central Committee Archive) f. 77, op. 1, d. 1, l. 8.

15. *Spravochnik partiinogo rabotnika*, vyp. 18, Moscow, 1978, l. 366. This figure corresponds to that calculated by a Western scholar ten years earlier; one wonders whether the Soviet editors did not decide to rely more on the painstaking research of this scholar than on their own records. See Thomas H. Rigby, *Communist Party Membership in the USSR, 1917–1967* (Princeton, 1968), 52.

16. J. Arch Getty, *Origins of the Great Purges: The Soviet Communist Party Reconsidered, 1933–1938* (New York, 1985), 58–64, 86–90.

17. See, for example, GARF, f. 9414, op. 1, d. 1138, l. 6.

18. See, for example, GARF, f. 9414, op. 1, d. 1139, ll. 88–89; d. 1140, l. 161.

19. See, for example, Robert Conquest, Letter to the Editor, *American Historical Review* 99 (1994), 1038–40, and 1821.

20. See, for example, GARF, f. 8131sch, op. 27, d. 70, ll. 104, 141; f. 9414, op. 1, d. 20, ll. 135, 149.

21. "Vestnik Arkhiva Prezidenta Rossiiskoi Federatsii: I.1995," *Istochnik*, no. 1, 1995, 117–30.

22. V. V. Tsaplin, "Arkhivnye materialy o chisle zakliuchennykh v kontse 30-kh godov," *Voprosy istorii*, nos. 4–5, 1991, 157–60.

23. See Oleg V. Khlevniuk, "Prinuditel'nyi trud v ekonomike SSSR, 1929–1941 gody," *Svobodnaia mysl'*, no. 13, 1992, 73–84.

24. See E. M. Andreev, L. E. Darskii, T. L. Khar'kova, *Istoriia Naseleniia SSSR 1920–1959 gg.*, vypusk 3–5, chast' 1 of *Ekspress-informatsiia, seriia: Istoriia statistiki* (Moscow, 1990), 31, 37; V. N. Zemskov, "Ob uchete spetskontingenta NKVD vo vsesoiuznykh perepisiakh naseleniia 1937 i 1939 gg.," *Sotsiologicheskie issledovaniia*, no. 2, 1991, 74–75.

Index

Agranov, Ya.: on Kirov assassination, 74–
75; and Yezhov, 166; arrest of, 268n5; bi-
ographical sketch, 246
Akulov, I.: at January 1933 meeting, 49;
biographical sketch, 246
Alekseev, P.: expelled from Central Com-
mittee in June 1936, 174
Alliluyeva, N., 222, 255n8, 266n61
All-Union Communist Party (Bolsheviks).
See Communist Party
All-Union Leninist Communist Union of
Youth (VLKSM). *See* Komsomol
All-Union People's Economic Council
(VSNKh), 247, 249, 250
Andreev, A.: at January 1937 plenum of the
Azov–Black Sea Territorial Committee,
143–50, 266n2; on removal of Shebol-
daev, 145; at February–March 1937
plenum of the Central Committee, 155;
and purge of regional leaders in 1937,
177; and fall of Postyshev, 201–2, 204,
273n8; and census statistics, 277n24; bi-
ographical sketch, 246
Ashukina, E.P., 46
Association of State Publishing Houses
(OGIZ), 250
Astrov, V.: confronted by Bukharin, 151,
267n19
Azov–Black Sea Territorial Committee:

on attitudes of expelled members,
93

Bauman, K.: and fall of Yezhov, 210–15
Beria, L.: and fall of Yezhov, 210, 211, 213,
224; and NKVD, 210, 211, 215; on appeals process, 216; biographical sketch,
246
Bliukher, V.: fall of, 206; biographical
sketch, 246
Bolshevik Party. *See* Communist Party
Budenny, S.: at February–March 1937
plenum of the Central Committee, 160;
on expulsion and arrest of Tukhachevsky
and Rudzutak, 173; biographical sketch,
246
Bukharin, N.: positions on NEP, 23, 24, 26,
28; versus Trotsky, 25; on United Opposition, 26; and Stalin, 27, 28, 43, 134,
138; as theoretician, 27; and the right opposition, 28, 31, 37; recants, 31–32, 52;
and Riutin Platform, 33, 36, 43, 153; and
A. P. Smirnov case, 51; and party unity,
51; and Pravda, 56; and Yezhov, 123;
and Zinoviev-Kamenev show trial, 132,
133, 197; Yezhov on antiparty activities
of, 133, 134, 153; and confrontations
with accusers, 133, 138, 151; and December 1936 plenum of the Central

Bukharin, N. (*continued*)
  Committee, 134, 135–39 passim; fall of, 151–64, 171; and February–March 1937 plenum of the Central Committee, 151–64, 201; expelled from party, 158, 159, 160; fate of, compared to Postyshev's and Yenukidze's, 164; begins confessing, 171; background of, 217–18; biographical sketch, 247
Bukharin-Rykov-Yagoda show trial (1938): compared to Zinoviev-Kamenev show trial, 207; description of, 207–8
Bulganin, N.: biographical sketch, 247
Bullit, W., 171
Bykin, Ya., 179

Central Committee of the Communist Party: Secretariat of, 2, 24; circular of 1939 on physical pressure, 3, 253n2; paranoia within, 3, 58, 190, 234; slogans of, 11; and variant texts, 11, 97–98, 212; problems of local control, 15, 60–61, 88, 96, 262n63; on grain requisitions, 27; and right oppositionists, 28; A. P. Smirnov case, 46–47; on purging of libraries, 56–57, 87; on arrest procedures, 59–60, 88, 211; and party purges, 64–65; on Kirov assassination, 77–79, 111; and Yezhov, 79; and Kremlin Affair, 80–87 passim; and verification of party documents, 92; and review of appeals of persons expelled from the party, 97–103 passim, 148, 200; and regional party secretaries, 118; decimation of, 174, 178–80; Stalin on impact of terror on, 179; and observation of norms of democratic centralism in 1937, 179–80; and 1937 elections to the Supreme Soviet, 181; rituals of (*see* Communist Party—rituals)
Central Committee plenums: December 1930, 31–32; January 1933, 45, 46, 47, 49–54, 64–65; June 1935, 80–82, 85, 111, 134; June 1936, 85, 97–105 passim, 111–12, 147, 205, 263n17; December 1936, 134–39, 208, 266n58; February–March 1937, 103, 116, 118, 265n22, 130, 141, 144, 147–50 passim, 151–64, 165–67, 168–69, 201, 208; January 1938, 197–205 passim, 206
Central Committee's Department of Culture and Propaganda: Stalin's control of, 57, 87
Central Control Commission (CCC): and A. P. Smirnov case, 76. *See also* Commission of Party Control (KPK)
Central Party Archive of the Soviet Communist Party, 17–18

Chastushki, 39
Cheka, 22, 61, 224, 225
Chief Administration of State Security (GUGB). *See* NKVD (of USSR)
Chubar, V.: Molotov on interrogation of, 194; arrest of, 210; executed, 215; biographical sketch, 247
Collectivization: purpose of, 28; consequences of, 30, 31, 36, 45, 57, 241; and Riutin Platform, 35–36; mass arrests during, 57; and police troikas, 59; and excess deaths during the Stalin era, 243
Comintern. *See* Communist International
Commissariat of Justice, 58, 62
Commissariat of Water Transport: and fall of Yezhov, 209
Commission of Party Control (KPK): and Yezhov, 80, 209; and arrest procedures, 88; and Gagarina case, 89
Communist International, 2, 171
Communist Party: self-destruction of, 8; development of, 8; self-image of, 9, 12, 41; schisms within, 9, 43, 97; traditions of, 9, 140, 158; worldview of, 9, 16, 68; documents of, 16, 17; and Marxism-Leninism, 21; and legacy of Civil War, 22, 43; and NEP, 23; on class war, 29, 66; response to famine, 45–46; and arrest of members, 88–89; and relations with police, 90, 166; and party elections of May 1937, 147, 168–69; and 1937 elections to Supreme Soviet, 181
—Central Committee. *See* Central Committee of the Communist Party
—Congresses: Tenth, 22; Seventeenth ("Congress of Victors"), 65–66, 69, 73, 74, 80, 83, 87, 158, 233
—Criticism and self-criticism: and ritual, 47–48, 92; from below, 118–19; Stalin on, 144; suppression of, 147, 168; and Azov-Black Sea Territorial Committee, 147
—Discipline: development of, 8–9, 29–30; and the right opposition, 28, 31; and Smirnov case, 52; and literature, 56; and the left opposition, 114; and destruction of elite, 130–31; and confessions, 134, 137; role in terror, 232
—Ritual: disarming as, 31, 134, 152, 155, 156; purpose of, 32, 78, 147, 201, 229, 233; apology rituals, 47–48, 50–51, 82, 84, 85, 138, 145, 146, 205; self-criticism ritual, 47–48, 92; and plenums of the Central Committee, 98, 134, 137, 145, 158, 202; and show trials, 112, 113, 207–8; and confession, 137; and denunciations, 145; and mass shootings, 195

—Unity: development of, 8; threats to, 26, 32, 137; appearance of, 51, 64–65
—Vigilance: and Kremlin Affair, 83; on the local level, 87, 92–93, 96–97; Yezhov on, 101–2; perversion of, 102; and February–March 1937 plenum of the Central Committee, 168; and spread of repression, 177–78; and January 1938 plenum of the Central Committee, 197, 200
Council of People's Commissars: 60, 174, 178, 245
Cult of Personality. See Stalin (Dzhugashvili), I.

Dekulakization: launch of, 28; consequences of, 30

Eikhe, R.: at February–March 1937 plenum of the Central Committee, 182; appointed to troika in Western Siberia, 183; arrest of, 210; biographical sketch, 247
Eismont, N. B., 46–47; biographical sketch, 247. See also Smirnov, A. P.: case of
Eismont-Tolmachev-Smirnov group, 33. See also Smirnov, A. P.: case of

Family circles: and 1933 purge, 64; and verification of party documents, 91, 96; and Sheboldaev, 143; and party elections of May 1937, 168–69; and NKVD, 169
Famine: cause of, 30, 31; Party response to, 45–46; and "excess" deaths during the Stalin era, 243
Far East of USSR: NKVD chief of, defects, 209; and police troikas, 258n21
Fascism, 11, 62, 109, 113, 141
Five Year Plan: purpose of, 28–29; atmosphere of, 30; results of, 30
Frinovsky, M., 123; biographical sketch, 247

Gagarina, V. V., 89
Gamarnik, Ya., 169; biographical sketch, 247
Goliakov, I., 216
Gulag: estimated population in Stalin era, 239, 242

Ikramov, A., 179
Industrial Party trial of 1930, 59
Institute of Red Professors: and Bukharin, 151
Interrogation procedures, 3, 172, 193–94
Izvestia, 103

Judicial policy: and socialist legality, 57; Law of August 7, 1932, 58, 277n12; trends in, 60–63, 66–70, 79, 87–89, 215–16; revolutionary legality, 69; on arrest procedures, 70, 210; Law of 1 December 1934 (Kirov Law), 72, 110, 264n4; and extralegal organs governing repression, 89, 120, 185–87, 270n59; Article 58, 95; and local control, 97; legalism and legality, 172

Kaganovich, L.: memoirs of, 18, 234; and Bukharin, 31–32; on reform of police, 69; and Kremlin Affair, 81, 83; on Yezhov, 109, 123–24; and Zinoviev-Kamenev trial of 1936, 112; and assassination plot against, 112; and confrontation of Sokolnikov by Bukharin and Rykov, 133; at December 1936 plenum of the Central Committee, 135, 137; and repression of former oppositionists, 141; at February–March 1937 plenum of the Central Committee, 161; at January 1938 plenum of the Central Committee, 203–4; on Stalin, 237, 275n6; and purge of Smolensk party organization, 269n33; biographical sketch, 247
Kalinin, M.: and December 1936 plenum of the Central Committee, 136; and February–March 1937 plenum of the Central Committee, 156; and petitions from victims, 191; biographical sketch, 247
Kalygina, A., 179
Kamenev, A.: position on NEP, 24, 26; on Trotsky, 25, 26; in United Opposition, 26; fall of, 27; and Riutin Platform, 54; and Kirov assassination, 75–76, 78, 110–15 passim, 235; and Kremlin affair, 80, 85–86; execution of, 112; implicates Bukharin, Rykov and Tomsky, 132; and Sokolnikov's denunciation of Bukharin and Rykov, 133; biographical sketch, 247
Kamensky, G., protests against spread of repression, 269n42
Khataevich, M.: expelled from Central Committee, 179
Khrushchev, N.: on Riutin Platform, 35; on Kirov assassination, 72, 74, 260n6; at February–March 1937 plenum of the Central Committee, 160, 161; Molotov on, 171; biographical sketch, 248
Kiev Regional Committee of the KP(b)U (Communist Party of the Ukraine): Postyshev removed from post of first secretary, 201, 205

Kirov, S.: as liberal alternative, 54, 72, 74; biographical sketch, 248

Kirov assassination: repercussions of, 62, 71, 72–74, 77–79; involvement of Stalin in, 72–76, 141; 1980s Politburo investigation of, 73; 1956 Khrushchev commission on, 74, 260n6; Secret CC letter on Kirov assassination, 77–78; and Kremlin Affair, 80–81; and destruction of Trotskyists, 110; and Zinoviev-Kamenev trial, 110, 111, 112, 113; and Yagoda, 122; and Bukharin and Rykov, 153

Kolkhozy: conflicts in, 17; arrests of members, 60, 187

Komsomol: purge of, 215

Kork, S., 169

Kosarev, A.: at the February–March 1937 plenum of the Central Committee, 155, 160, 167; biographical sketch, 248

Kosior, S.: at December 1936 plenum of the Central Committee, 136, 140; at February–March 1937 plenum of the Central Committee, 154, 160, 167, 182; arrest of, 210; executed, 215; biographical sketch, 248

Kremlin Affair, 80–87, 110

Krupskaia, N., 131, 172; biographical sketch, 248

Krylenko, N.: biographical sketch, 248

Kuchkin, I., 132, 266n51

Kuibyshev, V. V.: on unity, 21; on recantation, 32; on Bukharin and Rykov, 32; on terror, 54; on the OPGU, 62; biographical sketch, 248

Kulaks: definition of, 12, 28; as targets of grain requisition, 28–29; attacks on, 29, 30, 57, 60; Stalin orders repression of former, 165, 186–87

Kulikov, M., 138

Larina, A.: fate of, 163–64, 274n25

Left Opposition: and NEP, 23–24; and Zinoviev-Kamenev trial, 113–14; and nomenklatura, 114. See also United Opposition

Lenin: political programs of, 10–11; democratic centralism, 22; adoption of NEP, 23; struggle for succession after, 24

Lepa, A., 179

Litvinov, M., 160, 161

Liushkov, G.: defection of, 209

Lominadze, V.: expelled from CC, 32; biographical sketch, 248

Machine Tractor Stations, 46, 177

Main Concession Committee, 247–48

Malenkov, G. M.: and verification of industrial cadres, 126; at January 1937 plenum of the Azov–Black Sea Territorial Committee, 146; on verifications, 148–49, 150; and fall of Postyshev, 202, 204, 205; biographical sketch, 248

Mekhlis, M., 265n20

Memoir literature: problems of, 17. See also Kaganovich, L.; Molotov (Skriabin), V.

Mensheviks, 165

Metro-Vickers trial: significance of, 59

Mikhailov, M.: removed from Central Committee, 174–76

Mikoian, A.: on Bukharin, 153; at February–March 1937 plenum of the Central Committee, 153; at January 1938 plenum of the Central Committee, 203

Moiseev (Yershistyi), I.: appeal to Molotov, 131–32

Molchanov, G.: criticized at the February–March 1937 plenum of the Central Committee, 166; arrest of, 167; criticized at NKVD conference, 268n5; biographical sketch, 248

Molotov (Skriabin), V.: memoirs of, 18, 75, 193, 234; and Bukharin, 32, 135, 136, 137, 155–56, 157; on mass repression of the peasantry, 59; on Kirov assassination, 75; and Moiseev's appeal to, 131; at December 1936 plenum of the Central Committee, 135–36, 137, 141; on repression of former oppositionists, 141, 142; and February–March 1937 plenum of the Central Committee, 155–56, 157; and Seventeenth Party Congress, 158; and purge of military, 170–71; and mass operations in the regions, 178; on democratic centralism during purges, 179–80; on repression of family members of victims, 192; on interrogation of Rudzutak, 193; and justification of repression, 193–94, 196, 208, 216; on interrogation of Chubar, 194; at January 1938 plenum of the Central Committee, 203–4; and fall of Yezhov, 210, 211, 214; on relations between Yezhov and Stalin, 215; biographical sketch, 248–49

Nevsky, V., 133

New Economic Policy: debates on, 23–24, 26; problems of, 27

Nikolaenko affair, 148, 267n14

Nikolaev, L.: and assassination of Kirov, 71

Nikolaeva, K., 160, 161

Nikolsky, I. V.: role in A. P. Smirnov case, 46

NKVD (of USSR): and Special Board, 4, 63, 215, 233; image of, 16; establishment of, 61; and Kirov assassination, 72, 73, 74–75, 78–79, 109, 110; and Yezhov, 79–81, 83, 122–28 passim, 165–68, 209–15; and Kremlin Affair, 80, 82–83, 86, 110; on judicial norms, 88–89, 210–11, 215; and verification of party documents, 90, 262n56, 262n66; and Zinoviev-Kamenev trial, 103; and fall of Yagoda, 122–26 passim, 165–67; and investigation of Bukharin and Rykov, 159–61 passim; and 1937 order for repression of anti-Soviet elements, 165, 187; and search for Trotskyists, 166, 168, 170, 178; Zakovsky on leadership of, 166; and release of prisoners, 177, 215–16; and troikas, 183, 185, 187, 210, 243, 270n59; and quotas for repression, 185, 238; and January 1938 plenum of the Central Committee, 200; and Zhuralev, 211; and Politburo, 211, 213; and Beria, 211, 213, 215; the Special Political Department of the Chief Administration of State Security (GUGB), 248

Nomenklatura: role in terror, 8–9, 231–32; origin and definition of, 9, 253n8; and Stalin, 9, 65–66, 85, 102, 103, 116–19, 139–44 passim, 197–201, 232–34, 237; worldview of, 9, 114, 137, 201, 229–30; conflict within, 9–10, 32, 46, 66–67, 84, 91, 96–97, 99, 233; reactions to Riutin Platform, 34, 35, 39, 45; threats to, 40–41, 43–44, 45, 70, 86, 115, 144; on oppositionists, 53, 81–82, 112, 113, 114; and variant texts, 56, 98, 99, 101, 102, 213, 234; corporate identity of, 113–14, 233–34; and consequences of February–March 1937 plenum of the Central Committee, 116, 158, 168; and personality cults, 117; and criticism from below, 118–19, 168; and self-destruction of, 131, 143, 178–80; and repression of former oppositionists, 139–42; and NKVD, 169; and purge of military, 174; blamed for excesses, 197, 200; and Politburo, 198; and death of Stalin, 239–40, as elite in post-Soviet Russia, 240

OGPU: and Riutin group, 34; on counter-revolutionary organizations, 54; and the creation of the special board, 54; and excesses, 55, 57, 62; powers of, 57, 60; abolition of, 61

Olberg, Valentin, 109, 264n1

Old Bolsheviks: opposition from, 64; destruction of, 71, 72, 75, 111, 171; worldview of, 217–18; and Stalin, 237; and Stalinist leadership, 237

Ordzhonikidze, G. ("Sergo"): suicide of, 93–94, 151; vote to expel Piatakov, 129, 131; and arrest of Piatakov, 129–30; and terror, 130; and sabotage in People's Commissariat for Heavy Industry, 130; at December 1936 plenum of the Central Committee, 138; and Seventeenth Party Congress, 158; biographical sketch, 249

Organizational Bureau. See Orgburo

Orgburo: origins of, 24

Osinsky, N.: expelled as a candidate member from Central Committee, 174; biographical sketch, 249

Patronage: and succession struggles, 24; function of, 91

Petrovsky, G., 160, 161; biographical sketch, 249

Piatakov, G.: arrest of, 3, 17, 123, 128; and Zinoviev-Kamenev show trial, 115; and fall of Yagoda, 123; and expulsion of Sokolnikov, 126, 131; expelled from Central Committee and party, 128, 131; and self-destruction of nomenklatura, 130–31; Ordzhonikidze on, 131; and confrontation with Bukharin, 138; biographical sketch, 249. See also Piatakov-Sokolnikov-Radek show trial (1937)

Piatakov-Sokolnikov-Radek show trial (1937), 151, 207

Politburo: as ruling caste, 10; strategies of, 10, 97; mentality of, 16, 42, 43; origins of, 24; and Trotsky, 25; on grain requisitions, 27; on right opposition, 28; factions within, 28, 54; and Bukharin, 56, 151, 152; on arrests of specialists, 58; and troikas, 59, 206, 210, 258n21, 270n59; on judicial procedure, 62, 210; on Kirov assassination, 62, 71, 73, 260n17; and Kremlin Affair, 86; on party expulsions, 102; on liquidation of Trotskyists, 110; on death penalties, 112; and expulsion of Piatakov, 128–31; appeals to, 131–32; and repression of former oppositionists, 141–42; on Sheboldaev, 145; on Postyshev, 147, 150; and arrest of Yagoda, 167; and 1937 elections to Supreme Soviet, 168, 181–84 passim; on Gamarnik and Aronshtam, 175–76; awards Order of Lenin to Yezhov, 174; and purge of regional leaders, 176–77; orders show trials of livestock saboteurs, 178; and repression among CC members,

Politburo (*continued*)
178–80; establishes quotas for repression, 185, 206, 238; and nomenklatura, 198; attempts to control repression, 210–11; on the OGPU and NKVD, 212; and Stalin, 237

Political Bureau. *See* Politburo

Postolovskaia, A., 148

Postyshev, P.: and party expulsions, 101, 102; demotion of, 104, 105, 143, 147; and Postolovskaia, 148; protected by Stalin, 149–50; fate of, compared to Bukharin's and Yenukidze's, 164; fall of, 201–5; Shkiriatov and fall of, 205; executed, 215; Andreev and fall of, 273n8; biographical sketch, 249

Pravda: slogans in, 11; and Bukharin, 23, 56; and variant texts, 98; and fall of Yezhov, 213

Preobrazhensky, Ye., 38

Primakov, V., 170

Procuracy of the USSR: establishment of, 61; in arrest procedures, 88, 210; and investigative procedures, 210–11

Ptukha, V., 179

Purge of *1933* (Chistka): targets of, 64; effects of, 64–65; Yezhov's role in, 80

Radek, K.: arrest of, 3; and Riutin Platform, 34; on A. P. Smirnov case, 52–53; and Zinoviev-Kamenev show trial, 115; trial of, 151; and the algebra of confession, 208; biographical sketch, 249

Red Army: purge of, 17, 169–74, 206; and torture of generals, 172; and conspiracy in, 172, 206, 268n14; purge of military and onset of terror, 174; circular concerning expulsion of party members in, 206

Red Terror, 22; second Red Terror of *1937*, 185–86

Riutin, M.: and Bukharin, 33; career of, 33; arrest of, 34; biographical sketch, 249

Riutin Affair. *See* Riutin Platform

Riutin group: secret meetings of, 33; destruction of, 34, 39; composition of, 255n20

Riutin Platform: creation and dissemination of, 33; critiques of Stalin, 33–35; significance of, 34, 35–38, 43, 114; and Khrushchev, 34; and Trotsky, 37; and fall of Yagoda, 123, 265n34; and Bukharin, 153

Rudzutak, Ya.: on Eismont-Tomachev-Smirnov case, 47, 48, 53; and Stalin, 50, 66; and tsarist prisons, 140; expulsion from party and arrest of, 172, 173; Budenny on arrest of, 173; Molotov on interrogation of, 193–94; execution of, 210; biographical sketch, 249

Rumiantsev, I.: expelled from Central Committee, 176; biographical sketch, 249

Rykov, A.: position on NEP, 23; on grain requisitions, 28; fall of, 28, 151, 153, 158, 159; in the right opposition, 28, 31; and A. P. Smirnov case, 51; and Zinoviev-Kamenev show trial, 115, 132; and confrontations with accusers, 133, 138; and December *1936* plenum of the Central Committee, 134, 137, 138, 151; and February–March *1937* plenum of the Central Committee, 154–64 passim; expelled from the party, 160, 162; biographical sketch, 249. *See also* Bukharin-Rykov-Yagoda show trial (*1938*)

Secret Police. *See* NKVD; OGPU

Sedov, Lev: and Trotskyists, 38–39

Shakhty trial of *1928*, 59

Sheboldaev, B.: and apology ritual, 143, 145; demotion of, 145–46; Andreev on, 150; protected by Stalin, 150; expelled from Central Committee in June *1937*, 176; biographical sketch, 250

Shkiriatov, M.: and Bukharin, 32, 154; on A. P. Smirnov case, 47–49 passim; on oppositionists, 49; on counterrevolutionary organizations, 49, 50, 52; on jokes as weapons, 49–50, 52; on excessive legalism, 71, 89; as head of Party Control Commission, 149; and fall of Postyshev, 205; at February–March *1937* plenum of the Central Committee, 154, 160, 161; biographical sketch, 250

Shliapnikov, A.: and censorship, 56; biographical sketch, 250

Show trials. *See* Bukharin-Rykov-Yagoda show trial (*1938*); Piatakov-Sokolnikov-Radek show trial (*1937*); Zinoviev-Kamenev show trial (*1936*)

Shvernik, N., 160

Smirnov, A. P.: case of, 33; activities of group, 45, 46, 47, 48; statements of Eismont, 46; attacks on, 47; confrontation with Eismont, 47; significance of, 52; expulsion, 53; punishment of Eismont, 53–54; biographical sketch, 250

Smirnov, I. N.: and Trotsky, 39, 112; biographical sketch, 250

Socialist Revolutionary Party (SR), 135, 186

Sokolnikov, G.: arrest of, 3; and Trotsky, 38; expulsion from Central Committee and party, 126, 131; and investigation of Bukharin, 133; and confrontation with Bukharin and Rykov, 133; biographical sketch, 250

Stalin (Dzhugashvili), I.: role in terror, 6, 59–61, 66–68, 69–70, 169–96 passim, 214, 232–34 passim, 274n46; and party purges, 6, 64, 96, 97–98, 101, 102, 148; personality cult of, 6, 48, 49, 233; mentality of, 6, 16, 236; as chief of CC personnel, 9, 24; and the nomenklatura, 9, 10, 37, 50, 87, 104, 105, 116–19, 139–42 passim, 197–201 passim, 232–34; on extraordinary grain requisitions, 23; and Lenin and Leninism, 24; and style of leadership, 25, 49, 231–38 passim; versus Trotsky, 25–26, 35; on socialism in one country, 25–26; on United Opposition, 26; and Bukharin, 27, 138, 134–36, 159–64 passim, 217–30 passim; on oppositionists, 28, 32–33, 81; on peasants, 28, 59–60; reaction to Riutin group, 34, 35–36; and a "liberal" faction, 54; and purge of historical profession, 55–56; and Culture and Propaganda Department of the CC, 57, 87; and "Dizziness with Success," 57; on kolkhoz property, 58; and NKVD Special Board, 63; at 17th Party Congress, 65, 69, 83, 87, 233; and Kirov's assassination, 71–77 passim, 109; and Kremlin Affair, 80–81, 85; on suicides, 93; and variant texts, 97–102 passim, 104; and Yezhov, 98–99, 102, 196, 209, 211, 212, 217–30 passim, 274n41; on Yenukidze, 103; on Zinoviev-Kamenev 1936 trial, 103, 112, 113; and investigation of Bukharin and Rykov, 133, 159–60; and December 1936 plenum of the Central Committee, 136, 137, 139; and February–March 1937 plenum of the Central Committee, 148–50 passim, 158–61 passim; and Postyshev, 149–50, 202, 205; at Bukharin's confrontation with Astrov, 151; and suicide of Ordzhonikidze, 151; and A. Larina, wife of Bukharin, 163–64; and arrest of Yagoda, 167; and purge of military, 169–74; and troikas, 177; and the decimation of the Central Committee, 178–80; and petitions from victims, 191; and repression of family members of victims, 191–92; at January 1938 plenum of the Central Committee, 199; and Old Bolsheviks, 237; biographical sketch, 250

Stalin Constitution, 233

Stalinism: and terror, 7, 71; and criminalization of anti-Soviet agitation, 12, 49–50, 54; and deviations from party line, 12, 41; as discourse, 12–15, 48, 56, 194, 228; as a belief system, 13, 42; as a revolution, 28–30, 33, 232; historical treatment of, 72–74, 75; characterized, 239–40

Stalinist leadership: mentality of, 3, 5, 8–9, 10–15 passim, 41, 43, 114, 228, 232, 236; style of rule, 11, 48, 98, 113, 232, 239; and collectivization, 28; on Riutin Platform, 35–37; popularity of, 40–41; on oppositionists, 47, 113; and literary censorship, 55; and control of judicial sphere, 65–66; and prison camps, 140; and motives behind mass terror, 191–92; and mass shootings, 195; and Old Bolsheviks, 237; and death of Stalin, 239. See also Nomenklatura

Stetsky, A., 250

Suicide: as antiparty weapon, 93, 94, 137; as a result of verifications, 93; and S. Ordzhonikidze, 93–94, 151; and M. Tomsky, 122, 132; and Gamarnik, 169

Supreme Soviet of the USSR, 181

Syrtsov, S., 32, 253n9

Tivel, Alexander, 1–6, 191, 238, 253n3

Tivel, Eva, 2–6 passim

Tolmachev, V. N., 33, 46, 272n85

Tomsky (Yefremov), M.: position on NEP, 23; fall of, 28; on grain requisitions, 28; in right opposition, 51; defense of A. P. Smirnov, 51; suicide of, 122, 132; and Zinoviev-Kamenev show trial, 132–36 passim; biographical sketch, 250

Troikas: activities during collectivization, 59; and Politburo, 59, 206, 270n59; and Andreev and Stalin, 177; activities and composition of in 1937–38, 184, 185–88 passim; abolished by Politburo, 210; and the Far East, 258n21; history of, 270n59

Trotsky (Bronshtein), L.: critique of nomenklatura system, 9; on NEP, 24; on party democracy, 25; on Stalin, 25, 37–38, 72; fall of, 26–27; and Riutin Platform, 35, 37, 39; in exile, 38, 81, 109; and Lessons of October, 55; censored, 56–57, 87; and Kremlin Affair, 86; and Zinoviev-Kamenev trial, 110, 112; biographical sketch, 250

Trotskyists: search for, 9, 39, 90, 119, 121, 148; definitions of, 12, 41, 111, 115, 120, 168, 207; activities of, 38, 40; and

Trotskyists (*continued*)
Riutin Platform, 38; I. N. Smirnov and,
39, 112; and rightists, 73, 161, 207; and
Kirov assassination, 110; and Zinoviev-
Kamenev trial, 110–12 passim; discursive function of concept, 111, 198, 199;
and nomenklatura, 114; execution of,
121; and rise of Yezhov, 126; and arrest
of Piatakov, 128–29; and Azov–Black
Sea region, 143, 145; and Ukrainian Regional Committee, 143; Stalin on, 148;
Andreev on, 155; in military, 170, 206
Tukhachevsky, M.: arrest and execution of,
169–74 passim; biographical sketch, 250

Uborevich, I., 169
Uglanov, N., 251, 266n52
Ukrainian SSR: and fall of Postyshev, 143
Union of Marxist-Leninists. *See* Riutin
group
United Opposition, 26–27

Vareikis, I., 179, 270n53
Verifications of party documents, *1935–36*
(proverka): purpose of, 89, 96; results of,
90–91, 93, 96, 262n57; significance of,
91; in comparison to hunt for Trotskyists, 121–22, 148–49; appeals resulting
from, 147–48; Malenkov on, 148–49;
Stalin on, 148–49; and Azov–Black Sea
Territorial Committee, 150
Victims of repression: camp population estimates, 67, 241–42; executions by year,
1921–38, 67; yearly estimates on number of arrests, *1921–38*, 67; aggregate arrest figures, 241–42; executions during
the Great Terror, 242–43; on total number of excess deaths in the *1930s*, 243–
44; and issues requiring further research,
244
Voroshilov, K.: and Bukharin, 31, 154; on
Tomsky, 53; at February–March *1937*
plenum of the Central Committee, 154;
and Tukhachevsky affair, 169, 170; and
fall of Yezhov, 209, 211; biographical
sketch, 251
Vyshinsky, A.: on revolutionary legality, 69;
and procedural norms, 76, 95–96, 215;
on Trotskyists, 110; in Zinoviev-Kamenev
trial of *1936*, 112, 132; and confrontation of Sokolnikov by Bukharin and
Rykov, 133; and NKVD, 215; biographical sketch, 251

Workers' and Peasants' Red Army (RKKA).
See Red Army

Yagoda, G.: and Kirov assassination, 75,
109, 110, 122, 260n17; fall of, 76, 86,
110, 122, 123, 125, 126; and Kremlin
Affair, 82, 83; on Zinoviev-Kamenev trial
(*1936*), 103, 110; on liquidation of Trotskyists, 110; replaced by Yezhov as head
of NKVD, 122–26 passim; and February–March *1937* plenum of the Central
Committee, 166–67; biographical
sketch, 251. *See also* Bukharin-Rykov-
Yagoda show trial (*1938*)
Yakir, I.: arrested and indicted for treason,
161, 169, 171; biographical sketch,
251
Yaroslavsky, E.: and purge of libraries, 57;
at February–March *1937* plenum of the
Central Committee, 182; biographical
sketch, 251
Yenukidze, A.: and Kremlin Affair, 80–87
passim; and fall of Yagoda, 122; fate of,
compared to Bukharin's and Postyshev's,
138, 164; expulsion from party of, 235;
arrest and execution of, 235; biographical sketch, 251
Yezhov, N.: on Trotsky, 39, 109, 256n24;
on Riutin Platform, 43; on Trotskyists,
43, 90, 92, 110–11; and Kirov assassination, 74, 76, 81, 109–11 passim; career of, 79–81, 86, 217–30 passim; on
Kremlin Affair, 81–82, 84; on expelled
party members, 88–89, 93, 98–105; on
the NKVD and the Party, 90; on verification of party documents, 90–91, 92,
262n62; and June *1936* plenum of the
Central Committee, 97–105 passim;
and Stalin, 98–99, 102, 196, 209, 211,
212, 217–30 passim, 274n41; Zinoviev-
Kamenev trial of *1936*, 103, 109–10,
111; and fall of Yagoda, 110, 165–68;
appointed NKVD chief, 122–28 passim;
and Piatakov, 129; and appeals to, 132;
and Bukharin, 133, 141, 151, 153, 158,
160, 164, 217–30 passim; and December *1936* plenum of the Central Committee, 134–42 passim; and fall of Rykov, 153, 158, 160; and February–
March *1937* plenum of the Central
Committee, 153–58 passim, 160, 161,
164, 166; and A. Larina, wife of Bukharin, 164; purged NKVD, 166–68; and
cadres for NKVD, 168; and family circles, 169; and purge of Trotskyists in
military, 170; receives Order of Lenin,
174; and Yezhovshchina, 196; fall of;
209–15; and Astrov, 267n19; biographical sketch, 251

Yezhovshchina: definition of concept, 196; as description of repression, 196–97

Zakovsky (Shtubis), L., 123, 166
Zhdanov, A.: and Culture and Propaganda Department of the CC, 57; on the OGPU, 62; and repression of former opposition-ists, 141; on party democracy, 147, 182, 267n9; at February–March 1937 plenum of the Central Committee, 168, 198; and party elections of May 1937, 168, 182, 183; and fall of Yezhov, 209, 274n30; bi-ographical sketch, 251
Zhukov, I.: and proposal to expel Piatakov from Central Committee, 131; and Feb-ruary–March 1937 plenum of the Cen-tral Committee, 167; expelled from Central Committee and party for coun-terrevolutionary activities, 174, 176; bio-graphical sketch, 251

Zhuravlev, V.: and fall of Yezhov, 211, 213; biographical sketch, 251
Zinoviev, G.: as party boss of Leningrad, 2; as chief of Comintern, 23–24; on NEP, 24; on Trotsky, 25, 26; in United Opposi-tion, 26; fall of, 27; and Riutin Platform, 34; and Lenin, 53; censored, 56–57, 87; and Kirov assassination, 75, 78, 79, 110–15 passim, 235; and Kremlin Affair, 81–82, 85; execution of, 112; biographical sketch, 251
Zinoviev-Kamenev show trial (1936): sig-nificance of, 2–3, 85, 112–13, 115, 264n11; preparations for, 103, 110–12; conduct of, 111, 112; and investigation of Bukharin, Rykov and Tomsky, 132–33, 137–38; compared to Bukharin-Rykov-Yagoda show trial, 207